Marilyn Wood

SOCIAL STUDIES
IN SECONDARY
EDUCATION

Social Studies in Secondary Education

DAVID G. ARMSTRONG

TEXAS A&M UNIVERSITY

Macmillan Publishing Co., Inc.

NEW YORK

Collier Macmillan Publishers

LONDON

Macmillan Publishing Co., Inc.
866 Third Avenue, New York, New York 10022

Collier Macmillan Canada, Ltd.

Library of Congress Cataloging in Publication Data

Armstrong, David G.

 Social studies in secondary education.

 Includes bibliographies and index.
 1. Social sciences—Study and teaching (Secondary)—
United States. I. Title.
H62.5.U5A75   1980   300'.7'1273   78–21035
ISBN 0–02–303980–9

Printing: 1 2 3 4 5 6 7 8   Year: 0 1 2 3 4 5 6

DEDICATION

To John R. Rogers High School, Spokane, Washington

PREFACE

THE SOCIAL STUDIES MIGHT BE DESCRIBED as a collection of enthusiasms in search of a purpose. Some have said that the social studies has suffered relative to other school subjects because of a lack of agreement concerning its elemental function. This concern for a clear conception of purpose has stimulated much spirited debate, but little movement toward consensus.

Regarding discussions centering on the purpose of social studies instruction, this book seeks a middle ground. The position that there is, or even ought to be, a single central purpose around which social studies programs are organized is rejected, as is the view that the purposes of social studies instruction are as broad as the purposes of the school. Rather, the social studies is viewed as serving a limited number of central purposes. Knowledge of this range of purposes is seen as providing a context for social studies educators' artistry as they design programs that strike a reasoned balance between students' individual needs and imperatives of the cultural milieux within which these students live.

Social studies teachers, if they are to make reasoned decisions about their programs, need to know both "where the social studies has been" and "where the social studies may be going." The first two chapters introduce special problems associated with social studies instruction, describe historic trends in the field, and suggest a basic framework that can be used to determine emphases of individual programs.

The five chapters in the second section of the book focus on aspects of the instructional planning process. General guidelines and specific examples are introduced that relate to content organization, long-term and short-term planning, identification of individual student characteristics, evaluation of students' performance, and classroom organization.

Concerns of the tax-paying public related to "getting their money's worth"

vii

from education have placed new pressures on schools to provide unequivocal evidence of students' progress. One consequence of this development has been a renewed interest in teaching basic skills. The three chapters in the third section focus on some relevant social studies skills. Procedures are introduced for dealing with students' reading difficulties, providing students with ways of locating and organizing information, and familiarizing students with skills associated with the general area of graphic literacy.

In the fourth section, three chapters are devoted to information related to strategies and techniques of instruction. A basic framework for systematic sequencing of instruction is introduced. Detailed examples illustrate the application of a number of effective teaching techniques.

The five chapters in the fifth section have been included to illustrate the great range of special topics and themes found in social studies programs. Clearly these five chapters do not provide anything approaching a comprehensive treatment of all topics featured in social studies programs today. For example, though not described here, themes such as women's studies and Holocaust studies have a place in the social studies program in many schools. The themes in this section were selected because they tend to be fairly representative of the range of special topical offerings in the secondary social studies program. To those interested in social studies teaching even this small sample should suggest the desirability of preparing for "breadth" as well as "depth" in their college and university preparatory programs.

Material derived from history and the social sciences continues to receive emphasis in most secondary social studies programs. The three chapters in the sixth section focus on these academic disciplines. Special problems associated with teaching contents from the individual disciplines are highlighted. Additionally, some contemporary approaches to organizing discipline-based instruction are introduced.

The final chapter focuses on the social studies as a profession. Sources of general professional information are introduced, and several organizations of interest to social studies teachers are described. There is a heavy emphasis on the personal responsibility of the individual social studies teacher for his or her own professional growth and development.

This book could not have been written without the support and willing help of many kind people. My special thanks go out to Raymond F. Tirrell of State University College, Oneonta, New York. His meticulous readings (and rereadings) of various drafts of individual chapters were of invaluable assistance as the writing process went forward. Thanks, too, are due to Jesus Garcia of Texas A&M University and James B. Kracht of Illinois State University for their willingness to respond to preliminary versions of several chapters.

Beth Van Cleave spent many tedious hours typing and retyping the manuscript. My very special thanks go out to her for a dedication to a task which, I am sure, she must have thought destined to "go on forever." Appreciation also is extended to Mary Faulkner, Molly Herbst, and Mary Sue Keahey for their help with manuscript preparation.

Finally, my heartfelt thanks to my wife, Nancy, and my son, Tim, who gracefully put up with a husband and father who was forever going back to the office "to work on the book."

DAVID G. ARMSTRONG

CONTENTS

Overview

Chapter 1

AN INTRODUCTION TO
THE SOCIAL STUDIES

3

Chapter 2

PATTERNS OF
CURRICULUM ORGANIZATION

14

Preparing for Instruction

Chapter 3

IDENTIFYING AND
ORGANIZING CONTENT

29

Chapter 4

PLANNING SOCIAL STUDIES UNITS AND
DAILY LESSON PLANS

47

Chapter 5

DIAGNOSING STUDENTS

71

Chapter 6

INTERACTING WITH LARGE GROUPS
AND SMALL GROUPS

88

Chapter 7

ASSESSING STUDENTS' LEARNING

106

Social Studies Skills

Chapter 8

DEALING WITH READING DIFFICULTIES
IN THE SOCIAL STUDIES

133

Teaching Strategies

Chapter 13

SELECTING INSTRUCTIONAL TECHNIQUES

230

Selected Themes

Chapter 14

DECISION MAKING
AND VALUES

255

Chapter 15

CULTURAL HERITAGE STUDIES

278

Chapter 16

LAW-FOCUSED STUDIES

296

Chapter 17

MORAL EDUCATION

315

Chapter 18

UTILIZING THE LOCAL COMMUNITY

330

Source Disciplines

Chapter 19
HISTORY AND GEOGRAPHY
349

Chapter 20
POLITICAL SCIENCE AND ECONOMICS
375

Chapter 21
SOCIOLOGY, PSYCHOLOGY,
AND ANTHROPOLOGY
391

The Profession

Overview

Chapter 1

AN INTRODUCTION TO THE

SOCIAL STUDIES

As they grow toward maturity, young people learn two great lessons. First, they learn that their unique and individual qualities are cherished. Second, they learn that they live in a social world that imposes limits on what they can do. The social studies seeks to help students strike a reasoned balance between self-centered personal development and unthinking acquiescence to the whims of others.

In earlier times there was sparse need for a special social studies program designed to help young people come to terms with their world. In traditional societies, wisdom of the elders was passed on to the young by word of mouth and on special ceremonial occasions. So long as basic survival skills remained little changed from generation to generation, this scheme worked well. The wisdom of the elders clearly was relevant for members of the younger generation.

Today this situation is much changed. New generations find themselves confronted by challenges undreamed of by their fathers. The "conventional wisdom" of experience has little to tell young people coming to maturity in an age unimaginably different from that experienced by their forebears two and three generations ago. There is some evidence that the rate of technical and social change is accelerating. This means that tomorrow's parents may have even more difficulty in communicating with their children than today's parents experience when fielding questions relating to digital computers and silicone chips.

Preparing students for a world in which change is a "given" is an important responsibility of the social studies program. If we are to help students communicate with a broad spectrum of people, it is especially important to make the point that a given change does not

3

affect all people in the same way. Consider, for example, the father who continues to lather up in the morning with a brush and a shaving cup even though pressurized cans of shaving cream have been on the market for years. Consider, too, the perhaps surprising fact that, despite the technical availability of the opportunity, a majority of the population has never been on an airplane.

Despite tremendous changes that have made possible a range of human activity little imagined a generation or two ago, for many people patterns of living are little altered. Various reasons have been suggested to explain why some people adapt more readily to change than others. Some people see change as a threat and are doubtful of their ability to cope with an unfamiliar technology. In Alvin Toffler's (1970) phrase, they suffer from "future shock." Still others see the change and understand how to deal with it but simply prefer to go on doing things in the "old way."

This preference for the familiar is a widespread phenomenon. It is by no means restricted only to a rejection of change. For many adults, preference for the known and familiar circumscribes a set of concerns and interests ranging little beyond their local community. Large numbers of people, even in the last quarter of the twentieth century, lead personally satisfying lives while never venturing more than two or three hundred miles from their birthplace. The fact that the technical opportunity exists for far-ranging travel by no means suggests that many or even most people have the economic resources or the inclination to take advantage of the opportunity.

This reality comes as a shock to many beginning social studies teachers. As well-read, well-traveled individuals, they have broad interests. Most social studies teachers can make a quick personal connection to a drought in Western Europe, to street crime in New York, or to historical precedents of proposed gun control legislation. But many students come to school with much narrower interests. Furthermore, many of their parents appear to be coping quite nicely with life's demands while sharing few, if any, of the enthusiasms of the social studies teacher.

This situation poses a serious difficulty for the social studies instructor. Indisputably, social survival is feasible for individuals with only the narrowest range of concerns and interests. Further, people with only a limited view of reality may well be very comfortable and resist exposure to new and potentially unsettling information. The character Benton Collingsworth in A. B. Guthrie's *Arfive* reflected on this point:

> There was the contrast between fact and faith in a personal god. There was the chasm between broad belief and narrow, between the embrace of the universe and the catch-hold of—all right—superstition . . . The members wanted the clean choice of bliss or brimstone. Answers they wanted, absolute answers to the unanswerable. . . .[1]

[1] A. B. Guthrie, Jr., *Arfive* (Boston: Houghton Mifflin Company, 1970), p. 77. Reprinted by permission of Houghton Mifflin Company and Brandt & Brandt Literary Agency, Inc.

Like the people in Guthrie's novel, many parents shy away from an "embrace of the universe" and restrict their interests to a more localized world they can understand. Given a rather limited range of concerns, they have worked out answers to life's problems so as to provide a sense of personal security. They—and their sons and daughters in the schools—are little inclined to develop serious interests in broader issues that might threaten their view of how the world "works." By no means all students are characterized by a limited range of interests, but their numbers invariably come as a surprise to beginning social studies teachers. Several studies have pointed out the nature of the problem social studies teachers face as they seek to broaden the personal and social studies horizons of their students.

A study by Fernández, Massey, and Dornbusch (1976) revealed that the social studies enjoy an esteem among students that, at best, could be described as modest. They surveyed more than 700 urban high school students and more than 600 suburban high school students in the San Francisco Bay area. Students were asked to describe their feelings about the general worth of high school courses in (1) English, (2) mathematics, and (3) social studies.

Students were found to believe that competence in their social studies classes was much less important for success in their future occupational roles than competence in their English and mathematics classes. This view was reinforced by similar beliefs on the part of parents, counselors, and friends. The investigators noted that, because students viewed social studies classes as unimportant, they were unwilling to expend a great deal of effort on their studies in this area. Supporting this conclusion, students were found to view their social studies classes as being less difficult than their English or mathematics classes. Further, there was a widespread belief among students that if they did "poor work" in their social studies classes, they still would receive an acceptably high grade.

The investigators concluded that students' tendencies to view social studies instruction as unimportant and academically "soft" were rooted (1) in students' lack of *specific* understanding of the knowledges and skills central to the social studies and (2) in students' failure to see any personal benefit deriving from lessons in social studies classes. On the other hand, basic skills in mathematics and English were perceived as "obvious and specific" and as having a direct link to personal experience. The investigators made the following suggestions to social studies teachers:[2]

1. Each teacher should know his or her specific objectives in each social studies course.
2. The importance of the objectives for the student's own future should be communicated.
3. There should be continuing assessment of the extent to which the objectives are being attained, and the results of these assessments should be told to students.

[2] Celestino Fernández, Grace Carroll Massey, and Sanford M. Dornbusch, "High School Students' Perceptions of Social Studies," *The Social Studies* (March/April 1976): 56.

4. It should be made clear to the students how the long-term goals of social studies relate to their own aspirations.

Conclusions of the Fernández, Massey, and Dornbusch investigation parallel those emerging from a study by Sleeper (1973), who examined adolescents' feelings regarding the importance of history. Sleeper found that adolescents attached importance to a given past event in terms of how directly they believed the event to have influenced the present.

Adolescents, Sleeper discovered, tend to separate past reality into two broad categories. One category is basically autobiographical in nature. It includes those events the adolescent sees as having direct and personal impact on his or her own life (the experience of an ancestor fighting in World War I, for example). The other category includes a distinct and separate body of knowledge known as "history." Most students have much greater interest in events in the autobiographical category than in the formal history category.

Sleeper pointed out that only a small minority of students, unaided, are able to make a connection between the autobiographical past and "history." For example, though a student might be highly interested in exploits of his or her great-grandfather on the western front, that same student may not connect this autobiographical series of events with a formal classroom study of World War I in a history course. An implication of Sleeper's study is that students are unlikely to view history as an important school subject unless teachers help them recognize the connection between what they are studying and their own autobiographical pasts.

In summarizing what is known about student attitudes toward the social studies program, one may say that (1) generally the social studies enjoy only a modest esteem and (2) a good deal of the problem seems related to students' failure to see any personal benefit or importance deriving from what is taught. These findings suggest the importance of finding out what students believe and value as a beginning point for instruction. To build a bridge between subject matter and student, the teacher must identify characteristics of students early.

Beginning social studies teachers are sometimes astonished at the range of interests and understandings of a group of students in a given class. Diagnoses of student characteristics at the beginning of a school year frequently will bring to light some startling misconceptions. One of the author's former students, a high school senior, argued vehemently that Ho Chi Minh was the president of Mexico—this during the late 1960s, when the media were providing saturation coverage of the Vietnam War. In addition to shaky information, diagnoses may reveal students with relatives actively involved in public affairs, with ancestors who were present at historically important events, and with pen pals in foreign countries. All of this information can help the teacher build a logical connection between social studies topics and students' personal points of view and interests.

Student characteristics provide a beginning point for social studies instruction.

This is not to suggest, though, that students' interests, alone, should shape the entire instructional program. To follow that path would be to suggest that the isolated development of each individual student was the primary goal of the social studies. On the contrary, the social studies seek personal development within a *social context;* that is, social studies teachers are interested in promoting both individual development and social responsibility. Consequently, information about individual students provides not program organizers but rather logical entry points for teachers' instruction. These beginnings attempt to motivate students by capitalizing on their interests and capabilities. Unless a connection to students' needs and interests is established, attempts to broaden the dimension of students' concerns stand little chance for success.

Historically, a number of approaches have been tried as social studies educators have attempted to help students better understand themselves and their world. An understanding of "where social studies have come from" can help illuminate present practices and suggest likely future patterns. In the next section, historical trends in the social studies will be reviewed.

A Short History of Programmatic Trends in the Social Studies

In the colonial era, social studies instruction reflected a good deal of social and moral concern. Students learned the general nature of their duty and obligation to the community. Instructional practices drew heavily upon insights from the Bible. There was a great deal of interest in developing "acceptable" attitudes and patterns of behavior.

In the years following the American Revolution, social studies programs leaned less heavily on Biblical sources. Though lessons were less frequently based on the Bible, still learning materials tended to be very moralistic in tone. Textbook authors of the period devoted considerable attention to topics such as "good breeding" and "proper manners."

During the first half of the nineteenth century, history became important as a separate subject in secondary schools. In elementary schools, geography was introduced as a major feature of the social studies program. Within these subject areas, abundant attention continued to be given to questions of "proper" behavior. But, in time, the prescriptive morality served up to students within the frameworks of these disciplines began to give way to more emphasis on contents that were more purely "historical" or "geographic" in nature. A new concern for the social sciences as specialized fields of study began to develop. But, throughout most of the first half of the nineteenth century, a fair observer probably would have noted a generally heavier emphasis on instruction devoted to teaching "proper" behavior than on instruction centering on findings and methods of social scientists.

In the second half of the nineteenth century, political science was introduced as a separate subject. History and political science were taught primarily in the high schools. Geography continued to be favored in elementary school programs. Though less prevalent than earlier, still some emphasis continued to be given to topics designed to teach students "proper" behavior.

In the early years of the twentieth century, geography became a common subject in the secondary as well as in the elementary schools. Concerns for "Americanizing" the vast numbers of immigrants arriving from southern and eastern Europe resulted in a much broadened view of the role of the political science course. During this period, political science courses in many secondary schools were transformed into "civics," a course that placed heavy emphases on institutional arrangements characterizing American government. The course, many believed, would help new immigrants develop a sense of loyalty to their adopted country. During this period, social studies programs emphasized both citizenship and contents derived from the social sciences. As evidenced by the establishment of the new "civics" course from the disciplinary cloth of political science, the concern for citizenship was perhaps the most influential force during this time.

This basic trend continued during the 1920s. Before 1920 some schools had added special courses in economics and sociology. Growth of these courses as separate subject offerings was slowed during the 1920s as a new course, "problems in democracy," increased in popularity. "Problems of democracy," a hybrid course drawing content from several academic specializations, absorbed a good deal of the material previously taught in separate economics and sociology courses. "Problems of democracy" introduced a novel element to the secondary social studies program. For the first time, students were asked to deal with pressing *current* social problems. Opportunities developed for teachers to encourage students to engage in problem-solving activities as the class considered important issues of the day. In terms of their orientation, social studies programs in the 1920s presented a very mixed pattern.

A mixed bag of focusing themes continued to characterize social studies programs in the 1930s. During this period, educators became increasingly interested in issues relating to the personal development of students. Guidance and counseling services in the schools expanded tremendously. In social studies education the interest in individual development was reflected in program descriptions. For the first time, social studies programs tended to be described in terms of how they would promote the personal development of students rather than in terms of the subjects or topics to which students would be exposed. This new interest in individual development was reflected in Charles Beard's classic, *A Charter for the Social Sciences*. Beard commented that social studies programs should enhance students' abilities

> to understand, analyze, bring information to bear, to choose, to resolve, and to act wisely. Competence in the individual, not dogma, is our supreme objective.[3]

[3] Charles A. Beard, *A Charter for the Social Sciences* (New York: Charles Scribner's Sons, 1934), p. 96.

Expanding on the idea that social studies programs should be described in terms of their influences on students, the Educational Policy Commission (EPC), with its goals of 1938, greatly influenced the emphases of social studies curricula. The EPC goals identified commitment to a democratic way of life as the most important outcome of education. This end was to be achieved as educators helped students develop competencies in the areas of (1) self-realization, (2) human relationships, (3) economic efficiency, and (4) civic responsibility. As Price (1968) has noted, these four areas of competency were much used by social studies curriculum committees in the 1940s and 1950s as they worked to formulate statements of program purpose.

During the 1940s and into the middle 1950s, social studies programs tended to be more oriented toward citizenship development and decision-making skills development than toward the social sciences. The citizenship development emphasis reflected a belief of many social studies educators that there was a common set of characteristics needed by effective citizens in a democracy. The four competency areas described in the 1938 Educational Policies Commission report were used by many social studies program developers as a basis for suggesting that all students needed to accept a certain set of core values.

The thrust toward prescribing a common set of values for all was blunted somewhat by a continued interest in the individual development of students. This interest provided a counterpoint to the view that students should be indoctrinated to accept a common set of attitudes. The concern for individualism in the schools was reflected, at least in some social studies programs, in social studies teaching that considered the role of student attitudes and values. Some interest in examining the values' basis of decision making began to characterize the social studies classroom. Although these valuing processes did not receive the intensive consideration that was to come their way in the 1960s and 1970s, still the concern for individual development prompted some programmatic commitment to the development of decision-making skills.

Throughout most of the 1940s and 1950s, the social sciences were regarded simply as sources of information. Teachers viewed them as storehouses of specific details that, as the occasion demanded, might be drawn upon as lessons were developed designed to help students better understand themselves and their world. Very little attention was given to introducing students to the techniques of the social scientist. The emphasis was on the findings of the social scientist rather than upon the techniques he or she used in arriving at conclusions.

1957, the year the Soviets launched Sputnik I, was a watershed year for American education. A public that had been benignly complacent about what was going on in the schools became intensely interested in what schools were doing to and for students. Whether accurate or inaccurate, a suspicion flourished that the schools had become "soft" and that academic programs compared unfavorably with those in other parts of the world. Schools' emphases on individual development were attacked by critics who felt such practices represented an unacceptable trading away of more "respectable" content. Many rallied to the phrase "education is too important for educators."

In social studies education, these concerns stimulated many distinguished scholars from university departments of history, economics, geography, political science, sociology, psychology, and anthropology to interest themselves in secondary school curricula. Many of these individuals involved themselves in curriculum development projects undertaken with a view to strengthening social studies courses in the public schools. A number of outstanding curricula resulted from these efforts. Central to many of these new curricula was the idea that students ought not to be taught only the "findings" of historians and social scientists but that they should be taught the "processes" these professionals use in arriving at their conclusions as well.

Given a theoretical rationale by Jerome Bruner's 1960 dictum that any concept could be taught to a child of any age in an intellectually responsible way, university specialists involved in curriculum development efforts in the late 1950s and the 1960s broke loose from their fear that some content might be too difficult for secondary school students. Freed from this concern, they proceeded to develop programs aimed at producing high school graduates able to function intellectually much as junior versions of Ph.D.'s in colleges and universities. From 1957 until the late 1960s, most new social programs placed a heavy emphasis on the social sciences.

In the late 1960s two major sets of circumstances resulted in diminished enthusiasm for academic discipline-oriented programs. First of all, few teachers were well grounded in the techniques used by historians and social scientists in processing raw information to arrive at conclusions. In their college classes, most had been exposed only to "findings" of historians and social scientists. Very few had been personally involved in the production of new knowledge using the techniques of academic professionals. When teachers who themselves had little or no training in examining raw information using the techniques of academic professionals were asked to teach new programs assuming a knowledge of these techniques, there were problems. Though there were some efforts to provide inservice training, the vast majority of teachers was not reached. Many teachers simply could not cope with the contents of the academic discipline-oriented curricula of the 1960s.

Perhaps even more important than the teacher training issue was a failure of many of these curricula to consider the issue of student interest. Many of these programs assumed that nearly all students would share the enthusiasm experienced by the experienced historian or social scientist as he or she works with raw data en route to developing new knowledge. Not only did many students fail to share an interest in these activities, they also considered the purpose of such instruction as irrelevant to their own concerns. Many wondered why, at a time when inner cities were erupting and debate over America's role in Vietnam was a consuming public interest, the emphasis in their social studies classes was on techniques for analyzing and interpreting raw data.

For many students, the academic discipline-oriented social studies programs with their emphasis on "value free" inquiry made little sense. Racism, poverty, an unpopular war—all cried out for a public examination of values on which decisions were being made. Many young people believed not only that values issues should be considered in social studies classes but also that they ought to play a *central* role in social studies instruction.

A programmatic response to these concerns was a renewed interest in how social studies programs affect individuals. These concerns stimulated a good deal of professional attention to questions relating to the role of personal values in decision making. In the late 1960s and into the 1970s, many newer social studies programs reflected heavy emphasis on development of students' decision-making skills.

Economic problems of the middle and late 1970s suggested beginnings of another potential shift in programmatic emphases in the social studies. The middle 1970s were years characterized by high unemployment and high rates of inflation. By the late 1970s some of the unemployment difficulties had eased, but inflation continued to be a serious problem. As a consequence of these difficulties, many Americans sensed their standard of living to be deteriorating. These circumstances led to intensive scrutiny of governmental expenditures of all kinds, including moneys earmarked for education. The taxpayers' revolt that began in California with the passage of Proposition 13 emphasized that increasingly standards of "cost effectiveness" would be applied to social studies programs (as well as to other educational activities).

The drive for "cost effectiveness" resulted in part from a widespread belief that declining scores of high school graduates on standardized tests was a result of inefficient educational management. Some observers noted that scores seemed to move inversely to public expenditures for education. Critics suggested that the schools were "asking more and giving less." This view resulted not only in a tightened hand on budgets for school programs (including social studies programs) but also in an increasing insistence that educators be held accountable for student learning.

In the social studies, this trend suggested new emphases on skills and other social studies areas where students' learning could be easily tested and scores reported for public consumption. Additionally, new emphases on "career education" and "law-focused education" began to emerge. The former suggested to the public that the social studies were not a "frill" and that there was a concern for the "real world" the student would enter upon graduation. Law-focused courses helped social studies educators counter the suggestion that they were irresponsible fomenters of dissention. Law-focused programs provided a vehicle for teachers to deal with public controversy within a "respectable" framework.

Trends of the late 1970s and early 1980s are still too close at hand to permit broad-ranging generalization. It does seem probable, given present social and economic conditions, that there are prospects for stabilized (if not actual decreased) funding for social studies programs. These conditions suggest that heavily monitored and meagerly funded social studies departments may seek to place heavier emphases on specifying in advance "proper" outcomes for students in response to a public demand for accountability. Such a reaction would suggest a renewed emphasis on citizenship development. A move toward increased attention to citizenship development at the expense of programs reflecting other orientations is far from a certainty at this time. But circumstances suggest that a more restricted range of social studies programs may be in the offing.

Summary

The social studies attempt to strike a balance between personal needs of individual students and social needs of their culture. As students are encouraged to work out a reasonable compromise between personal desires and social responsibilities, social studies teachers attempt to broaden the range of their interests. By exposing students to people, places, and issues beyond the parochial limits of the school and the community, the social studies program emphasizes the interdependent nature of the human community.

A difficulty that frustrates many beginning social studies teachers concerns the limited range of concerns of many secondary school students. Many of these students, taking a cue from the rather restricted interests of their parents, simply are little concerned with people and events beyond their own limits of personal experience. Conclusions such parents and their children may have reached about issues may well "make sense," given the conditions in the local community. Given this reality, it is quite natural that large numbers of students initially display little interest in a broader world where answers that "make sense" in the local community may have to be reevaluated. Students, like adults, tend to resist exposure to experiences that might threaten conclusions that, for the most part, seem to "work."

As an entrée to stimulate student interest in social studies, it is desirable to connect instruction to personal experiences and interests of students. This implies a need for the teacher to diagnose student characteristics in order to identify interests and possible basic misconceptions. Given this information, lessons can be constructed that take advantage of identified student characteristics.

Historically, the social studies have responded to changes in social, political, and economic conditions. Today we are witnessing a concern for cost-effective education. In the social studies, this may result in emphases on instruction focusing on topics lending themselves readily to assessment techniques that yield numerical results. Quite possibly, programs easily accommodated to standardized testing may be favored over others in which learning outcomes cannot be measured so conveniently. There is no certainty that this will happen, but present trends suggest that this may indeed be the end result.

References

Beard, Charles A. *A Charter for the Social Sciences*. New York: Charles Scribner's Sons, 1934.

Fernández, Celestino; Grace Carroll Massey; and Sanford M. Dornbusch. "High School Students' Perceptions of Social Studies." *The Social Studies* (March/April 1976): 51–56.

Guthrie, A. B., Jr. *Arfive*. Boston: Houghton Mifflin Company, 1970.

Price, Roy A. "Goals for the Social Studies." In *Social Studies Curriculum Development: Prospects and Problems*, edited by Ronald O. Smith, pp. 33–64. 39th Yearbook of the National Council for the Social Studies, 1969. Washington, D.C.: National Council for the Social Studies, 1968.

Sleeper, Martin E. "The Uses of History in Adolescence." *Youth and Society* (March 1973): 259–274.

Toffler, Alvin. *Future Shock*. New York: Random House, Inc., 1970.

Chapter 2

PATTERNS OF CURRICULUM

ORGANIZATION

SOCIAL STUDIES PROGRAMS HELP students understand themselves in terms of their relationship to the world they live in. To achieve this end, two major objectives guide the work of curriculum developers. On the one hand, there is an attempt to highlight the unique qualities of people as individuals. On the other hand, there is an effort to underscore the collective character of people as social beings. Taken together, these objectives provide direction to the development of programs designed to help students determine their role as individuals in a multiperson world.

A variety of organizational schemes have been tried by social studies educators as they have attempted to promote student growth in the areas of personal and social understanding. An examination of social studies programs today might well suggest a confused hodgepodge to a casual observer. In some schools, history, geography, and certain other social science disciplines are taught much as they were thirty, forty, and even fifty years ago. In other schools, programs have been built around pressing social problems. In some others, students are free to choose from as many as fifty two-week to four-week "mini-courses" organized around a bewildering variety of topics. Though social studies programs reflect a tremendous diversity, there are discernible organizational patterns. In the sections that follow, some of these will be identified.

Emphases of Social Studies Programs

Bruce Joyce (1972) suggested that three major emphases are found in social studies programs. These emphases include (1) *personal education,* (2) *citizenship education,* and (3) *intellectual education.*

The *personal education* emphasis includes those portions of social studies courses directed toward promoting students' self-understanding. Lessons might include concerns for personal growth and development, personal values in decision making, and encouragement of individual students to assume leadership responsibilities. The *personal education emphasis* establishes a high priority for learning experiences designed to help students come to terms with themselves.

Benefits and responsibilities of individuals in a society are a major concern of the *citizenship education* emphasis. *Citizenship education* does not imply that there are certain "must" attitudes that all students should share. Rather, the intent is to emphasize individual development as this process goes forward within social limits. This lesson implies that commitment to individualism carries within itself the need for active social participation. Because of the emphasis on the social context within which individual development unfolds, *social education* may be a more descriptive term for this emphasis than *citizenship education.*

The *intellectual education* emphasis refers to those parts of social studies courses focusing on the academic disciplines of history and the social sciences. Lessons consider both findings of historians and social scientists and techniques these scholars use in arriving at their conclusions. Many traditional social studies textbooks are heavily oriented toward an *intellectual education* emphasis.

Learning Outcomes of Social Studies Programs

In addition to the relative attention given each program emphasis, social studies programs and lessons vary in terms of the kinds of learning outcomes sought.

	Understandings	Skills	Attitudes and Values
Personal Education			
Social Education			
Intellectual Education			

Figure 2–1. Social Studies Program Characteristics Matrix. (Source: This matrix appeared originally in Tom V. Savage, Jr., and David G. Armstrong, "Zeroing-In: Targeting Social Studies," *The Clearing House* (January 1974): p. 279. Reprinted with permission of Heldref Publications.)

Jarolimek (1977) pointed out that social studies learning outcomes can be divided into three general categories. The first category of learning outcomes includes what Jarolimek calls *understandings*. The second category is concerned with helping students master certain *skills*. The third category has to do with a focus on students' *attitudes and values*.

The three categories of learning outcomes suggested by Jarolimek can be combined with the three program emphases described by Joyce to generate a matrix. This matrix provides a framework for identifying various program types. Program types are defined in terms of their emphases and attention to specific learning outcomes. This matrix is depicted in Figure 2–1.

The Social Studies Program Characteristics Matrix

Each of the nine cells of the matrix describes a certain set of program practices. Each is characterized by a specific emphasis and a specific learning outcome. Each cell might be thought of as a single instructional "target" of the total social studies program. The general character of the social studies program in a given district might be inferred by determining the relative attention given to each of the nine matrix "targets."

There is no expectation that every social studies program will, or even ought to, reflect equal emphasis on each target. But a comprehensive program will include at least some attention to all nine targets. General characteristics of learning experiences associated with each target are described in the following pages.

PERSONAL EDUCATION—UNDERSTANDINGS

An important function of the instructional target designated *personal education— understandings* is helping students to develop a solidly grounded sense of personal identity. Instructional activities attempt to help students grow in terms of their awareness of personal implications of past, present, and possible future events. This social studies target promotes student recognition of forces that shape their own unique qualities. Questions such as the following guide course and lesson planning in this area:

1. What are patterns of individual development in our society? In others?
2. How do individual actions affect the larger society?
3. How does the larger society affect individual actions?
4. To what extent is "individual behavior" defined by the expectations of others?
5. What is unique to the individual other than his or her first name, his or her family name, and other "labels" applied to him or her by social convention?

PERSONAL EDUCATION—SKILLS

The target of *personal education—skills* seeks to help students develop behavior patterns that will help them to work comfortably and productively with others.

At one level, because each individual's contributions influence the quality of life of an entire society, responsible work and study habits are encouraged. Inquiry skills that help students develop defensible solutions to problems are emphasized. Special attention is devoted to the improvement of students' abilities to communicate their ideas clearly. Questions such as the following guide course and lesson planning in this area:

1. What steps are involved in arriving at a supportable decision?
2. What are the characteristics of effective written and oral communication?
3. How does the quality of work of an individual affect the quality of life in a society?
4. How can work be organized so that it can be accomplished in a way that is efficient and personally satisfying?
5. How can arguments be altered to fit the special needs of the audience being addressed?

Personal Education—Attitudes and Values

A central purpose of the target of *personal education—attitudes and values* is helping each student to develop a positive self-concept. This requires the development of learning experiences designed to assist students in recognizing their own values. Alternative value options are emphasized. Students are helped to identify priorities they have established among values they hold and to recognize the values' basis of their decisions. Questions such as the following guide course and lesson planning in this area:

1. What are values, and how are they identified?
2. What kind of behaviors can be identified that indicate the relative importance an individual attaches to different values?
3. What can an individual do to identify his or her own values priorities?
4. How are individual values affected by culture?
5. What is the relationship between values and individual decisions?

Social Education—Understandings

The target of *social education—understandings* seeks to help students understand the expectations placed on them by the society of which they are a part. Learning experiences highlight institutional arrangements that have evolved over time to define relationships between individuals and societies. Consideration is given to present arrangements and to potential future changes in the individual-society relationship. Also, students are helped to identify ways in which they personally can shape the direction of the larger community. Questions such as the following guide course and lesson planning in this area:

1. How is individual development both supported and limited by societies?
2. What specific institutional arrangements have evolved in this society to define

individual-society relationships? What arrangements have evolved elsewhere. How are these differences explained?

3. How stable are present individual-society relationships in this society? Elsewhere? How can differences be explained?
4. What likely future patterns in individual-society relationships might be expected here? Elsewhere? Why might there be differences?
5. What impact can the individual have on the larger society here? Elsewhere? How are differences explained?

Social Education—Skills

Effective group participation is a primary concern of the social studies known as *social education—skills*. Learning experiences focus on developing students' abilities to work productively with others to make collective decisions. Emphases include development of expertise in such areas as facilitating discussions and negotiating acceptable compromises. Questions such as the following guide course and lesson planning in this area:

1. What are alternative ways of organizing groups? What are strengths and weaknesses of each?
2. How can individuals best contribute to a group effort? What sort of individual behavior contributes to the ability of a group to arrive at a decision?
3. How can participation of members in groups be maximized?
4. How does the negotiation process go forward? What rights and obligations characterize individuals engaged in negotiation?
5. What strategies can the individual employ to maintain group cohesiveness? Under which conditions should these strategies be employed?

Social Education—Attitudes and Values

Instruction guided by the social studies target of *social education—attitudes and values* attempts to help students to recognize basic social values characterizing their own society. Influences that these values have on individual behavior are emphasized. In addition, students are exposed to attitudes and values of other cultures. Students are encouraged to compare and contrast attitudes and values in their own society with those of other societies. Questions such as the following guide course and lesson planning in this area:

1. What basic social values characterize this society? How do those values affect individual attitudes and values?
2. What specific features of this society reflect basic social values?
3. How do values in other societies differ from values in this society?
4. How do people in other societies establish priorities for their attitudes and values? How do people in this society do this? How are differences explained?
5. To what extent can differences in behavior of individuals in different societies be explained by dissimilar sets of cherished attitudes and values?

Intellectual Education—Understandings

Learning experiences directed toward the social studies target of *intellectual education—understandings* are characterized by emphases on the findings of historians and social scientists. Facts, concepts, and generalizations from these academic specialists may provide a focus for instructional practices. Lessons are directed toward helping students master knowledge that has been developed by professional scholars in history and the social sciences. Questions such as the following guide course and lesson planning in this area:

1. What key topics have attracted concerted professional interest by historians and social scientists?
2. What frameworks have historians and social scientists used to organize the presentation of their findings?
3. Which key facts, concepts, and generalizations have been highlighted by historians and social scientists?
4. Which alternative interpretations of important topics have been made by historians and social scientists?
5. How can ideas deemed important by historians and social scientists be presented in a form that appears relevant to students?

Intellectual Education—Skills

The social studies target of *intellectual education—skills* seeks to acquaint students with methods of historians and social scientists. There is a heavy emphasis on the *processes* as opposed to the *products* of research. Learning experiences are directed toward helping students develop defensible data-gathering procedures and scientific inquiry skills. Questions such as the following guide course and lesson planning in this area:

1. What are the sources of raw information used by historians and social scientists?
2. How do historians and social scientists organize raw information?
3. What steps do historians and social scientists follow in reaching conclusions? How can the "validity" of their conclusions be checked?
4. What special skills are needed by historians and social scientists?
5. How can processes used by historians and social scientists be applied to nonacademic problems?

Intellectual Education—Attitudes and Values

Learning experiences focusing on the social studies target of *intellectual education—attitudes and values* are designed to help students develop positive feelings toward the systematic approaches used by historians and social scientists in generating new knowledge. Instruction promotes student appreciation of rational approaches to problems out of a conviction that such approaches are likely to result in personally and socially productive solutions. There is a heavy emphasis on giving students opportunities to demonstrate their commitment to systematic problem-solving procedures. Questions such as the following guide course and lesson planning in this area:

1. Which personal problems of students are likely to provide a good focus for the practice of systematic problem-solving skills?
2. Which problem-solving techniques used by historians and social scientists are students most likely to find useful in working out solutions to personal problems?
3. What arguments can be made supporting the use of systematic problem-solving approaches similar to those used by historians and social scientists?
4. Which social problems that are important to students might be used as a focus for lessons designed to help students appreciate the usefulness of systematic problem-solving approaches?
5. What advantages of scientific problem-solving techniques might be pointed out to students?

Identifying Social Studies' Organizational Patterns

A comprehensive social studies program provides learners with at least some instruction directed toward each matrix "target." Clearly, however, there will be significant differences in emphasis from program to program. This diversity reflects a healthy attention to differing needs of individual districts, schools, and students. Although a certain programmatic uniqueness from district to district is desirable, there is a need for social studies educators to avoid developing extremely unbalanced programs that might focus all instructional efforts on only a very limited number of "targets."

There is evidence that unbalanced programs do exist in some places. For example, some very traditional programs tend to be heavily oriented toward the single target of "intellectual understanding." Learning experiences in such situations may demand little of students beyond simple recall of information. Unless there is some consideration of "intellectual skills" and the *processes* of knowledge production, students will not be encouraged to develop more sophisticated thinking skills.

A lack of systematic attention to social or personal concerns, moreover, may convince students that social studies classes are fundamentally irrelevant. Students have merely to look around to observe people who are getting along very well indeed with little knowledge of any academic discipline. Given this reality, a social studies program centered heavily on the single target of "intellectual understandings" may prove a "hard sell" to students.

There are dangers, too, in weighting programs too heavily in either the areas of "social education" or "personal education." In the case of social education, unbalanced programs may promote the idea that individuals are hopelessly controlled by the social groups of which they are a part. Such an emphasis may well suggest to students that they have no personal responsibilities for their own actions.

Programs centering too heavy on personal education may lead students to develop very self-centered views of reality. Students may develop an unhealthy commitment to a destructive individualism in which personal actions are seen as having no relationship to the social milieu in which they occur. Further, an absence of learning experiences directed toward the target of intellectual education denies students access to basic information that can form the basis for reasoned individual action in a multiperson world.

Program balance is achieved only when some emphasis is accorded each target area. Acceptable programmatic variants include all those in which the goal of social competence can be seen clearly as guiding program organization. Programs directed toward the goal of social competence seek to help students utilize academic knowledge to make decisions with an understanding of their likely personal and social consequences.

In an attempt to serve the general goal of social competence, many traditional social studies programs have been organized around courses drawing heavily upon the academic disciplines of history and the social sciences. Such course patterns have been maintained by the force of tradition and by teacher preparation programs that have emphasized work in these subjects. The following list of courses by grade levels exemplifies a typical discipline-centered pattern:

Grade 7: State History.
Grade 8: United States History.
Grade 9: Geography.
Grade 10: World History.
Grade 11: United States History.
Grade 12: Economics/Political Science.

Some programs organized around the academic disciplines are quite strong. The better ones maintain a desirable balance among "targets" associated with "intellectual education," "social education," and "personal education." Less desirable programs organized around disciplines overemphasize intellectual "understandings" at the expense of other important areas.

Hunt and Metcalf (1968) suggested that the social studies program be organized around "problematic areas of culture" as an alternative to the academic disciplines. A *problematic area of culture* is an area of culture about which people may hold conflicting, contradictory opinions and about which many people have not made up their minds. As examples of problematic areas of culture that might replace academic disciplines as course titles in secondary social studies, Hunt and Metcalf (1968) suggest the following:

1. Power and the Law.
2. Economics.
3. Nationalism, Patriotism, and Foreign Affairs.
4. Social Class.
5. Race and Minority Group Relations.
6. Sex, Courtship, and Marriage.

According to this organizational scheme, students are encouraged to use information from history and the social sciences as the basis for making judgments about these problems. These decisions are to be made only after careful consideration of personally held attitudes and values. Learning experiences directed toward "social education" targets fit in particularly well with this scheme. Strong programs with this orientation also do a good job of serving targets associated with intellectual education and personal education. Weak programs of this type tend to deal superficially with contents from the disciplines that can help students deal meaningfully with critical social issues. Some, too, give sparse attention to the need to attend to students' individual as well as social development.

A third organizational scheme appeared in many secondary schools in the late 1960s and early 1970s. This scheme might best be described as a cafeteria-style curriculum. The term *cafeteria-style* refers to the freedom given students to choose from a wide variety of course offerings made available in this organizational arrangement. Developed in response to student activism and accompanying charges of programmatic "irrelevancy" in the social studies, many poorer examples of cafeteria-style curricula have been characterized by a hodgepodge of short two-, three-, four-, or five-week courses known as minicourses. In some schools, except for a few state-mandated graduation requirements, minicourses have come to comprise the entire social studies curriculum. The following titles are examples of those found in social studies programs reflecting a cafeteria-style curriculum:

Great Generals from Caesar to MacArthur.
Improving Sensitive Verbal Communication.
Cultural Settlement Patterns in Illinois.
America's Four Great Religions.
Consumers and the Law.
Social Problems Through Sociodrama.
Who Started World War I?
War and Technology.

On the positive side, cafeteria-style curricula have had the potential to respond well to targets focusing on personal education. In many programs, new minicourses have been offered in response to surveys of student interest. This has provided a potential, at least, for addressing social studies programs to genuine areas of student concern. Some of the better programs have attended to targets relating to intellectual education and social education as well. With regard to intellectual education, some programs have required students to take a series of minicourses that, when completed, would assure exposure to some organized content from history and the social sciences. Others have been careful to provide some minicourse topics that have focused on persistent social problems and that have been directed toward targets with a social education orientation.

Because of its essentially fragmented character, the cafeteria-style curriculum has great potential for reducing social studies instruction to a trivial level. Certainly, this need not happen, but the typically heavy emphasis on personal education suggests a potential, at least, for such programs to respond perhaps too quickly to the whims of the moment.

In the final analysis, the pattern of organization of the social studies program is not, by itself, a sufficient criterion of excellence. Outstanding programs and very poor programs can be found that have been organized around academic disciplines, around problematic areas of culture, and around minicourses. Titles and sequences of courses reveal little about the quality of a program. The key to quality resides in the nature of the learning experiences provided *within* courses. So long as courses, however titled and sequenced, promote the development of learners' understandings, skills, and attitudes and values in the areas of intellectual education, social education, and personal education, then the social studies program can be described as worthy.

An assessment of a given social studies program must be tempered by the recognition that the simple existence of a structure of courses including contents promising *possibilities* for comprehensive learning experiences by no means suggests that comprehensive learning experiences will be provided in *practice*. Maintenance of a comprehensive social studies program demands systematic review to assure that good intentions are truly reflected in good practice.

Likely Trends in Organizational Patterns of Social Studies Programs

Though diversity probably will continue to characterize organization of social studies programs, pressures are at work that may make it more feasible for many districts to center programs around academic disciplines than around problematic areas of culture or minicourses. These pressures relate to typical patterns of teacher training and to increasing public demands for teacher "accountability."

The "problematic areas of culture" approach assumes that teachers will be able to pull relevant insights from a number of disciplines that students can use as a basis for decision making. Regrettably, very few teachers are prepared by training to sift through information from a variety of disciplines in a systematic way. Most secondary teachers have majored in history. A smaller number have majors in political science, geography, and other social and behavioral sciences. Very few are intellectually comfortable in situations calling for them to deal with sophisticated content in more than a single academic major.

One might argue that if teachers are deficient in terms of their ability to manipulate contents from a variety of subjects, the college and university preparation programs should be modified. Indeed, such a modification might make a good deal of sense. But, given the reality of a higher education culture where honor goes to those who make their contributions within the confines of a single academic discipline, prospects for change seem slim. Very few rewards are likely to accrue to professors who break with tradition by attempting to institute a truly interdisci-plinary undergraduate program. Indeed, tenure and promotion problems of professors holding appointments in more than a single department are legendary in academic communities. So, though an intellectual case might well be made for truly interdisciplinary university-level training, social and political realities within higher education will probably frustrate attempts to reshape undergraduate education in this direction.

The trend toward increasing public concern for "accountability" or "cost effectiveness" in education may well augur an era of diminished enthusiasm for both programs organized around problematic areas of culture and programs organized around minicourses. A major concern of individuals concerned with escalating costs in education is that instruction be efficient. Any determination of a course's efficiency assumes a capability of comparing students' achievement in a course taught under one set of conditions with students' achievement in a similar course taught under a different set of conditions. Further, it assumes a broad consensus about which content is "basic" and how it should be measured.

Programs organized around problematic areas of culture and minicourses tend to include courses that vary tremendously from school to school. Consequently, it is difficult for evaluators to make comparisons between schools and programs. What, for example, does one conclude if, in School A, seniors average 89.3 per cent on a test given at the end of a course on "Great Military Leaders of the Confederacy" and, in School B, seniors average 71.4 per cent on a test given at the end of a course on "Great Naval Battles and How They Have Shaped History"? Clearly, from a measurement standpoint, such a comparison is meaningless. The demand for "accountability" may tend to support installation of courses having more common threads of content to facilitate the desire to have a reasonable basis for comparing programs in different settings. Given the wide range of course titles and contents in programs organized around problematic areas of culture and minicourses, this push for accountability may well result in less public support for social studies programs of these types.

A likely consequence of the cost-effectiveness movement may be a renewed emphasis on courses and topics stemming from the academic disciplines of history and the social sciences. Years of scholarship in these areas have brought about at least some degree of agreement about which topics are important. Further, there has been a long history of development of testing procedures designed to assess students' skills and understandings in these areas. Although certainly such tests could be developed to assess performance in programs organized according to a "problematic areas of culture" or "minicourse" theme, funds for such undertakings are likely to be short in an atmosphere characterized by the suspicion that the cost of education may already be too high. Chances are that existing evaluation procedures will be favored. Given the focus of these testing devices on traditional content from the academic disciplines, it is likely that increasing pressures will be put on the schools to make contents associated with these disciplines key components of the social studies program. This result is by no means an inevitability. But, given present public concerns, prospects seem favorable for a renewed interest on topics associated with the disciplines of history and the social sciences.

Summary

A number of organizational schemes have evolved for social studies programs. Alternative focuses of programs can be illustrated graphically in a nine-cell matrix. On one axis this matrix features the three program emphases of (1) personal education, (2) citizenship education, and (3) intellectual education. On the other axis, this matrix identifies types of learning outcomes including (1) understandings, (2) skills, and (3) attitudes and values. Each cell of the matrix can be thought of as one important "target" of the social studies program. Comprehensive programs give some attention to all targets. This does not mean, however, that there are not variations in emphases on individual targets between and among social studies programs.

Three general types of course schemes have evolved. The most traditional type features courses and titles tied more or less directly to the academic disciplines of history and the social sciences. A second type features an emphasis on persistent problems. A third type emphasizes interests of students very heavily and is characterized by a heavy reliance on minicourses. Because of the nature of teacher preparation programs and because of increasing pressures on social studies educators to produce measurable results, there may be a trend back toward a heavier emphasis on courses and contents associated with the academic disciplines.

REFERENCES

HUNT, MAURICE P., and LAWRENCE E. METCALF. *Teaching High School Social Studies.* New York: Harper & Row, Publishers, 1968.

JAROLIMEK, JOHN. *Social Studies in Elementary Education.* 5th ed. New York: Macmillan Publishing Co., Inc., 1977.

JOYCE, BRUCE R. *New Strategies for Social Education.* Chicago: Science Research Associates, Inc., 1972.

SAVAGE, TOM V., JR., and DAVID G. ARMSTRONG. "Zeroing-In: Targeting Social Studies." *The Clearing House* (January 1974): 278–280.

Preparing for
Instruction

Chapter 3

IDENTIFYING AND ORGANIZING CONTENT

IDENTIFYING AND ORGANIZING CONTENT pose an important challenge to the talents of social studies educators. One response, though a dangerously inadequate option, has been to use topic titles contained within textbooks as an organizational framework. Such a practice suffers from several serious deficiencies.

Social studies texts, even within a given subject area, tend to reflect a tremendous diversity in terms of topics treated. Probably the least variety is observed within traditional secondary history texts organized according to a chronological development approach. But even history texts formatted according to a sequential exposition of events through time reflect some differences in terms of topic selection and treatment. Differences in authors' approaches are even more pronounced in texts treating a single social science discipline (anthropology, economics, geography, political science, or sociology).

Even if all social studies texts were organized according to predictable patterns, little would commend the practice of organizing contents around a topic title framework. Contents ordered by topic title fail to focus on what is truly central to planning an organizational framework. This key issue concerns what students are expected to derive from their experiences with these materials.

A satisfactory procedure for identifying and selecting social studies content requires a consideration both of the nature of the content to be mastered and the nature of the learning process itself. Subject matter content and learning process are related symbiotically. Considering either element in isolation from the other results in decisions about identifying and organizing social studies content that ignore the mutual-ity of the content structure/learning process relationship. An organizational approach that does recognize the importance of this relationship centers around the use of the "structure of knowledge" approach.

The Structure of Knowledge Approach

Developed from the work of such figures as Bruner (1960) and Taba (1962), the "structure of knowledge" approach seeks to identify critical elements to be learned from a given content area and to scale those elements in terms of their importance. The assumption is that a given element becomes "important" as it increases in its ability to provide students with information that transfers to situations other than the one in which it was learned. Thus, elements of a higher level of abstraction are regarded as "more important."

Elements of the structure of knowledge, listed in order of increasing specificity, are generalizations, concepts, and facts. Briefly stated, identifying and organizing social studies content according to a structure of knowledge involve (1) a determination of the generalizations to guide the direction of the overall program, (2) an identification of major concepts contained within or implied by those generalizations, and (3) selection of facts to illustrate and illuminate the generalizations and concepts. The relationship of these three elements is depicted schematically in Figure 3–1.

A more detailed explanation of the special characteristics of each of these elements will provide a better basis for understanding how each functions in the process of identifying and organizing social studies content.

GENERALIZATIONS

Fundamentally, generalizations are statements of relationship among concepts. A generalization's "truth" is demonstrated by reference to evidence. Generalizations

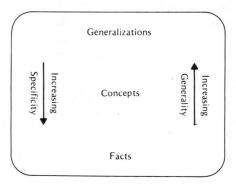

Figure 3–1. Relationship of Elements in a Structure of Knowledge

tend to organize a tremendous amount of information into a concise statement.

Generalizations are propositional in nature; that is, they are true only so far as available evidence continues to support their truth. Some generalizations may have to be modified at a later date when new evidence, not presently available, fails to support the truth implied by the generalization.

The following are examples of social studies generalizations:

1. When the quantity of goods available for purchase remains the same and the quantity of money in consumers' pockets increases, prices are likely to go up.
2. As a society becomes increasingly educated and industrialized, its birthrate declines. (Berelson and Steiner, 1967.)
3. The more demands a natural environment places on people for physical survival, the less attention people in that environment pay to supernatural phenomena. (Berelson and Steiner, 1967, pp. 24 and 25.)
4. Opinions that originate in an earlier period persist to be influential in a later period, both within a single lifetime and over generations. (Berelson and Steiner, 1967, p. 104.)

Note that these generalizations can all be converted to an "if . . . then" format. As can be seen from the preceding examples, generalizations are not always written in the form of an "if . . . then" statement. But nearly always they can be restated in this manner. This points up again the propositional tentative nature of generalizations. Generalizations always are characterized by their "testability," by a capability of having their validity assessed in the light of new evidence.

Generalizations represent terse, idea-dense consolidations of "truths" whose veracity is supported by the best information available at present. Generalizations, however, have at least the potential of being modified should new evidence develop at some future time that contradict the generalizations' "truth."

Generalizations are propositional statements of relationship among concepts that frequently are qualified by a condition. Take, for example, the following generalization from those provided in the list in the previous section: *As a society becomes increasingly educated and industrialized, its birthrate declines.*

Concepts in this generalization include: "society," "educated society," "industrialized society," and "birthrate." This generalization does include a necessary *condition* that must exist if the relationship among these concepts is to hold; that is, the birthrate declines under the *condition* that a society increasingly becomes educated and industrialized.

CONCEPTS

For students to understand the intent of the generalization just discussed, they need to have a solid understanding of the concepts included in the generalization. For students, an essential beginning is that they grasp the fundamental distinctions between concepts and generalizations.

Generalizations are propositional statements thought to be "true" because available evidence supports them. Concepts, on the other hand, are definitional. They are *stipulative* constructs. They "mean" what they "mean" not because of any supporting evidence but because they have been defined in a certain way. Concepts may be thought of as fulfilling a function similar to axioms in plane geometry. They are "givens" that are accepted as building blocks of levels of knowledge that are testable (generalizations).

The stipulative nature of a concept might be illustrated by the concept "moon dust" that we could define as (1) *a powdery substance,* (2) *gray in color,* (3) *found on the surface of the moon.* Should an astronaut land and find (1) *a powdery substance,* (2) *brown in color,* (3) *resting on the lunar surface,* he or she could not logically claim to have found "moon dust." The definition stipulates that moon dust is gray; therefore, the brown substance he or she found cannot be moon dust.

Concepts can be thought of as organizers that tie together a great deal of specific information under a given heading. As can be seen from the "moon dust" example, concepts are defined by reference to specific characteristics that each example of a given concept must have. These characteristics are referred to as *attributes* of a concept. "Moon dust" has the attributes of (1) being a powdery substance, (2) being gray in color, and (3) being located on the moon.

In the social studies, concepts present special problems because few are so simply defined as moon dust. Social studies teachers need to deal with very complex concepts such as "democracy," "culture," "socialization," "diffusion," "capital goods," and other abstractions with multiple defining attributes. Indeed, the problem is so nettlesome that a number of strategies described in another section of this book deals exclusively with procedures for teaching concepts.

Problems associated with concepts are particularly acute for teachers of high school juniors and seniors who have developed a certain social sophistication. These youngsters sometimes are able to use concept *labels* properly and in context even when they have totally inadequate understandings of the defining attributes of a concept.

Consider a high school teacher who poses a question such as "Tell me. Why do you think so many Hungarians wanted to come to the United States after the 1956 revolt?" An insightful student might reply, "They were attracted by our democratic institutions." The response with the reference to "democratic institutions" does have a logical connection to the question, and it may please the teacher. But the reply in no way can be taken as evidence that the student really understands the complex defining attributes of the concept *democratic institutions.* The alert teacher needs to be sensitive to the possibility that smooth student verbalism may not signal genuine understanding.

FACTS

Whereas concepts tie together a great number of specific phenomena and enable us to make some order out of very fragmented information, "facts" have no such general organizing characteristic. Concepts are universals that draw together all examples that are consistent with the stipulated attributes. Facts, on the other hand, are restricted to a particular time. Note the differences between the concepts and the facts presented in the following two lists:

Concepts	Facts
Monsoon wind	Lincoln was born in 1909.
Socialization	There are more than 12 million Methodists in the United States.
Inflation	Mountains cover 13.5 per cent of New Mexico.
Nuclear family	In 1960 there were over one million foreign-born Italians in the United States.
Executive clemency	King George V of England and Czar Nicolas II of Russia were related.
Growth pole	Wyoming has fewer people than Montana.
Folkway	Olympia is the capital of Washington.

Facts, because they tend to be tied to a specific set of circumstances, tend to have little transfer value from situation to situation. For this reason, identifying and organizing a social studies program around facts has little to commend it.

On the other hand, there is a need to caution against the protestations of some critics of facts who have suggested they should be eliminated completely from social studies programs. This position ignores the critically important function of facts in supporting the "truth" of generalizations. Facts provide the evidence that illustrates the veracity of generalizations.

In identifying and organizing content, then, the issue ought not center on the question of whether or not facts should be taught. Rather the discussion should focus on *which* facts to include. Generalizations selected for inclusion in a program provide bases for making that decision. If the facts illuminate the generalization, they are properly included. If, on the other hand, there seems no logical relationship between facts and generalizations, then inclusion of those facts in the instructional program cannot be defended. As an illustration, look at the following generalization and a list of facts being considered for inclusion in the program.

Generalization: As a society becomes increasingly educated and industrialized, its birthrate declines.

Possible facts that might be stressed are the following:

1. After large-scale steel production developed in Zoravia between 1890 and 1940, the number of live births declined from a pre-1942 level of 150 per 1,000 to 75 per 1,000.
2. Zoravia has built resort hotels overlooking Lake Balasuki in Sarimba Province that in 1976 brought in over $2 million to the government tourist bureau.
3. From 1900–1950 Zoravia increased its investment in education and industry tenfold, and the rate of population growth was cut in half during the same period.
4. Maltuccio City is the capitol of Zoravia.
5. Deposits of silver-bearing ores in southeastern Zoravia have been estimated by United Nations authorities to be worth the equivalent of $2.3 billion U.S.

Of the five facts presented, only facts 1 and 3 relate to the generalization. Although textual material might well include reference to facts 2, 4, and 5, for purposes of organizing for instruction, the teacher logically cannot insist that students deal with these facts that bear no relationship to the identified generalization. (Of course, were there other generalizations guiding instruction that did relate to items 2, 4, and 5, they properly might be emphasized.)

Selecting Program Organizers

Identifying and organizing content in the social studies involves, in order, a determination of (1) guiding generalizations, (2) concepts contained within or implied by those generalizations, and (3) facts that illuminate those generalizations. The focus on generalizations has several advantages. First, generalizations point to a specific learning outcome of instruction rather than to a chapter title or some other label that may have an unclear relationship to the specifics of intended student learning. Second, generalizations are broad consolidations of information that have great transfer value from situation to situation. They help students to apply knowledge in settings beyond the social studies classroom.

Depending upon the purposes of instruction, teachers may choose to develop their own guiding generalizations or to select them from other sources. Teacher-developed generalizations are most appropriate when instruction focuses on personal education and, to a somewhat lesser extent, on social education. This results because issues relating to these areas tend to cross lines of academic disciplines. Consequently, there may be a poor "fit" between generalizations attached to the disciplines and the focus of an instructional program in the area of personal education.

On the other hand, for many instructional programs with heavy emphases on specific academic disciplines, there are a number of excellent sources for generalizations that have been validated by the work of professional scholars. For example, Berelson and Steiner's *Human Behavior: An Inventory of Scientific Findings* (1964) is a treasure trove of generalizations developed from the behavioral sciences. Additionally, the Social Science Education Consortium in Boulder, Colorado, has monographs available with generalizations from social science disciplines.

Once generalizations are identified, they need to be arranged in terms of their importance according a logical plan. A casual examination of a list of generalizations, unfortunately, will not reveal which ought to be selected for heaviest emphasis. A certain artistry is required. But it should not be presumed that this artistry implies that *any* selection and arrangement of generalizations are equally appropriate. There are some guidelines that can be followed in selecting and establishing priorities for generalizations. Consideration needs to be given to each of the following:

1. Student characteristics.
2. Teacher characteristics.
3. Extent of available learning materials.

STUDENT CHARACTERISTICS

In the selection of one generalization instead of another for emphasis, the interests of students deserve consideration. When selected generalizations focus on issues of compelling concern to students, then it is relatively easy to develop lessons relating to these generalizations that students find motivating. When selected generalizations focus on issues and topics students regard as less relevant to their own concerns, the teacher faces a more difficult motivational task.

Certainly, some issues may be considered important enough to introduce to students even when initial levels of interest are low. Creative teachers are able to generate student enthusiasm through the development of a series of lessons that are so outstanding that the issue *becomes* "relevant" as instruction unfolds. Though television's "superteachers" manage this trick with ease once a week (indeed, sometimes a class of television students hopelessly deficient in basic skills has been so turned on by its "superteacher" that its members are observed quoting snatches from Kant's *Critique of Pure Reason* after only twenty minutes of the program have gone by). Regrettably, in the real world of teaching, such quick and easy transformations are the exception. Turning around a serious motivational problem requires dogged effort on the part of teacher. Although no one argues that the attempt should not be made, still, when alternatives are available regarding which issues might logically be selected to illuminate a given topic, it makes sense to opt for an issue that holds some initial interest for students. Generalizations focusing on such issues provide a sound basis for developing lessons students will find interesting.

In addition to the question of initial student interest, the complexity of concepts within alternative generalizations must be considered. This requires a simultaneous examination of the concepts themselves and of the students in a given class. For example, for some students, a concept from economic geography such as "growth pole" might be something never previously encountered. Others may have picked up a general understanding of the term, but nothing too specific. Still others may have a solid grasp of the concept.

This situation suggests that some diagnostic work is in order to determine students' levels of understanding of important concepts. A short diagnostic test might be prepared to assess students' levels of understanding (for example, the term *growth pole* might be included in a short matching test along with alternative choices of definitions). Another possibility would be some probing teacher questions to determine students' grasp of the idea ("Dennis, can you tell me what a 'growth pole' is?").

Ordinarily, generalizations that do not contain large numbers of concepts that are unfamiliar to students require less instructional time than those that do include many new concepts. Consider the following generalization:

> Urban areas grow out from a central core area in a pattern of concentric circles.

Suppose most of the students in the class are unfamiliar with the concepts "urban center," "core area," and "concentric circle." Given this situation, most students would be unable to derive meaning from the generalization. Certainly, there is nothing essentially wrong with selecting such a generalization. But the choice must be made with a full realization that development of student understanding will take time.

In addition to teaching the essence of the generalization, the teacher will have to build a solid base of understanding of the fundamental concepts "urban center," "core area," and "concentric circle." For teachers, the lesson is that generalizations including large numbers of unfamiliar concepts require more time to teach than those where basic concepts are familiar to students. Because time for instruction is limited, when alternative generalizations seem to serve a given focus topic equally well, it makes sense to organize instruction around those generalizations that will not result in students' being overwhelmed by the necessity of learning too large a number of totally unfamiliar concepts.

Teacher Characteristics

The personal background of the individual teacher must be considered in selecting generalizations to use as a basis for designing the instructional program. For example, a junior high school teacher with a solid background and a compelling personal interest in American social history properly should select a different set of guiding generalizations for a unit on the Civil War from that selected by another teacher with a solid background and compelling personal interest in American military history. Certainly, both teachers will wish to cover some common ground, but each can enrich his or her program by drawing upon individual strengths. Teachers become more excited about their teaching and more personally involved with their instruction when they draw upon their own interests and academic strengths.

These enthusiasms frequently translate into heightened levels of student interest in the program.

EXTENT OF AVAILABLE LEARNING RESOURCES

The nature and availability of learning materials that might be used to support instruction must be considered when selecting generalizations to guide instructional practices. Generalizations that focus on issues so specialized that only a limited range of student learning materials are available represent poor choices. Productive learning demands the availability of a range of books to supplement the text, films, tapes, speakers, and other informational resources. In selecting generalizations, it makes sense to choose those for which a wide array of support materials and learning resources are available.

The "availability" issue bears some emphasis. By "availability" is meant "availability for use in the classroom where instruction will take place or by students in that classroom." It is not wise to plan a program on the assumption that certain materials, not presently in hand, will be purchased in time for the beginning of the new program. Moneys targeted for materials purchase in May have a tendency to find their way to other uses before September. Until such learning resources are actually available for teacher and student use, it makes little sense to commit time to planning a program that assumes their availability. If instructional planning goes forward on an assumption that x will be available in the fall and x turns out not to be available, new plans will have to be made. Given the very heavy demands on teachers' time, it makes little sense to invest hours in preparing an instructional program that cannot be taught with instructional resources known to be on hand.

When a number of generalizations have been identified that might be used in organizing instruction related to a given topic, the process of identifying the generalizations that will be selected can be facilitated through the use of a "generalizations decision-matrix." This matrix allows for a visual representation of relative strengths and weaknesses of generalizations that are being considered. An example is provided in Figure 3–2.

In using the generalizations decision-matrix, the teacher places a check mark in boxes that describe identified generalizations in terms of their potential appeal to students, the difficulty of the associated concepts, and the teacher's background in areas related to each generalization. In Figure 3–2, sample checks have been made beside each of the twelve hypothetical generalizations that have been listed. By reviewing checks made in various categories, teachers can begin to make judgments about which generalizations might be stronger choices than others for selection as program organizers.

For example, assuming that all twelve of the generalizations listed in Figure 3–2 are appropriately related to a given topic, a teacher would do well to give

Possible Generalizations that might be selected to guide instruction related to a given topic	Interest of Students		Concept Difficulty		Teacher's Background in Area		Availability of Learning Resources			
	Hi	Lo	Hi	Lo	Substantial	Minimal	Textbook Only	Textbook/Library	Audio/Visual Media	Other
Generalization 1	x		x		x				x	x
Generalization 2	x			x	x		x			
Generalization 3		x	x			x	x			
Generalization 4		x	x		x		x			
Generalization 5	x			x	x			x		x
Generalization 6	x		x		x			x	x	
Generalization 7	x			x	x			x	x	x
Generalization 8	x			x	x			x	x	
Generalization 9		x	x			x	x			
Generalization 10		x		x	x			x	x	x
Generalization 11	x		x		x			x	x	x
Generalization 12		x		x	x			x	x	

Figure 3–2. Generalizations Decision-Matrix (with sample data checked)

first consideration to generalizations characterized by (1) a potentially high student interest level, (2) low concept difficulty, (3) substantial teacher background in the area of focus of the generalization, and (4) abundant learning resources. The checks on the Figure 3–2 matrix reveal that Generalization 7 meets all four of these criteria.

The next most attractive generalizations would be those characterized by (1) a potentially high student interest level, (2) high concept difficulty, (3) substantial teacher background in the area of focus of the generalization, and (4) abundant learning resources. The most important difference between generalizations in this category and those in the "highest priority" category is that generalizations in this second highest priority group tend to have concepts that are more difficult than those in the highest priority group. This probably means that more instructional time will be necessary before students develop a substantial understanding of the generalization and lessons flowing from it. But if one considers that their interest in the subject is high, teacher background in the area is substantial, and a wide variety of learning resources is available, these generalizations in this group have promise as program organizers. In Figure 3–2, Generalization 11 is in this category.

Somewhat less desirable than generalizations in this second category are those characterized by (1) a potentially high student interest level, (2) low concept difficulty, (3) substantial teacher background in the area of focus of the generalization, and (4) somewhat limited learning resources. Though many features commend the selection of these generalizations, the limited supply of available learning resources places some restraints on the teacher's ability to design a program that seeks to meet individual needs of students through the use of a wide variety of learning experiences. Although creative teachers can do remarkably well given even a very restricted list of learning resources, still it is generally true that such a limitation results in the development of instructional programs that prove less satisfactory than those supported by a wider variety of learning resources. In Figure 3–2, Generalization 5 falls into this category.

Beyond this third category is a fourth containing generalizations that might be described as falling somewhere between "desirable" and "undesirable" in terms of their usefulness as program organizers. Such generalizations may have a few strong points, for example, abundant learning resources or low difficulty concepts. But they also have some counterbalancing "negatives" such as potentially low student interest and a focus on an area about which the teacher might have only a minimal background. Although respectable instructional programs can be developed using such generalizations as a basis for organizations, they hold less promise as program organizers than generalizations in the first three categories. In Figure 3–2, Generalizations 1, 2, 4, 6, 8, 10, and 12 are in this category.

The fifth and final group of generalizations should not be selected as program organizers when any other options are available. Generalizations in this group are characterized by (1) a potentially low student interest level, (2) high concept difficulty, (3) minimal teacher background in the area of focus of the generalization, and (4) learning resources limited to the course textbook alone. Generalizations in this category have scant promise of functioning as organizers for instructional programs that will involve and excite students. In Figure 3–2, Generalizations 3 and 9 are in this "unacceptable" category.

To summarize, a teacher who had looked over the twelve generalizations listed in Figure 3–2 might establish the following priorities for selecting generalizations to serve as a focus for the instructional program:

Priority 1: Generalization 7
Priority 2: Generalization 11
Priority 3: Generalization 5
Priority 4: Generalizations 1, 2, 4, 6, 8, 10, and 12
Priority 5: Generalizations 3 and 9

Use of the generalizations decisions-matrix assists teachers in establishing priorities for the selection of generalizations to guide program organization. But it does not help answer the question of how many generalizations ought to be selected. There is no quick and ready answer to the "how many" question. The issue turns on the interaction of two variables. First, the length of time to be devoted to the topic must be considered. Second, the depth of treatment of individual issues within the topic must be weighted.

In most cases, the number of generalizations required to organize a *four-week* block of instruction on the French Revolution will be fewer than the number required to organize a *semester-long* course on urban geography. Yet, because of variability associated with intensity of treatment of issues within a given topic area, there is no *inevitable* increase in the number of generalizations needed to organize a block of instruction that will require, for example, three weeks of instructional time over the number of generalizations needed to organize another block of instruction requiring, perhaps, two weeks of instructional time. If intensity of instruction is greater during the shorter two-week block of instruction, more organizing generalizations might be required than might be needed for a three-week instructional experience where expected learning outcomes are more modest.

If one is to make a reasoned decision about the number of generalizations needed to organize instruction on a topic, the focus must go beyond a consideration of the subject matter to be conveyed. The issue of intensity really reduces to the question, What should students be expected to take away from this experience? This question suggests an important focus on the process of thinking as well as on the content of learning.

The Thinking Process and the Selection of Organizing Generalizations

The amount of time spent on instruction relating to a given generalization varies according to decisions made about the nature of anticipated student learning. For example, if there is an interest in building only basic understandings with respect to Generalization A, but an interest in developing students' abilities to apply and analyze information deriving from Generalization B, then more instructional time will be required focusing on information related to Generalization B than on information related to Generalization A. This results because "applying and analyzing" are more complex mental processes than "developing basic understanding." Therefore, these abilities evolve more slowly and require more instructional time.

A useful tool for determining the complexity of alternative learning outcomes has been developed by Bloom and his associates (Bloom et al., 1956). They developed a "cognitive taxonomy" or hierarchy of thinking skills that were assigned priorities in terms of their sophistication. Ordered from simplest to most complex, the elements of the *Taxonomy* (Bloom et al., 1956) are the following:

Knowledge
Comprehension
Application
Analysis
Synthesis
Evaluation

KNOWLEDGE

"Knowledge" is the simple recall of previous information. Nothing more is required of the individual operating at the knowledge level than simply calling to mind and reproducing something that has been learned. The following are examples of questions that demand only knowledge-level thinking:

1. What is the capital of Michigan?
2. Who was the seventeenth president of the United States?

COMPREHENSION

"Comprehension" involves a focus on more than just a single element of knowledge and may require the individual to change the form of previously learned material or make a simple interpretation. The following are examples of questions requiring comprehension-level thinking:

1. Using this chart, explain the trend of wholesale prices over the last four years.
2. Summarize the plot of the story in your own words.

APPLICATION

"Application" requires that information learned in one setting be used in an unfamiliar context. The following are examples of questions requiring application-level thinking:

1. Using a scale of 1 inch = 500 miles, determine the point-to-point distance between Boston and Houston.
2. Using a table of random numbers, obtain a sample of 100 junior boys, and develop a profile of their interest in social studies.

ANALYSIS

"Analysis" requires an examination of a given phenomenon that involves a consideration of its constituent parts. The following are examples of questions requiring analysis-level thinking:

1. Look at the results of the presidential balloting. Identify and explain patterns of voting of blacks, Spanish-surnamed voters, and voters from at least two other important minority groups.
2. When it was written, how did the U.S. Constitution respond to the economic interests of certain classes of people?

SYNTHESIS

"Synthesis" requires students to put together pieces of separate information into a new configuration ("new" at least to the person doing the thinking). The following questions demand synthesis-level thinking:

1. What might have occurred had General Lee won a smashing victory at Gettysburg?
2. What differences might occur in the nature of decisions made by the General Assembly of the United Nations were member countries allotted votes proportional to their populations?

EVALUATION

"Evaluation" requires students to make judgments in the light of criteria. The following questions demand evaluation-level thinking:

1. Which of these two plays most closely follows the "rules" of French classical drama? How do you interpret the rules? What are the bases for your decision?
2. Which of these two candidates is best equipped to be president, and upon what evidence is your decision based? In your answer, define the phrase "best equipped." Describe qualities of the "good" president and the process or processes you used to identify these qualities.

These taxonomical categories provide useful planning guidelines to the teacher attempting to decide how much instructional time ought to be spent on various issues. In general, when learners will be expected to analyze, synthesize, or evaluate, more instructional time will be required than when they will be asked only to operate at the levels of knowledge, comprehension, or analysis.

The difference in time required to teach for learning at the various levels of the taxonomy has implications for the selection and organization of generalizations to guide program planning. For example, in a program where the teacher hoped that nearly all instructional activities would result in students' being able to function at the levels of analysis synthesis, and evaluation, fewer generalizations might be needed to organize program planning than in a situation where few instructional activities would be designed to promote these sorts of higher-level outcomes. Programs that are *entirely* oriented toward promoting higher-level thinking or entirely *oriented* toward promoting lower-level thinking are of some hypothetical interest, but they rarely occur in the real world of social studies teaching. Most social studies teachers establish some priority areas where they hope to produce students capable of analysis, synthesis, and evaluation (or, at least, application). Other areas are treated less thoroughly, and students are required to demonstrate less sophisticated levels of thinking.

Realizing that most programs represent something of a mix in terms of levels of thinking expected of students as a consequence of their exposure to the program, one should give serious thought to which generalizations to treat first in an instructional sequence. Generally, because of the time required to develop higher-level thinking abilities, instruction focusing on generalizations that organize content about which students will be expected to analyze, synthesize, and evaluate should begin early in the program. This will allow time for the development of these very sophisticated thinking skills and for the reinforcement of important basic information throughout the course. But sequencing of instruction related to individual generalizations does not depend *only* on expected levels of student thinking.

Suppose, for example, a teacher had identified the following five generalizations (adapted from Berelson and Steiner, 1967) to serve as program organizers for a six-week block of instruction on "urbanization." Further, assume that a decision had been made to provide students with instruction demanding them to analyze, synthesize, and evaluate information related to Generalizations 1, 2, and 3. (This would suggest a lower priority for information related to Generalizations 4 and 5. Presumably, less instructional time would be devoted to these lessons.)

Generalization 1: As regions become more urbanized, levels of literacy and years of formal education of the population tend to increase.

Generalization 2: When urbanization occurs rapidly, as in developing countries, differences in status among various social classes tend to increase.

Generalization 3: As an area becomes more urbanized, there is a tendency for the area to be characterized by a higher degree of political stability.

Generalization 4: Industrialization in a country brings with it increased urbanization.

Generalization 5: As an area becomes more urbanized, tolerance for religious diversity increases.

In identifying an appropriate sequence for instruction related to these generalizations, in addition to the issue of expected student outcomes, one must consider whether there is any "natural order" suggested by the language of the generalizations. In this case, the answer is no. Content related to each generalization could be taught before or after content related to any other of the five without doing violence to logic.

Another consideration concerns the numbers of concepts in any one generalization that are also contained in others. It is particularly important to determine if there is a single generalization among those that have been targeted for instruction leading to the development of students' higher-level thinking abilities that has many concepts in common with other generalizations of this kind. In the case of these sample generalizations, only the concept "urbanization" is common to

Generalizations 1, 2, and 3. Consequently, no case can be made for teaching any one of these generalizations before teaching the others.

Because there appears to be no "natural order" implied by Generalizations 1, 2, and 3 and because none of the three contains a large number of concepts common to the others, no very strong case can be made for teaching one of these generalizations before the others. In making the sequencing decision, the teacher might well consider interests of students, availability of learning materials, and his or her own preferences. So long as adequate instructional time is provided for students to develop the higher-level thinking abilities sought in learning experiences oriented around Generalizations 1, 2, and 3, the sequence in which they are taught probably will not be the most important determinant of student success during this block of instruction.

Using Selected Generalizations to Organize Content for Instruction

Once decisions have been made regarding which generalizations will provide a focus for instructional planning, the process of organization can go forward in a systematic way. Major concepts related to each generalization can be identified. Key facts can be identified that illuminate the concepts and the generalization to which they are related. Materials for students can be identified as well as materials that can enrich the background of the teacher.

In organizing a block of instruction on a given topic, for example, urbanization, one will find it useful to lay out each generalization and major related concepts as headings on a matrix. The matrix can be used to write in information related to key facts and specific sources of student and teacher information as they are identified during the planning process. Many teachers find it convenient to draw the matrix on a wall-sized piece of butcher paper and write in information with a felt-tipped marker. This provides plenty of room to include as many details as a teacher may desire. (As a rule, it is better to "overplan" than to "underplan" an instructional program.)

Consider, for example, a teacher who has made a decision to teach a block of instruction on "Problems of Urban Areas." One of the selected generalizations is the following:

> When urbanization occurs rapidly, as in developing countries, differences in status among social classes tend to increase. [Adapted from Berelson and Steiner, 1967]

Figure 3–3 illustrates how a generalization planning matrix might be developed for the part of the "Problems of Urban Areas" instruction focusing on this generalization.

Note in Figure 3–3 that not *every* concept included in the generalization has been included. The identification of "major concepts" results from a consideration of (1) the concepts most clearly related to an understanding of the generalization

```
Topic:              Problems of Urban Areas

Generalization:     When urbanization occurs rapidly, as in developing countries, differences
                    in status among various social classes tend to increase.

Major Concepts:     Urbanization, developing country, status, social class
```

Major Concepts	Urbanization	Developing Country	Status	Social Class
Key Facts				
Information Sources for Students				
Information Sources for the Teacher				

Figure 3–3. Generalization Planning Matrix

and (2) the concepts about which students may lack any depth of understanding. Given these two criteria, one or more concepts included in a given generalization may not be appropriate for inclusion as a "major concept" in the generalization planning matrix. For example, the concept "differences" probably represents an idea that is familiar to most secondary social studies students. It makes little sense to spend time planning for instruction directed to a concept of this type that students understand already. To do so robs valuable instructional time from lessons directed toward helping students grasp such complex and difficult concepts as "status" and "social class."

Once the generalization planning matrix has been prepared, the teacher can begin surveying available learning resources that might provide useful information for teaching and reinforcing the identified "major concepts." Surveyed resources might include textbooks; library books and periodicals; audio and visual media of all kinds, and community resources including speakers, museums, and points of interest that might be appropriate for students to visit. Key facts that might be used to enhance students' understanding of the major concepts can be identified as this review of learning resources goes forward. When specific learning resources and key facts are identified, they should be written in the matrix. The completed matrix presents a good overall guide to the kinds of content that should be highlighted and the kinds of relevant information resources that are available.

The generalization matrix for the topic "Problems of Urban Areas" depicted in Figure 3–3 focuses on just one of the generalizations selected to guide instruction on this topic. Additional planning matrices would be developed for each of the remaining generalizations selected to function as program organizers.

Information organized in generalization planning matrices provides a useful beginning point for preparing the more specific instructional units that will focus on each generalization. These units will include much more detailed information including (1) specific student objectives (what students should learn from the instruction provided), (2) instructional techniques to be used, and (3) methods for evaluating the success of the program. Daily lesson plans will be developed from these units. Detailed procedures for preparing units and daily lesson plans will be introduced in the chapter entitled "Planning Social Studies Units and Daily Lesson Plans."

Summary

Generalizations, concepts, and key facts can be used as a design framework for organizing social studies instruction. A number of sources for generalizations are available. In addition to their relevance to the focus topic, selection of generalizations demands consideration of (1) students' interest, (2) the teacher's background and interests, and (3) availability of learning resources that can be used to support lessons related to the generalization.

Once generalizations have been selected, instruction on a given subject can be organized through the use of a generalization planning matrix. This tool enables teachers to identify major concepts necessary for an understanding of the generalization and to pinpoint key facts that might enrich student understanding. Further, the matrix allows for the organization of related informational resources of interest both to students and to the teacher. A set of completed generalization planning matrices related to a given subject prepares the groundwork for more specific unit and daily lesson planning.

REFERENCES

BERELSON, BERNARD, and GARY A. STEINER. *Human Behavior: An Inventory of Scientific Findings.* New York: Harcourt Brace Jovanovich, Inc., 1964.
———. *Human Behavior: Shorter Edition.* New York: Harcourt Brace Jovanovich, Inc., 1967.
BLOOM, BENJAMIN S., ed. *Taxonomy of Educational Objectives: Handbook I: The Cognitive Domain.* New York: David McKay Co., Inc., 1956.
BRUNER, JEROME S. *The Process of Education.* Cambridge, Mass.: Harvard University Press, 1960.
TABA, HILDA. *Curriculum Development: Theory and Practice.* New York: Harcourt Brace and World, 1962.

Chapter 4

PLANNING SOCIAL STUDIES UNITS AND DAILY LESSON PLANS

S ELECTING A LIMITED AMOUNT OF material for instructional emphasis presents thorny problems for social studies teachers. Although identification of focus topics restricts the array of possibilities somewhat, still a very large number of options remains within those topic areas. One very simple, but inadequate, solution to this difficulty is a decision to allow the table of contents in a textbook to dictate the order and the emphasis of instruction.

Though this solution has an appeal on the basis of its apparent low demand on teacher planning time, it is not practical for several important reasons. First of all, even assuming an unusual class of students who had no reading difficulties, problems may well ensue because most text chapters contain a bewildering array of detailed information. Few students have the skills, when dealing with new material, to distinguish consistently between critically important and inconsequential details. Because of their shaky control over the concepts being presented in new textual materials, many students are quite as likely to key on the irrelevant as on the relevant information.

To avoid this pitfall, professional teachers give considerable thought to organizing instruction in such a way that significant information is highlighted in a systematic manner. The textbook becomes in their hands not an organizer of instruction but rather a data source that is used to support information that has been identified as "high priority." The planning framework that many teachers have found successful as an organizer of instructional experiences is the *unit*. The unit provides an organizational scheme for instruction that enables teachers to identify priority emphases, to communicate these emphases to students, and to plan learning experiences that support these emphases.

The unit can be thought of as a bridge between general goals of a broad subject and day-by-day instruction in the classroom. Units provide guidelines that seek to assure that instructional practices are directed individual generalizations that have been identified as effectively summarizing the content of a given topic area. The length of instruction covered by a given unit plan varies. In general, the unit represents an instructional span longer than several days' lessons, but shorter than a school quarter or semester.

Components of the Instructional Unit

A large number of frameworks for the development of instructional units have been developed. The scheme to be introduced here is representative of those unit plans. In terms of its basic components, the instructional unit has seven basic parts. These are

1. A topic statement (Civil War, Drugs and Youth, Revolution, and so on)
2. Focusing generalization(s)
3. Major concepts and subconcepts
4. Performance objectives
5. Key facts
6. Instructional techniques
7. Needed materials

THE TOPIC STATEMENT

Selection of a topic statement depends on the individual course being taught. In some instances, topics may reflect nothing more than chapter titles in textbooks. In others, topics may be much broader than those chapter titles. In still others, the teacher and the students may jointly identify the topic area. In general, then, the topic statement identifies the general area of concern or focus of the unit.

FOCUSING GENERALIZATION(S)

The focusing generalization represents an effort to add a measure of specificity to instructional planning once a topic area has been identified. The nature of the focusing generalization will vary, depending upon whether the unit is directed primarily toward intellectual education, social education, or personal education. The focusing generalization summarizes in a concise way a great deal of information related to the unit topic. The focusing generalization, as a statement of relationship among concepts, serves to highlight the major concepts that will be a major center of concern in the unit.

Major Concepts and Subconcepts

Concepts are organizers that tie together large quantities of information under a common heading. Many of the major concepts will be included in the statement of the focusing generalization. Subconcepts include important terms that are subordinate to the major concepts and that, in many instances, must be understood by learners before they can deal adequately with the major concepts.

Performance Objectives

Performance objectives represent one of the most critical decision points for teachers in unit planning. Performance objectives represent explicit statements of what students are to be able to do as a consequence of instruction and how learning is to be measured. As a protocol for writing performance objectives, the ABCD format is useful.

A = the *Audience* (Who will be doing the learning?)   C = the *Conditions* (What will the format of testing or assessment be?)

B = the *Behavior* (What must the student do to demonstrate his learning?)   D = the *Degree* (How well must the student perform to achieve the objective?)

The following is a correct example of a performance objective illustrating each of the major components:

>   A   B
> *Each student* will *compare patterns of black ghetto expansion in Seattle and Chicago*
>   C   D
> on an *essay examination* in which *at least five specific characteristics of the ghetto growth pattern in each city are described.*

The audience. The audience component of a performance objective presents few difficulties. It simply involves an identification of the specific person or persons at whom the objective is directed. In most cases, performance objectives are directed toward a class of learners. In these situations, the audience is described as "each student," "students," "learners," or by some other like terminology implying that all individuals in the group are to work toward attainment of the objective. In some instances, performance objectives may be directed toward a single individual or a group of individuals. In such cases, the audience component of the performance objective properly refers to "Elsa's group," "Herman Smith," or to whomever the teacher is directing the objective.

The behavior. The behavior component of a performance objective seeks to describe the outcome of learning in terms of observable student behavior. This requires the selection of verbs that imply an observable behavior of some kind. This, in turn, has necessitated some adjustments in thinking in the social studies where in times past desired outcomes largely were described in nonobservable terms. For example, sentences such as "Students will appreciate the democratic decision-making process" or "Students will learn to understand the causes leading to the outbreak of the Civil War" were features of social studies curriculum guides not too many years ago.

In dealing with the behavior component, one must decide upon the observable behaviors that, clustered together, may be taken as evidence of more abstract verbs such as *appreciate* and *understand*. The decisions as to which specific verbs will be selected have an arbitrary element about them that distress many beginning teachers. But the task should be undertaken confidently in the realization that grading based on a nonspecific, nonobservable verb such as *understand* is likely to be far more arbitrary and less reliable than grading based upon a set of verbs implying directly observable behavior. Once observable behaviors have been identified, instructional planning becomes simplified because expected student outcomes are stated in clear, precise terms.

The following are examples of verbs that might be selected for inclusion in the behavior component of a performance objective:

apply	differentiate
compare	evaluate
compute	identify
contrast	point out
describe	select
determine	state

The verbs that are selected will vary according to the cognitive level of the performance objective and the general purpose being sought. A much more extensive treatment of the process of selecting specific verbs to replace verbs such as *understand* and *appreciate* is found in Norman E. Gronlund's *Stating Objectives for Classroom Instruction*, 2d ed. (New York: Macmillan Publishing Co., Inc., 1978).

The conditions. The conditions component of a performance objective refers to the conditions of assessment. These assessment conditions, in a large number of instances, will be an examination or a test of some type. But, under certain circumstances, assessment may consist of teachers' casual observations of student behavior or of oral interchanges between teachers and students. In the selection of the appropriate assessment conditions, it is essential to consider the behavior being sought. For example, if the behavior is simply to "name the capitals of five states," an objective test of some kind is much more appropriate than an essay. The behavior calls for simple recall of specific information. There is nothing to be gained by permitting students to let their thoughts wander on an essay when the objective is directed at the recall of discrete, specific information that can be adequately tested on a simple true-false, multiple-choice, or other form of an easily corrected objective test. On the other hand, if the performance objective calls upon students to suggest implications for the American economy of a quintupling of the price of oil from the Persian Gulf, an essay would be a perfectly apt choice and a true-false test probably would be a very poor choice. The point is that if students are expected to become competent in a given behavior, the conditions of assessment must be constructed in such a way that they truly have an opportunity to demonstrate that behavior. The entire issue of matching assessment procedures to identified behaviors will be treated at greater length in the chapter entitled "Assessing Students' Learning."

The degree. The degree component of a performance objective describes the level of competence a student is expected to demonstrate before he or she will be credited with attainment of the objective. For true-false, multiple-choice, matching, and completion items, the degree is ordinarily expressed as a minimum percentage of items that must be correct for the student to achieve the objective. For example, consider the following: The statement "Each student will identify Confederate generals in the Civil War by responding correctly to 80 per cent of the multiple-choice items" establishes the degree of proficiency that must be demonstrated. The degree selected is arbitrary, though the 80 per cent figure has been widely used and has some research support as being favorably regarded by students (Block, 1972).

When multiple-choice, true-false, matching, and completion items are used, research by Novick and Lewis (1974) suggests that a minimum of ten items be provided for each performance objective. When smaller numbers of items are used, there is a question regarding the reliability of the measurement. The ten-items rule suggests, then, that, on an examination designed to test students' proficiency on five separate performance objectives, about fifty items would be appropriate.

The degree component of a performance objective takes a somewhat different form when essay questions are used. Clearly, a percentage is not appropriate. For example, a statement such as "Each student will discuss causes of the outbreak of World War I on an essay with 80 per cent accuracy" is meaningless. The statement implies that there is a limited number of "causes," that authorities have identified these by consensus, and that the teacher has the capability to count the number identified by the student against the discrete number of agreed-upon causes. Obviously, there is no such list of "causes" that has been cast in concrete by the authorities. For essay questions demanding interpretive responses, the use of percentage to establish the degree of proficiency desired is unacceptable.

In a performance objective including an essay, degree is indicated by a very precise statement regarding the nature of the information to be provided. Frequently, this is done by describing the types of evidence to be included and the number of examples to be included. Provision of this information in the performance objective provides the teacher with a rational basis for grading responses to essay questions. Further, when teachers share the statements of performance objectives with students at the beginning of a unit, students have useful guidelines as they work through the material with a view to preparing for the examination. The following is an example of an appropriately stated performance objective involving an essay item (the degree component is underlined):

> Each student will discuss the probable impact of a sudden appearance of a chain of mountains averaging 10,000 feet in height extending from Chicago to Cleveland on an essay examination. Each essay must include references to *a minimum of three distinct pieces of evidence related to each of the following categories: (1) the impact on transportation networks, (2) the impact on climate, and (3) the impact on the industrial base in the area to the north of the mountains.*

Performance objectives for varying cognitive levels. Performance objectives in a unit need to be developed at different levels of cognitive difficulty. Unless there is a systematic attempt to promote student thinking at various levels, there is a tendency for instruction and student intellectual performance to stagnate at lower cognitive levels. This results because instruction directed toward higher-level thinking processes puts heavier demands both on students and on teachers. For the teacher, for example, it is much easier to develop and correct tests designed to assess knowledge and comprehension than to assess analysis and synthesis. Unit plans need to be guided by performance objectives that assure an instructional focus on higher as well as lower level cognitive processes. Major headings of Bloom's (1956) cognitive taxonomy and representative performance objectives for each level are presented below.

Knowledge
Each student will identify the capitals of the nations of Europe on a matching test with at least 80 per cent accuracy.

Comprehension
Each student will interpret data on a graph depicting voting patterns in a particular precinct in general elections years by responding correctly to eight of ten "true-false" items consisting of statements related to information on the graph.

Application
Each student will determine the shortest air distance between Houston and Buffalo, using a map with an inches-to-miles scale. To be counted correct, responses must be within fifty miles (more or less) of the actual shortest air distance.

Analysis
In a three-to-five page essay, each student will comment on a letter written by John Hancock to James Madison. Each essay will point out how the letter reveals (1) basic political beliefs of Hancock, (2) basic political beliefs of Madison, and (3) at least three issues considered important by these two individuals.

Synthesis
In an essay not to exceed six pages in length, each student will discuss significant social, political, and economic consequences that might result were a line of mountains,

with peaks in the 10,000- to 14,000-foot range, suddenly to appear between Shreveport, Louisiana and Waco, Texas. References should be made to social, political, and economic consequences both for people living south and for people living north of this new chain of mountains.

Evaluation

Each student will make judgments about the relative appeal of New Orleans and Chicago as settlement sites in the United States for nineteenth-century immigrants from (1) Sweden, (2) Poland, (3) Italy, and (4) France. Judgments will be made on a unit essay test. Responses must include an explanation of criteria used in making judgments and a minimum of four pieces of evidence regarding these criteria for each of the above countries.

Performance objectives in the affective domain.   In addition to a development of cognitive performance objectives, there is a need to develop some affective performance objectives as well. Were instructional planning to focus only on cognitive outcomes, it might be possible for students to acquire a great deal of specific information but, at the same time, develop a real distaste for the subject. Because social studies teachers hope students will develop a continuing interest in social studies-related topics, they are concerned with the affective as well as the cognitive impact of their instruction. In a more general sense, emphases on affective objectives reflect social studies teachers' concern for how their students feel about themselves and the world they live in.

Unlike cognitive objectives, where students' performances can be measured quite directly, students' performances on affective objectives cannot be measured directly. Rather, they must be *inferred* from behaviors that are observable. For example, there is no way to measure directly a person's "love of baseball," but frequency of attendance at baseball games is measurable. From observations of this behavior it is possible to infer that someone who spends lots of time at the ball park is characterized by a "love of baseball."

In the social studies, affective performance objectives seek to measure changes in observable student behaviors from which changes in attitudes and values can be inferred. In planning units, this typically involves a measure of the rate of incidence of a behavior at the beginning and at the end of the unit. Changes of behavior that seem to reflect more enthusiasm for issues introduced in the unit are taken as evidence of achievement of the affective performance objective. The following is an example of an affective performance objective:

> Students, on a preference rating sheet, will rate social studies (as compared to English, mathematics, and science) as high at the end of the unit as at the beginning of the unit, or higher.

The uses of performance objectives.   Performance objectives serve two important functions. First of all, they provide a basis for teachers to select instructional materials and plan instructional activities in a purposeful way. They provide a rationale for making decisions to include or not to include specific learning activities.

If learning activities support the purposes implied by the performance objectives, they are appropriate; if they do not, then they ought not to be included in the instructional program.

The second function of performance objectives is to provide students with a clear sense of direction. For this function to be fulfilled, students must be provided with copies of the performance objectives for the unit *before* instruction begins. With copies of the performance objectives available to them, students are able to work more purposefully through the learning experiences associated with the unit. Performance objectives help them separate relevant and critical information from irrelevant or unimportant background material. Considerable research evidence exists that suggests students who are provided with performance objectives learn more than students who do not enjoy that advantage (Ferre, 1972; Taylor et al., 1973; Huck and Long, 1973; Morse and Tillman, 1973). Given this evidence and the possibilities for "information overkill" inherent within many social studies materials, it makes good sense to provide students with performance objectives before they begin work on new units.

KEY FACTS

Once performance objectives for a unit have been developed, it is necessary to identify a number of key facts that must be made clear to students if they are to attain those objectives. Facts have had something of an ill-starred history within social studies education. Because of instances of some poorly designed programs requiring students to deal with long lists of disjointed factual material, some critics have suggested that facts should be eliminated entirely from the social studies program. But that response results really more from a misuse of facts than from any inherent deficiencies within facts that make them totally inappropriate for systematic inclusion in a social studies program.

The issue is not whether facts should or should not be taught, but rather *which* facts should be taught. Once performance objectives are developed, there is a decision-rule for including or rejecting given factual information. If a given fact can help illuminate material implied by the performance objective, it is worthy of inclusion. Indeed, these key facts may be essential to helping students attain the performance objective. A social studies instructional program that includes no facts at all is likely to be characterized by very little substance. Much of the teacher's artistry is explained in the ability to select sufficient key facts to elucidate new material without providing so many that the seeds of confusion are sown.

INSTRUCTIONAL TECHNIQUES

Instructional techniques are to the teacher what tactics are to the military planner. They are specific procedures that, tied together collectively into strategies, are designed to help learners master the performance objectives that guide instructional practices during a unit. Beginning teachers sometimes ask for lists of "good" instructional techniques. The question is inappropriate. No instructional technique is "good" or "bad" in all situations. The worth of an instructional technique depends upon its effectiveness in helping students develop competence that leads them to master the performance objectives that have been identified for a given unit. If an instructional technique helps large numbers of youngsters to achieve success in a given situation, it is a good technique for that situation. If an instructional technique results in a high incidence of failure in a given situation, clearly that technique was a failure in that situation. The success or failure of a given technique is contextual. Therefore, comments that "Lecturing is bad" or "Simulations are good" are inappropriate. Few instructional techniques are likely to be "good" in all situations, and, likewise, few are likely to be "bad" in all situations.

In determining which instructional techniques ought to be selected for use in a given unit, one must take care to select a technique that is consistent with the cognitive level of the performance objective it is supposed to support. For example, if the performance levels seeks to bring youngsters to a level of intellectual competence characterized by the ability to make reasoned analyses of unfamiliar situations, the instructional techniques selected must provide them with opportunities to practice and develop those kinds of intellectual skills during the instructional process. A performance objective calling for analytical thinking cannot possibly be adequately supported by an instructional technique characterized by uninterrupted lecture and totally passive student reception of information. If the desired end is higher-level thinking, then very careful attention must be paid to selecting instructional techniques and organizing them into strategies that will provide youngsters with experiences designed to develop higher-level thinking abilities. This issue will be treated in more detail in the chapter entitled "Selecting Instructional Techniques."

NEEDED MATERIALS

Once other components of an instructional unit have been identified, needed materials must be determined. In practice, identifying needed materials frequently occurs simultaneously with identification of the instructional techniques to be used. Many instructional techniques depend for their success on the availability of certain materials.

In identifying needed materials in unit planning, one should be as specific as possible. It makes little sense, for example, to refer simply to "an article on capital punishment." When the time comes to teach the unit, it will be necessary to have an article in hand, and it is much easier to select something appropriate ahead of time rather than under the press of events when the unit is actually being taught.

Another important consideration in identifying needed materials is variety. Students vary enormously in their capacity to profit from individual materials. This is particularly true where prose materials are concerned. Beginning teachers frequently are shocked by the difficulties large numbers of learners experience with reading even relatively unsophisticated materials. Consequently, in identifying needed materials, the teacher should select prose materials that present similar information at widely diverging levels of verbal sophistication. Further, films, audiotapes, videotapes, and other nonprose materials should be located that present information to students via a mode other than reading. The range of selected materials, ideally, will provide some opportunity for every student to utilize learning materials that he or she can handle successfully. This ideal is not always met, but it should be kept in mind as materials are identified during the unit planning process.

An Abbreviated Unit Planning Framework Inspired by a Textbook Chapter

As has been noted, instructional planning that depends for sequence and content on the chapters of a social studies text is likely to result in programs that do little to help students make sense out of the tremendous quantity of information presented in the text. Ideally, a unit planned by the teacher with a clear focus on guiding generalizations and major concepts and subconcepts represents a much more responsible framework for instructional planning. When the teacher identifies the generalizations and concepts, there is a far greater likelihood of instructional techniques' being selected to highlight these generalizations and concepts than when instruction proceeds simply in accord with the page-by-page and chapter-by-chapter layout of a textbook. Though texts certainly do contain important generalizations and concepts, unless the teacher takes the time to identify them and organize his or her instruction to highlight them, they may remain obscure to students.

Though few would dispute that teacher-made units represent a more responsible framework for organizing instructional planning than the table of contents of a textbook, the reality of teaching is that textbooks, with temptingly available tables of contents, are readily at hand whereas teacher-made units are not. When one considers the tremendous time pressures under which secondary teachers work, there is little to be wondered at the attractiveness of organizing instruction according to the chapter-by-chapter development of the text rather than spending long hours preparing tailor-made instructional units.

A compromise that has a good deal to commend it centers around developing abbreviated units inspired by topics introduced in chapters in the text. This procedure has the advantage for beginning teachers of providing them with a known source of student information once the unit is complete. For more experienced teachers, this technique provides a basic organizational pattern that identifies priority areas that can be enriched by materials drawn from the source files they may have put together over the years.

For students, instruction based on textbook-inspired units has the advantage of pointing out clearly the significant concepts and subconcepts they are expected to learn. This helps them key on relevant rather than on filler or background information. Further, as teachers' instructional techniques are selected with a view to helping students learn the information that has been identified as important, there is likely to be a clear relationship between classroom activities and the demands of the final examination.

In planning an abbreviated unit around a textbook chapter, the teacher begins by scanning the chapter and identifying a major generalization or two that effectively summarizes the contents. Once this has been done, major concepts and subconcepts are identified. Next, performance objectives are developed in sufficient number that all identified major concepts and subconcepts are included. Then some key questions are developed that can be used to highlight major concepts and subconcepts and to suggest possible instructional techniques that can help students master these ideas.

Once a chapter has been broken down in this way, it is possible to bring in additional resource material to support the performance objectives that have been identified. This kind of planning can result in the individual textbook chapter's becoming but one of a number of information sources that students can use as they grow toward an understanding of the major concepts and subconcepts.

With respect to the textbook itself, it becomes a much more efficient information source for students when such an organizational plan is followed. Once performance objectives have been developed and provided to students, they have a guidance system to use in working through the textual material. The performance objectives direct them toward the essential information and, by implication, away from the less essential background information. (Many will read this anyway, as a supplement, but not at the expense of the more important material.)

In summary, the steps of textbook-based unit planning are

1. Identify focus generalization(s).
2. Identify major concepts and subconcepts.
3. Develop performance objectives that relate to all major concepts and subconcepts. (A single performance objective may deal with several concepts.)
4. Develop key questions to guide selection of instructional techniques and identification of additional learning resources.

In planning textbook-based units, sometimes beginning teachers are fearful of "leaving out too much." If the author, a learned scholar, put the information in, "Isn't it important?" they reason. Well, yes, all the information included probably was important to the author. But he is a learned professional in the area, and his grasp on the fundamentals is so solid that he can afford to let his interests run across a broad horizon of concern. But most secondary students have little

Focus Generalization

Over time, there has been a general improvement in living conditions because of important changes in social and cultural life.

Major Concepts	Subconcepts
living conditions	geographic mobility
social life	social mobility
cultural life	educational trend
	medical progress
	technological progress

Major concepts:	Living Conditions		Social Life	Cultural Life		
subconcepts:	geographic	social		educ.	med.	tech.
(related performance objectives)	po 1	po 1 po 2	po 3	po 4	po 5	po 2

Performance Objectives

1. Each student will point out patterns of population change in the United States between 1945 and 1960 by responding correctly to eight of ten multiple choice items.

2. Each student will identify changes in working conditions and job opportunities between 1945 and 1960 by responding correctly to eight of ten true-false items.

3. Each student will describe in an essay at least six new leisure-time activities that developed between 1945 and 1960. For each activity cited, at least two reasons, supported by appropriate evidence, must be included explaining why this particular activity became popular during this time.

4. Each student will prepare a short essay in which he or she assesses the impact of political and social events between 1945 and 1960 on educational progress. At least three specific educational changes should be noted. For each change, there should be an explanation including the roles of both social change and political change on the educational change.

5. Each student will prepare a short essay in which he or she indicates how educational, social, and political changes between 1945 and 1960 influenced medical practices. At least four changes in medical practices should be noted. For each change in medical practice that is cited, an explanation of the roles of educational change, social change, and political change in promoting the change in medical practice should be included.

Key Questions

1. Why did millions of people move to the West and the South during the 1950s?

2. What major population shifts took place after 1945? How do you explain those shifts?

3. How did work patterns change after World War II? What causes for these changes can you suggest?

4. How did Americans use their leisure time during the postwar period? How do you explain differences between prewar and postwar uses of leisure time?

5. Why did some people resist school desegregation during the 1950s? How would you compare general characteristics of "resistors" and "nonresistors?"

6. What impact did Sputnik I have on American education? How would you compare and contrast groups of people who (1) benefited from these changes or (2) did not benefit from these changes?

7. Why did the post-World War II seem to be characterized by so much educational crisis? How would you evaluate motives of people who suggested that "education is too important for educators"?

8. Why did polio almost disappear in the United States in the 1950s? How would you compare roles of government health agencies, private research groups, and actions of talented individuals in "conquering" polio?

9. Why were Americans doing less physical work at their jobs between 1945 and 1960 than in years previous to that time? How do you evaluate the social consequences of this reduction in the amount of physical work?

Figure 4–1. (above and left) Example of a Textbook-based Planning Unit

depth even in very basic issues. Consequently, lacking help from the teacher, they will have difficulty in differentiating between trivial and crucial details. Given this situation, a decision by the teacher to delimit the focus in textbook unit planning to major issues of concern represents a solidly professional decision.

An example of a brief teacher-developed textbook-based unit is presented in Figure 4–1. Note that the unit is short. These textbook-based units can be developed without a heavy price in terms of teacher planning time. (Note that this unit has been completed just to the point that the teacher would begin to identify suitable instructional techniques and additional supportive resources. These have not been identified for inclusion here.)

Preparing a Complete Instructional Unit

After they have had experience in planning abbreviated textbook units, many teachers move on to develop complete instructional units. These may be quite independent of topics treated in textbook chapters. Textbooks often fail to deal with issues teachers deem important. Faced with this situation, teachers have little choice other than to organize their own instructional plan independent of the textbook. The instructional unit offers a responsible framework for an effort of this type.

Teachers frequently are pleasantly surprised at how well instructional units they develop themselves are received by students. One reason for the success of teacher-made units is that teachers have a much better understanding of the needs or capabilities of their students than any textbook author could be expected to have. Additionally, as architects of the unit, teachers are likely to include instructional techniques and learning materials in which they have personal confidence. Given the conditions attendant on the creation of instructional units, there is little to be wondered at students' generally favorable reaction to them.

Professional unit planning takes time. Though many teachers have done exemplary work in preparing units during the school year, most find the task to be very demanding and better accomplished during the summer. It is better, particularly for beginners, to identify areas during the school year around which they would like to develop instructional units and to wait until the end of the school year before beginning the actual work. Unit production proceeds much more efficiently when the demands of paper correction and daily lesson planning must not be attended to along with the host of additional responsibilities that are expected of the typical secondary school teacher.

Once a decision to begin work on a complete instructional unit has been made, the following seven components, as introduced earlier in the chapter, must be included:

1. A topic statement.
2. Focusing generalization(s).
3. Major concepts and subconcepts.
4. Performance objectives.
5. Key facts.
6. Instructional techniques.
7. Needed materials.

A sample of a unit including these components is provided in Figure 4–2.

Systematic Analysis of Unit Components

An instructional unit should be more than simply a collection of randomly associated parts. Individual components each should play a distinct and identifiable function. The necessity suggests the desirability of a procedure that permits the intended function of each unit component to be seen easily. As a beginning, it is useful to code each unit component so that it can be identified both in terms of its broad function and in terms of what it, specifically, purports to contribute to the unit. A typical coding system was used to tag components in the sample unit introduced in Figure 4–2.

Note that uppercase Roman numerals (I, II, III, IV, V, and VI) were used to identify individual performance objectives. Arabic numerals were assigned to each key fact (1, 2, 3, 4, 5, 6, 7, 8, 9, 10, 11, 12). Capital letters identified each instructional technique (A, B, C, D, E, F, G, H, I, J, K). Lower-case letters were assigned to each needed material (a, b, c, d, e, f, g, h, i, j, k). There is nothing definitive about the particular coding system that was adopted for use in the sample unit. Any number of others would have served equally well.

Once a set of component identifiers has been established, the teacher planning the unit has the potential for doing two very important things. First, the teacher gains the potential for examining unit components to assure that all necessary

Topic Statement

Social Stratification

Focusing Generalization

Social stratification in the United States has implications for how individuals play out their life roles in American society in terms of their prestige, their access to wealth, and their general social mobility.

Major Concepts and Subconcepts

Social Stratification
- objective investigation
- subjective investigation
- reputational investigation
- role
- role conflict
- esteem
- prestige

Status
- ascribed status
- achieved status

Differentiation

Social Class Structure
- caste system
- open-class system

Social Mobility
- vertical mobility
- horizontal mobility
- career mobility
- intergenerational mobility

Performance Objectives

I. Each student will describe three approaches to the investigation of social stratification in a unit essay question. Each essay will contain names of the three approaches and at least four distinguishing characteristics of each.

II. Each student will point out examples of ascribed status and achieved status on a true-false test with at least 80 per cent accuracy.

III. Each student, in a unit essay test, will discuss five indicators of status. For each indicator cited, at least two examples will be provided demonstrating how that indicator can be used to gauge status.

IV. In a short essay, students will provide a working definition of *differentiation* and will point out at least four separate examples of the operation of differentiation in American society.

V. Each student will distinguish between a caste system and an open-class system in a unit essay examination. Each essay will include at least two similarities and three differences between the two systems.

VI. Each student will distinguish among vertical mobility, horizontal mobility, career mobility, and intergenerational mobility by responding correctly to at least 80 per cent of the multiple-choice items on a unit test.

Figure 4–2. Example of an Instructional Unit

Key Facts (These facts have been selected as illustrative. Other facts, perhaps a more extensive list, might be appropriate in the judgment of the teacher preparing the unit.)

1. *Studies by the National Opinion Research Center have revealed that the prestige of occupations in the United States remains quite stable over time. These studies demonstrated that professional occupations continually are ranked higher in esteem than are unskilled occupations.

2. For purposes of governmental statistics, a household is defined as "poor" when its money income falls below a given dollar level. This actual dollar amount is changed periodically to account for price inflation.

3. In the United States the median educational level is increasing. Today over one half of the adults have more than twelve years of schooling.

4. The *Statistical Abstract of the United States* (1968) reported that in 1960, except in the case of school teachers, an increase in median years of schooling was associated with an increase in median annual earnings.

5. A recent sampling of business leaders revealed that 57 per cent had a college education. A generation earlier the figure was 32 percent.

6. In identifying status, W. Lloyd Warner considered (1) occupation, (2) sources of income, (3) house type, and (4) dwelling area.

7. W. Lloyd Warner identified six social classes: upper-upper, lower-upper, upper-middle, lower-middle, upper-lower, lower-lower.

8. In assessing the status of alternative sources of income, W. Lloyd Warner developed this hierarchy: inherited wealth, earned wealth, profits and fees, wages, private assistance, public assistance.

9. One recent study found that 70 per cent of Americans regard themselves as middle class and only 22 per cent regard themselves as lower class. Yet 60 per cent earn a living by doing work of a type generally associated with the lower class.

10. Plans of a given high school student to attend or not to attend college have been found to be closely associated with both his or her family's status and his or her academic ability.

11. A 1962 study found that there was little relationship between first jobs of sons and occupations of their fathers.

12. Of high school graduates ranking in the top fifth of their classes academically, 82 per cent of those who are children of parents ranked in the upper one fourth economically will go to college the first year following graduation. But of high school graduates in the top fifth of their classes academically who are children of parents ranked in the lower one fourth economically, only 37 per cent will go on to college in the first year after graduation.

Instructional Techniques (These refer primarily to what will be going on in class. There is an assumption that students have been asked to read relevant material and view or listen to available audio and video tapes. These techniques are provided as illustrative, not definitive. The developer of the unit is free to exercise the option to include whichever instructional techniques seem to have good potentials for helping students master the performance objectives.)

A. Bring to class a large number of photographs cut from newspapers and magazines showing people of varying social classes. Put photographs up on a wall where they can be seen clearly. Using a concept diagnosis-concept formation strategy, ask students to

1. Name as many things as they can that come to mind when they see the photographs. (Write responses on the board, on butcher paper, or on an overhead projector transparency.)

2. Put into categories some of the things they have mentioned and that you have written on the board and to develop a name for each category (clothing, hairstyles, and so on).

Next point to certain of the photos as exemplifying people with upper-class characteristics. Ask the students to look at just the photos of upper-class people and to tell you what these people are like in terms of the categories developed earlier (clothing, hairstyles, and so on). Do the same for photos of middle-class and lower-class people. As a summary, ask students to summarize differences and similarities of individuals in the upper class, the middle class, and the lower class.

Figure 4–2. cont'd.

B. Prepare and deliver a short lecture focusing on social stratification, status, and differentiation.

C. Show the McGraw-Hill film "Social Class in America." Follow up with an interpretation of data questioning sequence:

- What did the film say about characteristics of the lower-class boy? What was his life like? (Same for middle-class and for upper-class boy.)

- What similarities and differences did the boys have? Are these differences "real," or were these differences just made up for the purposes of the film?

- How do you personally feel about the life of each boy?

D. Divide the class into three groups. Assign each group to investigate social stratification from a different perspective, as follows:

- *Objective group.* The objective group will observe people in the mall area of a shopping center. They will attempt to discern interests and interactional patterns of observed individuals, using observation alone. From these observations, they will attempt to infer social class, income levels, and other characteristics of individuals observed.

- *Subjective group.* The subjective group will interview individuals and ask them directly where they place themselves in the social class structure.

- *Reputational group.* The reputational group will present interviewees with a list of hypothetical people (perhaps ten or so in number). This list will include name, occupation, and annual salary. People interviewed will be asked to rank each individual on the list in terms of his or her social class standing.

Once each group has completed its work, information will be shared and will be debriefed. Some of the following questions are appropriate:

- What similarities and differences are there in reports of the three groups?

- How do you account for the differences?

- In which group's report would you place most faith? Why?

E. Use a concept attainment strategy to help students develop a sense for the distinction between ascribed status and achieved status. Be sure to have a sufficient number or examples and nonexamples of each concept available in case students are slow to pick up the defining characteristics of each. The following questioning sequence is appropriate:

- Say the term *ascribed status* after me. (Students repeat term.)

- This is an example of ascribed status. (Describe example to students.)

- This, too, is an example of ascribed status. (Describe example to students.)

- This is *not* an example of ascribed status. (Describe nonexample to students.)

- Now, I'll describe three examples without telling you whether each is or is not an example of ascribed status. When I finish, I want you to tell me the examples of ascribed status and the examples that are not instances of ascribed status. (Students respond as directed.)

- Who will give me a definition of ascribed status in his or her own words? (A student volunteer responds.)

  (Follow same general pattern for achieved status.)

F. Prepare and deliver a short lecture focusing on social class structure.

G. Prepare a short tape of two short case studies presented in the first person. One should be entitled "I am Amar," and the other should be entitled "I am Robert." Amar is a fourteen-year-old Brahmin living in India in 1870. Robert is a fourteen-year-old American living today.

In each tape, the boy (Amar or Robert) should describe (a) what his father does, (b) what his present house looks like, (c) what he hopes to be doing in twenty years, and (d) what kind of a house he expects to live in in thirty years. The tape should contrast differences between the Indian caste system and its tendency to maintain patterns of living within castes over generations and the American open-class system that permits life-styles to vary enormously between different generations of the same family.

Figure 4–2. cont'd.

At the conclusion of the tapes, debrief the class. Focus on distinctions between a caste system and an open-class system.

- What similarities do you see between Amar and Robert?
- What differences?
- What impact does the caste system have on Amar? The open-class system on Robert?
- What advantages and disadvantages do you see for each system?
- How do you suppose such different systems could have evolved?
- And so on.

H. Prepare and deliver a short lecture focusing on social mobility.

I. Instruct students to keep notebooks for one week made up of clippings from newspapers and periodicals focusing on psychological effects of a sudden change in social status. (For example: What happens to the executive who is forced to go on welfare?) At the end of the week, debrief the class and ask students to share their materials. Attempt to help students formulate some generalized statements via a questioning exercise:

- What common threads seem to run through all of these stories?
- What does social mobility pose a potential psychological threat?
- How could a person become comfortable with himself after a sudden change in social status?
- And so on.

J. Deliver a very short lecture focusing on vertical mobility and on horizontal mobility. Divide students into two groups. Assign one group to prepare a short role-playing exercise illustrating a situation in which an individual (or individuals) are involved in a change of status involving vertical mobility. Assign the other group to prepare a short role-playing exercise illustrating a situation in which an individual (or individuals) are involved in a change of status involving horizontal mobility. Ask each group to present its respective role-playing exercise. Debrief with a questioning sequence:

- What special problems are associated with vertical mobility?
- What special problems are associated with horizontal mobility?
- How would you compare the relative difficulty of adjusting to vertical mobility as opposed to horizontal mobility? Why?
- How could a person prepare himself to cope with changes associated with either horizontal mobility or vertical mobility?
- And so on.

K. Suggest to students that they find out what the occupations of their paternal grandfathers were. Ask students to write on a piece of paper the occupations of their fathers and the occupations of their grandfathers. (To avoid any potential embarrassment, ask students not to put their own names on these papers.) Collect the papers, and on the board, on butcher paper, or on an overhead transparency, list all the pairs of fathers and grandfathers and their occupations. Debrief with a questioning sequence.

- What does this information tell us about the stability of occupations from one generation to the next?
- In general, do jobs held by the fathers tend to be higher or lower in status than jobs held by the grandfathers?
- Can you make any general statement about the relationship or lack of relationship between occupations followed (in this country) by different generations of the same family?

Needed Materials (These materials have been selected as illustrative. A given teacher might find a much different list to be appropriate. The focus here should be on materials to be used by students.)

a. Charles Allyn. *Sociology: An Introduction*, pp. 517–599.

Figure 4–2. cont'd.

b. Judson R. Landis. *Sociology: Concepts and Characteristics*, pp. 35–36, 67–77.

c. Suzanne Harris Sankowsky. *Sociology for High School*, pp. 290–308.

d. Sociological Resources for the Social Studies. *Class and Race in the United States.*

e. W. Lavern Thomas and Robert J. Anderson. *Sociology: The Study of Human Relationships*, pp. 121–146.

f. Descartes and Company. *Social Progress through the Generations.* 8 mm. film loop. (4 minutes)

g. Sociological Associates, Inc. "Social Stratification." Audio cassette. (15 minutes)

h. "Social Classes in Mid-America: A Prospectus for the Twilight Years of the 20th Century." Audio Cassette. (Speech delivered by A. Cecil Turner, Chicago, 1977). (25 minutes)

i. Newmann and Berg Associates. *Life of the "Upper-Uppers."* Sound 16 mm. film. (30 minutes)

j. R. N. Hanrahan Films. *Father* Unlike *Sons.* Sound 16 mm. film. (23 minutes)

k. McGraw-Hill Films. *Social Class in America.*

Figure 4–2. cont'd.

pieces are there before instruction begins. Second, after the unit has been taught, the teacher has the capability to identify individual weak spots within the unit plan that guided instruction. To accomplish either of these things, however, the teacher must organize the codes developed to identify individual unit components in such a way as to permit easy visual analysis. A very useful technique for doing this is illustrated in Figure 4–3. Data in Figure 4–3 have been taken from the sample unit introduced in the preceding section.

When codes are displayed as in Figure 4–3, visual inspection can reveal whether all performance objectives are supported by key facts, by instructional techniques, and by needed materials. Further, any concepts or subconcepts for which no learning experiences have been designed readily become apparent. Use of such a scheme in unit planning assures comprehensiveness of unit planning. In an analysis of the data presented in Figure 4–3, it is clear that more instructional attention is going to be devoted to some issues than to others. For example, more key facts and instructional techniques have been selected to support the subconcept of "horizontal mobility" than the concept of "intergenerational mobility." This pattern need not necessarily be cause for concern. Clearly, some portions of the unit merit more attention than others. The teacher's artistry comes in making these sorts of decisions. In this instance, the unit planner judged "horizontal mobility" to be a more important concept for learners than "intergenerational mobility." However, should the chart ever reveal a concept or subconcept for which no performance objectives or key facts or instructional techniques or needed materials had been identified, then there is a clear need either to provide these missing elements or eliminate that major concept or subconcept as a major focus of the unit.

| | Topic |
| | **SOCIAL STRATIFICATION** |

Focus Generalization(s): Social stratification in the United States has implications for how individuals play out their life roles in American society in terms of their prestige, their access to wealth, and their general social mobility.

Major Concepts and Subconcepts	Performance Objectives	Key Facts	Instructional Techniques	Needed Materials
Social Stratification	I	1, 2, 6, 7	A, B, C. D	a, b, c, d, e, g
objective investigation	I	1, 2, 6, 7	A, B, C, D	a, b, c, d, e, g
subjective investigation	I	1, 2, 6, 7	A, B, C, D	a, b, c, d, e, g
reputational investigation	I	1, 2, 6, 7	A, B, C, D	a, b, c, d, e, g
role	I	1, 2, 6, 7	A, B, C, D	a, b, c, d, e, g
role conflict	I	1, 2, 6, 7	A, B, C, D	a, b, c, d, e, g
esteem	I	1, 2, 6, 7	A, B, C, D	a, b, c, d, e, g
prestige	I	1, 2, 6, 7	A, B, C, D	a, b, c, d, e, g
Status	II, III	3, 4, 5, 6	B, E	a, b, c, d, e
ascribed status	II, III	3, 4, 5, 6	B, E	a, b, c, d, e
achieved status	II, III	3, 4, 5, 6	B, E	a, b, c, d, e
Differentiation	IV	6, 7	A, B, F	a, b, c, d, e, h
Social Class Structure	V	7, 8, 9	C, D, F, G	a, b, c, d, e, h, i, k
caste system	V	7, 8, 9	C, D, F, G	a, b, c, d, e, h, i, k
open-class sytem	V	7, 8, 9	C, D, F, G	a, b, c, d, e, h, i, k
Social Mobility	VI	10, 11	G, H, I, J, K	a, b, c, d, e, f, j
vertical mobility	VI	10, 11	G, H, I, J, K	a, b, c, d, e, f, j
horizontal mobility	VI	10, 11	G, H, I, J, K	a, b, c, d, e, f, j
career mobility	VI	10, 11	G, K	a, b, c, d, e, f, j
intergenerational mobility	VI	11	K	a, b, c, d, e, f, j

Figure 4–3. Representing Relationships among Unit Components

Once the instructional unit has been taught, the chart fulfills a useful function in helping the teacher to analyze the weak points and the strong points of a unit. Because individual components are identified so clearly, the teacher can analyze patterns of "misses" on the unit examination to identify performance objectives that proved most troublesome to students. Once these have been determined, a number of questions can be asked. For example,,was the performance objective itself appropriate, or did it demand too much of students? Were sufficient key facts provided? Were instructional techniques appropriate? Were materials provided for learners sufficiently diverse? And so on.

By engaging in these kinds of analyses, the teacher can identify weaknesses of individual unit components, and the unit can be modified accordingly before it is taught another time to a different group. The ability to examine individual parts of a unit helps teachers to refine their abilities to analyze their instructional practices and moves them away from a natural tendency to condemn an entire unit of work as "bad" or "unsuccessful" when, in fact, only small portions of the unit were responsible for the difficulties.

Unit planning, then, professionalizes the instructional process. Given careful attention to systematic unit construction, social studies teachers convey to students their expectations and provide learning experiences that clearly relate to those expectations. Instruction based on teacher-made units has great potential for adding a spirit of purposefulness to social studies classes and for helping students to make sense out of new and potentially confusing information.

Planning Daily Lessons

The unit lays out the "grand design" for several weeks' instruction. The daily lesson plan identifies the substance and sequence of instruction within a given class period. Each day's lesson focuses on only a portion of the larger body of content contained within the unit of which it is a part.

Beginning social studies teachers sometimes are inclined to overlook the importance of daily lesson planning. They observe experienced teachers functioning very well using only very sketchy notes as a basis for organizing each day's teaching. For these older, more experienced professionals, much of the sequence and pattern of the day's instruction has become a matter of familiar habit. Beginners have not time to develop these almost automatic responses to changes in the ebb and flow of the lesson as it unfolds. Consequently, without good plans available that describe in some detail the sequence of events that should occur during a lesson, instruction may look disorganized. Timing can be an especially nettlesome problem. Many beginning social studies teachers, perhaps a bit nervous, have rushed through in twenty minutes a lesson they had expected would last an hour. Good planning can prevent (or at least reduce the likelihood of occurrence) of such situations.

For new social studies teachers, it is better to overplan than to underplan. It is much easier to cut back some material than to stretch a lesson to "fill an hour." This means that daily lessons ought to be highly specific in terms of the directions provided to the teacher and long enough that these necessary details can be included. Lesson plans running on for several pages are perfectly appropriate, especially for beginners.

A number of formats are available for lesson plans. Many schools provide teachers with forms adopted for use in individual districts and buildings. Although variations do exist, most tend to include a fairly standard set of components. Figure 4–4 illustrates a lesson plan reflecting elements common to many lesson plan formats.

Lesson plans ought not to be prepared more than a day or two in advance of instruction. It is hard to judge the rate at which a given group of students will

Subject: Social Stratification

General Purpose: This lesson is designed to help students understand that, in many cases, social status of individuals can be inferred by their clothing, mannerisms, patterns of speech, and food preferences.

Lesson Objective: Each student will be able to cite two or three examples of how physical appearance and habits of individuals may reflect their relative social status.

Sequence of Teacher Activities

1. Short introduction to the general concept of "social stratification." (15 minutes) Conclude this phase with some questions such as

   • What kind of categories do you use to sort people into groups?

   • Why do you focus on those sorts of things?

   • Do people everywhere use the same sorts of standards when they make decisions about the relative status of different people?

   • Why do you think people do make judgments about the "relative" worth of others? What leads you to this conclusion?

2. Divide the class into four groups. Assign one group to look at differences in *clothing* of selected individuals. Assign a second to look at differences in *mannerisms*. Assign a third to note differences in *patterns of speech*. Assign a fourth to examine differences in *food preferences*.

3. Provide students in the first group with a series of photographs of different kinds of people. Provide students in the second group with a second set of photographs illustrating reactions of people who have just learned they are lottery winners. Provide students in the fourth group with a tape recording containing speech selections from people in various social groups. Provide students in the fourth group with restaurant menus from restaurants in "poor," "middle-class," and "wealthy" sections of a city.

4. Assign one individual in each group to be the recording secretary. Ask each group to examine materials to see what might be revealed about characteristics of different kinds of people. Allow twenty minutes for this part of the lesson.

5. Reunite class as one large group. Briefly introduce and discuss concepts "lower class," "middle class," "upper class." Draw data chart on the board as follows:

	clothing	mannerisms	speech	food
Lower Class				
Middle Class				
Upper Class				

6. Debriefing. Ask recording secretary from each group to write information in appropriate categories that members of the group discovered during the exercise. Discussion questions:

   • What similarities do you notice in practices of people in all three social classes?

   • What differences do you note?

   • How do you account for these differences?

   • And so on.

Figure 4-4. Sample Lesson Plan

Sequence of Student Activities

1. Students will respond to questions focusing on "social stratification."

2. Students will participate in groups as directed.

3. Students will participate in debriefing exercise centered around a data chart. They will analyze similarities and differences of preferences of people in different social classes. They will make copies of the completed data chart to keep for review.

Materials Needed

1. Chalkboard, chalk, photographs of different kinds of people, photographs of lottery winners, recordings of voices of different people, menus from different kinds of restaurants.

Evaluation Procedures

Daily: At the end of the period or at the beginning of class tomorrow, individual students will be asked to suggest several indications of an individual's social class. Each student asked should be able to provide two or three examples.

Final: On a unit posttest, each student will discuss at least five indicators of status. This essay will include at least two examples illustrating how given indicators can be used to gauge status.

Figure 4–4. cont'd.

be able to work with new material. Student interests will vary, too, and the professional social studies teacher accommodates the program to take advantage of those interest. To maintain the flexibility to meet these varied sets of circumstances, teachers should not plan lesson plans days and weeks ahead of instruction. (They *can* be, but the chances of a given class being at precisely the predicted point two and three weeks after the plan has been written are remote.)

Summary

This chapter has introduced frameworks for developing textbook-based units, teacher-made units, and lesson plans. Systematic instructional planning gives an order that students sometimes perceive as lacking in their social studies classes. Further, units organized in such a fashion that interrelationships among components are clear permit teachers to assure that their instructional practices are truly directed toward their stated objectives and to assess the impact of individual parts of the total instructional program.

The construction of systematic units in no way should become a vehicle for rigid, stultifying instruction. Many options for very creative lessons are possible within any unit plan. The unit should be regarded as a context within which teacher creativity can be developed. Professional social studies teachers are both flexible and creative, but their purposes are always clear both to themselves and to their students. The unit planning and lesson planning frameworks introduced here are appropriate organizers of those purposes.

REFERENCES

BLOCK, JAMES H. "Student Learning and the Setting of Mastery Performance Standards." *Educational Horizons* (Summer 1972): 183–191.

BLOOM, BENJAMIN S., ed. *Taxonomy of Educational Objectives: Handbook I: The Cognitive Domain*. New York: David McKay Co., Inc. 1956.

FERRE, ALVIN VICTOR. Effects of Repeated Performance Objectives upon Student Achievement and Attitude. Ed.D. Dissertation, New Mexico State University, 1972.

GRONLUND, NORMAN E. *Stating Objectives for Classroom Instruction*. 2d ed. New York: Macmillan Publishing Co., Inc., 1978.

HUCK, SCHUYLER W., and JAMES D. LONG. "The Effects of Behavioral Objectives on Student Achievement." *The Journal of Experimental Education* (Fall 1973): 40–41.

MORSE, JEAN A., and MURRAY H. TILLMAN. "Achievement as Affected by Possession of Behavioral Objectives." *Engineering Education* (June 1973): 124–126.

NOVICK, MELVIN R., and CHARLES LEWIS. "Prescribing Test Length of Criterion-Referenced Measures." In *Problems in Criterion-Referenced Measurement*. Edited by C. W. Harris, M. C. Aikin, and W. J. Popham. Los Angeles: Center for the Study of Evaluation, UCLA, 1974.

TAYLOR, CURTIS, et al. "Use of Inferred Objectives with Non-Objective Based Instructional Materials." Tempe, Arizona: Arizona State University, Research Sponsored by Air Force Human Resources Laboratory, Williams Air Force Base, Arizona Flying Training Division, October 1973.

U.S. BUREAU OF THE CENSUS. *Statistical Abstract of the United States: 1968*. 89th ed. Washington, D.C.: U.S. Government Printing Office, 1968.

Chapter 5

DIAGNOSING STUDENTS

O NCE DECISIONS HAVE BEEN MADE regarding content and units have been organized, attention needs to be directed to the individual characteristics of students in the classroom. Of course, the instructional unit itself is likely to have been developed only after a reasoned consideration of the nature of the students to be served. But necessarily this kind of planning goes forward based on assumptions regarding what "typical" or "average" individuals in the class might be expected to do with a given set of learning experiences. Clearly within these norms, enormous differences exist among individual students. Instruction that proceeds without an attempt to identify individuals whose competencies range well above and below the limits of the "averages" may fail to meet the needs of a sizable number of students in the class. Use of a few simple diagnostic procedures can result in information that can provide a profile of the competencies of each individual with regard to the demands of a proposed new unit of work.

Diagnosis must be accomplished quickly and efficiently; otherwise, valuable time is lost that might be expended more defensibly on instructional activities. Overly elaborate diagnostic procedures frequently provide more information than is required for minor program modification. Frequently, too, such procedures yield information that is only tangentially relevant.

For example, suppose a teacher had designed a unit that, in part, called upon students to identify examples of "glittering generalities" while listening to radio commercials. Diagnostic information related to students' reading skills would have little potential for identifying individuals likely to experience difficulty with this exercise. Diagnostic information relating to listening skills or to understanding of the concept "glittering generality" would be much more appropriate. Appropriate diagnosis, then, requires a clear focus on the kinds of demands a new instructional situation is likely to place on students. When diagnosis provides information relevant to those demands, it merits a commitment of teacher time. When such relevance cannot be established, teacher time is much more judiciously spent on other tasks.

Determining a Focus for Gathering Diagnostic Information

In determining which sorts of diagnostic information ought to be gathered in advance of teaching a new unit of work, one must identify demands of that new unit with some precision. A convenient way to accomplish this task is to refer to the performance objectives. Recall that the performance objectives of a unit specify what students are expected to be able to do by the conclusion of the instructional sequence. By focusing on these anticipated terminal student performances, one can identify some relevant knowledge, skills, and attitudes that might be related to these performances. Consider, for example, the following performance objective that might have been developed for a textbook-based unit:

> Each student will prepare a short essay in which he or she assesses the impact of political and social events between 1945 and 1960 on educational progress. At least three specific educational changes should be noted. For each change, there should be an explanation including both the role of social change and of political change on the educational change.

A teacher might be interested in gathering the following kinds of diagnostic information related to this objective.

Knowledge	Skills	Attitudes
political event	Written expres-	Interest in
social event	sion skills	educational change
educational change		Interest in historical analysis

Certainly, many more specific and relevant knowledge, skills, and attitudes might be identified. For a given objective, there is no definitive list. The amount of information sought will vary in accordance with what an individual teacher believes to be necessary. This judgment results from a consideration of what a teacher suspects students may not now know but need to know for success on a new unit of work. The decision to identify the items listed under *knowledge, skills,* and *attitudes* for the performance objective cited here as an example might have resulted from an analysis something like the following.

Knowledge. The performance objective seems to assume that students have some prior familiarity with the concepts "political event," "social event," and "educational progress." Most probably have picked these terms up, but a few may still not have a clear understanding of what each implies. Conceivably, some might have trouble with the concept "role" as it is used in the performance objective. But that term is not really central to the basic concern of the performance objective. Further, students did not experience great difficulty with the term when it was introduced earlier. For that reason, it probably would not be terribly productive to spend time gathering diagnostic information focusing on this concept. Other terms stated or implied by the objective should not prove too troublesome.

Skills. The performance objective demands that students display their new learning in an essay. This presupposes at least a minimal ability to write grammatical and logically developed prose. Some students may have some difficulties in this area that may suggest a revision of the performance objective to permit another form of assessment for some members of the class. The potential for difficulty is severe enough here that it is worth doing a quick diagnostic check to identify individuals with severe deficiencies in writing skills.

Attitudes. Though most students in this class have been in the course long enough to make their general feelings toward history and, more particularly, historical analysis clear, still there are a number of new transfer students who are question marks in this regard. A quick procedure designed to elicit their feelings will probably be worth the time and effort. Additionally, as previous units have not dealt specifically with the issue of educational change, general levels of interest in the topic are unclear. Because this issue is central to the new unit, an effort to determine the general level of initial student interest in the topic will be a worthwhile expenditure of teacher time.

Clearly, the quantity of diagnostic information relating to knowledge, skills, and attitudes will vary greatly from situation to situation. Most teachers, at the beginning of the school year, have a much less adequate understanding of the capabilities and interests of individual students than they have later in the year. Consequently, more systematic attention to gathering diagnostic information is to be expected at the beginning of the year than later. Further, when new units relate sequentially and logically to units just concluded, there is less need for diagnostic activities than when new units bear little resemblance to previous work.

The central concern, then, of diagnostic activity is to identify those knowledge and skills students will need if they are to have reasonable prospects for success on new units of work. Additionally, there is an interest in determining students' general attitudes toward the topics to be treated in the new unit. This whole diagnostic enterprise seeks to assure the teacher that his or her impressions regarding what students know and feel are accurate. A number of sources of information may provide insights that are useful in this regard. But, as will be noted in the following section, some of these sources probably will provide much more reliable information than others.

Sources of Diagnostic Information

In the selection of sources of diagnostic information, it is necessary to seek out those that provide information relating to knowledge, skills, and attitudes that are relevant to information needs implied by the performance objectives included within the new unit of work. Greatest faith should be placed in those information sources that have become available as a result of something students have done in the classroom of the teacher gathering the diagnostic data. The following sources of information meet these requirements:

1. A teacher-made diagnostic test specifically focusing on identified knowledge and skills.
2. Teacher-kept anecdotal records.
3. Teacher-student conferences
4. Teacher-kept checklists on student behaviors.
5. Interest inventories relevant to the new unit.

Teacher-made diagnostic tests. Of the options available as sources of diagnostic information regarding knowledge and skills needed in a new unit of work, teacher-made diagnostic tests are to be preferred over all others. These diagnostic tests, specifically prepared with a focus on identified knowledge and skills, provide information that is more clearly relevant to specified needs than any other data source.

In the preparation of diagnostic tests of this type, a key word is *brevity*. Diagnostic information must be gathered quickly and evaluated quickly so that whatever adjustments to the program there are can be made and instruction can go forward. As a rule of thumb, no more than one or two class periods should be consumed by the administration of diagnostic procedures before actual introduction of the new unit begins. This time constraint means that short, to-the-point, and easily corrected tests are to be preferred. When forced choice items including multiple-choice and true-false questions are chosen, no more than six questions should be asked about each knowledge or skill area that has been identified from an examination of performance objectives. Keeping the number of items relatively few assures that tests can both be developed and corrected without a heavy expenditure of teacher time.

Recall that, for the performance objective provided earlier in the chapter as an illustration, a number of knowledge and skills were identified about which the teacher might be interested in gathering diagnostic information. Under the heading of *Knowledge*, "Political event," "Social event," and "Educational change" were designated as concepts students would need to know before they could profit from learning experiences to be introduced in the new unit. Under the heading of *Skills*, a concern for determining students' competencies in the area of "Written expression skills" was identified.

With regard to the concepts of "political event," "social event," and "educational change," several diagnostic testing options are open to the teacher. At one level, the teacher may be interested only in determining whether students are able to identify correctly examples and nonexamples of these concepts. If this is the case, then short objective test items are appropriate. For example, short multiple-choice, matching, or true-false items will meet this need very well.

On the other hand, the teacher may be interested in determining whether students have picked up an erroneous conception of the basic definitional characteristics of these concepts. Of course, should this be the case, students would fare very poorly on the objective tests mentioned above. But these tests alone fail to explain to the teacher the precise nature of the erroneous "reality" the students have generated in creating their own inappropriate conception of these terms. To obtain information specifically related to the nature of such conceptual deficiencies, the teacher will find the short essay question appropriate. Properly constructed, the essay question can provide students with an opportunity to explain their own understanding of knowledge necessary for success on a new unit of work. Responses can be quickly checked for adequacy by the teacher. When conditions permit, this same information can be gathered appropriately also from oral responses of students, presented either directly to the teacher or presented to the teacher in the form of audio recordings.

In the area of *skills*, objective test items such as true-false and multiple-choice tests are inappropriate. A skill requires a demonstration of a competency that cannot be assessed properly by using a forced-choice testing procedure. Although many teachers may have abundant evidence of past student work reflecting competencies in skill areas (old papers, for example) and may not wish to develop a formal testing procedure to gather diagnostic information of this type, when such information is not readily, available diagnostic testing must be designed to provide the student with an opportunity to *demonstrate* the skill being assessed. For example, if the skill identified relates to oral reading, opportunities for oral reading must be provided. In the case of the skill identified as related to the performance objective used here as an illustration, the skill of "written expression," the appropriate diagnostic testing procedure would be to provide students an opportunity to generate a sample of their writing.

Some examples follow some diagnostic tests that would be appropriate as sources of information regarding the knowledge and skills identified as necessary for success on a new unit of work that included the performance objective cited earlier in the chapter:

DIAGNOSTIC TEST A:
POLITICAL EVENT

Directions: True-False. Each of the following statements is either a "true example" of a *political event* or a "false example." Place a + in the blank provided before each "true example." Place a 0 in the blank provided before each "false example."

_____1. The United States and Japan signed a peace agreement at the conclusion of World War II.

_____2. From 1945 to 1965 the percentage of unwed mothers in the United States population increased.
_____3. From 1945 to 1975 there was a change in men's hairstyles. In 1975 men's hair, on the average, was worn two inches longer than in 1945.
_____4. The incidence of polio in children decreased markedly between 1945 and 1975 because of the development and distribution of the Salk vaccine.
_____5. The United Nations met in San Francisco and adopted the United Nations Charter.
_____6. Jimmy Carter was elected president of the United States in 1976.

DIAGNOSTIC TEST B:
SOCIAL EVENT

Directions: Multiple-Choice. For each of the following items, circle the letter before the most appropriate response.

1. All of the following are examples of a "social event" *except*
   a. The Declaration of Independence was signed in 1776.
   b. The automobile changed American dating habits.
   c. The completion of the transcontinental rail system changed coast-to-coast travel habits.
   d. The National Organization of Women disseminated information directed toward opening up more professional options for women.
2. Which of the following is the best example of a social event?
   a. United States' recognition of the sovereignty of Israel.
   b. The change in undergraduate life after World War II that occurred when veterans came back to the college campus by the thousands.
   c. Woodrow Wilson's election to the presidency in 1912.
   d. The Cuban Missile Crisis of 1962.
3. The World War II "baby boom" could best be described as
   a. A social event.
   b. A political event.
   c. A geological event.
   d. None of the above.
4. All of the following are examples of "social events" *except*
   a. Admission of Hawaii and Alaska to the union as states.
   b. A decrease in average family size after birth control pills became widely available.
   c. A change in the ethnic makeup of inner city neighborhoods between 1930 and 1975.
   d. A decline in readers' preference for Gothic novels between 1945 and 1978.
5. The best example of a social event in the following list is
   a. Franklin Roosevelt's defeat of Alf Landon in 1936.
   b. Redistribution of national wealth after the introduction of a federal income tax.
   c. The U.S. treaty with Mexico over boundary disputes.
   d. The passage of the Kansas-Nebraska Act.

6. Invention and widespread distribution of a new pill that would increase the average life expectancy to ninety-five years would best be classified as
   a. A social event.
   b. A political event.
   c. A geological event.
   d. None of the above.

DIAGNOSTIC TEST C:
EDUCATIONAL CHANGE

Directions: True-False. Each of the following statements is either a "true example" of an *educational* change or a "false example." Place a + in the blank provided before each "true example." Place a 0 in the blank provided before each "false example."

_____1. A larger percentage of the U:S. population can read now than in 1920.
_____2. Team teaching, a situation in which two or more teachers have responsibility for instructing the same group of students, first became popular in the late 1950s and early 1960s.
_____3. The government of France made a decision to give up membership for France in the North Atlantic Treaty Organization.
_____4. More elementary schools today are built according to an "open space" plan than were built according to that plan in the 1950s.
_____5. Montana became a state in 1889.
_____6. The federal government pays a higher percentage of total educational costs today than in 1945.

DIAGNOSTIC TEST D:
POLITICAL EVENT, SOCIAL EVENT, AND EDUCATIONAL CHANGE

Directions: Short answer essay. Write a short paragraph on *each* of the following terms: *political event, social event,* and *educational change.* Explain what each term means, as you understand it, in each of your three paragraphs.

DIAGNOSTIC TEST E:
WRITTEN EXPRESSION SKILLS

Directions: Essay. Write a one-page essay on the following topic: *The Most Important Issue Facing the American People Today.* Be sure to proofread your paper before submitting it.

Diagnostic tests are administered with a view to identifying students lacking knowledge and skills they are assumed to know as prerequisites for a proposed new unit of work. If planning of the new unit has gone forward only after a careful consideration of what students have been exposed to previously and how well they have mastered this material, few students are likely to be found deficient in the identified prerequisite knowledge and skills. But there will be a few who have failed to acquire these knowledge and skills, and diagnostic testing can pinpoint them.

In utilizing information gathered from diagnostic testing, the teacher needs to formulate a decision-rule to establish a score that signals a need for special attention for a given student. A workable, rule-of-thumb procedure for diagnostic tests of the true-false, matching, or multiple-choice varieties is to presume that students

TABLE OF PRESCRIPTIONS

Knowledge	*Skills*
Political Event Option A: Read a short, one page handout focusing on this term. Option B: Listen to a five-minute discussion on an audio tape focusing on this term. Option C: Schedule a teacher-student conference to discuss this term.	*Written Expression Skills* Option A: Complete short program in the school writing competencies laboratory. Option B: Complete programmed instructional material focusing on written expression. Option C: Schedule a teacher-student meeting to work on special writing problems.
Social Event Option A: Read a short, one-page handout focusing on this term. Option B: Listen to a five-minute discussion on an audio tape focusing on this term. Option C: Schedule a teacher-student conference to discuss this term.	
Educational Change Option A: Read a short, one-page handout focusing on this term. Option B: Listen to a five-minute discussion on an audio tape focusing on this term. Option C: Schedule a teacher-student conference to discuss this term.	

making errors on one half or more of the items need help. Where short answer essay items are used, the teacher must make a more subjective judgment. In the case of essays focusing on "political event," "social event," and "educational change," students whose answers reflect an understanding of those terms severely at odds with the working definition of the teacher ought to be identified as in need of special assistance. In the event that the essay demands a representation of a skill such as "written expression skill," a subjective judgment can be made in terms of what a minimally acceptable performance might be. For example, a decision might be made to suggest help for all those students making more than ten mechanical errors in the passage.

Once decisions have been made regarding how students needing help will be identified using diagnostic tests, it is necessary to determine the nature of the help to be provided these students. Before the diagnostic tests are administered, a "table of prescriptions" ought to be developed. The table of prescriptions suggests several possibilities for providing help for students identified as deficient in selected knowledge and skill areas. See the "Table of Prescriptions" on page 78.

Once a diagnostic test has been given, the teacher then identifies students needing help, selects from among options on the table of prescriptions, and prepares a special program of help for each of those youngsters. For purposes of illustration, assume that Roberta Jones was found to have difficulty with the concepts "social event" and "educational change" and also to be deficient in terms of her "written expression skills." Looking at the table of prescriptions, her teacher might select the following options and place them on a "student prescription card" including such information as the following reproduced below: (This information can be placed conveniently on a four-by-six-inch card.)

ROBERTA JONES

Problem Areas	Prescription
Social event	Read short, one-page handout.
Educational change	Schedule teacher conference with Roberta to discuss this term.
Written expression skills	Have Roberta complete programmed material on this topic. Then schedule a teacher conference with her to assess progress in this area.

Maintenance of student prescription cards helps the teacher keep track of precisely what has been recommended for each student. Of course, materials mentioned must be prepared and ready to go. In general, handouts and other prescription options ought to be designed in such a way that they can be completed relatively quickly. These students need to get the necessary help as rapidly as possible to permit them to move into the new program without delay. When simple definitions and explanations of terminology are involved, printed materials ought not to be more than a page or two in length. Longer materials tend not to be time-efficient and often provide much more information than is really needed for a student to acquire a basic understanding.

Teacher-kept anecdotal records. Though teacher-made diagnostic tests are probably the most useful source of diagnostic information because of their ability to focus specifically on special knowledge and skills needs associated with a proposed new unit of work, other sources, too, can provide useful information. One of these sources is the anecdotal record. An anecdotal record is simply nothing more than a written summation of a classroom incident or some other episode involving an individual student. Anecdotal reports of a given incident need not be long. A few pertinent sentences describing the essence of the situation will suffice. It is a good idea to write down the information as soon as possible after the incident to assure that the passage of time does not interfere with recollection of specific details.

Frequently, teachers keep anecdotal records when they wish to maintain a running account of a behavioral problem. But the episodes recorded need not be limited to issues associated with discipline. For example, if a given youngster opens up and becomes an active participant in a discussion as a result of something the teacher did, it makes sense to record that information for future reference. Anecdotal records on individual students can be kept on cards or on notebook paper. Usually, information for no more than a single student is kept on one card or sheet. An anecdotal record focusing on a student's attitudes might look something like the following:

ROBERTA JONES: ANECDOTAL RECORD—FOCUS:
CLASSROOM PARTICIPATION.

Date	Episode
3/6	No response from Roberta to a number of questions directed both from me and by our student discussion leader.
3/8	No response from Roberta during first part of the discussion. But when discussion moved toward a consideration of professional roles for women, she volunteered three comments.
3/13	Roberta participated freely during group discussion on possible barriers to women interested in entering the profession. She

Date	Episode
	appeared to gain assurance when some others in the class nodded in approval of some of her remarks.
3/17	Roberta participated much more frequently than in the past on all issues covered during the discussion. She seems to have picked up on the idea that other students are interested in and respond well to what she has to say.

Specific comments made in an anecdotal record can be made long or short as is appropriate for the given situation. Additionally, there will be great variances in the length of a given anecdotal record focusing on a single issue for one student. Sometimes sufficient information can be gathered in just a few days. On other occasions, particularly when an attempt is being made to establish sound baseline information about a particularly vexing behavioral problem, anecdotal information may be gathered over a considerable period of time. The effort is directed toward gathering sufficient *useful* information, however long that might take.

Teacher-student conferences.   The teacher-student conference represents another useful diagnostic data source that, appropriately used, can provide a great deal of information to the teacher. This procedure is suited particularly well to dealing with those students who do not feel comfortable in expressing themselves in a large group setting and whose performances on teacher-made tests do not seem to reflect accurately their real understandings. With such individuals, teachers frequently can gather a great deal of information from a short, comfortable, personal conversation.

To be effective, the teacher-student conference requires planning. The teacher needs to consider specific issues to be discussed in advance; otherwise, there is a likelihood that the conference will drift far afield from the concerns that suggested that a conference was desirable in the first place. Clearly, once the conference is underway, these issues ought not to be converted to just so many "canned" questions that the teacher asks one after the other. There is a need for questions and comments to go forward in a natural manner and for serious consideration and response to be given to what the student says. But the focus of the meeting should be kept in mind so that the teacher can redirect the conversation in such a way that major concerns are not forgotten.

Once a conference has been concluded, the teacher should make a brief written summation. This procedure assures that information that came forth from the teacher-student conference will not be forgotten days or weeks later when there might be occasion to consider once more how a given student may meet some challenges relevant to issues that were discussed. Teachers deal with so many students and so many issues during a given day that, unless a systematic attempt is made to record information, much is likely to be forgotten or, at best, only selectively remembered. A summary of a teacher-student conference can be kept in a variety of forms. A few notes on an 8½-by-11-inch sheet or on a 4-by-6-inch index card work well. Some teachers even record comments and file the cassette tapes for future reference. A sample of a teacher-student conference summation follows:

ROBERTA JONES:
TEACHER-STUDENT CONFERENCE 3/22

Roberta and I chatted this afternoon for about twenty minutes about her participation in class discussion. I mentioned that I have been pleased by her increasing interest in participating during the past several weeks and that I have noted a real improvement in this area. She mentioned that she has been interested in some of the women's rights issues we have been dealing with. She indicated an interest in pursuing a career in the law as something she would really like to do.

I noted that a law career was a fine career objective. Pursuing this idea, I mentioned that lawyers have to be very knowledgeable in a variety of areas. I mentioned my pleasure at Roberta's interest in involving herself more actively in *all* discussions we have been having, not just those dealing with women's rights issues, and that I hoped this active involvement would continue.

Roberta admitted that she was becoming "turned on" by the favorable reactions she had been getting from some of the other students when she participated and that made her feel good about taking part. She seemed to appreciate, too, the idea that if she really hopes to make a contribution to the women's movement, she will have to immerse herself in a great number of topics that might not seem immediately relevant to women's issues.

Conference summations can be as brief or as lengthy as the individual teacher deems appropriate. The idea is for the teacher to gather for the record as much information as is necessary to recall the specifics of the conference at a later date. Clearly, the amount of information will vary in terms of the length of the conference, the topics discussed, and the ability of the individual teacher to recall details without the aid of a written or taped record.

The glaring weakness of the teacher-student conference as a diagnostic data source is its very high costs in terms of teacher time. A typical secondary school teacher may work with 170 students a day. If a twenty-minute teacher-student conference were set up for each student, the teacher would have to spend more than fifty-six hours to meet with each individual. Clearly such an allocation of time does not represent a defensible utilization of the teacher's talents. Consequently, the teacher-learner conference needs to be reserved for use only with individuals about whom relevant information cannot be obtained in more time-efficient ways.

Teacher-kept checklists.   Another alternative diagnostic data source is the teacher-kept checklist. Frequently used to establish information about the rate of occurrence of a specific undesirable student behavior, the checklist is not limited to providing details regarding issues relating to classroom control and discipline. For example, a checklist can be used to determine frequency of students' participation in classroom discussions as measured by their willingness to raise their hands to be recognized.

Only rarely is it feasible to keep a checklist on behaviors of an entire class. Such an undertaking requires too much of a teacher's observational talents. Conducting a class session and, at the same time, checking off appropriate incidences of targeted behaviors on a checklist for thirty-five separate youngsters demands too much of the teacher. Consequently, the teacher-kept checklist ordinarily is used to track the behaviors of only a few individuals about whom the teacher may have serious concerns. The following is an example of such a teacher-kept checklist:

TEACHER-KEPT CHECKLIST.
TARGETED BEHAVIOR: HANDS RAISED TO ANSWER QUESTION
DURING A GIVEN CLASS SESSION.

	Dates				
	4/1	4/2	4/3	4/4	4/5
Roberta Jones	11	111	1		11
Elma Nolan	1111	1	111	11	111
James Smith	11			1	
Peter Wiley			1		

Once the teacher-kept checklist has been completed, the teacher can review the information to pinpoint youngsters who may need some special attention. For example, in the illustrated teacher-kept checklist, Peter Wiley raised his hand seeking recognition only once during this week of instruction. This may trigger a decision to set up a teacher-student conference or some procedure to gather additional information with a view to helping him become a more frequent and a more comfortable classroom participant.

Interest inventories relevant to a new unit. Although teacher-made diagnostic tests represent the preeminent diagnostic data source for gathering information relevant to knowledge and skills that students are presumed to have acquired prior to the initiation of a new unit of work, interest inventories are the most appropriate tool for gathering information about relevant attitudes. Attitudes have some peculiar characteristics that present measurement problems different from those associated with knowledge and skills. Attitudes cannot be measured directly in the same sense that knowledge and skills can. (For example, if one is interested in the skill of making underhanded free throws, he or she simply asks his or her students to make a given number of free throw attempts, records the baskets and misses, and makes a judgment.) Attitudes must be inferred from behaviors that are likely to reflect the existence of an attitude that supported those behaviors.

For the purpose of diagnosing attitudes, the interest inventory works well. An interest inventory is a simple procedure according to which students are asked to rank their preference for Item A as opposed to their preference for Items B, C, D, and so on. From the ranking of A, an attitude can be inferred. For example, if A is ranked higher than all the other options, the attitude of "liking or enjoying A" is inferred. If A is ranked lower than the other options, the attitude of "disliking or not enjoying A" is inferred. The following is an example of a typical interest inventory relevant to a proposed new unit of work:

INTEREST INVENTORY

Directions: On the list that follows is a list of some topics we may be studying during the remainder of the term. Place the number 1 in the blank before the topic that most interests you. Place a 2 before the second most interesting topic. Continue in the same way concluding with an 8 in the blank before the topic you consider to be least interesting.

_____ Interest in analysis of population shifts.
_____ Interest in interpretation of political speeches.
_____ Interest in educational change.
_____ Interest in small-group interaction patterns.
_____ Interest in historical analysis.
_____ Interest in evolution of technology in the arts in the nineteenth century.
_____ Interest in the impact of the automobile on American courting patterns and on French courting.
_____ Interest in _____ (you fill in topic).

A review of the results of an interest inventory can give the teacher an understanding of how individual students feel about topics that may be central to a proposed new unit of study. No specific prescriptions are provided in advance of instruction when a given student or students are found to have attitudes unfavorable toward topics to be considered in a new unit. To speak of "prerequisite attitudes" has a heavy-handed, authoritarian ring about it that is antithetical to the purposes of the social studies. Certainly, teachers may hope to change students' attitudes in certain directions (we do not want them leaving our courses hating social studies more at the end of the course than at the beginning), but those remain changes that are *hoped for*, not mandated or required for success on a given unit of instruction. If simply overwhelming numbers of students seem to be "turned off" by the topic of a proposed new unit, that unit should be reevaluated. Is the material absolutely essential? Or, alternatively, would another unit more in line with students' interests responsibly serve just as well? Should a decision be made to go forward with a unit about which students' attitudes are largely negative, the teacher must work very hard to establish student interest through the provision of highly motivating learning experiences as the unit of instruction unfolds. The hope is that, at the conclusion of the unit, students' feelings toward the topic will be more positive than was the case at the beginning.

Summarizing Diagnostic Information for a Class of Students

Once diagnostic information has been gathered, some teachers find it convenient to summarize information about all students in a class on a *class profile sheet*. A class profile sheet permits a quick visual assessment of strengths and weaknesses of an entire group of youngsters. A number of frameworks for organizing information on a class profile sheet can be devised. A workable sample is illustrated in Figure 5–1.

The sample class profile sheet depicts a typical display of diagnostic information. Note that there are relatively few students with severe problems in the knowledge and skill areas. Happily, too, few attitudinal problems regarding the material to be covered in the new unit were found. If unit planning has gone forward after a careful consideration of the interests and capabilities of the students to be served, there should be relatively few individuals who need special help on knowledge and skills they are presumed to have acquired prior to the beginning of the new unit. The purpose of diagnosis is to identify these few and provide quick remedial assistance to them so that they will have a realistic chance for success once instruction on the new unit begins.

Diagnosis: A Final Caution

Diagnosis of students followed by appropriate prescriptions can assure that a higher percentage of students will experience success when new units of work are presented than when such diagnosis is lacking. It is vital, however, that diagnosis be kept

	Knowledges			Skills	Attitudes	
	Political Event	Social Event	Educational Change	Written Expression	Interest in Educational Change	Interest in Historical Analysis
Adams, P.	—			—		
Blair, S.	—	—	—	—		
Corey, B.						
Dann, P.		—	—			
Eanes, R.						
Foley, N.						
Gaston, L.						—
Henry, Q.			—			
Ivey, L.	—					
Jones, D.						
Karr, F.	—					

KEY: — indicates either need for remediation or, in the attitudinal area, a negative attitude in the area indicated.

Figure 5–1. A Class Profile Sheet (a partial sheet for a real class of 35)

in its proper perspective, particularly in regard to the time consumed by the diagnostic procedures themselves. Diagnosis must be accomplished expeditiously. Sometimes beginning social studies teachers delude themselves that, by spending more time gathering diagnostic information, they will be able to provide a learning situation in which every student masters every bit of the relevant material. Regrettably (perhaps not regrettably), the variability among human beings assures that no "fail-safe" instructional system can be devised in which the total needs of every individual are accommodated. Consequently, expenditure of a great deal of time diagnosing students is not likely to result in tremendously improved learning on the part of the students served. In fact, such practices may be counterproductive in that every class hour devoted to diagnostic practices results in a class hour taken away from instructional activities.

However, when diagnosis of students proceeds quickly and efficiently and results in immediate provision of appropriate, immediate remediation prescriptions to students, diagnosis has an important role to play in assuring students' success on new units of work. Properly done, diagnosis of students provides the teacher with valuable information that increases the likelihood of student mastery of new material. Improperly done, the process takes time away from important instructional activities and denies students the "percolation" time they need to make new material truly their own.

Summary

Diagnostic information provides teachers with a basis for matching their instructional practices to individual student characteristics. In general, diagnostic information can be gathered that relates to students' knowledge, skills, and attitudes. A number of procedures can be used to obtain needed information. Some of these require a heavy investment of teacher time. This suggests that teachers should not attempt to gather comprehensive diagnostic information about each student. Although a certain amount of information about each individual in the class is desirable, time considerations suggest that only selected students or groups of students be the focus for a truly comprehensive diagnostic effort. Too much time spent on diagnosis robs valuable minutes and hours from other important teaching tasks. On the other hand, properly done, the diagnostic process can yield information that can make classroom instruction more effective.

Chapter 6

INTERACTING WITH
LARGE GROUPS
AND SMALL GROUPS

I MPORTANCE OF GROUP EXPERIENCES IN social studies classes cannot
be overestimated. Social studies classes seek to provide students with
insights centering on the interactive relationship between the individual
and his or her own social group. Given this focus, it is only natural
that most learning experiences in social studies classes involve students
organized in groups, either large or small. Of all the subject areas
within the secondary school curriculum, the social studies probably is
least amenable to "packaging" in programmed instructional modules
(or in other isolated self-study formats) that demand that individual
students complete their work isolated from any kind of interactive
contact with others.

Interaction patterns in social studies classes occur in two major kinds
of settings. On the one hand, the teacher works with an entire group
of youngsters as a unit. In this "large-group setting," all individuals
in the class are provided with more or less the same sorts of learning
experiences. There may be some attention to providing variations to
meet individual differences (providing some youngsters with reading
materials written at less challenging levels of difficulty, for example),
but generally most youngsters will have similar learning experiences
in such arrangements.

Alternatively, instruction may occur in a "small-group setting." Given
this arrangement, a class of students is divided into several groups.
Groups may or may not be pursuing common objectives. This format
lends itself more readily to providing learning experiences tailored to
specific needs of individuals within the classroom. It also requires a
good deal more teacher planning. This results because the teacher,

rather than planning learning experiences for a single group (as in a "large-group setting"), must make detailed plans for learning activities for as many as four, five, or even six groups of youngsters. When a teacher is willing to make a commitment to careful planning, small-group learning can be very productive. On the other hand, when such planning fails to occur, small-group experiences may be considerably less productive than instruction in a large-group setting. In sections that follow, guidelines will be provided both for instruction in large groups and instruction in small groups.

Large-Group Instruction

Large-group instruction is neither "good" nor "bad" in any kind of an absolute sense. It is as simplistic to argue that large-group instruction is "always bad" as it is to suggest that small-group instruction is "always good." The worth of any scheme for organizing instruction is associated with the quality of the planning and the execution of the instructional experiences rather than with any mystique attached to the name of the procedure.

For beginning social studies teachers, it makes good sense to become proficient at organizing successful large-group lessons before committing too heavily to small-group experiences. Learning flowing from a single carefully planned large-group experience may be much more productive than that resulting from a number of small-group experiences that have not benefited from careful organization and design.

In planning for interaction in a large-group setting (involving the entire class), the teacher needs to think through answers to the following questions before instruction begins. For beginners, it is a good idea to take time to jot down brief answers to these questions as part of the process of preparation:

1. What is the purpose of this lesson?
2. What is the role of the teacher to be?
3. What are students to be doing?
4. What kind of teacher-to-student and student-to-student interactions are desirable?
5. Is there something specific students should have completed at the end of the hour?
6. What should students do who finish early?

With regard to the "purpose of the lesson," it is necessary to do little beyond reviewing the basic unit plan and the appropriate objectives. Assuming a daily lesson plan has been prepared, a quick check on the basic lesson objective will be in order. This whole procedure is designed merely to reinforce the teacher's focus on the central point that he or she will be attempting to make. A brief written note might be written, for example, indicating the following central "purpose":

I want students to be able to provide me with at least three explanations for the great stock market crash of 1929.

When the teacher takes time to refocus his or her thinking on this purpose ahead of actual instruction, there is less likelihood of instruction getting diverted into a nonproductive channel. Although certainly interests and comments of students need to be listened to sensitively, still there comes a time when instruction must be brought back to the basic purpose of the lesson. This needs to be done skillfully and to be tied, when possible, to the points made by the student. But it *does* need to be done. Clarifying the specific purpose of the lesson ahead of time is helpful to the teacher in redirecting a class back to the central purpose of the lesson. Many beginning social studies teachers are unprepared for how quickly and easily a "seasoned" group of high school students can ask questions and make comments resulting in forty minutes of discussion about the teacher's "island-hopping" days in the Pacific instead of forty minutes of discussion focusing on the "Crash of '29."

Preplanning also must consider the intended "role of the teacher." If there is to be some lecture, about how long will the lecture last? What will be done next? What kinds of transition statements will be made as shifts occur from one phase of the instructional hour to another? Exactly what will the teacher be doing during each phase (sitting at the desk, working at the chalkboard, walking among students answering questions, and so on). As the actual lesson develops, there must be some flexibility in the teacher's activities. For example, a lecture scheduled to last ten minutes must not be hurried to meet that planning guideline if student questions and teacher clarifications cannot be handled conveniently within those limits. Planning the role of the teacher seeks to establish reasonable limits for the teacher's activities during the instructional period.

In preplanning, careful attention must be paid to "what students are to be doing." If there is to be a short lecture, for example, will students be asked to take notes? If yes, what will they be asked to do with those notes? Will students be involved in some assigned seat work? If yes, exactly what is it they will be asked to do? What kinds of equipment must they have? Where will they get it if they do not have it? In general, what will a student who is productively engaged be doing at various times during the class hour?

If there is some intention to have a discussion during the period, "what patterns of interaction are desirable?" Will the teacher manage the discussion? That is, will questions be directed to him or her and then be answered? Will the teacher ask all the questions and ask for volunteers? Will the teacher ask the questions and call on specific students? Or, as an alternative, will the discussion flow more freely from student to student without any necessity of passing comments through the teacher? If this mode is adopted, how will the discussion be "kept on track." There is no "absolutely correct" or "absolutely incorrect" way to plan and manage patterns of interaction. But the teacher does have an obligation to think through a scheme with which he or she is comfortable so that appropriate guidelines can be provided to students. When students are provided with guidelines or ground rules, discussions have a much higher potential for being productive learning experiences than when they go forward in the absence of such a framework.

In the event that students will be involved in some directed study during the period, the teacher needs to determine whether there is "anything specific that students should have completed at the end of the period." If the teacher has such an expectation, it should be communicated to the students as they begin work. Students probably will be much more productive when they know that the teacher has a certain expectation that something specific will be accomplished before the end of the period.

A chronic problem, particularly for beginning social studies teachers, is the student who "finished early." When students are asked to complete a given task, there will always be a few who complete their work long before most of their other classmates. Frequently, these will be bright individuals who have little difficulty in working through even fairly challenging material. Of course, there will be a few others, not so academically talented, who also complete assigned work relatively quickly (perhaps more quickly than they should). Teachers need to have something specific planned for these "early finishers." They might be asked to begin work on another assignment, directed to a learning center in the classroom where supplementary materials are available, or provided with an opportunity to visit a departmental or school resource center. For the teacher, the important thing is to make a determination ahead of time regarding what these people should do. With this kind of preplanning, the teacher can announce to the class the specific options open to those who finish early.

Advantages and Limitations of Large-Group Instruction

Especially for beginning teachers, large-group instruction has the advantage of restricting the range of planning that must be done before instruction begins. With the focus ordinarily on a class of students, lesson planning goes forward on the assumption that students will be pursuing a common objective. Of course, sensitivity to individual differences does mandate attention to providing alternative learning materials, for example, to slow readers. But though the learning materials are varied, the general theme of an instructional class period tends to be similar for all students.

Large-group instruction can help build students' sense of belonging. Skillful teachers build positive group allegiances in large-group settings. ("All right, we are the fourth-period class, and together we are going to refight the Civil War!") As students grow in terms of their identification with the interests and purposes of a large group of students, there are opportunities for teachers to help them increase their sense of self-esteem. A student who makes a point in a discussion in a large-group setting and is rewarded with collective nods of twenty-five or thirty heads develops a real sense of this ability to influence others.

On the limitations side of the ledger, large-group instruction does not accommodate itself as well to meeting individual differences as well as small-group instruction. True, materials used may vary to meet some individual differences. But, basically, objectives of a given lesson tend to be pretty much the same for all students in a class. Given the range of abilities and interests represented in a typical secondary classroom, many students simply may not be reached when all instruction takes place in a large-group setting.

Additionally, because of the large number of students involved, classroom discussions have a tendency to become teacher-dominated. Student-to-student exchanges may be severely restricted out of a necessity to keep the noise level down so that students who have been recognized by the teacher can be heard. Skillful social studies teachers develop ground rules that do result in more frequent student-to-student comments. But, given the nature of large-group settings, there is a clear danger of communication flowing almost exclusively to and from the teacher.

Finally, motivation may be a problem when all instruction takes place in a large-group setting. Generally, instructional experiences in this setting tend to restrict students' abilities to talk to one another, their freedom to move from place to place, and the range of topics considered "appropriate." Given these limitations, many students may find their classroom experiences tedious exercises to be "survived" rather than to be "enjoyed." Simple survival has little to commend it as a motivating device for secondary school social studies classes.

Small-Group Instruction

Small groups have been defined in various ways. For the purposes of this discussion, a definition suggested by David Wright will serve well:

> A small group is a collection of 3 to 15 persons who share common interests and responsibilities in a face-to-face situation which fosters and promotes substantive interaction.[1]

A number of advantages has been suggested for organizing social studies students into small instructional groups. Wells (1972) has suggested that small groups help students break away from an excessive dependency on the teacher as an information source. As small-group work progresses, students are said to become increasingly confident of their own abilities to identify appropriate information. The decision-making processes students go through in small-group work are thought to parallel those used by adults as they make reasoned decisions at home and at work.

Wright (1975) has pointed out that individuals working together in a small group can generate a larger number of ideas than individuals working independently. Further, the quality of these ideas is likely to be higher than those developed by

[1] David W. Wright, *Small Group Communication: An Introduction* (Dubuque, Iowa: Kendall/Hunt Publishing Company, 1975), p. 4.

individuals working alone. Individuals working in groups are likely to develop a stronger sense of personal commitment to decisions made by the group than to decisions they might make by themselves. Finally, work in small groups provides ample opportunity for active verbal participation and, in some cases, for physical movement. These factors are associated with higher levels of student motivation than are instructional settings in which students' active oral contributions and freedom of movement are more severly restricted.

Small-group instruction has its limitations as well as its strengths. For example, group development takes time. Students come to small groups (in most cases) from a history of exposure to large-group instruction. Students take time to adjust to the small-group mode. This adjustment phase takes time away from other, potentially more productive learning experiences.

Small groups can waste a great deal of time when directions are not clear. Beginning social studies teachers frequently are astonished at how much time students can consume bickering over issues as basic as the basic goals of the group. With proper preparation, these sorts of inefficiencies can be eliminated. But, left unattended, potentials for time wasting in small group settings are high.

Another danger of small groups concerns the composition of individual groups. Because groups involve small numbers of students, it is possible (quite likely, even) that some groups may include students with very similar points of view. In a problem-solving situation, such groups probably will do little more than reinforce biases existing before the group exercise started. Again, careful planning by the teacher can avoid this situation. But the teacher must know his or her class members well in order to avoid pointless reiteration of preexisting student beliefs.

PLANNING FOR SMALL-GROUP LEARNING

Successful small-group learning experiences require very careful planning. Individual groups probably will be working in different parts of the classroom. Under these conditions, it is impossible for the teacher to be constantly close at hand to answer questions. Students then must be provided with clear guidelines regarding the task of their group and their individual responsibilities within the group. Small-group learning experiences that have not benefited from patient and careful preplanning may well produce more confusion than learning. As a means of avoiding this unhappy possibility, careful attention needs to be given to (1) the question of appropriate group size, (2) physical or geographic arrangements of individuals within the group, (3) purposes of the group and responsibilities of individuals in achieving these purposes, and (4) group development exercises.

GROUP SIZE

There is no easy answer to the question of what the optimal size for a small learning group is. James (1951) found that in natural conversational settings (for example, during a half time at a football game or intermission at an opera), 71 per cent of the people were engaged in conversational groups consisting only of two people. Twenty-one per cent were involved in groups of three, 6 per cent in groups of four, and only 2 per cent in groups of five or more. He postulated that this situation results because, as more people join in a conversation, the number of potential speakers and listeners grows so rapidly that it becomes difficult to maintain a coherent conversation in which all parties feel an active sense of participation (some interactional possibilities are shown in Figure 6–1). Consequently, there is a preference for small conversational groups.

It is impossible, or at least not very practical, to take James's (1951) findings and attempt to structure small-group learning around groups of two people. Although the evidence suggests that a vast majority of people prefer two-person conversational groups, not much advantage accrues to an instructor who finds himself or herself faced with fifteen groups of two students each rather than with a single group of thirty. Most teachers find it convenient to assign from four to seven students to a group. This permits some ease of management in

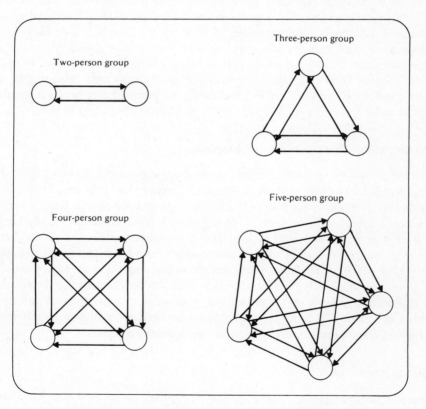

Figure 6–1. Interactional Possibilities for Groups of Different Sizes

that four to five groups can be organized in a reasonably isolated fashion in different parts of the classroom. An implication of this practice, derived from James (1951), is worth noting. There is nothing naturally cohesive about a four-to-seven student group. Recall that, given natural unstructured settings, most will prefer groups of two. Given this reality, unless very careful attention is given to identifying the purpose of the group and the specific responsibility of each student, there is a tendency for a teacher-made group of four to seven students to "fragment" into several chatting subgroups of two students each.

Physical Placement of Individuals in Groups

In addition to identifying purposes and individual responsibilities within small groups, teachers make decisions regarding physical or geographical arrangements of individuals within groups that influence behavior of students in these groups. If a teacher, for example, wishes certain students to exercise a leadership function, they will be better able to fulfill their responsibilities if the physical arrangement of the group allows them to sit at the end of a table rather than along the side. In general, leadership roles are most easily exercised from a "point position" within a group's physical arrangement. On the other hand, should the group be designed with a view to shared responsibility, a circular arrangement is likely to be a productive choice. Clearly, in this setting, no individual is at a point position, and the physical arrangement lends itself to a freer exchange of ideas. (Should a circular arrangement be chosen, it is a good idea to provide tables for students to sit around or at least some small table in the middle. A completely open circle poses a psychological threat to some students and makes them reluctant to participate.) Positions of leadership in three configurations are illustrated in Figure 6–2.

Distances between individuals in a group form another important consideration. In general, distances should be kept as short as possible. Increasing distance between students is associated with increasing inhibitions. Comfortable conversation cannot occur when distances between speakers in a small group go much beyond three feet. Greater distance necessitates uncomfortable (for many students, at least) increases in volume. Rather than participate under such conditions, many students will opt to say nothing.

Purposes of Groups

Regardless of their purposes, all small groups require the teacher to give attention to several key issues in planning for instruction. First of all, the general goal or objective of the group needs to be communicated to the students in the group. Next, specific student responsibilities need to be explained. (Who will be chairperson? Who will be the recorder? Who will keep track of materials? And so on.) The basic sequence of events that will be followed as the group pursues its objectives needs to be identified. Finally, the teacher needs to think through his or her role in working with the group.

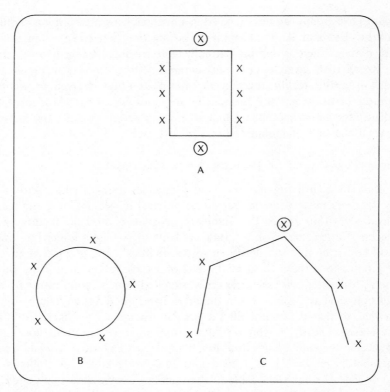

Figure 6–2. Positions of Leadership in Three Configurations (leadership positions are circled)

Obviously, responses to these considerations will vary, depending upon the purposes of the individual group. The kinds of groups that can be devised to provide productive learning in social studies classes are limited in number only by the teacher's own creative design capabilities. In sections that follow, some examples are described for three small-group types: (1) the tutoring group, (2) the investigative group, and (3) the selected options group.

The tutoring group.   The basic purpose of the tutoring group is to provide information to students who may (1) experience problems in learning in large-group settings or (2) be capable of dealing with content going beyond that presented in a large-group setting. In other words, tutoring groups can be used both for remediation and for enrichment. In a sense, a tutoring group can be viewed as a smaller version of a large instructional group. The teacher plays a directive leadership role. He or she goes over content much as might be done with a much larger group of students.

Students in a tutoring group are encouraged to ask questions and make comments as the explanations unfold. Because of the small number of individuals involved, students who may feel reluctant to speak up in large-group settings feel more comfortable in assuming an active role. Additionally, as students are relatively few in number and are seated close to the teacher, levels of student interest and attention tend to be high when tutoring groups are used.

Preparation for a tutoring group does not involve a great deal of adjustment for students. In many respects, their activities will be quite similar to what they do in large-group instructional settings. They may feel somewhat exposed at first in that they cannot get "lost in the crowd" when such a small number of students is involved. But a few supportive statements from the teacher can generally put such anxieties to rest.

For the teacher, preparation is not terribly different from what goes on in getting ready for large-group instruction. However, there is one important difference. A tutoring group demands almost all of the teacher's energies and concentration while it is in progress. This means that students not involved in the group being served must be productively engaged in a way that will not result in frequent disruptions of the teacher's leadership role in the tutoring group. Arrangements might be made, for example, for some students to work in the departmental or school media center, some to work with a teacher's aide, and some to work quietly on some independent seat work. Clearly, such arrangements need to be made in advance of any attempt to lead a tutoring group. When such arrangements have been made and the teacher is free to devote all of his or her energies to the group of students being served, the tutoring group can provide a rich learning experience for social studies students.

Investigative groups. The central purpose of the investigative group is problem solving. Students work together to develop reasonable solutions to situations with which they are confronted. Investigative group learning can help students become more familiar with rational, step-by-step decision making.

In the preparation of students for work in investigative work, they need to be told that the purpose is to provide them with thinking skills that will be useful to them throughout their lives. They should be introduced to the elements of a systematic decision-making sequence. The one that follows is representative of a number of such scientific schemes that have been introduced from time to time:

1. Identify the issue.
2. Suggest tentative solutions.
3. Test tentative solutions against evidence.
4. Accept or revise tentative solutions after examination of the evidence.

Students need to be assigned specific responsibilities for their work in the investigative work. A *group leader* might be identified to take general charge of the investigation. A *group secretary* or *recorder* can be assigned to take notes as the group works through its investigation of the issue. Sometimes teachers find it useful to appoint a *devil's advocate* charged with challenging emerging conclusions. This individual can help a group avoid making decisions too hastily.

The teacher's role, then, begins with an explanation of the decision-making sequence and assignment of specific responsibilities. Next, an issue must be provided. One can be supplied by the teacher, a list of alternatives can be provided and students be allowed to choose, or students themselves can be permitted to identify an issue with no teacher assistance. For students who have had little experience in investigative group work, it is a good idea for the teacher, at least, to provide some general suggestions with regard to appropriate issues.

Once the issue has been identified, the teacher must make certain that sufficient learning materials are available for students to use as they attempt to test their tentative solutions. Unless a responsible selection of materials is available, students may well reach some strange and unsupportable conclusions.

As the exercise unfolds, the teacher needs to circulate among the group to ensure that the basic decision-making process has been understood and that each student understands what his or her own responsibilities are. During a debriefing at the conclusion of the exercise, the role of the teacher is to challenge conclusions, call for evidence, and ask why certain other interpretations might not be better than those generated by the group. This phase must be handled sensitively. Students are not familiar with the role of generating interpretations themselves. To encourage their self-confidence, the teacher needs to make supportive comments about their efforts while, at the same time, suggesting the possibility that other interpretations might also be worthy of consideration.

Selected options groups. Selected options groups provide students with opportunities to pursue one of several alternative learning experiences made available to them during a given instructional period. Generally, selected options groups involve the use of learning centers. Learning centers are selected areas of the classroom, typically four to six in number, where students may go to receive instructions and materials necessary for completing a given learning activity. Ordinarily, each learning center has a different focus. For example, in a U.S. history class studying the Civil War, there might be centers focusing on "Great Battles," "Economic Causes," "European Alliances of North and South," "Politics in the Union and Confederate Capitals," and "Expansion of Transportation Systems."

In selected options groups, students are not necessarily assigned to work with a certain group of other students. Rather, they might be instructed simply to complete all of the assignments at each learning center by a certain time. During each instructional hour, they might, on their own, decide the center at which they wish to work. Under these conditions, members of the group at each center may vary from day to day.

The teacher must spend a great deal of time preparing learning centers before beginning lessons based on selected options groups. Materials must be provided, and, equally important, instructions at each center must be made clear enough so that students can understand what they are to do, with only an occasional necessity to ask the teacher for clarification. Further, the teacher needs to think through some operating guidelines. For example, what is the maximum number of people who should be permitted to work at one center? What about "early finishers?" What patterns of movement between centers are the most desirable? Decisions made regarding these and other issues must be made clear to the students.

As instruction goes forward, the teacher rotates from center to center to assure that students understand directions and are moving forward in a productive manner. This pattern of movement affords the possibility of close personal work with individual students that simply cannot be accomplished comfortably in large-group settings. Though the "costs" are high for selected options groups in terms of teacher planning time, the opportunity for close teacher-student involvement has the potential for providing motivating and productive learning experiences for students.

PREPARING STUDENTS TO WORK IN SMALL GROUPS

Secondary students need to be prepared for small-group work. As has been noted previously, many have not had a great deal of experience working in anything other than a group of thirty or thirty-five students. Because of their unfamiliarity with an instructional setting consisting of four, five, six, or seven students, many students approach small-group learning with initial doubts and even some anxiety. They are not quite sure just what behaviors will be expected of them.

Small-group learning experiences are likely to be much more productive when the teacher takes time to plan some small-group familiarization exercises for students. These exercises should precede work focusing on major instructional issues. Several examples of techniques that have proved successful in allaying students' anxieties and warming them up to the idea of small-group work are introduced in the following sections.

Two-by-twos. "Two-by-twos" is an exercise that works very well as an "icebreaker" when a teacher wishes to use some small-group techniques with a class of students who do not know one another well. Many teachers use the technique on the first or second day of class in a new school semester.

For purposes of illustration, assume the teacher has a class of thirty-two students. The exercise flows through a series of steps as indicated:

Step 1

> *Teacher:* All right now, I want each person to stand up, walk around, and find someone he or she doesn't know very well. If you find a perfect stranger, that's just great! You have thirty seconds to find someone. Ready . . . go!
> [Students quickly find a partner.]

Step 2

Teacher: I want each of you to find out three important bits of information from your partner. Number one: What is your partner's name? Number two: When is your partner's birthday? Number three: What would your partner do today if he or she were suddenly given $1,000? You have two minutes to exchange this information. Remember what your partner tells you.
[Students follow these instructions. Teacher calls a halt after two minutes.]

Step 3

Teacher: Now things are going to get interesting. I want each pair of you to get together with another pair to form a group of four. When you have your groups formed, I want one person to begin. He or she should tell people in the group the three things he or she learned about his or her partner. Remember those are (1) his or her name, (2) his or her birthday, and (3) what he or she would do with a surprise $1,000. I want everyone in the group to share this information about his or her partner. This time I want you to try to remember these three things not just about your partner, but about everyone in your foursome. You'll have four minutes for this one.
[Students follow directions. Eight groups of four students each result. Teacher calls a halt after four minutes.]

Step 4

Teacher: This time I am really going to challenge you. I want each group of four to get together with another group of four to form a group of eight. Do the same thing in the group of eight as you did in the group of four; that is, take turns providing information about one another until everyone has been familiarized with the three bits of information about everyone in the group.
[Students follow directions. Four groups of eight students result. Teacher calls a halt after about six minutes.]

Step 5

Teacher: Now we are going to see who the real memory artists are. Let's have each group of eight get together with another one to form a group of sixteen. Follow the same process as before. You'll have about eight minutes for this one.

Step 6

Teacher: We have now arrived at the "grand finale." Let's have the two groups of sixteen form one large group of thirty-two and go through the

same process. Let's form a big circle to do this. I think eight minutes will be about enough time.
[Students follow directions. One large group of thirty-two results. Teacher brings exercise to a halt after about eight minutes.]

Step 7

Teacher: Who will take the plunge and try to name everyone in the group? Wait a minute. That's too easy. Who'll provide all three items of information about everyone? Sue, you want to try it. Fine, go ahead. [Other students will make attempts in turn. Group ordinarily cheer on and applaud those who succeed. A surprisingly large number will.]

Two-by-twos does a fine job of breaking down students' initial anxieties. An astonishing number of students will be able to name the entire class at the end of the exercise. The exercise builds a real sense of cohesiveness and speeds up the "settling in" period classes of students go through as they try to become comfortable with a new situation. Students who are comfortable with one another tend to become much more quickly involved in productive small-group work.

Inside-outs. Another warm-up for small-group work, inside-outs, is designed to build students' skills as a discussant in a small group. In inside-outs, the teacher divides the class into two groups. In a class of thirty-two, each group will have sixteen members. Sixteen chairs are arranged in a circular fashion, and one group sits in them. This group is called the "inside" group. Each member of the other group, the "outside" group, is assigned to observe and take notes on what one member of the inside group does. Then the inside group is given a controversial topic and told to talk about it in a reasonable, responsible way. For example, the group might be told to discuss the following proposal:

Resolved that from this date forward women in the U.S. armed forces should be assigned to front line combat duties on the same basis as men.

Members of the outside group watch the individuals assigned to them and take notes on the following points.
To what extent did the person observed

1. Take an active part in the discussion?
2. Make comments that built logically on what the previous speaker said?
3. Summarize something said by a previous speaker?
4. Make comments keeping the group from jumping to premature conclusions?
5. Make supportive comments about something someone else said?
6. Provide real evidence to support a statement he or she made?

After the "insides" have carried on a discussion for about ten minutes, the two groups switch, that is, the former "outsides" become "insides." The new "insides" take up the discussion, and the new "outsides" take notes. This phase goes on for about ten minutes. At this time, the teacher leads the class in a debriefing discussion. Information gathered by the notetakers is discussed. The teacher highlights techniques associated with small-group membership. Students who have gone through this exercise tend to become much more productive in their small groups than others who have not benefited from this kind of training.

Listening skills exercise. Many social studies teachers, particularly beginners, are dismayed at student comments in small groups that reflect a lack of careful listening to what others have said. Listening skills are not automatic, and time spent helping students sharpen these skills can result in more productive small-group membership.

A listening skills exercise many social studies teachers have found useful involves identifying an issue or series of issues about which large numbers of students disagree. The issue can be a matter of public policy or something much narrower in scope affecting only the students in a particular school. The issues should be very divisive ones about which students have fairly strong feelings. Some possibilities might be suggestions that

1. Athletic budgets be equally divided between traditional male sports and traditional female sports.
2. More women than men be appointed to jobs as sportswriters on the local newspaper to make up for past job discrimination against women.
3. Low-cost federally subsidized housing for the poor be built in the center of a neighborhood of $125,000 houses.
4. Busing be instituted between the central city and the affluent suburbs for the purpose of achieving racial balance.
5. The draft be reinstituted in place of the all-volunteer army.

Once issues have been selected and individuals identified on both sides of them, the listening skills exercise can begin. The teacher selects a pair of individuals, one supporting one of the propositions and the other opposing it. Each of the two students is told to sit down and, as calmly as possible, tell the other individual what his or her basic position is and what the basis of his or her position is. Once one individual finishes, the other does the same thing, telling the other side of the story. When this phase of the exercise is completed, the teacher calls first of all on the person taking the "pro" position on the issue. This person is asked to stand up and tell the class not his or her own position (the "pro" position), but rather the position of the individual he or she listened to, an individual favoring the "con" position. The person holding the "con" position listens carefully. At the end, the individual holding the "con" verifies the extent to which the person with the "pro" position accurately represented the "con" position. Next, the process is repeated as the individual holding the "con" position explains the "pro" position while the class and the individual holding the "pro" position listen attentively.

This exercise sharpens students' listening skills. They must push their own biases aside as they pay close attention to what individuals holding contrary views are saying. The exercise broadens students' understanding of issues and enhances their effectiveness as listeners in small groups.

SMALL GROUPS: FINAL CONSIDERATION

Small groups can provide students in social studies classes with motivating and highly productive learning experiences. But because students typically have not had much experience in small-group settings, some initial student doubts and concerns are to be expected. It is not sufficient for teachers to plan for the *content* of small-group learning experiences. Rather, planning must also be designed with a view to familiarizing youngsters with the *process* of small-group learning. More specifically, the structure of small-group learning must be explained. Students need to know the purposes of the group, the step-by-step procedures to be followed in achieving those purposes, and their individual responsibilities in the group. Given this information, small-group learning experiences add a stimulating dimension to instruction in the social studies classroom.

Combining Large- and Small-Group Instruction

Skilled social studies teachers do not rely exclusively on either large-group or small-group instruction. Rather, they seek flexibility by combining the two approaches to meet their needs. The two approaches by no means are incompatible. Careful planning must precede any attempt to implement such a combination.

When a social studies teacher is interested in developing a planning scheme that will accommodate both large- and small-group instruction, one way to begin is to assign each student in class to one of several groups. On some days those groups will meet as small groups. On other days all small groups will be combined into one large-group section. To illustrate how such a plan might operate, let us assume a typical classroom of thirty students. These students could be divided into six groups as follows:

Group A = 5 students	Group D = 5 students
Group B = 5 students	Group E = 5 students
Group C = 5 students	Group F = 5 students

The teacher might be interested in providing students with three basic kinds of learning settings. One of these might be a typical large-group setting in which information could be dispensed and certain kinds of discussions conducted. A second setting might involve the teacher working more closely with only fifteen students at a time. A third setting might involve groups of students working independently at several learning centers provided in the classroom. A planning scheme for a single week that would provide these three kinds of settings might look something like the following:

Monday	Tuesday	Wednesday	Thursday	Friday
A—Large group	A—Center	B—Center	A—Large group	B—Center
B—Large group	C—Center	D—Center	B—Large group	D—Center
C—Large group	E—Center	E—Center	C—Large group	F—Center
D—Large group	B—Group of 15	A—Group of 15	D—Large group	A—Center
E—Large group	D—Group of 15	C—Group of 15	E—Large group	C—Center
F—Large group	F—Group of 15	E—Group of 15	F—Large group	E—Center

This scheme represents simply an example of the almost endless variety that can be generated. The key principle in planning directed at combining small-group and large-group instruction is to focus on the small group rather than the large group as the unit of planning. For example, given this plan where the class was broken down into groups of five, the teacher would be able to plan a learning experience for as few as five students at a time. Perhaps Group A might go to the library on Monday, Group B on Tuesday, and so forth, until all students had gone. Given the focus on the small group, real flexibility can be built into instructional planning in the social studies. This kind of flexibility can be the vehicle for providing learning experiences that serve well the varying interests and needs of secondary school social studies students.

Summary

Both large-group instruction and small-group instruction have their place in social studies classes. Both organizational schemes have their strengths and their weaknesses. Success in both large-group and small-group instruction requires careful attention to planning. Success or failure of a given organizational scheme relates much more directly to the quality of this planning than to any features unique to either large-group or small-group instruction.

Small-group instruction places more demands on the teacher than does large-group instruction. Careful attention must be directed toward planning experiences for several groups of learners who may be pursuing quite different objectives within a given instructional period. Monitoring of student activities occurring simultaneously at several locations requires careful thought and consideration.

As most students have had much broader experience learning in large groups than in small groups, planning for small groups needs to attend to familiarizing students with small-group learning as a process. Group participation skills, in particular, need to be developed. Several exercises are available that teachers can use to familiarize students with some of the challenges of small-group learning.

Many social studies teachers combine large- and small-group learning experiences. This procedure has the advantage of providing a desirable degree of variety and flexibility for the social studies program. Such plans may be relatively easily developed provided that the small group, rather than the large group, is used as the basic unit of consideration for instructional planning.

REFERENCES

JAMES, JOHN. "A Preliminary Study of the Size Determinant in Small Group Interaction." *American Sociological Review* XVI (1951): 474–447.

WELLS, ELIZABETH H. "An Organizational Pattern for Small Groups in an American History Course." Monograph. Baltimore: The Johns Hopkins University Center for Social Organization of Schools, 1972. ERIC system number ED 073 024.

WRIGHT, DAVID W. *Small Group Communication: An Introduction.* Dubuque, Iowa: Kendall/Hunt Publishing Company, 1975.

Chapter 7

ASSESSING STUDENTS'
LEARNING

T HE PROCESS OF COMBINING ASSESSMENTS and judgments of students' work results in evaluation. Evaluation plays a pivotal role within social studies education. Indeed, issues relating to measuring and judging students' progress are so important that proper evaluation has been said to serve as a "conscience of the social studies" (Armstrong, 1977). Careful, professional evaluation serves as a "conscience" in the sense that it assures that programs deliver in practice what they promise in statements of intent. Proper evaluation, for example, demands that students demonstrate problem-solving capabilities at assessment time when the sequence of instruction claims to have involved them in "problem-solving activities."

Social studies teachers are involved in assessment activities that can be divided broadly into the two general categories of "informal assessment" and "formal assessment." Informal assessment occurs when students' performances reflect an improvement that the teacher subjectively perceives to be an improvement over past performances, but for which no formal documentation is gathered. For example, social studies teachers often notice that students become much more comfortable with the pronunciation of Russian names after they have spent some time studying Russian history. Informal assessment does not result ordinarily in the teacher's taking some action to record information about individual students for future reference. Rather, informal assessment results in a cluster of perceptions the teacher develops from casual observations relating to relative levels of development of individual students. The general area of informal assessment presents few serious difficulties for beginning social studies teachers.

Formal assessment presents social studies teachers with a greater challenge than informal assessment. This challenge results from a combination of three factors. First of all, formal assessment is preplanned and requires teacher preparation of testing procedures. Second, results of testing must be recorded in a systematic way. Third, these records of student performance must be converted to grades or other reporting mechanisms at various times throughout the school year. Formal assessment is time-consuming; and, because of its association with grades and other progress reporting practices, it is an area of high student concern. Indeed, many students are so concerned with evaluations based on teacher assessments and practices that they infer the purposes of a course from the nature of testing practices alone.

This situation has serious implications for the teacher. For example, if a program is described to students as being designed to develop "higher-level interpretation skills," but tests call on students only to identify isolated pieces of information on true-false tests, insightful students quickly learn that the "real" objective of the course is to teach them isolated pieces of information. The teacher may "talk" a good case for developing "higher-level interpretation skills," but his or her assessment procedures telegraph to students that in his or her heart of hearts the real interest lies in "pushing facts."

Because of the tremendous power of adopted evaluation procedures as a shaper of students' perceptions regarding purposes of courses, it is imperative that extraordinarily careful attention be paid to developing assessment procedures that are consistent with the described goals and objectives of those courses. Frequently, inexperienced social studies teachers make the mistake of allocating a great deal of preparation time to identifying and preparing engaging presentation techniques and a very short time preparing assessment instruments. Shorting preparation time for appropriate assessment procedures results in slipshod testing that may produce student attitudes about what is important that are totally at odds with the teacher's intentions. The most carefully constructed strategies of organized instructional techniques directed toward helping students become "better problem solvers" will not result in students' prizing problem-solving behavior if final tests require no demonstration of problem-solving competencies. Credibility demands that, when only factual recall is sought, testing should demand factual recall and that when higher-level thinking abilities are sought, testing should demand higher-level thinking abilities.

Seeking Congruence Between Instructional Intent and Assessment[1]

In arranging for parallelism between instructional intent and assessment procedures, one might find that a logical place to begin is with the performance objectives.

[1] This material has been extracted from David G. Armstrong, "Evaluation: Conscience of the Social Studies," *The Social Studies*, 57 (March/April 1977): 62–64. Copyright (1977) Helen Dwight Reid Educational Foundation. Reprinted with permission of Heldref Publications.

The evaluation component of a performance objectives is described by the "conditions" (kinds of testing procedure) and the "degree" (how well students must do to achieve credit for their performance) components of a performance objective. As a means of assuring that evaluation as reflected in the "condition" and "degree" component of each objective is appropriate, a logical beginning involves the development of a table of objectives written in such a way that only the "audience" [the individual(s) doing the learning] and the "behavior" (what the student must be able to do as a consequence of instruction) components are included. Using this procedure, one would arrange these objectives in terms of increasing levels of cognitive difficulty. This arrangement is based on the assumption that a base line of information must be known by learners before they can be expected to demonstrate higher-level thinking skills. An abbreviated sample of a table of objectives, with content objectives drawn from geography, is presented in Figure 7–1.

Once objectives have been identified and ordered in tabular form, evaluation procedures can be identified that require learners to engage in thinking skills at the level of complexity implied by each objective. In determining which evaluation procedures ought to be included, one needs to make reference to the cognitive level of each objective.

For program objectives written at the knowledge, comprehension, and application levels, assessment procedures are appropriate that require students to provide predetermined "proper" or "correct" responses. Tests of this type include matching,

Knowledge
> Each learner will define the term *capital city*.

Comprehension
> Each learner will describe the process of *chain migration*.

Application
> Each learner, using a provided mileage scale, will determine approximate distances between selected pairs of U.S. cities.

Analysis
> Each learner will compare and contrast patterns of black ghetto expansion in Seattle and Chicago.

Synthesis
> Each learner will describe possible consequences for settlement patterns in Seattle and Chicago that might result from a sixfold increase in the present price of gasoline.

Evaluation
> Each learner will make judgments about the relative appeal of Chicago and Seattle as final settlement sites for nineteenth-century immigrants from (1) Sweden, (2) Poland, and (3) Italy.

Figure 7–1. Table of Objectives (including only "audience" and "behavior" components)

fill-in-the-blanks, true-false, and multiple-choice tests and other variations of these basic themes. Of these possibilities, measurement specialists tend to prefer multiple-choice items. Some research work of interest has suggested that about ten test questions be developed for each knowledge, comprehension, and application objective and that a criterion of eight correct out of these ten be accepted as a reasonable indication of mastery (Novick and Lewis, 1974).

For program objectives requiring learners to demonstrate the ability to engage in higher levels of thinking, including analysis, synthesis, and evaluation, the essay represents the most appropriate choice as an assessment procedure. Multiple-choice items can be used to test thinking at the level of analysis, but they are difficult and time-consuming to construct. For most teachers, the essay represents a better choice.

In spite of the commitment of many social studies professionals to encouraging students to engage in higher-level thinking processes, the essay examination is not used as widely as it might be. Part of the reluctance of some teachers to use essay examinations stems from the belief that responsible correction demands too much time. Additionally, such tests may seem to be difficult to correct because achievement criteria are frequently not as clear as in the case of multiple-choice, matching, and true-false tests. (It is a simple matter to insist that learners must get 80 per cent of the items on a true-false test correct in order to pass. A statement that learners must pass an essay examination with 80 per cent accuracy is meaningless.)

The situation with regard to essay examinations is not beyond resolution. Both the problem of correction time and the problem of elusive criteria can be remedied by careful attention to the wording of essay items. Specifically, the instructor's expectations must be described as precisely as possible in the essay's question statement. Consider the two following questions:

A. Write an essay in which you explain reasons for the outbreak of World War I.
B. Write an essay explaining your interpretations of the causes of World War I. In your essay include references to the following areas: (1) economics, (2) secret treaty arrangements, and (3) persistent national rivalries. For *each* of these three areas, cite at least five incidents, episodes, or conditions that support the position you are taking.

Given Item A, students likely will ramble. Correction time increases (1) because of the necessity to look for insights that may lie buried among pages of irrelevancies and (2) because of an uncertainty about the specific responses that will be rewarded with a high grade or a kind remark. On the other hand, Item B provides the instructor with a specific set of guidelines as he or she begins grading the students' work. Because criteria are clear, the process of scanning papers becomes more focused and can be accomplished with more dispatch than was the case with essay A.

Development of essay items that include clearly described criteria takes time, but this time is certain to be less than that required to correct (responsibly) essay tests lacking precise statements of criteria. Certainly, no case can be made for the other time-saving alternative—the inappropriate use of true-false or matching items to assess students' abilities to demonstrate higher-level thinking skills.

Now that the general sorts of assessment procedures that are appropriate for objectives demanding different levels of cognitive functioning have been identified, the next step requires the identification of the specific evaluation procedures to be used with each listed objective. Using the objective included in the table objectives depicted in Figure 7–1, one can develop a second table of complete performance objectives (including the "conditions" and "degree" components). Figure 7–2 illustrates such a table.

Knowledge

> Each learner will define the term *capital city* by responding correctly to at least eight of ten items on a multiple-choice test.

Comprehension

> Each learner will identify steps involved in the process of *chain migration* by responding correctly to at least eight of ten items on a multiple-choice test.

Application

> Each learner, using a provided mileage scale, will determine approximate differences between selected pairs of U.S. cities by responding correctly to eight of ten multiple-choice items.

Analysis

> Each learner will compare patterns of black ghetto expansion in Seattle and Chicago in an essay. Responses must include comparisons between the two cities in terms of each of the following factors: (1) topography, (2) density of black settlement in areas adjacent to ghetto areas, (3) density of black population in the entire urban area, (4) attitudes of city officials toward black ghetto areas, (5) specific legal barriers to ghetto expansion, (6) patterns of employment among ghetto residents, and (7) degree of political organization within the ghettos.

Synthesis

> Each learner will describe possible consequences for settlement patterns in Seattle and Chicago that might result from a sixfold increase in the present price of gasoline. Responses will be provided in an essay that must include specific comments regarding each city concerning possible changes relating to (1) highway networks, (2) fixed rail transport, (3) water transport, (4) single-family dwelling developments, (5) high-rise apartments, and (6) real property prices in (a) the central business district, (b) residential districts in the city, (c) the close-in suburbs, and (d) the distant suburbs.

Evaluation

> Each learner will make judgments about the relative appeal of Chicago and Seattle as final settlement sites for nineteenth-century immigrants from (1) Sweden, (2) Poland, and (3) Italy. Responses will be provided in an essay. For each city (Seattle and Chicago) and each country (Sweden, Poland, and Italy) specific comments must be included relating to criteria developed and described by the learner.

Figure 7–2. Addition of Assessment Procedures to Develop Complete Performance Objectives from Objectives Listed in Figure 7–1

Careful matching of assessment components to the "audience" and "behavior" components of performance objectives helps students to infer program purposes that are consistent with teachers' intentions. This congruence also helps the teacher to assessment procedures to instructional purposes, helps students to infer proper program purposes, and helps teachers to monitor and evaluate the effectiveness of their practices. To maximize the effectiveness of these performance objectives, the teacher should duplicate them and provide them to students at the beginning of an instructional sequence. If they familiarize themselves with the nature of the objectives and the expected assessment procedures, levels of achievement at assessment time are likely to be enhanced.

Tests for Assessing Cognitive Performance of Students

Figure 7–3 summarizes the relative appropriateness of some selected testing techniques for assessing students' performances at various levels of cognitive difficulty.

Essay Tests

Essay tests are properly used to assess students' abilities to function at the levels of application, analysis, synthesis, and evaluation. Indeed, essays have the potential for assessing knowledge-level and comprehension-level learning as well, but the essay is a much less efficient assessment vehicle for gathering information relating to student performance at those levels. This results because, whereas both knowl-

	Knowledge	Comprehension	Application	Analysis	Synthesis	Evaluation
Multiple-choice	x	x	x	x		
Matching	x	x				
True-False	x	x				
Fill-in-the-blanks	x	x				
Essay			x	x	x	x

KEY: An x implies that test items of this type represent an appropriate choice.

Figure 7–3. Selecting Appropriate Testing Procedures for Assessing Learning Scaled According to Levels of Cognitive Difficulty

edge-level testing and comprehension-level testing are designed to elicit specific "correct" answers from students, the essay yields responses that are not so easily interpreted in terms of their being "right" or "wrong." Consequently, when a teacher wishes to determine only whether students have acquired a specific piece of information, a multiple-choice test (or other procedure demanding a fixed, easily corrected "right" or "wrong" response) represents a better choice.

However, when the purpose of testing is to determine students' higher-level thinking competencies, the essay is the test instrument par excellence. The essay permits students to pull information freely from a variety of sources and organize it into meaningful patterns in response to the question. It assumes student mastery of basic knowledge and presumes an ability of the student to manipulate that information in a manner that suggests higher-level thinking abilities.

Though the essay expects the learner to put information together in a unique manner (unique in terms of its actual organization and presentation, if not in substantive content), that does not mean that there are to be no standards against which the excellence of a given essay response can be judged. As was illustrated earlier in the chapter with the example relating to World War I, a good essay item describes clearly the categories of information that must be included. This means, for example, that a question ought not simply to direct students to "write an essay on the depression," but that rather the question should be refined to include delimiters resulting in a question such as "Write an essay on the depression in which you cite specific impacts on small farmers, on urban workers, and on small businessmen." Addition of these categories provides a framework for students' writing without requiring them to develop a single correct response. The addition of this kind of specificity to essay questions speeds correction time and tends to improve the quality of student answers by reducing the tendency to ramble.

Student essays are improved, further, by directions that limit their length. An essay limited to three pages may well be more tightly organized and include more substantive content than an essay eight or ten pages in length. Given a page limitation, students are much more inclined to give some thought to planning the development of their response than when no such limits are provided. When no such limits are imposed, many students seem to think that there is "virtue in volume." They may strive for quantity rather than quality in their response. The illustration provided in Figure 7–4 demonstrates an acceptable set of instructions for an essay examination.

Clearly, the essay is not an appropriate format for all students. Some lack the basic composition skills necessary for success on an exercise of this kind. This deficiency in writing skills does not necessarily imply that students cannot process information at higher cognitive levels. Such students can be provided with an opportunity to demonstrate their compentencies in higher cognitive thinking areas through the use of oral examination. Questions and directions for oral examination of this type can parallel those for essay examinations. There is a limitation of the use of such oral examinations imposed by physical conditions of teaching.

United States History — Mr. Williams

Your name ______________________________

Essay Question

Directions: You are to write an essay on the following topic:

"Public Reactions to Woodrow Wilson's League of Nations Proposal"

In your response include at least three specific references to general reactions of individuals within each of the following groups: (1) United States Manufacturers, (2) Middle-Class Citizens in the "Farm Belt" and (3) the Eastern Press.

Limit your answer to no more than three pages. Please write legibly. You have been provided with a fourth piece of paper you might wish to use to plan the development of your essay before you begin writing.

Figure 7–4. Formatting for an Essay Examination

Whereas a large number of students can take essay examinations at the same time in a given classroom without interfering with one another's work, an oral examination usually requires a one-on-one situation with the teacher working with a single student at a time. Arranging for time to work with a single student requires special teacher planning. Consequently, the oral examination, practically speaking, cannot be used as much as the teacher might desire. But when conditions can be arranged, the oral examination does represent a viable alternative for testing higher-level thinking abilities of students with severe writing deficiencies.

As a summary, the following points should be kept in mind when essay examinations (or oral examination) are given:

1. Use should be restricted to testing higher levels of cognitive thinking (application, analysis, synthesis, and evaluation).
2. Specific directions should require students to provide information within a restricted number of categories.
3. A limitation should be set in terms of maximum length.
4. Students should be encouraged to spend some time organizing their thoughts before beginning the exercise.

Multiple-Choice Tests

Multiple-choice tests enjoy high esteem among measurement specialists. They can be written to test students' abilities across a wide range of cognitive difficulty. Further, they are applicable to almost any subject area and to most topics within a given subject area. Finally, tests consisting of multiple-choice items, when properly constructed, have been found to be characterized by high reliability; that is, the same kinds of students tend to receive consistent patterns of scores on repeated administrations of the test.

Multiple-choice tests can be used to test students' capacities at the cognitive levels of knowledge, comprehension, application, and analysis. For the higher levels, particularly in the case of analysis, construction of multiple-choice items is a time-consuming, somewhat cumbersome process. Many teachers prefer to give essay examinations to test students' functioning at this level. But when developmental time is sufficient and the teacher is so inclined, nothing prevents the use of good multiple-choice items to test analytical talents of students.

Construction of multiple-choice items at the knowledge level can be accomplished quickly. Knowledge level items demand simple recall of specific pieces of information. Ordinarily, a single word or very short phrase will do. The following item exemplifies an appropriate knowledge-level, multiple-choice item:

The capital of the State of Montana is

    a. Butte.
    b. Helena.
    c. Missoula.
    d. Polson.

Comprehension-level items demand more sophisticated cognitive functioning. Comprehension involves an understanding of a number of elements contained within a given situation that are related to one another in a specific and predictable way. Comprehension requires simultaneous recall of all of these elements and an ability to perceive their proper interrelationship. The following item exemplifies an appropriate comprehension-level, multiple-choice item:

In a story, your younger brother read that Mr. and Mrs. Jones visited their attorney to see about a codicil. Your brother asked you what *codicil* meant. You explained that a codicil is a

    a. Legal document that is added to a will to modify it.
    b. Preliminary paper filed in a divorce case.
    c. Name given to a decision appealed according to code law.
    d. Legal seal used to emboss official court documents.

Application-level items require students to apply information they have learned in one setting to a novel situation. For example, students may have been taught how to read mileage scales on maps. An application exercise may require them to determine mileage between two points on the map, using the provided mileage scale. The following item illustrates another proper example of an application-level item written as a multiple-choice question:

A dramatic, one-dollar-an-hour increase in the federal minimum wage would most likely result in

    a. An increase in demand for employees to work at the new rate and a decrease in the supply of employees willing to work at the new rate.

    b. A decrease in demand for employees to work at the new rate and a decrease in the supply of employees willing to work at the new rate.

    c. An increase in demand for employees to work at the new rate and an increase in the supply of employees willing to work at the new rate.

    d. A decrease in demand for employees to work at the new rate and an increase in the supply of employees willing to work at the new rate.

Analysis-level items require students to infer information not studied directly by looking at components of a whole. They are required to elicit clues from available information that they can use to render an appropriate decision in terms of the provided responses. The available information must not itself provide the needed answers directly. Often in analysis-level items, basic informational material is made available to the students as they take the test. An example of such an item follows:

> If Ford was no genius, he had nonetheless unusual qualities and qualifications indispensable for the role he almost unwittingly assumed. He had great native shrewdness, patience, an iron will, an all-consuming interest in machines—a passion that had grown steadily stronger within him from his boyhood on a Michigan farm onward—and considerable mechanical experience acquired in nine years at the Edison Illuminating Company. He possessed also a kind of idealism, warped in later life by his overwhelming power, but as late as 1916 expressed in chartering and sending his "Peace Ship" to Europe to bring the war there to an end. In 1898 when he succeeded in building a two-cylinder engine that drove a bicycle-tired buggy down Detroit's back streets, it was a triumph of persistence. A shed behind the little house where he lived was his workshop, in which, for lack of money and the necessary power-driven tools, he shaped by hand some parts of his engine. His refusal to be bested by circumstances that would have beaten down most men showed a force of character that marked him through life.[2]

Several assumptions are revealed in these remarks. One of these assumptions is that

[2] Reprinted with permission from Constance McLaughlin Green, "Detroit, A Biological Sport," *American Cities in the Growth of a Nation* (New York: Harper Colophon Books, 1965), p. 201. Copyright 1965 by Constance McLaughlin Green.

1. Great power is, of itself, an admirable human trait.
2. Tenacious pursuit of a goal is associated with ultimate triumph.
3. Luck, rather than personal character, is the most important determinant of success.
4. Single-minded passion stands in the way of successful innovation.

Good multiple-choice items require ample preparation time. A common deficiency when such items are developed in a hurry is a set of incorrect answers that are so implausible that most students mark the correct answer even when their control of the material is marginal. Incorrect answers, or distractors, must be prepared with care to assure that they provide reasonable alternative responses for students who do not truly understand the information about which they are being tested.

Another frequently seen error involves development of distracters that do not combine grammatically with the first part, or stem, of the question. Consider the following example:

Surveys reveal that for lunch most Americans prefer an

1. Apple.
2. Candy bar.
3. Plum pudding.
4. Taco.

Because the article *an* agrees with only one of the four possible response choices, most astute students will mark item number "1" as the correct item. This situation is easily remedied by changing the item stem to read: "Surveys reveal that for lunch most Americans prefer a (an) . . ." This modification assures that, from a grammatical standpoint, nothing should prevent a student from choosing any one of the four possible responses.

In summary, multiple-choice items represent a sound choice for a wide variety of assessment needs. The following points should be kept in mind when considering their use:

1. Use should be restricted to testing cognitive thinking at the levels of knowledge, comprehension, application, and analysis.
2. Preparation of analysis-level, multiple-choice items is a very demanding task. In many cases, the essay represents a more attractive option for testing at this level.
3. Care must be taken to assure that incorrect responses, or distracters, represent reasonable choices for students who really do not have a good grounding in the material.
4. Grammatical agreement between the item stem and each alternative response is essential.

True-False Tests

True-false items are much more limited in their application in the social studies than are multiple-choice items. Partially, this results from the difficulty of identifying things that can be identified as "true" or as "false" in any absolute sense. Certainly, no test designed to assess students' abilities to make inferences can rely on true-false items. But when restricted to assessing students' competencies to process information at the levels of knowledge and comprehension, true-false items may be an appropriate choice. For example, in the social studies students frequently are asked to work with information presented to test their ability to comprehend information presented in this fashion. The following example illustrates such a use of true-false items.

INDEXES OF MEDICAL CARE PRICES: 1960–1974

Year	Physicians' Fees	Dentists' Fees	Semi-private Hospital Room
1967	100.0	100.0	100.0
1968	105.6	105.5	113.6
1969	112.9	112.9	128.8
1970	121.4	119.4	145.4
1971	129.8	127.0	163.1
1972	133.8	132.3	173.9
1973	138.2	136.4	182.1
1974	150.9	146.8	201.5

Source: U.S. Bureau of the Census, *Statistical Abstract of the United States: 1975*, 96th ed. (Washington, D.C.: U.S. Government Printing Office, 1975), p. 71.

Directions: Use the given table of information as a basis for determining your answer. For items that are *true*, place a + in the blank provided. For items that are *false*, place a 0 in the blank provided.

_____1. Physicians' fees by 1974 had increased more from the 1967 base year than had costs of semiprivate hospital rooms.

_____2. Between 1967 and 1974, dentists' fees increased more than physicians' fees.

_____3. In 1974, the cost of a semiprivate hospital room had more than doubled from the cost in 1967.

_____4. Dentists' fees increased *less* rapidly between 1972 and 1973 than between 1973 and 1974.

Directions to students in true-false tests must be made very clear. Notice in the example provided that students have been directed to mark a + for *true* responses and a 0 for *false* responses. This procedure assures clarity when the teacher is correcting the papers. The more traditional practice of having individuals mark a *T* for *true* and an *F* for *false* can lead to correction problems. Carelessly written *T*'s and *F*'s are easily confused.

In summary, true-false items represent an appropriate choice for testing certain knowledge-level and comprehension-level understandings. The following points should be kept in mind when a consideration is given to the use of true-false items:

1. Use of true-false items should be restricted to testing cognitive thinking at the levels of knowledge and comprehension.
2. Directions for true-false items should provide clear information that directs students to mark responses in such a way that the teacher has no trouble deciding whether a given item has been identified as *true* or *false*.
3. Use of true-false items should be used only with respect to information that is genuinely true or false. They should not be used with material open to subjective interpretation.

MATCHING TESTS

Matching items represent an appropriate choice for assessing students' knowledge and comprehension-level capabilities. Most frequently, matching tests are used to determine the degree to which students have mastered new terms or are familiar with important individuals and their actions. Problems associated with matching tests relate primarily to formatting consideration. Properly constructed, they are a valuable addition to the teacher's repertoire of assessment procedures.

Several considerations deserve attention in constructing matching items. The first of these relates to the questions of the scope of a given set of matching items. It is desirable that a set of matching items be related to a common theme. For example, a test consisting of ten matching items might focus on the organizing theme "Revolutionary War Leaders."

Commonly, the terms or names are provided in the list on the left side of the page and the definitions or identifying statements on the right side of the page. As a rule of thumb, there should be from one-quarter to one-third more options in the list on the right side of the page than there are terms or names on the left side of the page. For example, in a matching test with ten terms on the left side, thirteen potential answers might be provided on the right side. If there are not more potential answers than names or terms, a student automatically misses two terms when he or she incorrectly identifies one of them. (For example, if a student incorrectly identifies answer *C* as the response to term 1 rather than as the response to term 3, which is correct, he or she will have incorrect answers both to term 1 and term 3.)

It is essential that all terms and possible responses be placed on a single page. When lists run over to a second page, many students will fail to see the terms and possible responses on the second sheet. Consequently, scores may not accurately reflect students' levels of attainment.

Clear directions are a must. Specifically, students must be directed to take the letter (or other code) identifying a given response and write that letter in the appropriate place provided by the term or name in the left-hand column. If this

---

Name _____

Matching

Directions: Find the correct definition of the terms on the left in the list on the right. In the blank provided before each term, write the letter identifying the appropriate definition.

Topic: "The Market Mechanism"

_____1. law of demand
_____2. law of supply
_____3. elastic demand
_____4. equilibrium price
_____5. law of diminishing returns
_____6. inelastic demand

A. Greatly increases or decreases as the price of a good increases or decreases.

B. Each succeeding unit of any good satisfies a less intense desire than the previous one.

C. Demand for a good remains the same whether the price increases or decreases.

D. An increase in the price of any good tends to bring a larger quantity to the market as soon as it can be made available.

E. The desire plus the ability and willingness to pay for an economic good.

F. The price established by the interaction of demand and supply where the quantity offered for sale equals the quantity people are willing to buy.

G. The higher the price, the less of a product people will buy. The lower the price, the more of a product people will buy.

H. An area where buyers and sellers meet for the purpose of buying or selling given commodities.

I. The amount that is offered for sale at any given price and at all possible prices.

J. Expenses that change significantly with changes in the number of units produced.

---

is not done, students are likely to draw lines connecting terms and names on the left with responses on the right. If the test is a lengthy one, this results in a messy spider web of lines that make correction a very difficult, if not an impossible, task. The matching test on page 119 is an example of proper formatting.

In summary, some general considerations in the development of matching items are the following:

1. Use should be restricted to testing student competencies at the levels of knowledge and comprehension.
2. One-fourth to one-third more definitions should be provided than there are terms to be defined.
3. Items should be organized around a common theme.
4. Clear directions should be provided so that students do not draw lines connecting terms and selected responses.

Fill-in-the-Blanks Tests

In general, fill-in-the-blanks items represent a weak testing format. In large measure, this results because of reliability problems associated with tests consisting of items of this type. These reliability difficulties stem from problems associated with making clear correction decisions regarding which student answers should be counted as correct. For example, if the expected answer to a fill-in-the-blank item is "nation," should "country" also be accepted? If "country" is acceptable, then what about "fatherland"? Lack of a consistent decision-rule to govern correction raises doubts as to what a given score on a fill-in-the-blanks test means.

An additional difficulty centers around the question of spelling. Are misspelled responses to be accepted? If the answer to that question is no, then is the test truly a measure of the social studies content, or is it a measure of spelling ability? If the answer to the question is yes, then how great a margin of spelling error is acceptable? If *natian* is an acceptable variant of *nation,* how about *natn* or *notin* or even *nottin'?* The decision of how far to go in accepting spelling errors is a difficult one, and few teachers are able to apply a consistent standard.

When fill-in-the-blanks tests are used, they should be restricted to testing students' competence at the levels of knowledge and comprehension. (Even presuming to test "comprehension" with such tests may be stretching the limits of the genre.) Blanks that are to be filled in must make logical sense in terms of additional information provided in statements within which they appear. For example, a fill-in-the-blank item such as the following can lead to nothing but student despair:

_____ relates to _____ under the conditions of _____ and _____.

Given such an item, the student cannot possibly obtain a proper context that would cue him or her to even the general category of answers being sought by the teacher.

A modification of the fill-in-the-blanks format that overcomes some of the difficulties associated with the procedure provides students with a list of terms they may use in filling the blanks. When such a work list is provided, students may be required to spell the terms correctly to receive credit. More terms may be provided in the list than students will need to complete the blanks contained in the test. They should be advised, however, that all necessary terms are contained within that list and that only those terms will be acceptable for use during the testing procedure. The following example illustrates this modification of the fill-in-the-blanks format:

Name _____

Fill-in-the-Blanks

Directions: Several blanks appear in the following short paragraph. Below the paragraph, you will find a list of terms. Select appropriate terms from that list, and write them in the proper blanks. All answers required will be found in the list of terms.

The cost of a free market transaction to people not involved in that transaction is termed (a) (an) _____. In response to this phenomenon, government may enter the market to help shift the supply curve back to (a) (an) _____. In an instance when the government does take such an action, the _____ would exceed the marginal private cost. Something that can be consumed by one individual without reducing the amount available to others is called (a) (an) _____.

externality	pure public good	marginal social cost
social optimum	marginal private benefit	bootstrapping

In summary, the following points should be kept in mind when consideration is being given to possible use of fill-in-the-blanks items.

1. Use should be restricted primarily to situations when multiple-choice, true-false, or matching items cannot be used.
2. Use should be restricted to testing students' abilities at the levels of knowledge and comprehension.
3. Enough information should be contained within each statement to cue student regarding the general nature of the response being sought.
4. Consideration should be given to providing students with a list of terms from which to select responses.

Assessment in the Affective Domain

As noted in the chapter entitled "Diagnosing Students," measurement of student development in the affective domain is of a different character from measurement of cognitive achievement. Specifically, affective change cannot be measured directly.

It must be inferred from other behaviors that can be measured directly. Further, attitudes are something social studies teachers hope to affect in a positive way, but that ethically they do not and should not seek to impose.

Assessment in this area seeks to measure changes in attitudes as those changes can be inferred from student behaviors. One useful procedure for accomplishing this task centers on the use of the interest inventory, introduced earlier in the chapter on diagnosis. A comparison of students' interest before and after a given unit of instruction provides a measure of attitudinal shift. For example, suppose that a social studies class were given the following inventory both at the beginning and at the end of the semester:

Name _____

Subject Preference Inventory

Directions: In the blank provided, place a number 1 beside the school subject you like best. Place a number 2 beside the subject you like second best. Continue in the same way until you conclude with a number 5 before the subject you like least.

_____ science
_____ English
_____ social studies
_____ physical education
_____ mathematics

At the end of the semester, class and individual preference changes can be computed. A change in relative preference for social studies as opposed to other subject areas would be one indicator of a positive attitudinal change brought about by the social studies class. However, a finding of "no change" need not be taken in a negative way. For example, if there was a reasonably high preference for social studies in the beginning, great changes in terms of increased preference should not be anticipated. However, when noticeably large declines in social studies preference are observed, then there may be some cause for concern.

Comparisons between two administrations of a preference inventory represent only one possibility for obtaining comparison data related to potential changes in attitudes. A number of other measures can be devised. For example, changes in circulation patterns of library books in social studies related areas can be noted. Changes in the number of favorable comments regarding bulletin boards can be charted. One museum, interested in the impact of its various displays, even keeps track of the number of noseprints on the glass in front of the several attractions. Similar schemes can be adapted to classroom use.

Whichever procedures are adopted, it must be recognized that these measures are not assessing attitudes directly, but only behaviors thought to be associated with those attitudes. There is a much larger inferential jump in suggesting that a change between two administrations of a preference inventory reflects a change in attitude than there is in suggesting that a solid performance on a multiple-choice tests reflects the acquisition of a cognitive competency. But when limitations of attitudinal assessment procedures are recognized and the tools are placed in a proper perspective, they provide a useful and a worthy source of information. Professional social studies teachers use these techniques to great advantage to provide a check on how their programs affect student attitudes. If students attitudinally are found to be ill-disposed toward a given program, its cognitive impact is likely to suffer as a consequence. Therefore, a complete program of assessment requires collection of information related to both the cognitive and the affective domains of learning.

Using Assessment Data to Make Judgments About Programs

When instructional programs have been organized according to a systematic framework, for example, one like that introduced in the chapter entitled "Planning Social Studies Units and Daily Lesson Plans," then results of student testing can be used to make judgments about programs as well as about individual student progress. In the scheme introduced in that chapter, major concepts were identified, performance objectives were developed, key facts were pinpointed, instructional techniques were described, and needed materials were delineated. If students' scores on items related to one of the performance objectives are poor, then a number of explanations are possible.

As concepts and subconcepts associated with that performance objective are identified clearly, one explanation may be that these concepts and subconcepts are inappropriate for this particular group of students. For example, perhaps these concepts assume prior knowledge that these students simply did not have before the beginning of the instructional unit.

Another explanation for the low scores may reside in the nature of the performance objective itself. Perhaps it demanded a level of cognitive functioning going beyond students' present abilities. If test examples related to the performance objective were designed to test analysis-level thinking, a revised version might include items designed to test application-level or comprehension-level thinking.

Still other possible reasons for the low scores may be the particular key fact selected, the instructional techniques identified, and the instructional material selected. Each of these possibilities would merit some serious investigation.

The point is that, by the systematic organizing of instruction, test scores can be related back to specific performance objectives. For example, assume that a test of thirty items were given. On the test, items numbered 1 through 10 referred to Performance Objective I, dealing with the major concept of "social stratification." Items 11 through 20 referred to Performance Objective II, dealing with "status." Items 21 through 30 referred to Performance Objective III, dealing with "differentiation." An examination of student scores might reveal the largest number of errors in items 11 through 20. This suggests that the greatest programmatic deficiency resided in instruction related to the major concept "status." Major efforts could then be directed to reexamining instructional practices associated with this concept. The rest of the program might well remain intact.

When instructional plans have been organized systematically, student test data can play an invaluable role in reviewing the impact of components of an instructional plan. Because test items are tied by number to individual parts of the unit, weak spots within the program can be identified easily. This procedure pinpoints places in need of attention. Frequently, a little readjustment will make a weak part of a program into one of its high points.

In the absence of systematic organization, there is a tendency to infer that the *total* program is deficient when student scores are low. Particularly in the case of relatively inexperienced teachers, there may be a tendency to want to abandon the entire program in such situations. This represents a horrendous loss in terms of teacher preparation time. Situations of this kind need not happen when planning is done systematically and individual test items are tied by number to specific parts of the instructional program. When this procedure is followed, disappointing test results in most cases can be traced to relatively minor deficiencies within the total program. Correction of these deficiencies is a minor task compared to that of rejecting the instructional unit in its entirety and starting again from scratch.

Using Assessment Data to Grade Students

Grading students is one of the most unpleasant tasks teachers face. Few experienced teachers look forward to grading time with relish. Indeed, concerns about grading and its alleged value or lack of value have been voiced for years. Occasionally, alternative reporting schemes have been devised, designed to provide parents with a more meaningful profile of their children's progress. But the longevity of these breaks from the tradition of assigning grades has not been impressive. In all but an isolated number of instances, innovative grading or reporting practices have faded, and "the old ways" have returned. Compelling as arguments against grading may be, the reality for most social studies teachers is that they will be in teaching situation where they will be expected to give letter grades.

Assuming that grades must be given, what considerations should go into a responsible grading process? Clearly, the system must be fair to students. If students perceive grading to be arbitrary or capricious, their level of work is certain to fall off. Secondly, grades ought to communicate something specific to parents; that is, an *A* in social studies ought to communicate something specific in terms of a student's performance that is different from what a *B* ought to communicate. Many traditional grading systems have not attended well to this consideration.

Often levels of competence implied by different grades have been poorly defined.

In general, three basic grading schemes have seen some use in secondary schools. These each have strengths and weaknesses of various kinds, particularly with respect to their ability to convey precise information regarding what a given grade means. These three general grading systems are (1) grading based on individual improvement over past performance, (2) grading based on individual performance as compared to group performance, and (3) grading based on individual performance as compared to a predetermined standard.

GRADING BASED ON INDIVIDUAL IMPROVEMENT

There is a humanistic appeal to the suggestion that students should be awarded grades on the basis of their individual improvement over past levels of performance. The idea is that students should be encouraged to do better and that they will be more motivated to achieve if grades are used to encourage improvement. Improvement is measured not against any absolute standard, but against the student's own past performance. Frequently, when such a system is used, teachers give students a pretest to determine entry-level understandings and then administer a posttest at the end of a unit of instruction. Grades are awarded on the basis of total amount of improvement as reflected in differences between pretest scores and posttest scores. The highest grades may be awarded to students whose posttest scores are not particularly remarkable, but who have achieved a tremendous increase in terms of their pretest scores. (For example, a student with a score of 10 on the pretest and 55 on the posttest has a 45-point gain. Though the gain is large, the 55-point total is still not notably high).

Several difficulties are associated with this grading approach. First of all, there is a phenomenon in measurement called "regression toward the mean." Essentially, this implies that scores on a given test that are either extremely high or extremely low are somewhat suspect; that is, those scores may be more a reflection of an error in measurement than an accurate assessment of the individual student's ability. There is evidence that, on subsequent testing, scores of individuals with extremely high scores and extremely low scores tend to move closer to the average score achieved by members of the class. For example, if Sandra Smith scored 15 on a pretest and Billie Frazer scored 95 and the class average was 59, there would be a very good chance that Sandra's extremely low score and Billie's extremely high score resulted, in part, from measurement error. It is quite likely that, without any exposure to formal instruction at all, Sandra would score higher than 15 on the posttest and Billie would score lower than 95 on the posttest.

Note the consequences of this "regression toward the mean" phenomenon when a decision has been made to base grades on improvement over a student's past performance. The individual with an extremely low pretest score will likely score higher on a posttest and, presumably, be rewarded with a grade commensurate with his or her improved performance. But this improvement in test scores may be totally unrelated to any real gain in knowledge. It may simply reflect a pretest score that was artificially low because of an error in measurement. On the other hand, the individual with an extremely high pretest score, may well score lower on the posttest because of the regression-toward-the-mean phenomenon. This lower score may not reflect any "slippage" in his or her knowledge during the instructional unit, but rather may be attributed to an error in measurement of the original pretest score. But whereas the individual with the extremely low pretest score is likely to get a high grade because of his or her supposed "improvement," the operation of regression toward the mean may result in the student with the high score on the pretest getting a low grade because his or her posttest score may not be even as high as his or her pretest score.

Another difficulty relating to the disadvantage at which this system places talented students is the "topping out effect." This results because there are only so many points on a given test, and a talented student may have scored very high on a pretest. Assume, for example, a pretest with 100 items. A very intelligent student might score 95, whereas a less acute student might score 50. The bright student (assuming the posttest has 100 items as well) can only improve by five points. The other student has the possibility of improving his or her posttest score by a full fifty points. Consequently, the bright student cannot possibly demonstrate as much improvement as his or her slower counterpart.

A final deficiency with grading based on personal improvement over past performance is the lack of a common referent for each letter grade. Though an *A* may imply great improvement in terms of differences between pretest and posttest performance, it suggests nothing about the level of competency of the individual receiving that grade. If, for example, a decision were made to award *A*'s to people with a forty-point difference between pretest and posttest scores, *A*'s would go both to Sidney Strom (pretest score = 17; posttest score = 60) and to Roberta Bell (pretest score = 51; posttest score = 95). Though both receive *A*'s, it is clear that the grades do not refer to a common level of competency.

In summary, for all that the notion of rewarding students on the basis of demonstrated improvement is attractive, the disadvantages of the approach suggest that it should be rejected. Other schemes are much more defensible from the standpoint of equity and from the standpoint of suggesting what specific level of competency a given grade implies.

Grading Based on Individual Performance as Compared to Group Performance

A grading practice that is more widespread than grading based on changes in individual students' performances on pretests and posttests awards grades on the basis of how well a given individual did as compared to other students in the class. This scheme awards high grades to students whose performances exceed the class average and low grades to students whose performances fall below the class average. Grading schemes, based on class averages, are referred to as "norm-referenced."

Norm-referenced grading is based on the finding that, in an entire population, academic abilities are distributed in such a way that most people are in the average range and smaller numbers are either well above or well below that range. Norm-referenced grading systems assign letter grades on the assumption that abilities in a given classroom parallel their distribution in an entire population of similar students. Figure 7–5 illustrates how a curve representing the distribution of abilities might be "sliced" for the purpose of assigning grades. Note in this scheme that A's are awarded to the top 3.6 per cent of the scores, B's are awarded to the next 23.8 per cent of the scores, C's to the next 45.2 per cent of the scores, D's to the next 23.8 per cent of the scores, and F's to the lowest 3.6 per cent of the scores. Other schemes arrange the percentages differently, but all assume abilities to be distributed in a pattern reflected in this normal curve.

A number of difficulties are associated with a norm-referenced grading system. First of all, the assumption that abilities in a given classroom represent the same pattern of distribution as abilities in the entire population of similar students is a shaky one. Simply stated, the number of students in a given classroom is too small to provide assurances that the pattern of abilities parallels that of the normal curve. Consequently, a grading system that awards grades on the assumption that there is a normal spread of abilities within a single classroom does not proceed from a solid logical base.

An additional difficulty with this system is that it awards grades with no regard to the quality reflected in scores on a test. For example, if the grading scheme implied by Figure 7–5 were used and a given class made an average of only 19 on a 100-item test and the highest score was only 29, this grading system would mandate that the top 3.6 per cent of those test scores be rewarded with grades

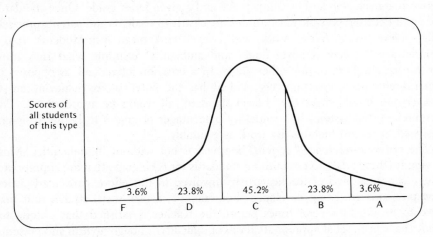

Scores of
all students
of this type

| 3.6% | 23.8% | 45.2% | 23.8% | 3.6% |
| F | D | C | B | A |

Figure 7–5. Example of a Normal Curve with Cut Points for Grading

of A (even though those scores would be, at best, no higher than 29). On the other hand, if a similar test were given and the lowest score achieved was 90, the person with the 90 and the others with the lowest 3.6 per cent of the scores would be rewarded (if that is the term!) with F's. The point is that an unbending norm-referenced system produces a distribution of grades that may bear little relationship to the actual amount of learning represented by each grade. Because class averages may go up and down from test to test and from course to course, it is difficult to determine what an A means in one situation as compared to what it might mean in another.

Though grading based on how an individual's performance compares with others in the class produces fewer inequities than grading based on personal improvements over past performance, the system's erroneous assumption of a normal distribution of talent within each classroom argues against its recommended use. Further, the failure of the system to provide a clear indication of the sorts of learner competencies implied by each grade suggests a need to look further.

GRADING BASED ON INDIVIDUAL PERFORMANCE AS COMPARED TO A PREDETERMINED STANDARD

Grading based on individual performance as compared to a predetermined standard generally is referred to as "criterion-referenced grading." The term *criterion-referenced* refers to the practice of assigning given letter grades in terms of how well individual performances measures up to a predetermined standard of excellence. Ordinarily, different standards are established for grades of A, B, C, and D. Usually, the F grade is awarded automatically when a student's performance fails to match up to the D grade standard.

A major advantage of criterion-referenced grading relates to the clear connection between a given standard of competence and a given letter grade. Once standards are set, it becomes possible to communicate clearly to students and parents precisely what A-level work, B-level work, and C-level work mean. For students, too, a criterion-level system removes doubt and ambiguity regarding what they must do to earn an A, B, or any other grade. In a criterion-referenced, as opposed to a norm-referenced, system, every student has the potential for achieving an A. If everyone should meet the A-level standard, all would be awarded A's. The norm-referenced system, by mandating percentages of grades to be given, is not designed to reward high-quality work as equitably.

The criterion-referenced system, however, is not without its difficulties. Most obviously, these relate to establishing standards for each grade that are appropriate. There is a great deal of teacher artistry involved in this effort, particularly when new programs are being developed. For example, a new social studies unit may have to be taught several times before the teacher is satisfied that criteria for grades have been set at appropriate levels of difficulty. Though no firm and prescriptive guidelines are available, a rule of thumb is to develop grading criteria that are sufficiently difficult to keep students from doing work hurriedly and carelessly but not so difficult as to make it all but impossible for them to earn *A* or *B* grades.

In this book, the use of performance objectives has been encouraged. Performance objectives contain within them certain criteria related to the achievement of the objectives themselves (the *conditions* and the *degree* components). But these criteria are not directly related to a letter-grading system. For the purposes of awarding letter grades, a system can be devised according to which criteria relate to *numbers* of performance objectives achieved. For example, assume that during a given grading period, students were exposed to work guided by thirty performance objectives. The scheme in Figure 7–6 typifies one that might be adopted to award letter grades.

Total Number of Performance Objectives = 30

Grade	Number of Perf. Objectives Achieved
A	27 to 30
B	24 to 26
C	21 to 23
D	18 to 20
E	17 or fewer

Figure 7–6. Use of Performance Objectives Achievement as a Basis For Awarding Grades in a Criterion-Referenced System

In the illustration in Figure 7–6, *A* grades are awarded on the basis of 90 per cent or more of the performance objectives being completed, *B* grades on the basis of 80 to 89 per cent, *C* grades on the basis of 70 to 79 per cent, *D* grades on the basis of 60 to 69 per cent, and *F* grades on the basis of 59 per cent or fewer performance objectives being achieved. The percentages used as cutoff points between grades are simply examples of those that might be chosen. Certainly, an individual social studies teacher would wish to adjust these figures to meet his or her own needs.

The organization of a grading scheme based on performance objective attainment makes the grading system clearly tied to the performance objectives used to guide the instructional program. When, as has been suggested, students are provided with copies of performance objectives before instruction on new material commences, they are likely to attend well to the substance of those objectives when they realize that there is a very real connection between attainment of objectives and their end-of-the-term grade.

Certainly, criterion-referenced systems are not perfect. But their ability to yield grades that communicate clearly information regarding levels of student achievement and their capacity to assuage students' fears that grading is capricious and arbitrary, commends the use of criterion-referenced systems.

Summary

This chapter drew a distinction between informal and formal assessment procedures. Because of difficulties experienced by new social studies teachers with formal assessment procedures, attention was directed primarily to that dimension of assessment. A system for providing congruence between instructional intentions and assessment procedures was introduced. Techniques to be used for assessing competencies at various levels of cognitive complexity were discussed.

With regard to specific assessment procedures, protocols were discussed for using and constructing essay tests, multiple-choice tests, true-false tests, matching tests, and fill-in-the-blanks tests. A general discussion relating to assessment in the affective domain was provided. Use of assessment data to make judgments about both programs and learners was discussed. Alternative procedures for assigning letter grades to students were introduced. A recommended procedure for using attainment of performance objectives as a basis for criterion-referenced letter grading was presented for consideration.

References

ARMSTRONG, DAVID G. "Evaluation: Conscience of the Social Studies." *The Social Studies* (March/April 1977): 62–64.

GREEN, CONSTANCE MCLAUGHLIN. "Detroit, A Biological Sport." *American Cities in the Growth of the Nation*. New York: Harper Colophon, 1965, pp. 193–215.

NOVICK, MELVIN R., and CHARLES LEWIS. "Prescribing Test Length of Criterion-Referenced Measures." In *Problems in Criterion-Referenced Measurement*. Edited by C. W. Harris, M. C. Aikin, and W. J. Popham. Los Angeles: Center for the Study of Evaluation, UCLA, 1974.

U.S. BUREAU OF THE CENSUS. *Statistical Abstract of the United States: 1975.* 96th ed. Washington, D.C.: U.S. Government Printing Office, 1975.

Social Studies Skills

Chapter 8

DEALING WITH
READING DIFFICULTIES
IN THE SOCIAL STUDIES

READING DIFFICULTIES OF secondary school students vex and challenge social studies teachers. Large numbers of middle school, junior high school, and senior high school students simply cannot read and understand a good deal of the print material made available to the schools by commercial publishing houses.

A little understood dimension of this problem is that variation in reading ability within a given classroom tends to increase with each ascending school grade. The social studies teacher working with an unsorted group of high school seniors probably will have students in class whose reading competencies vary across a much broader range than would be found in the typical first or second grade classroom. Not uncommonly, some seniors will be enjoying *War and Peace* for their own recreational reading while some others cannot handle material much beyond the picture book level. Selecting reading materials that have some potential for motivating and interesting individual students while, at the same time, not requiring skills hopelessly beyond their capabilities strains the ingenuity of even the most experienced social studies teacher.

Reading difficulties pose a tremendous problem because so much social studies content has been packaged and delivered in the form of print materials. Indeed, one specialist (O'Connor, 1967) has gone so far as to suggest that the social studies curriculum and the necessity to read are interwined so inextricably that reading skills properly ought to be considered the basic social studies skills. Jarolimek (1977), while citing other basic skills, places a high priority on reading skills associated with social studies content.

Some critics, including Neil Postman (1973), have contended that educators have continued to rely on the use of print materials out of habit rather than out of necessity. Others, agreeing that alternative technologies now permit the teacher to choose from among a broad range of options, continue to argue the importance of print materials for the social studies. As Smith (1973) has noted, the print medium permits ideas to become fixed permanently to the page, where they can be examined critically and evaluated carefully over time. Some visual modes, for example, live television, present ideas so fleetingly that sustained analysis becomes very difficult for individuals not blessed with extraordinary recall capabilities. Though almost no one would argue for an exclusive reliance on print materials, still their importance as resources for social studies students should not be underestimated. Because of this importance, difficulties associated with reading have been described as constituting a genuine "crisis" within social studies education (Chapin and Gross, 1973).

Major Dimensions of Reading Difficulties in the Social Studies

In general, difficulties associated with reading in the social studies sort into two broad categories. On the one hand, there are difficulties associated with the reading process itself that are independent of the content within given print materials. Some students simply lack basic decoding skills. On the other hand, some individuals who are at least minimally competent with respect to more general reading skills cannot deal with complex concepts contained in materials they are expected to read. They might be described as suffering from a conceptual deficiency rather than from a reading skills' deficiency.

Many attempts that have been made to address and remedy reading problems in the social studies have ignored the dualistic nature of these difficulties. For example, a number of readability formulas are available that teachers can apply to print materials to determine a rough estimate of grade-level readability. The idea is that materials that a given formula might identify as too challenging for a given group of students could be rewritten in such a way that reading difficulties would be minimized. Ordinarily, this involves shortening sentence length and reducing the complexity of the vocabulary. Although such approaches do have some merit, they do not deal adequately with the problem of conceptualization. If a student does not understand concepts contained in print material, a simplification of structural elements (for example, sentence length and vocabulary) alone holds scant promise of enhancing the likelihood he or she will understand the passage.

Indeed, an overzealous attention to problems associated with more general reading skills may actually impair student understanding of concepts. Traditional reading formulas, such as the Dale-Chall, for example, rely heavily on improving passage readability through a systematic reduction of vocabulary complexity and sentence length. A potential difficulty with this procedure is that reductions in vocabulary tend to purge abstract nouns. Yet abstract nouns—and words used to describe them—are the heart and substance of much printed social studies material.

The dilemma reduces to a situation where, on the one hand, a dramatic reduction in the level of readability may result in the elimination of key social studies concepts or, on the other hand, an increase in descriptive material related to important concepts may increase reading difficulty of the passage and make it incomprehensible to many students. In a consideration of the entire issue of reading difficulties in the social studies, the symbiotic relationship existing between factors associated with the general reading process and factors associated with conceptualization must be recognized. Regrettably, no definitive plan of attack has been formulated that spells out the optimal relationship between strategies designed to deal with general reading deficiencies and strategies focused on problems associated with conceptualization. What is clear, however, is that attention to both dimensions of the social studies reading problem is essential.

The Fry Formula and the Cloze Procedure

One of the two key dimensions of the social studies reading problem is general reading ability. General reading ability refers to the degree to which a given student or group of students possess the capability of reading print materials with which they are provided. Efforts directed toward remediation of deficiencies in this dimension assume that difficulties relate primarily to decoding problems experienced by students rather than to difficulties associated with content (concepts) included within the print material. As noted previously, rarely are students' problems exclusively associated with deficiencies in general reading ability (frequently, a conceptualization problem is present as well). But difficulties associated with general reading ability are an important contributor to student problems in this area, and it makes sense for the social studies teacher to have some knowledge of techniques that can be used to identify both general difficulty levels of materials as well as difficulties individual students might be expected to experience with those materials.

The Fry Readability Graph, developed by Edward Fry (1968), enables teachers to determine the approximate grade-level readability of a given example of print material. For example, a United States history text can be examined to determine whether the indicated grade-level readability is close to the intended eleventh grade level to which the book nominally is targeted. The Fry Readability Graph yields readability averages. It does not predict the likelihood of reading success for individuals within a classroom.

The Cloze procedure (Taylor, 1953) focuses more specifically on individuals. A teacher using the Cloze procedure extracts a representative sample from a book or from other print material of interest that is at least 250 words in length. Following prescribed rules, the teacher deletes every fifth word from the passage. Students are presented with the passage complete with blanks where words have been deleted. They are asked to write words in the blanks that "give the passage logical sense." Based on the number of words an individual student writes that are identical to the words in the original passage, the teacher is able to make a judgment about the degree of reading difficulty a given youngster might be expected to experience in reading the book or other print material from which the passage was extracted.

The following sections will describe in greater detail how both the Fry Readability Graph and the Cloze procedure might be used by social studies teachers.

THE FRY READABILITY GRAPH

In using the Fry Readability Graph (see Figure 8–1), one must remember that readability levels represent only class averages. For example, if some print material were found to be at a grade eight level of readability, that by no means suggests that any student in the eighth grade should be able to read it with understanding. The only implication that can be drawn is that the mythical "average eighth grader" should be able to handle the material. Even in the highly unlikely circumstances that a given teacher had a classroom full of eighth graders whose talents precisely matched the national norms, one would expect one half of the students to have reading abilities below the eighth grade level and one half to have reading abilities above the eighth grade level. Realizing that the Fry Readability Graph yields only an average, the social studies teacher must be cautious in making specific assumptions about how a specific student might cope with a given piece of print material.

Though the Fry Readability Graph cannot provide information related to how an individual might fare with, for example, a given text, it does provide useful comparative data. For instance, using the Fry Readability Graph, the social studies teacher can compare relative difficulty of alternative texts or materials that focus on the same general subject or topic areas. If students are known to be having reading difficulties, a reasoned decision can be made to choose the material that, according to information derived from use of the Fry Readability Graph, is characterized by a lower grade-level readability.

Another important use of the Fry procedure relates to teacher adaptation of difficult material. Frequently, very interesting articles appear in professional journals or in books that relate to topics being taught in social studies topics. Often the vocabulary and general writing style are too sophisticated for many secondary school students to handle. A teacher who understands that reading difficulty as measured by the Fry Readability Graph is increased as sentence length increases and as numbers of syllables in words increase, can rewrite the material in such a way that there are reductions both in sentence length and in the numbers of polysyllabic words. The Fry procedure can be applied to the rewritten version to determine whether there has been a significant reduction in measured grade-level

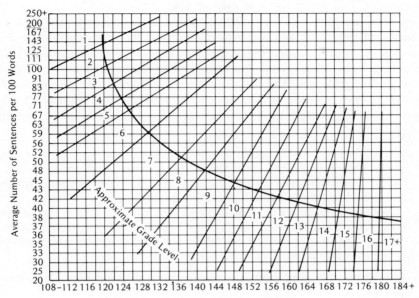

GRAPH FOR ESTIMATING READABILITY—EXTENDED

Average Number of Syllables per 100 Words

Expanded Directions for Working Readability Graph

1. Randomly select three (3) sample passages and count out exactly 100 words each, beginning with the beginning of a sentence. Do count proper nouns, initializations, and numerals.
2. Count the number of sentences in the hundred words, estimating length of the fraction of the last sentence to the nearest one-tenth.
3. Count the total number of syllables in the 100-word passage. If you don't have a hand counter available, an easy way is to simply put a mark above every syllable over one in each word, then when you get to the end of the passage, count the number of marks and add 100. Small calculators can also be used as counters by pushing numeral 1, then push the + sign for each word or syllable when counting.
4. Enter graph with average sentence length and average number of syllables; plot dot where the two lines intersect. Area where dot is plotted will give you the approximate grade level.
5. If a great deal of variability is found in syllable count or sentence count, putting more samples into the average is desirable.
6. A word is defined as a group of symbols with a space on either side; thus, *Joe*, *IRA*, *1945*, and *&* are each one word.
7. A syllable is defined as a phonetic syllable. Generally, there are as many syllables as vowel sounds. For example, *stopped* is one syllable and *wanted* is two syllables. When counting syllables for numerals and initializations, count one syllable for each symbol. For example, *1945* is four syllables, *IRA* is three syllables, and *&* is one syllable.

Note: This "extended graph" does not outmode or render the earlier (1968) version inoperative or inaccurate; it is an extension.

Figure 8–1. The Fry Readability Graph and Directions for Use. (Source: Edward Fry, "Fry's Readability Graph: Clarifications, Validity, and Extension to Level 17," *Journal of Reading*, 21 (December 1977), pp. 242–252.)

readability. If an appropriate reduction has been achieved, the rewritten materials can be duplicated and distributed to students.

To illustrate how such a rewriting exercise might be accomplished, let us assume a social studies class is focusing on issues related to conservation of energy. The teacher, alert to possibly relevant articles from current periodicals, might have discovered an article focusing on increased interest in home insulation. Thinking that such an article could supplement other materials presently available to the eighth graders in the social studies class, the teacher might select a 100-word sample from the article and use the Fry procedure to make a determination of approximate grade-level readability. Consider the following 100-word sample[1]:

> When President Carter proposed incentives for home insulation early this year as part of his energy program, Tom Heines started getting ready for the boom. At his Morristown, N.J. insulation-installing business, he doubled the size of his warehouse and ordered new trucks and insulation-blowing machines.
>
> And now, as the height of the boom approaches, Heines Insulators, Inc. has everything it needs—except insulation. "It's like having your ship come in and sink at the dock," says a rueful Mr. Heines, who is turning away business daily. Customers he does take face delays of six to eight weeks in getting their . . .

Looking at this 100-word sample, one sees clearly that there are 4.9 sentences and 160 syllables.

To determine estimated grade-level readability, find the line in Figure 8–1 that intersects the approximate point where 4.9 sentences lies along the left side of the graph (the side titled "average number of sentences per 100 words"). Next, move across the graph from left to right on an imaginary line that intersects point 4.9 on the left side. Move along this line until it intersects a line coming down from the top of the page from the point indicating 160 syllables. The intersection point of these two lines falls between the two lines cutting off the grade eleven readability level area. (That is, the point falls between lines separating grade eleven from grade ten on the left and grade eleven from grade twelve on the right.)

As the teacher wishes to use this material in an eighth grade class and the measured readability of the 100-word sample is grade eleven, there is a need to rewrite the material to reduce the reading difficulty. This can be accomplished by shortening sentences and, where appropriate, using shorter words. The teacher might set out to rewrite the material in such a way that an analysis of the rewritten material with the Fry procedure might yield a grade level of about seven or eight. Assuming that reading talent in this classroom were distributed approximately according to national averages, a reduction to a grade seven or eight level of

---

[1] This material was extracted, with permission, from Robert L. Simison, "Home-Insulation Shortage Is Worsening As Builders, Owners Snap Up the Material," *The Wall Street Journal*, September 27, 1977, p. 40, col. 1.

reading difficulty would assure that a large number of students would be able to cope with the materials. A rewritten version might look something like this:

> Early this year, President Carter proposed a tax savings for homeowners. He suggested lower taxes for people who insulated their homes. People in the insulation business looked forward to good times. Tom Heines of Morristown, N.J. doubled the size of his warehouse. He ordered new trucks and machines to blow in the insulation.
> Business has been almost too good. Mr. Heines finds his firm is short of insulation. He says, "It's like having your ship come in and sink at the dock." He has to turn away business every day. New customers must wait six to eight weeks to get. . . .

Note that this rewritten version also is exactly 100 words in length. The Fry Readability Graph is based upon samples of this length, and it is critical to use a 100-word sample in computing grade level of the rewritten version as well as in computing the approximate grade level of the original passage.

In this rewritten version there are 9.8 sentences and 148 syllables. Using the same procedure as followed with the original 100-word sample, plot an intersection point. This time that point falls between the lines cutting off grade seven readability. This means that the rewritten passage has a measured grade-level readability of about grade seven. Assuming that this teacher were teaching a group of fairly typical eighth graders, this result would indicate that for many of the youngsters the rewritten material should not pose severe reading problems. (The grade seven reading level, remember, is only an average estimation. Consequently, even some eighth graders may be expected to experience difficulty associated with reading in spite of the reduction to grade-level seven of the reading level in the rewritten passage.)

The Fry Readability Graph can provide very useful information when alternative textbooks are being considered. When the focus is on textbooks, ordinarily three 100-word samples are chosen from each textbook to be reviewed. Averages are computed from these three samples. These averages are used to determine approximate grade-level readability. Assume, for example, that examinations of three textbooks yielded the following figures:

	Textbook 1		Textbook 2		Textbook 3	
	No. Sents.	No. Syls.	No. Sents.	No. Syls.	No. Sents.	No. Syls.
Sample 1	5.2	146	3.6	160	3.8	170
Sample 2	4.3	151	4.0	158	3.0	165
Sample 3	6.0	154	3.8	164	4.0	167
	16.5	451	11.4	482	10.8	502
	3	3	3	3	3	3
Averages	5.5	150.3	3.8	160.7	3.6	167.3
Grade Level	9		12		college (grade 14)	

If, for example, these textbooks were being examined as possibilities for use in grade eleven United States History classes, Textbook 1 would seem to present potential readers with fewer problems associated with the reading process. However, it is doubtful that selection would be based only on the single criterion of reading difficulty. This textbook might not treat certain topics well or might have other deficiencies. But should other areas of concern be found to be well handled in this material, a good case might be built for selection of Textbook 1 over Textbook 2 or Textbook 3.

In addition to making use of its value as a tool in textbook evaluation, many social studies teachers find it useful to apply the Fry Readability Graph to materials they themselves develop for student use. Even directions provided to students at the heading of multiple-choice or true-false tests can be checked for readability difficulty, using this procedure. It is possible that some students do not do well on such tests because of their failure to understand the written instructions rather than because of an inadequate grasp of the information about which they are being tested.

In conclusion, the Fry Readability Graph can provide a good general picture of the relative reading difficulty of individual selections of printed material. The procedure has an advantage in that it can be applied relatively quickly, and ratings made by different individuals will likely produce similar results. A limitation is that the Fry procedure yields a measure of estimated grade-level readability expressed in terms of averages. The instrument does not provide a good indication of how an individual (as opposed to how a typical group of individuals) might be expected to fare, given an assignment to read a given selection. The issue of individual compatibility with given print material is assessed much more adequately through the use of the Cloze procedure, described in the following section.

THE CLOZE PROCEDURE

First introduced in 1953 by Wilson Taylor (Taylor, 1953), the Cloze procedure provides a means for determining an individual student's potential for experiencing reading-related difficulty with a given prose selection. Unlike the Fry Readability Graph, which yields rough measures of reading difficulty associated with group averages, the Cloze procedure provides information that relates not to groups but rather to individual students.

The Cloze procedure is simple to use. Basically, the teacher selects at random a sample of prose material from a selection being considered for use in the course. This may be a textbook, a reprinted article, or any other print material. The sample selected should be at least 250 words in length. Somewhat longer samples are to be preferred in that resultant scores will likely be more reliable. Follow these directions in using the Cloze procedure:

1. Identify a sample passage at least 250 words in length. Type the passage in such a way that every fifth word is omitted except when the fifth word is the first

word in a sentence. In such a case, omit the second word of the sentence. Then begin counting again and omitting every fifth word. Leave about fifteen typed spaces where words have been omitted to allow students to write in words that have been omitted.

2. Students should be directed to write in words in the blanks that give the passage logical "sense." In scoring, count as correct only words written in by students that are *exactly the same* as those in the original passage. Compute the percentage of correct words. For example, in a 250-word passage with fifty blanks, a student with forty-one words correct would receive a score of 92 per cent (41/50 = .92).

The percentage score a given student achieves should be interpreted as follows:

1. If a student scores 58 per cent or higher, he or she is operating at an *independent reading level* with respect to this material. This means that he or she should be able to read and master material from this selection with minimal need for teacher assistance. (Percentage figure from Bormuth, 1968.)

2. If a student's score falls between 44 and 57 per cent correct, he or she is operating at the instructional reading level with respect to this material. This means that he or she should be able to read and learn from this material provided that teacher assistance is furnished him or her, especially with the more difficult sections. (Percentage figures from Bormuth, 1968.)

3. If a student receives a score of 43 per cent or lower, he or she is operating at the *frustrational reading level* with respect to this material. Because of difficulties such an individual might experience with the selection, it is desirable to provide alternative reading materials demanding less sophisticated reading competencies (when they can be found or prepared) for the frustration-level reader. (Percentage figures from Bormuth, 1968.)

As an example of how a Cloze procedure might be developed, suppose a teacher was interested in using some materials from "Cultural Geography," the third unit in the High School Geography Project's *Geography in an Urban Age* (New York: Macmillan Publishing Co., Inc., 1969, p. 8). The teacher randomly selects a passage from a unit three chapter entitled "A Lesson from Sports."[2] That 250-word sample would look like this when rewritten with words deleted for a Cloze procedure:

Football was no longer _____ 1 in the streets of ____

_____ 2 . Many other towns followed _____ 3 . In 1314,

King Edward _____ 4 banned it as did _____ 5 James

I many years _____ 6 . This did not, however, _____ 7

young boys from playing _____ 8 game and schoolmasters decided

_____ 9 set up rules in _____ 10 attempt to protect the

---

[2] Reprinted, as adapted, by permission of the National Council for Geographic Education.

_____ from serious injury. These _____ limited a
   11   12

team's size _____ eleven players and prohibited _____
              13

_____ player from going in _____ of the ball to _____
   14   15

_____ it while his team _____ moving it
   16   17

down the _____.
        18

   As the English began _____ regulate the game more ____
                     19

_____, college and amateur teams _____ established.
  20   21

The game became _____ popular and has remained ____
                22

_____. In fact, today it _____ the most popular sport
  23   24

_____ the world. To the _____, it is "association
  25   26

football" _____ "soccer" and vast populations _____
        27   28

know no word of _____ call it "futbol" or "_____."
          29   30

   The first major variation _____ association football took place
                         31

_____ 1823 at Rugby, a _____ English school. Dur-
  32   33

ing a _____ match, a player named _____ Webb
      34   35

Ellis was discouraged _____ his lack of success _____
               36   37

kicking the ball so _____ picked it up and _____
              38   39

with it. Although Ellis _____ criticized greatly for his ____
                    40

_____ of football (soccer) etiquette, _____ spread about
  41   42

his run _____ the ball. Some players _____ that
        43   44

the choice of _____ or running might make _____
           45

_____ exciting addition to the _____.
  46   47

   However, it was not _____ the 1940's that this "____
                    48

_____ game" began to be _____ . . .
  49   50

Key

1. allowed	6. later	11. students	16. protect
2. Manchester	7. stop	12. rules	17. was
3. suit	8. the	13. to	18. field
4. II	9. to	14. a	19. to
5. King	10. an	15. front	20. carefully

21. were	29. English	37. at	45. kicking
22. very	30. foobal	38. he	46. an
23. so	31. in	39. ran	47. game
24. is	32. in	40. was	48. until
25. in	33. famous	41. breach	49. rugby
26. English	34. soccer	42. news	50. played
27. or	35. William	43. with	
28. who	36. with	44. felt	

In the correction of a Cloze procedure exercise, only student entries that are exactly the same as those in the key are counted correct. Spelling errors are acceptable so long as the clear intent was to write in the word listed in the key. Though the rule prohibiting credit for synonyms seems harsh, the percentage figures adopted as cutoff points separating independent reading levels, instructional reading levels, and frustrational reading levels have been adjusted downward to account for an enforcement of this rigid grading standard. By the requirement of correct responses to match up with those in the key, much ambiguity is removed from the correction process. This frees the teacher from deciding, for example, whether to accept *hat* for the key word *cap* or to deal with even more confounding possibilities such as *chapeau* or *bandanna*. Strict adherence to a standard of identity with the key words resolves such issues and makes the teacher's correction task much simpler.

The Cloze procedure provides a good indication of how each individual in the class might be expected to fare, given an assignment to read material from which the sample selection was extracted. These results can pinpoint students for whom supplementary reading materials of a less challenging nature ought to be provided. The Cloze procedure frequently is used by social studies teachers at the beginning of a new school term to determine how individual students might be expected to deal with the reading level of the course textbook (or textbooks). All too frequently secondary textbooks in the social studies are written at a level of reading difficulty that is simply beyond the capacity of many students. The Cloze procedure can help the teacher to get a picture of the dimensions of this problem as it exists within a given classroom of students.

The Cloze procedure, similar to the Fry Readability Graph, functions to provide a measure of difficulty students might be expected to have with the fundamental processes of reading. The procedure does not deal with the issue of how students might be expected to deal with concepts presented within given prose materials. This conceptualization issue is at least as large a contributor to students difficulties in learning from print materials as is deficiency in general reading skills. Some procedures to be introduced in the following section focus more specifically on possible responses to reading difficulties associated with conceptualization.

Using a Directed Reading Approach

Social students must deal with large numbers of abstract concepts, including such disparate terms as *culture, democracy, socialization,* and *immigration.* These concepts are complex, generally nontangible in nature, and only rarely expressed in words of one or two syllables. These concepts organize tremendous quantities of information, and no student can be expected to arrive at rich and deep understandings in his or her social studies classes if he or she has not acquired reasonably solid understandings of these terms. Certainly, little is to be gained by an overzealous effort to reduce readability levels by eliminating so many polysyllabic words that these important concepts are deleted from the material.

The limitation, then, of a single reliance on adjustment of grade level readability as a remedy for reading difficulties of students is that, carried to an extreme, content vital to the course can be removed. Difficult as the term *socialization* may be, still the concept conveys a host of understandings that cannot so easily be transmitted to students when the organizing label is eliminated. Consequently, efforts to deal with reading difficulties through an adjustment of sentence length and vocabulary complexity must stop short of the point of removing critically important content. This means that some potentially confusing terminology will remain within even rewritten material and that an approach is needed that will help students cope with some of these complexities.

In dealing with this situation, many social studies teachers have found it useful to use a systematic, step-by-step approach in introducing students to assignments that call for a good deal of reading. Typical of these systematic, directed reading approaches is the following four-part scheme:

1. Survey the content of the print material to be assigned, and identify potentially difficult concepts.
2. Take time to introduce these concepts to students in class and to use information students already know to illustrate these concepts.
3. Point out to students potential areas of difficulty in the text by reference to specific page numbers.
4. Establish a specific purpose or function for the reading assignment.

Given this sequence, there is a good chance that large numbers of students will be able to deal with concept-related difficulties as they complete their reading assignments. Subsequent sections will describe specific characteristics of each of the four components of the directed reading program.

Surveying the Content

When there is an intention of making a reading assignment, a preliminary review by the teacher of the material frequently can identify potential pitfalls for students. Basically, this effort ought to be directed toward identifying any concepts or terminology that might be confusing to students. Certainly, technical terms frequently fall into this category. But another important category involves terms that, by themselves, are not complex, but that are characterized by connotations that may be unique to the context within which they may be presented in the text. For example, terms such as *market* and *capital* have meanings associated with ordinary man-on-the-street usage that may vary considerably with the meanings attached to those terms by professional economists. The difficulty with such items is that students, familiar with everyday usage, may fail to recognize the restricted sense of the term being utilized by the writer of the textbook or article.

A list of potentially bothersome terms can be constructed as the teacher works through the material. This list can be written on the chalkboard or on an overhead projection transparency. Another possibility that may prove worthwhile involves a distribution of these items to each student on ditto or mimeo paper. When such a list has been made available to students, a short discussion may prove helpful to the teacher in diagnosing the extent of student understanding of each term. Questions such as the following might be considered:

1. What does this term mean?
2. Does it have any other meaning?
3. Can you use the term in a sentence?
4. How about another sentence illustrating another meaning?

After the list has been discussed, the second phase of the directed reading exercise can be initiated.

INTRODUCING AND ILLUSTRATING CONCEPTS

The second part of the directed reading exercise is designed to give students a feel for the terminology they will be needing to read the assignment. This is accomplished by providing them with experience seeing the terms in the context of a sentence, not just as isolated items on the list. As a preparation for this part of the exercise, a number of sentences need to be developed by the teacher that use the concepts that might prove difficult for students. These sentences ought to be similar to the kinds of sentences the students will find in their reading but not identical to them. For example, if *market* is one of the terms under consideration and the assigned reading material will be in the area of economics, teacher-prepared sentences should use the term as an economist uses it.

These sentences can be written on the board, on overhead transparencies, on large sheets of butcher paper, or in any other way that makes them conveniently available to students. The teacher should ask individual students to read the sentences and explain their meaning. A discussion should be used to clarify any problems with meaning that might become evident. At the conclusion of this part of the exercise, students' attention should be drawn to specific parts of the material to be read that might prove especially difficult.

Pointing Out Difficult Areas

After exercises have identified potentially difficult concepts and provided students with an opportunity for students to see these concepts illustrated in a context similar to that which they will find in their reading, it is time to direct their attention to the assigned material itself. Clearly, some sections will pose more difficulty for student readers than others. Those sections where terminology or usage are thought by the teacher to pose severe potential problems to readers should be called to students' attention. Special usages of terms and other features of these sections that might lead to misunderstanding need to be discussed in class before students are asked to read the material. Time spent in preparing students to cope with these challenging passages will pay off well in terms of enhanced student understanding.

Establishing a Purpose for Reading

After students have been alerted to potential pitfalls within certain sections of the assigned reading, it is time to move on to making the actual reading assignment. A frequent mistake of beginning social studies teachers is their failure to provide students with a specific purpose for a given reading assignment. A statement such as "Please read pages 31 through 44 for tomorrow" fails to communicate to the student the specific sorts of information he or she is supposed to derive from this commitment of his or her time. A more precisely stated purpose can serve as a motivator for students and can result in more significant understandings emerging from the reading exercise.

The best statements of reading purpose give students some indication of what they should derive from their reading and stimulate their interest in the material. For example, should a class be assigned to read some material on Ireland, the teacher (provided he or she has a source for such an item) might bring in a peat brick; display it to the students; and, in making the assignment, say, "Tomorrow, I want you to be able to tell me why peat is so important to the Irish and why we don't use more of it in this country."

Charts, photographs, war relics, artifacts, and other visual and tangible objects that relate to a reading assignment can provide an excellent departure point for the teacher as he or she prepares to describe to his or her class a specific purpose for reading some assigned material. Another approach many teachers have found useful takes advantage of the competitive enthusiasms of many secondary school students.

For example, in an economics class, a given set of readings might focus on the issue of inflation and governmental responses to the problem. In making the reading assignment, the teacher might establish purposes for reading as follows:

> In class tomorrow we are going to have a contest between you people on the left side of the room . . . that is everybody from Jane here over to that wall . . . and

you people on the right side. I want those of you on the left to come up with as many individual examples as you can of how government intervention in the economy has acted to solve the problem of inflation. I want those of you on the right to come up with as many examples as you can of how government intervention in the economy has tended to make inflation worse. Now, I won't take just opinion statements. You will have to have some evidence to back up your claims.

Regardless of the side you are on, you will find information in the Smith book (pages 71 through 83) and in the two pamphlets by Wooldridge and Taylor. [Teacher writes reading assignment on the board.]

When students are provided with a purpose for their reading, they have guidelines to use as they work through their assigned work that help them to focus on central and critical material. In the social studies, many textbooks (and other supportive materials, too) tend to be characterized by presentations of tremendous quantities of information within relatively few pages. Without some guidelines, students may well get lost in the forest of details and emerge from their reading with only very hazy notions about the contents of the assignment. When purposes are provided for students, they approach their tasks more psychologically secure in the knowledge that their efforts will be directed toward acquiring a better understanding of a more limited quantity of information.

In utilizing the directed reading approach in social studies classes, teachers help students to acquire a broader understanding of key concepts and to develop a sense of mission and purpose when they approach their reading assignments. The difficulty with the approach is that, if it is to be effective, there is a time demand placed on the teacher in terms of working through print materials to identify problem areas before assignments are made. Additional time is consumed in class as important concepts found in the reading to be assigned are to be discussed.

Certainly, these time costs merit serious consideration. Certainly, no argument can be made for irresponsibly taking too much time away from other important instructional tasks to prepare students for reading assignments. Yet a case can be made for allocating at least some time for an instructional purpose no broader than preparing students to profit from their assigned reading. The payoff for such an effort can be handsome both in terms of enhanced motivation for reading and increased understanding of course contents presented in print materials.

Summary

Reading in the social studies presents difficulties for social studies teachers associated both with general reading skills' deficiencies and with conceptualization problems. With regard to general reading skills, use of such techniques as the Fry Readability Graph and the Cloze procedure provides the teacher with a methodology for controlling average grade-level readability and for identifying problems individual learners might be expected to have with specific materials.

A difficulty with relying only on procedures designed to deal with general reading skills deficiencies is that most seek to enhance "readability" of given materials through processes involving reductions of sentence length and eliminations of polysyllabic words. Carried to logical extreme, these changes may result in the elimination of many key social studies concepts that cannot be expressed in words of one or two syllables. Consequently, there is a limit to the use of procedures designed to reduce grade-level readability in the social studies.

This limit suggests that many difficult concepts must remain in materials social studies students are asked to read. For this reason, specific attention must be directed to these difficult items before students are asked to read prose material containing these references. A directed reading approach is recommended according to which teachers identify potentially difficult concepts in new material before an assignment is made, discuss these terms with students, point out how these vocabulary items will be used in the assigned print material, and provide students with a clear purpose for reading the assignment.

REFERENCES

BORMUTH, JOHN R. "The Cloze Readability Procedure." *Elementary English.* (April 1968): 429–436.

CHAPIN, JUNE R. and RICHARD GROSS. *Teaching Social Studies Skills.* Boston: Little, Brown and Company, 1973.

FRY, EDWARD. "Fry's Readability Graph: Clarifications, Validity, and Extension to Level 17." *Journal of Reading* 21 (December 1977): 242–252.

HIGH SCHOOL GEOGRAPHY PROJECT. *"Unit 3; Cultural Geography." Geography for an Urban Age.* New York: Macmillan Publishing Co., Inc., 1969.

JAROLIMEK, JOHN. *Social Studies in Elementary Education.* 5th ed. New York: Macmillan Publishing Co., Inc., 1977.

O'CONNOR, JOHN R. "Reading Skills in Social Studies." *Social Education.* (February 1967): 104–107.

POSTMAN, NEIL. "The Politics of Reading." In *The Politics of Reading: Point-Counterpoint,* edited by Sister R. Winkeljohann, pp. 1–11. Newark, Delaware: International Reading Association, 1973.

SIMISON, ROBERT L. "Home-Insulation Shortage Is Worsening as Builders, Owners Snap Up the Material." *The Wall Street Journal.* September 27, 1977, p. 40, column 1.

SMITH, FRANK. "The Politics of Ignorance." In *The Politics of Reading: Point-Counterpoint,* edited by Sister R. Winkeljohann, pp. 43–55. Newark, Delaware; International Reading Association, 1973.

TAYLOR, WILSON L. "Cloze Procedure: A New Tool for Measuring Readability." *Journalism Quarterly* (Fall 1953): 415–433.

Chapter 9

LOCATING AND
ORGANIZING INFORMATION

S KILLS ASSOCIATED WITH locating and organizing information characterize secondary school students who do well in their social studies
classes. On the other hand, students with deficiencies in these important
skill areas frequently experience great difficulty in these courses. Because
of the importance of these skills and because not all students have
them when they leave elementary school, special attention needs to
be directed toward enhancing students' abilities to locate and organize
information. It is not sufficient to tell students *where* information is
available. Specific instructions need to be provided relating to *how*
the information is to be extracted and organized.

In very general terms, secondary students suffer not from an inadequate supply of information but rather from an oversupply of information. This situation results in great difficulty for the unsophisticated
student who lacks a systematic scheme for sorting the relevant from
the irrelevant information. Many beginning social studies teachers err
in assuming that their students have a broader base of information
at their command than many, in fact, do. For example, a startling
number of high school students do not know the difference between
"latitude" and "longitude" though these concepts likely will have been
introduced a number of times during their earlier school years. An
assignment premised on the belief that all students have a solid grasp
of these terms surely will yield levels of student performance falling
well short of the teacher's expectations. This situation points up the
necessity of considering *individual student characteristics* when asking
students to seek out information.

A second general consideration in directing students toward some specific information sources has to do with the *nature of the learning task*. If students are to be held responsible only for a general understanding of a topic, the kinds of learning materials to which they will be directed should be different from those when they will be held responsible for a more detailed understanding. Further, when students are asked to produce something requiring interpretation or application, certainly the learning material must be capable of providing them with necessary background information. Finally, the scope of the learning task must be considered. If a term paper is to be the end result, clearly more detailed learning resources will be required than when students will be asked simply to give a short five-minute oral overview to their classmates. In general, the range and variety of learning resource materials will increase as the sophistication of the learning task increases.

A third consideration that must be weighed in directing students to use specific learning materials relates to the *nature of the materials* themselves. For example, the mode of the materials must be considered. Are the materials printed? Are they audio materials? Are they tangible objects that students can be invited to handle? Levels of difficulty must be considered. For example, little is to be gained from asking students to listen to a speech by a speaker whose vocabulary is hopelessly beyond the level of the students' comprehension. Similarly, much print material that is very stimulating to the student who is a master reader will be unintelligible to the youngster with poorly developed reading skills. Unless learning materials are surveyed to determine their characteristics in advance of an assignment, a significant number of students probably will experience great difficulties as they attempt to complete their assigned tasks.

Once characteristics of individual students, of the learning task, and of potentially useful learning materials have been identified, students need to be directed to some specific information sources. Each of these sources has unique characteristics that must be considered preparatory to assigning students to utilize them for the purposes of acquiring specific information.

Locating Pertinent Information

The following sources are among those students might wish to use. They might locate information through

1. Personal experience.
2. Personal observation.
3. Interviews.
4. Listening.
5. Newspapers and journals.
6. Books.
7. Special retrieval systems and other sources.[1]

[1] Adapted from Gene E. Rooze and Leona M. Foerster, *Teaching Elementary School Social Studies: A New Perspective* (Columbus, Ohio: Charles E. Merrill, 1972), pp. 317–319. Copyright © 1972 by Bell & Howell Company.

In the following sections, characteristics of information sources falling within each of these seven general areas will be discussed.

PERSONAL EXPERIENCE

An important information resource frequently overlooked by beginning social studies teachers is personal experience of students. Many students, particularly in the upper grades of senior high school, hold down jobs requiring them to come into direct contact with governmental regulations and other issues that may well be relevant to social studies lessons. Still others may have lived in other areas of the United States or overseas. Such students have experienced directly realities that exist only in books, magazines, on television, or in the movies for many others. Drawing out contributions from individual students who have had such experiences enriches the social studies program for all.

Limitations, of course, do exist on personal experience as a source of information. For one thing, memory is often very selective. Those things a given individual remembers about a certain situation or event may not represent the whole story. To illustrate this point with their students, many teachers have had great success in (1) inviting someone from the central office staff to walk in quickly to ask the teacher a question in the middle of a class and (2) then asking students to write down their recollections of that individual's attire. Rarely is there consensus. The exercise makes the point that individual memory is not always a dependable information source.

To help individual students recognize potential difficulties with relying exclusively on personal experience for information (even in cases where there has been relevant personal experience), some teacher questions are in order. These questions are designed to help students develop more sophisticated skills in assessing the reliability and validity of information derived from personal experience. A number of questions might be asked, including the following:

1. Was the experience representative, or were there some very unusual and special conditions in this case?
2. How might we check on how typical an experience this was?
3. Is there evidence from other sources that corroborates the personal experience evidence?

In addition to calling upon students to share personal experience information with others, social studies teachers have a chance to provide opportunities for students to experience certain situations directly. For example, in some communities there are "mayor for a day" programs that invite direct participation of students in local government. Such programs as Boys' State and Girls' State closely simulate the reality faced by elected representatives to state legislatures. Some local history societies encourage participation of young people in the examination of original source materials being examined by members to shed light on selected aspects of the community's past. These situations represent fine opportunities for secondary school students to experience directly a large number of situations that may bear directly on their learning in the social studies. Certainly, social studies teachers have an obligation to encourage learning opportunities of this type.

Personal Observation

Another source of information for secondary social studies classes is personal observation. Personal observation differs from personal experience primarily in the intensity of involvement. In a personal observation situation, students themselves are not individually participating in what they are observing. They are close enough, however, to be able to note clearly what is going on.

Possibilities for providing students with opportunities to refine their skills of personal observation are legion. Meetings of city councils, school boards, planning commissions, and other governmental bodies provide outstanding opportunities for students to gather information for use in their social studies classes. Another variant on this general theme is the familiar school field trip. Field trips, properly organized, can yield up a rich harvest of student understandings.

A key to the success of all attempts to provide insights to students via personal observation is planning. Students need to be cued in advance to look for specific kinds of information. This kind of advance planning provides students with a scheme for sorting critical, relevant information from other data that, at best, are of secondary importance. Without such a guidance system, students may well be overwhelmed by the sheer volume of information available to them in an unfamiliar setting. Teachers, too, may well be frustrated when students, in a class discussion following a return from a visit to a session of the state legislature, appear to have profited little from the experience.

To remedy such situations, the teacher should establish a purpose for any observations students are to make. Frequently, key questions serve well to guide students' attention to relevant material. For example, suppose that a class of ninth graders were going to go on a field trip to look at some Indian burial mounds. The teacher might prepare the class as follows:

> *Teacher:* Tomorrow, we will be going to Two Waters to look at the Indian mounds. What I want all of you to do is to try to decide why the mounds are arranged as they are. There are a lot of theories, but the experts aren't sure. Let's see what we can come up with as a class. Now I want everybody to be prepared to answer the following questions when we come back. Write them down. Take notes tomorrow as you try to come up with some answers:
>
> 1. What is the general arrangement of the mounds?
> 2. How high are the mounds?
> 3. On which side of the field are most of the mounds located?
> 4. How could you explain this arrangement?
>
> We'll share answers to these questions in class the day after tomorrow, and, as I said, we'll try to work out our own theory.

Given this kind of preparation for an experience requiring personal observation, students go forth with good prospects for a profitable learning experience. They have some idea about what to look for, and the teacher has explained clearly that some specific learning is expected to be derived from the experience. A debriefing following a field trip preceded by good directions generally reveals that the personal observation experience has been a profitable exercise (and a motivating one) for students.

INTERVIEWS

The interview combines elements both of personal experience and personal observation. As a questioner, the student directly participates in and experiences the situation. As a listener, the student acts as an observer who notes responses of the individual being interviewed. Students who develop good interviewing skills are able to derive a great deal of profit from the experience.

Good interviewing skills result when students receive specific instruction regarding how an interview ought properly to be conducted. It is not enough to provide students with a general topic and the name of an individual to be interviewed. A specific purpose for the exercise must be established, and guidelines need to be prepared. Specific questions can be framed in advance to guide students as they conduct their interviews. Certainly, such questions need not be followed in a mechanistic fashion as the interview unfolds, but they can provide students with a general pattern of questioning to be followed. Assume, for example, that a class of students has been studying the depression. Arrangements might be made by the teacher for several students to interview some adults who had lived through this experience. The teacher might ask students to prepare for their interviews as follows:

> *Teacher:* Tomorrow, we will be conducting our interviews with the people from the senior citizens' center who have agreed to sit in the cafeteria and be interviewed about the depression. You each have the name of the individual you will be talking to. You may use a tape recorder if you wish, but be sure to ask the person you are interviewing if he or she minds having the interview recorded. If the person indicates that he or she might be uncomfortable with the recorder going, don't press the point. Simply say, "That's fine," and take a few written notes on what is said.
>
> Remember that the purpose of the interview is to find out how the depression affected these people personally. We don't want to get into causes of the depression. Let's all try to stick to finding out what the depression meant to these people individually. [Teacher writes, "How the depression affected me" on the board as a reminder to the students of the central purpose of the interview.]
>
> Now, let's spend some time thinking about kinds of questions to ask these people. [A discussion ensues.] All right, I think what we have decided is this. We ought to begin by asking specific, factual

kinds of questions that should be easy to answer. We want our people to be comfortable, and these questions should be relatively easy for them to answer. Only after a number of very specific questions have been asked should we ask some questions of an opinion or an interpretation variety. Let's put together a possible sequence. [A discussion ensues.] Fine. I'll put the list on the board:

1. Were you employed during the depression? What kind of job did you have? Was this the kind of a job you preferred?
2. What kinds of things did you do for recreation during the depression? Were these things different from what you did before the depression?
3. Did you get enough to eat during the depression? How did your diet differ from what you ate before the depression?
4. Do you think your situation during the depression was fairly typical? Was there anything special about your situation?
5. When do you think the depression ended? How did your life change then?
6. Looking at all of your experiences during the depression, do you think that the depression hurt or helped you later on in life?

These are samples of the kinds of questions you might be interested in asking. Of course, other issues may pop up during your interview that you may want to pursue. But make an attempt, whether you use these specific questions or not, to get some of the information that these questions are attempting to bring forth from those being interviewed.

Given this kind of preparation, students' interviews stand a good chance of keeping a reasonably good focus on issues that the teacher wishes to emphasize. Of course, given the dynamics of an interview, a good deal of additional information will come out as well. This information coupled with that suggested by the prepared questions will provide a rich learning experience for students. A set of key questions that are reasonably common to all interviewing students will result in a greatly improved potential for the debriefing session to be a good one. This results because several students have gathered different information related to common topics or themes. Debriefing, then, can compare and contrast remarks of individuals being interviewed in terms of their responses to similar kinds of questions.

Interviews need not require students to leave the school building or to complete their tasks outside of regular school hours. Many adults, if contacted by a teacher, will agree to come to the school to be interviewed by students. For example, as illustrated in the sample dialogue regarding the depression, retired people represent a very important information source for young people. They are free during the day, and many enjoy visiting with young people in the schools. Large numbers of retirees and other adults have not been inside of a school building for years, and scheduling interviews within school buildings can contribute to their understanding of young people as well. Such experiences can do a good deal of generation-gap bridging and can promote a more positive image of students in the larger community. Because of the potential benefits, social studies teachers need to work systematically to increase their students' competence in the important information gathering skill of interviewing.

LISTENING

The skill of listening is closely associated with students' success in their social studies classes. Formal lectures by the teacher as well as illustrative comments made both by teacher and students characterize a sizable portion of class time in social studies courses. When one considers this situation, it makes good sense to work with students to increase their ability to acquire information through listening.

Many students are not careful listeners. They may well hear what is said, but they have little facility when it comes to distinguishing between material that is important and material that is provided only as general background. To help students sharpen their skills in this important area, teachers must take care in making assignments for students to acquire information through listening.

More specifically, students ought to be provided with a general purpose for listening. Beyond this general purpose, it is a good idea to provide them with several specific listening tasks. A teacher interested in having students listen to a presidential news conference to be aired over live radio during the evening hours might give directions to his or her class something like these:

Teacher: The president is going to hold a press conference tonight that will be broadcast on radio at 7 P.M. our time. I would like as many of you as possible to tune in. I want you to focus your attention specifically on what he has to say about our country's energy situation. As you listen to the president, see whether you can find out about these questions:

1. Whom does the president blame for the crisis?
2. What does he see happening if the crisis continues?
3. Does the president blame anyone? If so, whom?
4. What specific steps does the president want to take?
5. Does the president identify any specific groups of people opposed to his plans? If yes, which groups?
6. What does the president say about the long-term consequences of failing to do anything?

Questions such as these provide guidelines for students as they attempt to gather information from listening to a speaker's remarks. Often it is desirable for both students and teachers to decide collectively on the kinds of information to be sought. Whether guidelines are jointly developed or not, there is evidence that providing students with some specific questions to guide their listening will result in a much more profitable exercise. Certainly, because listening skills are called upon so frequently in social studies classes, it makes good sense to provide students with opportunities to exercise these skills in a productive and an organized way.

Newspapers and Journals

Newspapers and journals are widely available and, properly selected, serve well as information sources for secondary school students. Although the large numbers of available newspapers and journals make student access to these materials relatively easy, these same large numbers suggest that there are large qualitative differences among these information sources. These differences may not always be apparent to students who may lack sophisticated reading and interpreting skills. Consequently, social studies teachers need to help their students refine their ability to make qualitative distinctions among various newspapers and journals.

One difficulty many secondary students have is coping with specialized presentation techniques characterizing certain widely circulated journals. The highly stylized prose of weekly newsmagazines, including *Time* and *Newsweek,* baffles many younger secondary students (and older ones, too, whose reading proficiency levels are not high). These individuals have a hard time extracting the "message" from the often elaborate stylistic package that carries it. A response to this difficulty that some teachers have found profitable is to develop a few special lessons designed to "acclimate" students to the prose style of the popular newsmagazines.

Such a lesson requires the teacher to identify a given focus event. The teacher either prepares a short, prose description of the event written in a straightforward style or finds a similarly unembellished newspaper account. Next a report focusing on the same event is found in one of the popular newsmagazines. Students are given an opportunity to read first the teacher-prepared (or newspaper) account and then the one from the newsmagazine. A series of debriefing questions follows:

1. What happened? (Students respond.)
2. What is different about the two accounts? (Students respond.)
3. Why did you find the second one more difficult? (Students respond.)
4. How is the author of the second account using words differently from the author of the first? (Students respond.)
5. Are both accounts communicating the same basic information? (Students respond.)

These questions are merely illustrative of those that might be asked. The questioning sequence is designed to help students see that different prose styles can be used to convey similar information. As a follow-up, students can be presented with a description of another incident as reported in one of the popular newsmagazines. To determine how well students have developed an ability to cope with the specialized reporting style, ask them either to describe the specific points being made or to write a report of the incident in a simple, unembellished way. Accuracy of these student efforts can be checked as a measure of their ability to cope with the newsmagazines' usages.

Another difficulty many secondary students have concerns their inability to detect biases of individual journals and newspapers. All too many labor under the illusion that because something has been printed, it must be unassailable "truth." To help break down this misconception, you will find it a good idea to make available to students specific materials written from clearly opposed philosophical positions. A number of journals identify regularly with either a "conservative" or with a "liberal" position. Exercises requiring students to read treatments of common issues in journals in both camps help them to develop an understanding that many periodicals are edited to reflect a particular point of view. Of the many possible pairings of suitable journals, one representative "conservative" journal might be the *National Review* and one representative "liberal" journal might be the *New Republic*. Debriefings of students after they have read treatments of a subject in two such periodicals can highlight how differing editorial slants are reflected in each article.

Newspapers and journal articles typically include a great deal more information than students will need to complete a given assignment. To avoid swamping students with details in asking them to read entire articles, you will find it a good idea to provide them with some guidance when assignments are made. This guidance can be directed toward pointing their attention to specific points. You might say, for example, "When you read the feature from the editorial page of the *Wall Street Journal*, take particular note of the arguments the author makes for giving the president more direct controls over the Federal Reserve System." Such an article might contain a great deal of information focusing on other topics. Given this kind of a focus statement, students spend their time more productively in searching out specific details.

Availability of materials is an important consideration in assigning students to read materials in newspapers and periodicals. Many beginning social studies teacher make the erroneous assumption that nearly all students will have a daily newspaper available to them at home. A surprisingly large number of American families subscribe to no newspaper and to no journals. Clearly, an assignment to read an account of a presidential news conference in "tonight's paper" puts a heavier burden on some students than on others. In an effort to assure reasonable access to materials, a supply of local newspapers and some periodicals ought to be available at the school. In many communities the local newspaper is made available to requesting schools at very modest rates. Certainly, a copy or two ought to be available in the library if not in individual classrooms.

Social studies teachers need to work closely with librarians to select journals and newspaper resources that can be used by social studies students. Of course, budgets vary enormously from school to school, but minimally an attempt ought to be made to include representative weekly newsmagazines such as *Newsweek*, *Time*, and *U.S. News and World Report*. As funds permit, the collection might be expanded to include journals of political comment such as *The National Review*, *The Nation*, *The New Republic*, and *The Spectator* (British). Other journals of interest to teachers of certain subject specializations within the social studies might include *American Heritage* (history), *Current History*, *Mankind* (world history), *Psychology Today*, and *Atlas* (selections from world newspapers). Directed toward a more general audience but frequently featuring articles of interest to social studies teachers and students are such magazines as *National Geographic, Smithsonian, Atlantic Monthly, Harper's, Saturday Review/World,* and *The New Yorker.* Clearly, these titles represent but a fraction of possibilities for a library collection that might prove useful to social studies students.

With regard to newspapers, one or two national newspapers such as the *Wall Street Journal* and the *Christian Science Monitor* might be considered. Additionally, where funding will permit, one or more large regional metropolitan dailies might be considered (or, at least, their Sunday editions). Some major dailies representing different geographical regions of the country are the Atlanta *Constitution,* Baltimore *Sun,* Chicago *Daily News,* Cleveland *Plain Dealer,* Dallas *Morning News,* Denver *Post,* Des Moines *Register,* Detroit *News,* Houston *Chronicle,* Kansas City *Star, Los Angeles Times,* Louisville *Courier-Journal,* Miami *Herald,* Minneapolis *Tribune,* New York *Times, Philadelphia Inquirer,* Portland *Oregonian,* St. Louis *Post-Dispatch,* Salt Lake City *Tribune,* Seattle *Times,* and the *Washington Post.*

Clearly, all of the named magazines and newspapers are directed toward an adult reading audience. Consequently, in making assignments requiring students to read these materials, you must weigh individual reading capabilities. For example, nothing is to be gained by assigning a student reading on a sixth grade level to attempt a sophisticated *New Yorker* article. For many students, assignments to journals and newspapers will not be desirable (except, of course, when the library has available some special periodicals designed especially for students with marginal reading abilities). But for students who can do the necessary reading, assignments focusing on journals and newspapers, properly delimited, can provide a rich and worthwhile learning experience.

BOOKS

Books represent one of the most frequently used information resources by students in social studies classes. The sheer number of books available hints at their great qualitative diversity. Consequently, assignments requiring students to extract information from books must be made after careful consideration of these variables. Further, such assignments must take into account individual differences in students' reading abilities. Finally, assignments must be made specific enough so that students' time can be expended efficiently.

Beginning social studies teachers sometimes make the mistake of assigning students to prepare a report based on "information to be found in anyone of a number of books in the library." Student work resulting from such vaguely worked directions is not likely to be of exemplary quality. Many students, despite years of exposure to lessons on "how to use the library," are not very proficient at finding library materials on their own. Still others have reading problems that interfere with their ability to profit from books once they are found. Yet another group may have the basic reading skills but may lack an efficient strategy for identifying relevant information in a given volume.

Several teacher responses can reduce the intensity of these difficulties. First of all, before any assignment is made regarding use of books in the school library, it is a good idea for the social studies teacher and the librarian to survey the collection to identify the availability of relevant titles. Many librarians will agree to pull these titles from the shelf and gather them together in one place for use of students in the class. Still others will allow the books to be removed to the social studies classroom where the teacher can oversee distribution.

Should time permit, the librarian and social studies teacher might have time to establish grade-level readability ratings for many of the frequently used volumes. For example, an eighth grade social studies teacher who regularly assigned students to give reports on Revolutionary War battles might work with a librarian to identify appropriate titles and to sort them into three categories according to measured reading difficulty. Using the Fry Readability Graph (Fry, 1968), one might describe titles as "difficult," "average," or "easy." "Difficult" titles might be those with a grade ten measured readability level or higher. "Average" titles might be those with a measured readability level ranging from seven to nine. "Easy" titles might be those with a measured readability level of grade six or below. These standards, of course, have been selected arbitrarily. Other cutoff points might be equally appropriate. Whatever standards are adopted to distinguish among categories, the scheme does allow for differentiating between and among volumes in terms of their difficulty. When such information is available, the teacher can assign individual students to extract information from books whose levels of reading difficulty are commensurate with those students' reading abilities.

Whether books have been sorted by reading difficulty level or not, it makes good sense to provide students with lists of specific titles that are relevant to the assigned task. When students have this kind of information, they can locate books more efficiently and can spend their time reading the material rather than looking for the material.

Assignments involving use of books must be made as narrow and tightly focused as possible. Individual volumes probably will contain much more information than a student needs to complete a task. To help the student avoid a frustrating search for information, the teacher should give him or her a specific charge and guidelines to use in locating the appropriate material. For example, an assignment to "find out about political difficulties of Thomas Jefferson before he became president" is so large and vague a charge that students would likely experience great difficulty in identifying appropriate information. Certainly, they would have great difficulty in determining when they had "done enough" to meet the teacher's expectations. On the other hand, an assignment to "point out four issues on which Thomas Jefferson was attacked while he was governor of Virginia and summarize the main points of his critics" provides students with a much more pointed focus. Students, given such a charge, should have little difficulty in identifying information in reference books that is relevant to the assignment.

Many students do not do a good job of scanning a book's table of contents and index to help them pinpoint information. It is clearly within the scope of the social studies teacher's obligations to take time to help students develop these skills. Time spent in class demonstrating how a given resource book might be scanned for information relating to a topic will pay handsome dividends in terms of increasing the efficiency of students' use of such materials. Beyond exercises illustrating use of the table of contents and the index, time might well be spent describing how paragraphs can be scanned to identify topic sentences and key items of information. In general, these classroom exercises need to be developed with a view to helping students understand that books, when used as information resources, rarely are read in their entirety. Rather, the efficient reader quickly locates relevant information, notes it, and moves on to consider other materials.

When systematic attention is directed to matching student reading abilities to appropriate titles and to developing sophisticated scanning skills, books can provide an especially fertile information source for social studies students. Because of the almost limitless range of information in books, they represent an information resource that can be tailored to meet the needs of almost any social studies program. Certainly, students should be encouraged to use them as they seek to broaden their perspectives respecting issues introduced in social studies class.

SPECIAL RETRIEVAL SYSTEMS AND OTHER SOURCES

Many libraries subscribe to services specializing in abstracting information relating to particular topics. Frequently, school budgets will permit subscriptions to one or more of these services by either the school library or by one or more individual departments. Several such services are of interest to social studies teachers who desire to make a wider range of information sources available to their students.

A number of secondary schools subscribe to *Facts on File* (distributed by Facts on File, 119 West 57 Street, New York, NY 10019). This service provides a weekly digest of world news. Specifically, information is organized under an easy-to-use topical index. The same organization distributes another service called *Editorials on File*, which features collections of editorials on various current topics of interest.

A similar focus on current information that is organized and indexed for easy use is provided by *Deadline Data* (available from Deadline Data, 100 Northfield Street, Greenwich, CT 06830). This source provides students with ready access to a host of information regarding topics of present interest.

A relatively new abstracting and indexing system specializes in television news. The *Television News Index and Abstracts* provides summaries of evening news broadcasts on all three major networks. Additionally, the service makes available, for a small charge, video and audio transcriptions of any newscast available in its library (beginning with August 5, 1968). (Address: *Television News Index and Abstracts*, Vanderbilt Television News Archives, Joint University Libraries, Nashville, TN 37203.)

Indexes of major newspapers are available. *The New York Times Index* and microfilms of daily and Sunday editions of that newspaper are found in many libraries. (Address: *New York Times Index,* P. O. Box 5792, Church Street Station, New York, NY 10249.) Sometimes local newspapers are available in microcopy. These materials make excellent additions to the school library and can provide students with especially good information when they are assigned to do research focusing on local issues.

Several sources provide information summaries relating to the individual social science disciplines. One of these, *Historical Abstracts,* contains synopses of information from world journals. (Address: *Historical Abstracts,* Bibliographical Center, Clio Press, Riviera Campus, 2040 Alameda Padre Serra, Santa Barbara, CA 93103.)

Of interest to economics teachers and sociology teachers is the annual publication *Statistical Abstract of the United States.* Containing a wealth of information on a variety of subjects, the *Statistical Abstract* is published each year by the U.S. Bureau of the Census (U.S. Bureau of the Census, *Statistical Abstract of the United States* [published annually]). A related publication that summarizes a great deal of historical data is *Historical Statistics of the United States, Colonial Times to 1970,* Bicentennial Edition (U.S. Bureau of the Census, 1975).

Sources of Information in the Social Sciences serves as a useful guide for locating places where specific issues are treated in the social science literature (Carl M. White and associates, *Sources of Information in the Social Sciences,* 2d ed. [Chicago: America Library Association, 1973]). A more general directory of information sources is *Information Resources in the United States: Social Sciences,* revised edition (*Information Resources in the United States: Social Sciences,* rev. ed. [Washington, D.C.: Library of Congress, 1973]).

Specific indexing systems and information introduced here represent only a fraction of those available. A trained librarian, working with a social studies teacher, doubtless would be able to point out many valuable additional sources of information. Collaborative efforts between librarians and social studies teachers can result in decisions to allocate available materials moneys to provide not necessarily extensive, but rather *useful* sources of information for students.

Whichever information sources are available, it is important that students learn how to use them. In many schools, cooperative efforts of social studies teachers and librarians work well to develop lessons designed to familiarize students with the use of available information retrieval systems. When students have mastered techniques of using these data sources, they grow in confidence and in efficiency as they work toward completion of assignments. Skills in using information retrieval systems increase students' range of options as they seek to go beyond more familiar sources in their quest for answers to questions of concern.

Organizing Information

Social studies students need to organize information once it has been located. Many have not mastered basics of note-keeping and have a very difficult time assigning priorities to specific informational items to which they have become exposed. A little time spent in social studies classes discussing possible systems for organizing information will enable students to derive more profit from materials and learning experiences that comprise the social studies program.

PREPARING OUTLINES

A number of effective systems for taking notes have been devised. One representative system relies exclusively on the use of a numbering scheme. According to this plan, major topics are indicated by a whole number as, for example, 1.0, 2.0, or 3.0. Subordinate topics are indicated by a number identical to that attached to the major topic with the exception that fractional figures after the decimal are changed. For example, the first two subordinate topics under the major topic indicated by 1.0 would be written 1.1 and 1.2. An example of such a scheme follows:

Focus subject: *The Nature of Murder*

1.0 No figures exist that establish how many murders that are committed are truly "premeditated."
2.0 The law defines "premeditated" in specific terms.
   2.1 The law assumes anyone carrying a weapon during a felony plans to use it.
      2.11 A killing during an armed robbery is considered to be "premeditated murder."
3.0 Over 70 per cent of murders involve members of the murderer's family.
   3.1 Most murders of family members seem to occur because of a momentary rage, not because of "premeditation."
4.0 Public distrust of murderers makes them less likely to be paroled than perpetrators of other crimes.
   4.1 The average criminal stays in prison 19.6 months. The average murderer stays in prison 78.7 months.

This sample represents a fragment of an outline prepared by a student listening to a lecture. The same technique can be used regardless of the source of information. Organized in this fashion, information can be easily retrieved. Information of a secondary nature can be readily identified.

Certainly, other frameworks for arranging notes in outline form would be equally acceptable to the one introduced here. The choice of the framework is a minor issue. The important decision is the one to commit class time to helping students develop their outlining skills. A technique many teachers have found useful in this regard involves playing a short recording of a lecture (or, more appropriately, just part of a lecture). Five minutes of lecture will do. Students are prepared for the exercise by being introduced to the outlining framework to be used. They are asked to outline the major points of the lecture as it is presented. During a debriefing session, the teacher can develop an acceptable outline of the remarks on the chalkboard. Discussion can focus on similarities and differences between the teacher's outline and those developed by individual students. Some teachers find it useful to play a second five-minute segment of tape after this initial exercise to provide students with another opportunity to practice their skills. Given this kind of systematic attention, most students can develop acceptable outlining competencies.

PREPARING NOTE CARDS

In addition to outlining, collecting information on note cards can be used by students to organize data. A good note card system functions to organize information in such a way that details focusing on specific topics or points of view can be identified easily. A number of systems are available for arranging information

Source: Garcia, Renaldo. *Mexican Migration to Colorado in the 1890's.* Aa2*
Denver: Pilsen Press, 1943.

Key points:

1. Mining was the primary attraction of Mexicans who moved to Colorado in the late nineteenth century.

2. Commonly, only men went. Families stayed in Mexico. Money was sent to these families to help meet living expenses.

3. Employers furnished housing, of a very low quality, for which Mexican workers paid out of their wages.

Note: This section of the card refers to (1) the topic, (2) the specific part of the topic to which data on the card refer, and (3) the number assigned to this specific card dealing with this particular part of the major topic. The first letter in the "Aa2" identifies the major topic. For example, topics such as the following might comprise those investigated at a given time:

A = Mexicans
B = Canadians
C = Caribbean peoples

The second letter in the "Aa2" identifies the particular part of the topic to which the data refer. Some possibilities here might be

a = relates to practices of individuals actually moving to U.S.
b = relates to anti-U.S. practices of individuals in own countries.
c = relates to U.S. responses to immigrants from these areas.

Thus, the notation "Aa2" means that the card refers to Mexicans and, more particularly, to lives of Mexicans who moved to the United States. The "2" indicates that this is the second card relating to Mexicans who moved to the United States.

Figure 9–1. Format for a Note Card

on cards. One such system enables students to sort individual cards into appropriate clusters either according to authors of source materials or by topics and positions taken regarding topics. A framework for a note card developed according to this system is depicted in Figure 9–1.

Students need to be provided with a format to follow in listing authors and titles for source materials they use. Some examples that might be provided to students follow:

(book) GARCIA, REYNALDO. *Mexican Migration to Colorado in 1890's.* Denver: Pilsen Press, 1943.

(journal) AVILA, MANUEL. "Politics of Exploitation: Anti-Mexican Laws in 19th Century Colorado." *Platte Historical Record* (April 1977): 220–242.

(newspaper) ILG, HECTOR. "Trial Record Reveals Old Judicial Error." New York *Press-Clarion* (June 10, 1967): 5, col. 2.

(speech) CABRERA, C. V. "An Unhappy Century: 100 years of Peonage of Mexicans in the United States." Address given at Naomi State University, Cleveland, on September 21, 1974.

(broadcast) NBC NEWS. "The Unlanded: Treatment of Mexicans in the Old West" (November 20, 1977): 7:00–8:00 P.M., E.S.T.

Perhaps even more frequently than they will wish to sort cards by author, students may wish to sort them according to major and subtopics. A notation system can be developed to allow them to do this. Note the use of such a system in the small box in the upper right-hand corner of the sample card depicted in Figure 9.1. A two-letter scheme can be used to identify major and subtopics. Capital letters can identify major topics, and small letters can identify subordinate topics related to those major topics. Examples of how such a scheme might be developed follow:

Major topics
A = Petroleum Resources
B = Coal Resources
C = Thermal Resources
D = Hydroelectric Resources

Subordinate topics
a = information in support of federal development of resources.
b = information opposed to federal development of resources.
c = information providing general background in which no basic "pro" or "con" position is taken regarding federal development of resources.

If this scheme is used, for example, the notation *Bb* written on a note card would indicate that the information dealt generally with the topic of coal and, more specifically, included information representing a position opposed to federal development of coal resources. There may well be a number of cards from a number of sources with information of this type. It may be convenient to number cards to keep track of the volume of evidence that is being gathered relating to a given position. This can be accomplished by adding an appropriate number immediately following the two-letter codes. For example, a card labelled *Bb5* would be the fifth card containing information relating to positions in opposition to federal development of coal resources.

This general scheme for organizing information on note cards provides students with a good deal of flexibility. They can organize and reorganize information they have gathered in terms of the particular needs they might have at a given time. Use of a systematic procedure for preparing note cards helps students focus more clearly on the purposes of various data they have gathered. It provides them with a means of discriminating among items of information that may have no real relevance to an issue and those that have a direct and legitimate relevance. In summary, when students are taught how to organize information on note cards, they become more sophisticated consumers of data. This sophistication goes hand in hand with the social studies teacher's desire to turn out students who are sensitive, perceptive, and capable of bringing potent information to bear on significant problems.

Summary

Success of students in social studies classes relates, in part, to their ability to locate and organize information. In asking students to seek out certain kinds of information, teachers need to consider (1) the capabilities of the individual student, (2) the nature of the task the student will be required to complete once information is in hand, (3) the various sources from which the needed information is in hand, and (4) the various sources from which the needed information potentially is available. Among possible sources of information are personal experience, personal observation, interviews, listening, newspapers and journals, books, and special retrieval systems. Once information has been gathered, it needs to be organized. Social studies teachers need not hesitate to spend time in their classes providing students with opportunities to learn several organizational systems. Time spent helping students master techniques of taking notes in outline form and in preparing note cards may well pay dividends as students become more sophisticated in their abilities to manipulate information they have gathered in a purposeful way.

REFERENCES

Fry, Edward. "Fry's Readability Graph: Clarifications, Validity, and Extension to Level 17." *Journal of Reading* (December 1977): 242–252.
Rooze, Gene E., and Leona M. Foerster. *Teaching Elementary School Social Studies: A New Perspective.* Columbus, Ohio: Charles E. Merrill Publishing Co., 1972.

Chapter 10

GRAPHIC LITERACY SKILLS

O NE OF THE MOST LONG-STANDING EXPECTATIONS OF the social studies program has been that it provide students with expertise in deriving information from charts, graphs, drawings, tables, maps, globes, and photographs. Writing in the thirty-third yearbook of the National Council for the Social Studies, Fraser and Johns (1963) pointed out that teaching students to interpret maps and globes was a major responsibility of the social studies and that teaching students to interpret visual data of other varieties was an important responsibility shared by the social studies and other school subject areas.

The developmental learning theorists Piaget and Inhelder (1956) have pointed out that many youngsters do not develop an adequate grasp of spatial relationships until age eleven or twelve. Towler and Nelson (1968) found that few youngsters before the age of twelve were able to develop a sure understanding of the concept of scale. An implication of these studies for secondary school teachers is that much work remains to be done in the area of teaching graphic literacy skills to their students. Sometimes there is an illusion that, because such skills have been *introduced* in the elementary grades, these skills have been mastered. But even when such skills have been well taught in the elementary grades, there is evidence that students cannot really develop a sure sense for their proper use before their secondary school years. Given this reality, it makes good sense to commit instructional time in social studies classes to teaching and reinforcing these skills.

For secondary students, the great strength of graphic display of information is its great weakness as well. Graphic displays condense tremendous quantities of information in a small space. This economy comes at a price. That price is associated with the large volume of sophisticated data carried by each element in the graphic display. To comprehend such a display, the viewer must have full knowledge of the data-carrying capabilities of each of a large number of separate parts. Further, he or she must be able to interpret intended meanings when these separate elements are presented in different configurations. For individuals who have these skills, the graphic display serves as a remarkably efficient transmitter of information. (Consider, for example, the paragraphs and pages of prose copy necessary to explain supply and demand functions in economics—functions that are briefly and elegantly depicted in drawings of supply and demand curves.) But when these skills have not been well developed, the graphic display has great potential for confusing rather than clarifying issues.

To help students develop more sophisticated graphic literacy competencies, classroom instruction needs to focus specifically on development of skills associated with learning from visual representations of information. Specific attention, in subsequent sections, will be devoted to procedures for helping students profit from learning experiences requiring the use of line graphs, bar graphs, pictorial representations, maps, and globes.

Line Graphs, Bar Graphs, and Pictorial Representations

Large quantities of numerical data can be summarized effectively through the use of line graphs, bar graphs, and pictorial representations. Teaching students skills associated with these visual presentation modes involves a two-step process. First, students must be introduced to basic design features of such graphic displays. For example, they need to be taught that, in line graphs, the vertical axis carries certain information, the horizontal axis carries other information, and the line itself represents a statement of relationship between measures scaled on both axes. This kind of basic information ordinarily does not present any great difficulties for students. A large example of a line graph—perhaps one on a transparency projected to cover a large section of a wall—and some teacher comments directing students attention to different components will suffice.

> *Teacher:* Note the horizontal axis. That's this one. (Uses pointer to indicate horizontal axis.) Note that each mark represents one calendar month. Note the vertical axis, the one going up and down. (Points out vertical axis). This axis depicts the number of families drawing welfare benefits. Each mark stands for 10,000 families. Note, for example, that the third mark up from the zero point stands for 30,000 families. The line drawn on the graph indicates changes in numbers of families on welfare from month to month. Note how the line goes down from February to March. That means that fewer families (20,000) were on welfare in March than in February (40,000).

Many secondary students who have no difficulty whatsoever in understanding basic functions of different parts of a line graph have considerable problems in the area served by the second part of the process of teaching about this particular method of graphic display. This second step of the teaching process seeks to prepare students to distinguish between line graphs that have been drawn responsibly and those that have not. By *responsibly* is meant that the graph presents a visual impression that is consistent with the data from which it is derived. A student who is unable to differentiate between a responsibly drawn graphic and one that distorts reality (perhaps to serve the special agenda of some interest group) may fall prey to those who would take advantage of his or her ignorance.

In helping students to learn distinctions between "proper" and "improper" graphic displays of data, many teachers find it useful to build a series of short lessons around a common set of data. Building on this common data set, one can construct graphic displays that, in some cases, accurately reflect this information and that, in others, inaccurately reflect this information. Consider, for example, a hypothetical company, Smartchips International, that in 1975 began manufacturing and selling digital watches. Suppose yearly sales figures were as follows:

    1975: 100,000 watches
    1976: 200,000 watches
    1977: 150,000 watches
    1978: 160,000 watches

A responsible depiction of these sales figure is portrayed in part A of Figure 10–1.

The line graph in Part A of Figure 10–1 is responsibly drawn in that the points connected by the line accurately reflect differences in the sales figure for each year. For example, sales in 1976 were twice those of 1975. On the line graph, the point for 1976 is twice as far from the zero point as is the point for 1975. The 1976 sales are twice the 1975 sales; distance on the graph to 1976 is twice that to 1975: this situation suggests that the visual impact of the graph parallels the "reality" of the figures upon which the graph was based.

Suppose this company, in reporting its annual sales figures, decided to use another popular visual form, the bar graph. A responsible bar graph might look something like the example provided in part B of Figure 10–1. Note that the bar for 1976 is exactly twice as tall as that for 1975. This difference again exactly parallels the difference in watch sales for the two years, 1976 sales being twice those of 1975.

Another favorite representational technique is the visual representation. Smartchips International might decide to draw outlines of digital watches to display sales differences in each year. A responsible example of this technique is presented in part C of Figure 10–1. In the case of a pictorial representation of this type, the *areas* of each drawn figure should relate proportionally to one another in the same way as yearly sales figures relate to one another. Part C of Figure 10–1 meets this standard; that is, the area of the watch depicting 1976 sales is exactly twice that of the area of the watch depicting 1975 sales. This parallels precisely

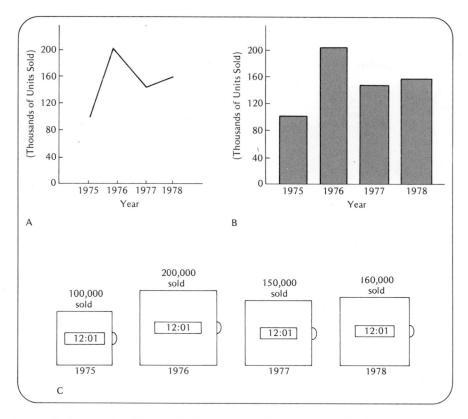

Figure 10–1. Examples of Responsible Presentations of Data via a Line Graph, a Bar Chart, and a Pictorial Representation

the fact that 1976 sales of 200,000 units were exactly twice the 1975 sales of 100,000 units.

Once students have been introduced to proper or responsible representations of numerical data, they can be introduced to techniques that, from time to time, have been used to create visual impressions that are not consistent with the data upon which graphic representations are alleged to have been based. A favorite technique for using a line graph to suggest a larger gain that the figures warrant involves eliminating part of the vertical axis and stretching the remaining portion to increase the vertical difference between points connected by lines. An example of two line graphs, one drawn responsibly and one drawn to reflect an irresponsible "stretching" of the vertical axis, is depicted in Figure 10–2.

Note in Figure 10–2 how the "responsible" line graph on the left indicates a rather modest rise in the line connecting points representing sales figures for 1977 and 1978. This accurately reflects the rather small increase in sales from 150,000

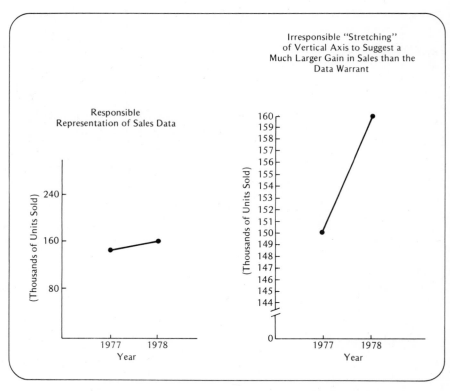

Figure 10–2. Line Graphs: A "Responsible" Example and an "Irresponsible" Example

units in 1977 to 160,000 units in 1978. On the other hand, a little deft and irresponsible draftsmanship has changed the vertical scale of the drawing on the right. This change in scaling has spread the vertical difference between points marking 1977 and 1978 sales. A careless observer might well conclude that the company had experienced boom times between 1977 and 1978 when, in fact, the increase in sales between the two years was less than 7 per cent.

An even more spectacular manipulation of this type occasionally is observed when data are reported using a bar graph. Figure 10–3 depicts a responsibly drawn bar graph on the left and one reflecting irresponsible distortion on the right. The bar graph on the right has had much of its midsection removed. Accompanying this change has been a "stretching" of the scale along the vertical axis. The result is a visual impression of a sales increase of over 100 per cent between 1977 and 1978 when, in fact, the real increase was less than 7 per cent.

Manipulation of pictorial representations is somewhat more subtle. Certainly, irresponsible pictorial representations initially are difficult for students to spot. An example of a correctly proportioned pictorial representation and one that suggests some irresponsible distortion are found in Figure 10–4.

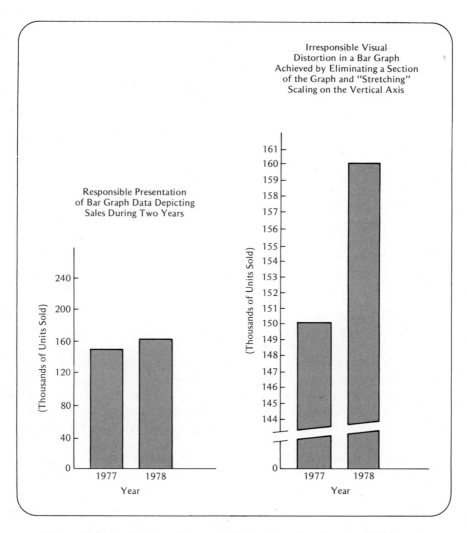

Figure 10–3. Bar Graphs: a "Responsible" Example and an "Irresponsible" Example

When pictorial representations are used to reflect changes in numerical data, the proportions between the areas of each figure should be the same as proportions between the numerical information being depicted. The pictorial representation of data on the left side of Figure 10–4 is responsibly executed. The 1976 "watch" is twice as large in area as the 1975 "watch," properly reflecting the 100 per cent difference in sales in the two years. But the pictorial representation on the right is an example of a frequently seen method of distortion. Instead of increasing the *area* of the 1976 "watch" to make it twice the *area* of the 1975 "watch," the artist has increased the length of each side of the 1976 watch to twice the

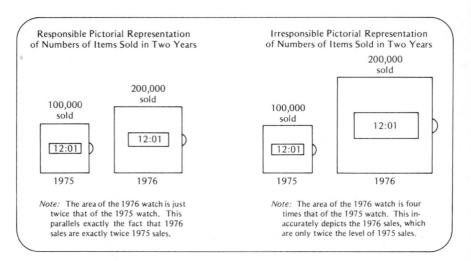

Irresponsible Pictorial Representation
of Numbers of Items Sold in Two Years

200,000
sold

200,000
sold

100,000
sold

100,000
sold

12:01

12:01

12:01

12:01

1975   1976

1975   1976

Note: The area of the 1976 watch is just twice that of the 1975 watch. This parallels exactly the fact that 1976 sales are exactly twice 1975 sales.

Note: The area of the 1976 watch is four times that of the 1975 watch. This inaccurately depicts the 1976 sales, which are only twice the level of 1975 sales.

Figure 10–4. Pictorial Representations: A "Responsible" Example and an "Irresponsible" Example

length of each side of the 1975 watch. This has resulted in a 1976 watch that is not twice as large in area as the 1975 watch but rather *four times as large in area.* (For example: If one has a square figure measuring 1″ on a side, the area is 1 square inch because $1'' \times 1'' = 1$. If each side is doubled, then we have a 2″ by 2″ figure whose area is 4 square inches because $2'' \times 2'' = 4$ square inches.) This kind of distortion suggests to an uncritical observer that the increase in sales in 1976 as compared to 1975 was significantly greater than the 100 per cent level revealed in the actual figures. After all, the 1976 "watch" is four times as large as its 1975 counterpart.

In viewing graphically displayed data, whether presented in line graphs, bar graphs, or pictorial representations, students must be taught to look beyond the visual display to the data upon which the display is based. This need not be difficult because, typically, the data are included in some form within the display. In looking at displays, students might well keep in mind the following questions:

1. Have the vertical axes of line and bar graphs been "stretched"?
2. Has the bottom or the midsection of the bar graph been removed to accentuate differences between top portions of the individual bars?
3. Are pictorial representations drawn in such a way that changes in areas of individual drawings are proportional to changes in data being depicted?

Trained to ask such questions, students quickly become sophisticated analysts of graphically displayed information. As a concluding activity to a lesson or series of lessons designed to increase students visual literacy, many teachers find it useful to ask students to develop graphic displays of their own from a common data set. Students might be asked to develop "responsible" as well as "irresponsible" representations. In a debriefing session, the class can examine individual student efforts with a view to distinguishing between those that accurately reflect the data and those that convey distorted impressions.

Special Problems with Visual Displays Built from "Indexed" Numerical Data

A special class of graphic displays causes students (and adults) a great deal of confusion. This confusion results not from problems associated with possible distortions in the visual display itself but rather from the special nature of the data upon which the display is based. These troublesome data are those whose units of value do not remain stable over time. The most common example is the dollar. There is an illusion (especially to unsophisticated students) that anything with a common name ought to mean the same thing regardless of any particular reference to time. But such a conception, with respect to the dollar, is untenable. Though the *name* stays constant, the *value* changes over time. Students need to recognize that five dollars in 1910 does not mean the same thing as five dollars in 1950 or five dollars in 1978. (That many students do not have such understanding is revealed in the "oohs" and "aahs" of students looking at 1902 Sears' catalogs and marveling at how "cheap everything was then." This assumption clearly reflects their mistaken belief that inflated late twentieth-century dollars are the same as 1902 dollars.)

To make comparisons equivalent across time when units, such as dollars, with unstable real values are concerned, economists commonly use "index numbers." Index numbers provide a common reference point. This reference point is usually expressed as 100.0. Data for other years are related back to this point by computing percentages of increase or decrease in real value from the common reference point.

Suppose, for example, there was interest in examining changes in consumer prices over a number of years. The year 1971 might be established as the common point of reference and assigned a value of 100.0. Investigation might reveal that prices in 1968 were 8 per cent lower than the 1971 level or, expressed another way, only 92 per cent as high. Thus, 1968 might be assigned a price index of 92.0. This would mean that, because of observed changes in the purchasing power of the dollar, it would have required only $.92 to buy in 1968 what it cost $1.00 to buy in 1971.

A study of pricing in 1975 might have revealed that prices in that year were 11 per cent higher than in the base year 1971. The year 1975, then, would be assigned an index of 111.0. This would mean that it required $1.11 to purchase in 1975 what $1.00 would have purchased in the base year of 1971.

Use of index numbers makes it possible to measure changes in "real" values over time. There is a tendency for students to be impressed with changes in "nominal" values because numerical differences are often striking. But "nominal" values indicate only changes in the number of units with a common name (for example, dollars) rather than changes in the true worth of those units.

For example, suppose members of a social studies class were investigating changes in wages between the early 1950s and the late 1970s. Among weekly wage differences that might have been found was the following:

WHOLESALE AND RETAIL TRADES—
AVERAGE WEEKLY WAGES

1953	$ 51.35
1976	133.39

Source: U.S. Department of Labor, Bureau of Labor Statistics, *Monthly Labor Review*, 100 (September 1977): 69.

Students looking at these figures, reflecting nominal changes in income, might well conclude that wholesale and retail trades workers had made enormous financial gains during the years from 1953 to 1976. Indeed, these figures suggest that weekly wages in 1976 were an impressive 159.77 per cent higher than in 1953. Appealing as this picture is, it does not mirror reality accurately. Though nominal dollar wages were much higher in 1976 than in 1953, those 1976 dollars did not buy as much, individually, as did their 1953 counterparts.

To get a more realistic picture of the relative economic well-being of wholesale and retail trades workers in the two years, one must refer to index numbers that can provide a basis for comparing the "real" value of the 1953 weekly wage against the "real" value of the 1976 weekly wage. To accomplish this, one might select the year 1967 as the base year and assign it an index value of 100.0. In fact, the U.S. Department of Labor's Bureau of Labor Statistics has used that year as a base and provides figures indicating the index numbers for the two years of interest, 1953 and 1976. Those figures are as follows:

CONSUMER PRICE INDEX (1967 = 100.0)

1953 =	80.1
1976 =	170.5

Source: U.S. Department of Labor, Bureau of Labor Statistics, *Monthly Labor Review*, 100 (September 1977): 77.

This consumer price index information means that in 1953 one could purchase for about $.80 what cost $1.00 in the base year 1967 and about $1.70 in 1976.

This information can be used to make a "real" comparison between the 1953 weekly wage of the wholesale and retail trades workers and their 1976 weekly wage. The comparison is made in terms of what the relative purchasing power of the weekly wages in both 1953 and 1976 would have been in terms of constant 1967 dollars. This computation is as follows:

$$\frac{\$51.35 \text{ (1953 weekly wage)}}{\$.80} = \$64.19 \text{ (purchasing power in 1967 dollars)}$$

$$\frac{\$133.39 \text{ (1976 weekly wage)}}{\$1.705} = \$78.23 \text{ (purchasing power in 1967 dollars)}$$

This comparison indicates the "real" difference in purchasing power of the 1976 wage as compared to the 1953 wage. This "real" wage gain reflects an increase of 21.87 per cent. The figure is impressive enough, but certainly it is far different from the 159.77 per cent increase that results when an illogical comparison is made between the nominal dollar wages in the two years.

Unless students understand the role played by indexing in equating dollar figures from different time periods, they may draw false conclusions from presentations of data in which one of the variables is dollars. For example, consider the students who were presented with the bar graphs on the left side of Figure 10–5 reflecting differences in *nominal* (or money) wages in 1930 and 1940. A student unaware of differences in the purchasing power of the dollar in 1930 might well conclude that, because of the decline in average wages from $1,368 in 1930 to $1,299 in 1940, the average wage earner was less well off in 1940 than in 1930.

The truth of the matter is that though average wages did decrease between 1930 and 1940, prices went down even faster than wages. A result of this set of circumstances was a 1940 dollar that would purchase considerably more than its 1930 counterpart. In fact, it took only $1.00 in 1940 to purchase what cost $1.10 in 1930. Given this information, the bar graphs on the right hand side of Figure 10–5 reveal that, because the 1930 dollar purchased less than the 1940 dollar, the average 1930 wage of $1,368 was equivalent to only $1,150 in 1940 dollars. This startling increase in the purchasing power of the individual dollar between 1930 and 1940 meant that, despite a decrease in *nominal* wages between 1930 and 1940, there was actually a gain in *real* wages between 1930 and 1940. Expressed in another way, the average wage earner in 1940 lived better than his 1930 counterpart even though he took home fewer dollars.

Unless students have an understanding of the operation of indexing, they cannot begin to understand how fewer dollars at the end of the week, the month, or year could ever have been associated with an increase in purchasing power. This situation is particularly difficult for secondary students whose formative years have been spent during times of price inflation rather than price deflation. Clearly, instruction in the use of index values is imperative if these students are to become sophisticated investigators of many important historical episodes, including the Great Depression.

Because indexing is initially a rather confusing idea for students, the process

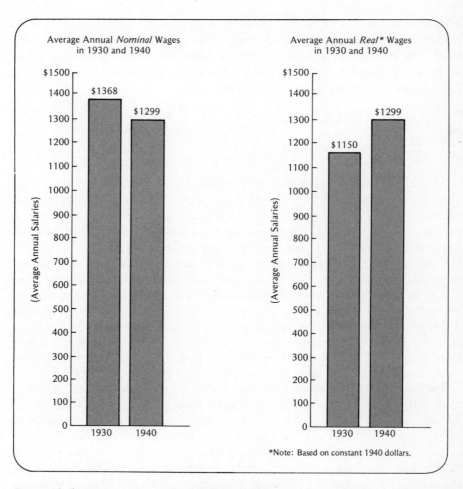

Figure 10–5. Differences between Nominal and Real Average Annual Wages in 1930 and 1940. (Source: Data adapted from U.S. Department of Commerce, Bureau of the Census, *Historical Statistics of the United States: Colonial Times to 1970* (Washington, D.C., 1975), pp. 164, 210–211.)

should be first introduced to students by using, perhaps, selected graphic representations employing indexed data as examples. Following this sort of initial exposure, students might be provided with sample data and asked to work up graphic representations of their own involving the use of indexing. Student efforts can be shared with class members in a debriefing session to reinforce the concept of indexing. Students who develop some interest in indexing (as well as in the whole general issue of graphic representation of information) might be directed to read and report on Darrell Huff's delightful *How to Lie with Statistics* (New York: W. W. Norton & Company, Inc., 1954).

Map and Globe Skills

Teaching students skills associated with the use of maps and globes is a major responsibility for social studies teachers. Though some attention to these skills is provided in the elementary grades, for reasons partially associated with chronological development, many secondary students come into the junior and even senior high school with very deficient map and globe skill competencies. Certainly, formal instruction focusing on enhancement of such skills ought to be included within the secondary social studies program.

Large numbers of secondary students have a poorly developed sense of geographic relationships. Relative locations of places in geographic space frequently are misunderstood. (Many secondary students are "shocked" to learn that Reno is west of Los Angeles and that the west coast of South America is in the eastern time zone.) Additionally, much confusion exists regarding relative physical sizes of different geographic places. (An astonishing number of secondary students believe that there is not much difference in size between the United States and the entire continent of Africa!)

Certainly, many factors contribute to student difficulties in dealing with geographic relationships of various kinds. Many, for example, have seen crudely drawn maps of the United States tilted in such a way that the entire west coast looks as if it were almost a straight line following a north-south meridian. Such maps create an impression that "any" city on the west coast, such as Los Angeles, must be west of "any" interior city, including Reno. Further, many students have been exposed to maps in school drawn according to a Mercator projection. This projection makes regions appear physically larger than their true sizes as distance from the equator increases. Consequently, Africa, spanning the equator, tends, on the average, to be more closely drawn in terms of its "true" size than North America, all of which is north of the equator. Years of looking at such maps may well contribute to students' lack of appreciation of real size relationships.

Another important force in shaping students' conceptions of geographic places is the degree of attention given individual places by the national media. For a number of reasons, some world places get much more television and newspaper coverage than others. Students, for example, are more likely to have a good grasp of the approximate location and relative size of France than they are of the Seychelles Islands. Indicative of this situation, one national network several years ago used to begin its evening news broadcasts with a recording of a message something like this: "Reports tonight and every night from our correspondents in Paris, London, Rome, Moscow, South America, and from wherever news is happening." An entire continent, South America, was equated in terms of importance with several large European cities.

Social studies lessons focusing on developing students' map and globe skills might well include the following major topics:

1. General characteristics of basic schemes for projecting a spherical surface on a two-dimensional plane.
2. Use of legends to extract information from maps.
3. Locating places through the use of coordinates.
4. Scaling and its effects on the level of abstraction of a map.
5. Purposes of various kinds of maps.

BASIC MAP PROJECTIONS

Perhaps the most basic information students must grasp in learning to use maps effectively is that no map transforms the areal data on the globe without distortion. Some schemes control the distortion more effectively than others, but none eliminates it. It is not physically possible to make a curved global surface flat without some "stretching." This "stretching" will result in a flat map surface that never conforms precisely to the curved surface from which it was derived. Students need to know how cartographers have dealt with this problem and the responses that have been developed for different purposes to minimize the effects of the inevitable lack of total congruence between the curved and the flat surface.

In general, mapping is accomplished through variations on three techniques of projection. These are (1) cylindrical projections, (2) tangential plane projections, and (3) conical projections. Variants on each of these themes are numerous, and once students have basic understandings of the basic principles involved, enrichment lessons might center on design characteristics of such complex projection schemes as the oblique azimuthal equidistant projection, Albers conical equal-area projection, the sinusoidal projection, the Bonne projection, and the Lambert azimuthal equal-area projection.

Cylindrical projections. In a cylindrical projection, a globe is wrapped with a cylinder in such a fashion that it is tangent to the globe around a great circle, ordinarily the equator. With the center of the globe used as the focus for the projection, points of the globe are projected on to the surface of the cylinder. When all points have been marked, the cylinder is unwrapped to reveal a flat map of the features represented on the globe. On the cylindrically projected map, lines of longitude will be depicted as parallel lines. This represents an accurate representation of the globe only at the equator (assuming the equator was selected as the point of tangency). On the globe, of course, lines of longitude are not parallel, but rather meet at the poles.

Further distortion involves the lines of latitude. On the cylinder, lines of latitude are unevenly spaced, growing farther apart with an increase in distance from the equator. On the globe, lines of latitude area are parallel. The result of the distortion involving lines of latitude and lines of longitude is that, as distance from the equator increases, areas are increasingly depicted larger than their true area. On Mercator maps, drawn according to a slight variation of this basic cylindrical-

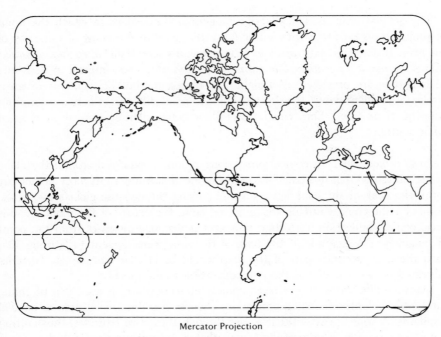

Mercator Projection

Note the distortion in the size of Greenland as compared to South America.

Figure 10–6. Example of the Mercator Projection. (Source: From *Elementary Topography and Map Reading* by Samuel L. Greitzer (New York: McGraw-Hill Book Company, 1944), p. 35. Copyright 1944 by McGraw-Hill Book Company. Used with permission of McGraw-Hill Book Company.)

mapping procedure, Greenland appears larger than South America. In fact, Greenland is only one ninth the size of South America. (See Figure 10–6.)

Students might be interested in investigating cylindrical central projections, cylindrical equal-spaced projections, and other modifications of the basic approach that have attempted to lessen the extent of distortions at distances from the equator. Students, too, might be interested in knowing that the popularity of the Mercator maps developed from their accurate depiction of locations in terms of coordinates of longitude and latitude. This accuracy makes them very useful for purposes of navigation.

Tangential plane projections. Tangential plane projection maps are characterized by a plane face's being placed tangent to a single point on the globe and points' being projected onto that place from a focal point either at the point directly opposite the point of tangency on the globe's surface or at the center of the globe. Frequently, such maps are used to depict polar regions. In such cases, the point of tangency becomes either the North Pole or the South Pole. Distortion on such maps increases as distance from the depicted pole increases.

The general term used to describe tangential plane maps in which the point of projection is on the earth's surface directly opposite the point of tangency of the plane is *stereographic projection*. Less frequently used than *stereographic projection* is *gnomonic projection*. *Gnomonic projection* is of some interest in that lines of longitude are projected as straight line representations of segments of great circles. Such maps depict the shortest point-to-point differences between locations lying on these lines. They can be useful for quick identification of short great circle routes.

Conical projections. In conical projections, a cone is wrapped around the globe in such a fashion that it is tangent to a given line of latitude. In its most elementary form, the peak of the cone lies on a line passing through the globe's two poles. Points on the conical surface are projected from the center of the globe. In this basic conical projection, distortion increases as distance increases from the point of tangency. For example, if the base of the cone were tangent to latitude 50°, then the most accurate part of the map would be at that latitude. As latitudes increased toward the 90° at the pole, distortion would increase.

Many modifications of this basic conical projection are in use. One of these, the Lambert conformal conic projection, chooses two lines of latitude as parallel standards. A cone is devised that passes through these two latitudes, thus cutting the globe's surface. There results a map that is accurate at two latitudes. Some

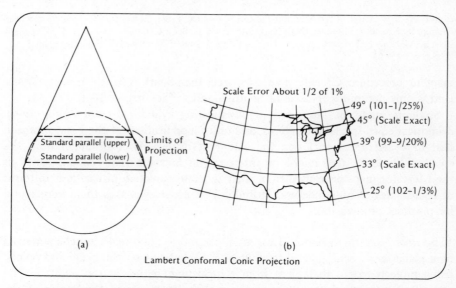

Figure 10–7. Example of the Lambert Conformal Conic Projection. (Source: From *Elementary Topography and Map Reading* by Samuel L. Greitzer (New York: McGraw-Hill Book Company, 1944), p. 45. Copyright 1944 by McGraw-Hill Book Company. Used with permission of McGraw-Hill Book Company.)

distortion exists between the two lines of latitude where the globe has been cut. But where areas are not of absolutely overwhelming size, the distortion is not excessively large. For example, in the construction of a map of the United States using such a system, error can be held to about 2 per cent or less. For an illustration of the use of the Lambert conformal conic projection, see Figure 10–7.

Sophisticated applications of conical projections called polyconic maps are frequently used for depicting north-south areas. In very simple terms, a number of conic projections are combined. These maps are very accurate along a line of longitude that is selected as the central mapping meridian. Accuracy declines as distance east and west of this central meridian increases. When a long, relatively narrow area is to be mapped, for example, Chile, this is a highly useful projection. On the other hand, it would not be a good choice to map the state of Tennessee.

A general comparison of the basic techniques of developing conical projections, tangential plane projections, and cylindrical projections is provided in Figure 10–8.

Map Legends

Map legends include special symbols that represent a kind of shorthand for identifying features depicted on the map. On political maps, frequently there will be symbols for state capitals and county seats and also some indication of the scale used in preparing the map. Other legends frequently include symbols for cities of various sizes; airports; and county, state, and national parks. Indeed, the possibilities are limited only by the imagination and inclination of the map maker. To derive maximum benefit from work with maps, students need to understand the symbol system used on the individual maps with which they are working. Time spent clarifying the meaning of these symbols generally results in enhanced students performance when learning activities require the use of maps.

Before students begin working with maps, a session with the entire class might center around discussion of the items mentioned in the legends of the maps students will be expected to use. If the maps are printed in texts, everyone can look on in his or her own book as the exercise unfolds. In other instances, a large wall-sized map that can be easily seen by all class members might be used. Still another alternative is an overhead transparency of the map(s) students will be using projected on a large screen in the front of the room. In a short lesson, the teacher can introduce students to symbols used and ask individuals to identify instances where such symbols are used on the map. ("All right, David, we know that red triangles indicate cities of over 100,000 people. How many such cities are there in Tennessee, and which are they?")

Students must understand that there is some variation in symbols used from map to map and that they should adopt the practice of immediately checking the legend to determine what each symbol represents when beginning work with a new map. They should be alerted, particularly, to watch for references on indicated

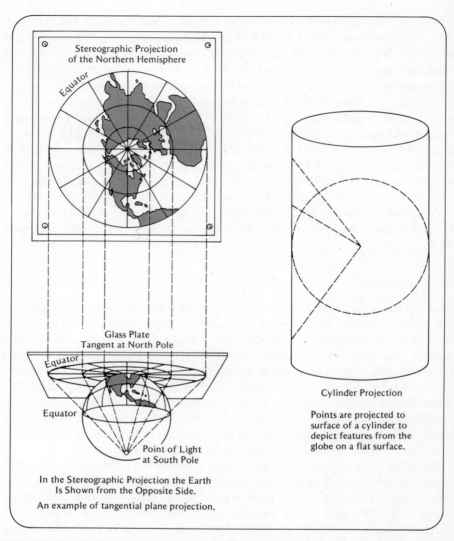

Figure 10–8. Illustrations of Projecting from a Spherical to a Flat Surface Using Cylinder Projection, Tangential Plane Projection, and Conical Projection

distance scales. On newer maps, distance scales more frequently are in terms of metric kilometers than English-system miles. A misunderstanding of this information can result in some very distorted conceptions of distances between places. (It is well to remind students that a kilometer is approximately six tenths of an English-system mile.)

Younger secondary school social studies students in middle and junior high schools often will profit greatly from exercises in which they are asked to develop

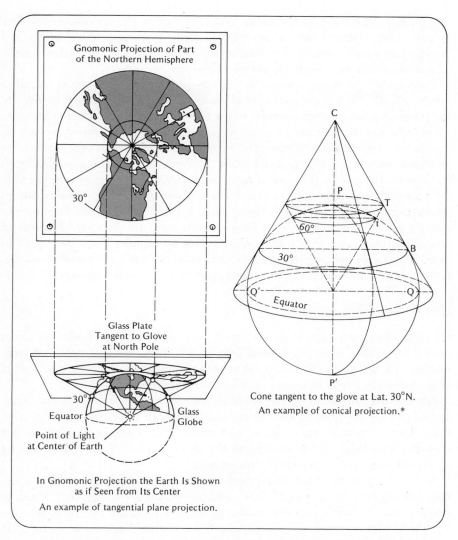

Gnomonic Projection of Part
of the Northern Hemisphere

30°

Glass Plate
Tangent to Glove
at North Pole

30°
Equator
Point of Light
at Center of Earth

Glass
Globe

In Gnomonic Projection the Earth Is Shown
as if Seen from Its Center

An example of tangential plane projection.

C

P
T
t
60°
30°
B
Q'
Equator
Q
P'

Cone tangent to the glove at Lat. 30°N.
An example of conical projection.*

Figure 10–8. cont'd. *(Source: The example of conical projection is from *Elementary Topography and Map Reading* by Samuel L. Greitzer (New York: McGraw-Hill Book Company, 1944), p. 42. Copyright 1944 by McGraw-Hill Book Company. Used with permission of McGraw-Hill Book Company.)

rudimentary maps of their own complete with a symbol system of their own devising in the legend. For example, a group of seventh graders might be asked to construct individual maps of the school grounds. They might be told its approximate dimensions and helped to determine an approximate scale that would enable them to get their maps on paper of a manageable size. As a concluding exercise, students can present their maps to the entire class and discuss the symbol system they devised. These systems can be discussed in terms of their practical utility and can open up a more general consideration of why professional map makers choose to include certain commonly encountered symbols.

The numbers of symbols found in a given map's legend can provide a rather rough indication of a map's instructional utility. Clearly, symbols ought to indicate the presence of information germane to the task students will be asked to perform. Maps with legends that are crowded with large numbers of symbols should be approached with caution. Frequently, such maps include tremendous quantities of information in a relatively small space. Students may experience difficulty in focusing on the specific dimensions necessary for success on a given learning task. As a general rule, it is wise to select less complex maps that include features related clearly to tasks students will be required to perform rather than information-dense maps. If the purpose is to help students learn the location of ranges of mountains, than maps with ranges of mountains will suffice. There is no need to cloud the issue by insisting that students deal with distracting information relating, for example, to locations of railroad lines, canal systems, and highways.

USING MAP COORDINATES

Locating places on maps is an important map skill. Many secondary students have a vague idea about the general system of latitude and longitude, but large numbers are not proficient in the use of map coordinates in locating places. Part of the difficulty results from some confusion in terminology.

For example, at different times students may have been exposed to the terms *line of latitude* and *parallel* without realizing that both were labels for the same thing. Other students may claim to understand what a *line of longitude* is but deny any knowledge of the meaning of the term *meridian*. Relationships among all these terms need to be clarified for students.

As a result perhaps of too much work with Mercator projection maps and too little with globes, many students have difficulty grasping the idea that distances between lines of longitude grow smaller as the two poles are increased, whereas lines of latitude are everywhere approximately equidistant from one another. (It is necessary to say, "Approximately" because the earth is not a perfect sphere, but rather somewhat flattened at the poles. Consequently, at the equator one degree of latitude is 68.708 statute miles, and at the poles it is 69.403 statute miles. This is a slight difference indeed, and for practical purposes it can be said that distances between two adjacent degrees of latitude are everywhere the same.) Confusion regarding lines of latitude may result because, on Mercator maps, lines of latitude are parallel and do not meet at the poles as they do on globes. Students should be provided opportunities to observe these intersecting lines on globes. Given this opportunity, they will grasp the idea that distances between lines of longitude decrease with increasing distance from the equator.

In working with students to teach them the use of map coordinates, teachers must introduce them to the system of measurement of lines of latitude and lines of longitude. With a large globe (or a good map if no globe is available), the system of measuring latitude from 0° at the equator to 90° north at the North Pole and 90° south at the South Pole can be introduced. Similarly, the concept of the prime meridian (line of 0° longitude) can be introduced along with the idea that measurements from this line extend incrementally 180° west and 180° east. Given an understanding of this basic information, students are nearly ready to begin locating places through the use of coordinates. As a final introduction, they must be introduced to the idea that degrees are each subdivided into sixty minutes (symbolically rendered by ') and that each minute is subdivided into sixty seconds (symbolically rendered by ").

Once students have this information in hand, the class and the teacher can identify a place or two on the globe or on a good map given only map coordinates. For example, the teacher might say, "All right, now let's see if we can find the place that is located at a latitude of 19° 25' 45" N and a longitude of 99° 07' 00" W." Ordinarily, it does not take students long to find Mexico City (and other places for which coordinates are provided).

A popular technique for reinforcing use of map coordinates, particularly with younger secondary school students, is the story with place names provided only in terms of map coordinates. Students are assigned to use globes or atlases to determine the names of the places referenced by the map coordinates. A very abbreviated version of this technique follows:

Directions: Read the following story. Fill in the blank with the name of the city described by the map coordinates. Use atlases on the back shelf to help you complete this task.

C. Worthington Jetsetter, the noted investment specialist, had received reports of problems in the coffee industry. Clearing his schedule for a week, he told his secretary to alert the pilot of his executive jet to prepare the craft for a long flight. At promptly 7 P.M., the jet took off bound for latitude 22° 53' 43" S and longitude 43° 13' 22" W. _____.
                                                                                a

As it developed, not much was really brewing in the coffee industry. But, C. Worthington did pick up intriguing rumors about a new gold strike thousands of miles away. Acting on a hunch, he ordered his jet to latitude 62° 28' 15" N and longitude 114° 22' 00" W _____. After securing
                                        b

several lucrative mining contracts here, C. Worthington decided a celebration was in order. Accordingly, he ordered his jet to latitude 48° 50' 14" N and longitude 2° 20' 14" E _____.
                                        c

In this city, C. Worthington learned about an opportunity to make a fortune in exotic animal skins. Ever seeking a "piece of the action," the executive jet was soon in the air bound for latitude 33° 52' 00" S and longitude 151° 12' 00" E _____. After putting together an amazing business
                        d

deal here, time had come for C. Worthington to return to headquarters to attend to his paperwork. The executive jet was boarded and soon took off for the long flight home to latitude 40° 26' 19" N and longitude 80° 00' 00" W. _____.
$$\overline{}_{e}$$

[For those who do not have an atlas handy, here is the key:]

a = Rio de Janeiro, Brazil
b = Yellowknife, Northwest Territories, Canada
c = Paris, France
d = Sidney, Australia
e = Pittsburgh, Pennsylvania, U.S.A.

SCALING: LEVELS OF MAP ABSTRACTION

Differences in scales of maps are sources of considerable difficulty for many secondary students. These relate both to problems associated with understanding the meanings of distance scales and with the more general problem of comprehending the relationship between a change of scale and the nature of the detail that can be mapped.

Unless students understand clearly the relationship between the distance scale indicated in the map legend and what is depicted, they may derive a very erroneous impression from their study of a map. For example, one very popular American atlas features very large maps of individual states. An entire page of space is devoted to each state. This means that Texas and, for example, Michigan occupy about the same amount of page space. Obviously, if one considers size differences of the two states, distance scales of the two maps are very different. In fact, on the Texas map, one inch is equivalent to about sixty statute miles. On the Michigan map, one inch is equivalent to only about thirty statute miles. Someone unfamiliar with these scaling differences might well get the impression that, because the size of the two printed pages are identical, Texas and Michigan occupy about the same area.

Clearly, given the example of Texas and Michigan, relatively few students would probably make this error. But what if less familiar territory were involved, perhaps Portugal and New Zealand? Without attention to scaling differences, mistaken impressions of relative areas of mapped territories may well result.

A more vexing problem for social studies teachers has to do with teaching students how scaling affects depiction of detail on maps. Some terminology that students (many of them at least) find confusing contributes to the difficulty. Cartographers refer to maps covering relatively small areas as *large scale* (for example, one unit on the map may equal 25,000 units on the ground). Similarly, they use the term *small scale* (for example, one unit on the map may equal 250,000 units on the ground) in describing maps covering large territorial expanses. Many students confuse the terms. Their logic is simply that *large scale* ought to go together with *large* places and *small scale* ought to go together with *small* places. Any discussion with students about scaling in which reference to *large-scale* maps and *small-scale* maps is to be made should be preceded by some teacher questions designed to ferret out any misconceptions regarding these basic terms.

In helping students understand the implications of covering increasing geographic territory through the use of small scales on coverage of details on the earth's surface, Boardman (1976) suggests the introduction of a systematic set of experiences for students. In essence, he proposes that, in learning to develop a sophisticated understanding of maps and their limitations, students first be presented with photographic representations of a very limited geographic extent. Next he proposes that high altitude photography of the same area be made available to students. Discussions at this point can center on the loss of detail in the high altitude as compared to the close-range photography.

The next step is to present students with local road and terrain maps depicting the same approximate area as included in the high altitude photography. Discussions can center on the loss of information and the added difficulty of intuiting details from symbolic rather than photographic notation.

The next steps involve the systematic introduction of new maps, each at a successively smaller scale and covering more and more territory. At each step, discussions can again center on the kinds of details that must be sacrificed in order to gain the additional territorial coverage.

Obtaining photographic maps of various points for such an exercise is not so difficult as might be supposed. The U.S. Geological Survey's EROS Data Center has available for purchase National Aeronautics and Space Administration photos of large numbers of U.S. points taken at altitudes ranging from about 50,000 to 65,000 feet. From the same source, photographs may be ordered taken by the Skylab spacecraft at an altitude of 270 miles. (For details and pricing information, write to EROS Data Center, U.S. Geological Survey, Sioux Falls, SD 47198.)

These photographs can be combined with maps from local chambers of commerce, state highway departments, and atlases to provide learners with lessons detailing the impact of systematically decreasing distance scales. Such a set of lessons can contribute greatly to students' understanding the limitations that must follow any decision to cover vast areas with small-scale maps.

KINDS OF MAPS

Secondary students tend to be most familiar with maps including political divisions and major highways. Though these maps are very important, many other kinds of maps are available that convey different kinds of information. Probably the largest major category of maps that do not have as a primary purpose depiction of political divisions is the topographic map. Topographic maps portray a limited area of land in such a way that physical features are depicted in such a fashion that scale and linear distance relationships among features are preserved. An important variety of the topographic map is the "contour map."

The contour map is concerned primarily with the depiction of elevations. This is accomplished by connecting points of equal elevation with lines. Each contour line, then, represents a given elevation. The map maker selects a common interval of distance between contour lines. Frequently five feet or ten feet are selected. For example, if a ten-foot interval were selected, then one contour line would connect elevations of 120 feet, and the next line would connect elevations of 130 feet (other lines would connect points of less than 120 feet at ten-foot intervals, that is at 110, 100, 90, 80, 70, 60, 50, 40, 30, 20, and 10 feet). On contour maps, each line contained by another contour line represents an elevation higher than the contour line within which it is contained. Actual elevations represented by individual contour lines are printed somewhere on the line to aid interpretation. By reference to this system of contour lines, a good idea of the nature of the terrain can be inferred.

Students need to be introduced to the concept that each contour line represents a change of elevation at an interval selected by the map maker. Further, they need to be cued to watch for changes in space between contour lines. When the contour lines are far apart, a very gradual change in elevation is signaled.

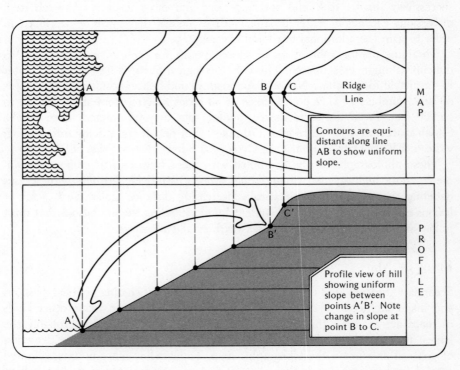

Figure 10–9. Relationship of Distances Between Contour Lines and Changes in Slope. (Source: From *A Workbook in Essentials of Map Reading and Interpretation*, 2d ed., by Robert E. Cramer (Berkeley, California: McCutchan Publishing Corporation, 1969), p. 101. Copyright 1969 by Robert E. Cramer. Reprinted by permission of the publisher.)

When contour lines are closely spaced, elevation is changing rapidly. An illustration of these relationships is included in Figure 10–9.

Other kinds of maps depict such things as distributional patterns of agriculture and industry, others indicate location of minerals, and still others reflect migration patterns of wildlife. In short, the range of maps is nearly as broad as the human imagination. Students deserve the opportunity to be exposed to a wide variety of maps in their social studies classes as they grow in their appreciation for the sophisticated representations of reality of the well-constructed map. Several additional, particularly unusual examples of mapping will be included in the chapter on teaching geography.

Summary

One of the objectives of social studies instruction is developing students' sophistication in reading and interpreting graphically presented data. With respect to graphs and charts, a number of common practices result in distortion of information. A common feature of many of these efforts is "stretching" scaling to make small changes appear to be large changes. Properly constructed charts and graphs give visual impressions that are congruent with the data upon which they are based.

Many secondary school students are deficient in terms of their map and globe skills. Many have been exposed to poorly drawn maps that have left a legacy of distorted conceptions of size relationships of different world areas and of spatial arrangements of different places on the earth's surface. Few students have a good understanding of various techniques for projecting a spherical surface (the globe) onto a plane to create a flat map. Cylindrical projections, tangential plane projections, and conical projections have characteristics that students need to understand in interpreting the accuracy of what they see on a map.

An additional problem for students with maps has to do with the question of scaling. Many students experience difficulty in visualizing differences in "reality" implied by two maps with different distance scales. Further, the "decay" of detail associated with small-scale maps is not appreciated by many students.

Difficulties students experience with learning from graphic representations of information merit systematic instructional attention. Because of reasons associated with chronological development, it is unreasonable to expect large numbers of secondary students to have good visual literacy skills when they begin their secondary school years. This fact, taken along with the social studies profession's traditional commitment to improving students' competency in this area, suggests the necessity for committing instructional time to lessons designed to help students become more sophisticated consumers of information presented in graphic form.

REFERENCES

BOARDMAN, DAVID J. "Graphicacy in the Curriculum." *Educational Review* (February 1976): 118–125.

CHAMBERLIN, WELLMAN. *The Round Earth on Flat Paper.* Washington, D.C.: The National Geographic Society, 1947.

CRAMER, ROBERT E. *A Workbook in Essentials of Map Reading and Interpretation.* 2d ed. Berkeley, California: McCutchan Publishing Corporation, 1969.

FRASER, DOROTHY M., and EUNICE JOHNS. "Developing a Program for the Effective Learning of Skills." In *Skill Development in Social Studies.* Edited by Helen McCracken Carpenter. 33d Yearbook of the National Council for the Social Studies. Washington, D.C.: National Council for the Social Studies, 1963.

GREITZER, SAMUEL L. *Elementary Topography and Map Reading.* New York: McGraw-Hill Book Company, Inc., 1944.

HUFF, DARRELL. *How to Lie with Statistics.* New York: W. W. Norton Company, 1954.

PIAGET, JEAN, and BARBELL INHELDER. *The Child's Conception of Space.* Translated by F. J. Langdon and J. L. Lunzer. London: Routledge and Kegan Paul, 1956.

TOWLER, JOHN O., and L. D. NELSON. "The Elementary School Child's Concept of Scale." *Journal of Geography* (January 1968): 24–28.

U.S. DEPARTMENT OF COMMERCE, BUREAU OF THE CENSUS. *Historical Statistics of the United States: Colonial Times to 1970.* Washington, D.C.: Bureau of the Census, 1975.

U.S. DEPARTMENT OF LABOR, BUREAU OF LABOR STATISTICS. *Monthly Labor Review* (September 1977).

Teaching Strategies

Chapter 11

INQUIRY AND THE
SOCIAL STUDIES

IN RECENT YEARS, "inquiry" has generated a great deal of discussion among social studies teachers. Professional journals in social studies education have dealt with the topic at great length. Few professional meetings have failed to feature a presentation or two on inquiry-oriented approaches. An increasing supply of materials for inquiry-based instructional programs has been made available by educational publishing houses.

All of this interest has resulted in the term *inquiry*'s being used in a variety of ways. Indeed, some of the definitions that have been suggested are mutually incompatible. For all of the confusion, some general threads of consensus do run through attempts to describe the term. There is broad agreement that inquiry-oriented instruction introduces content to students through an *inductive* process. Inductive learning proceeds from the specific to the general. For example, if the objective were to teach the concept "automobile," the teacher might provide students with photographs of automobiles, lead them through a series of questions designed to help them identify features common to all of the photographs, and urge them to develop their own description of the concept "automobile" complete with all the necessary defining characteristics.

Inductive learning contrasts with *deductive* learning, which proceeds from the general to the specific. For example, using a deductive approach to teach the concept "automobile," the teacher might begin by providing students with a complete definition of the term. Next understanding might be enriched by discussions focusing on photographs of automobiles. The aim of these discussions would be to highlight characteristics of the new concept, "automobile."

Though interest in inductive or inquiry teaching has blossomed in recent years, the approach has a long history in American education. As early as 1910, John Dewey suggested a sequence for a "complete act of thought" that included nearly all of the steps found in most modern suggestions for sequencing inquiry instruction (Dewey, 1910). With some variation, the following steps generally are followed in teaching a lesson according to an inquiry approach:

Step 1: Identify and describe the essential dimensions of a "problem."
Step 2: Suggest possible solutions to the problem or explanations of the problem.
Step 3: Gather evidence related to these solutions or explanations.
Step 4: Evaluate possible solutions or explanations of the problem in the light of evidence.
Step 5: Formulate a conclusion that is best supported by the evidence.

These steps highlight the basic objective of the inquiry approach. Specifically, the approach seeks to help students develop the sort of rational thinking abilities that will serve them well throughout their adult lives. The approach seeks to help students focus on issues, identify and evaluate evidence, and develop supportable conclusions. The key point with respect to the purposes of inquiry-oriented instruction is that the focus is on teaching students a thinking *process*.

Certainly, new *content* is conveyed during inquiry-based instruction, but interest in having students master the specifics of this content is secondary to the interest in having them internalize the *process* of making rational decisions.

Considerations for the Teacher in Planning for Inquiry

In the planning of a lessons or sequence of lessons organized according to an inquiry approach, careful consideration must be given to each step of the process. Careful attention to planning from the introduction of the problem to the culminating session in which students formulate conclusions lays the foundation for a productive learning experience for students.

TASKS FOR STEP 1 ("THE PROBLEM")

Selection of the problem is a very important consideration. Certainly, student motivation will be greater if the issue selected as a focus has some personal meaning. Of course, selection of the problem should not depend only on present interests and enthusiasms of students. But when it is possible to make a connection between students' interests and course contents in selecting the problem, students' initial reactions to the process will likely be more positive than when such a connection cannot be made. For example, in the choice of a problem relating to the evolution over time of common law precedents, a problem focusing on the changing legal status of students in schools with respect to their First Amendment rights is almost certain to be more appealing than a problem focusing on changing interpretations of the Commerce Clause in the nineteenth century.

Once a problem has been selected, a method of introducing it to the students must be devised. In some instances, the problem might simply be described. In others, students might be provided some raw data and, with the help of some focusing questions by the teacher, identify the problem during a class discussion. In other situations, videotapes, audiotapes, short prose selections, photographs with captions, role-playing students, and other options might be appropriate as vehicles for helping students grasp the essentials of the problem. It is essential that the problem itself be clearly understood by students. Lacking such understanding, they will not benefit from the remainder of the exercise.

TASKS FOR STEP 2 ("POSSIBLE SOLUTIONS")

During the Step 2 phase of the inquiry process, students will be asked to suggest possible solutions to the problem or explanations of the problem. Decisions need to be made regarding how students will respond and, even more importantly, how information will be recorded. Some teachers will opt for a simple classroom discussion technique, using a chalkboard to record student suggestions. Others prefer to organize students in groups to consider the problem and possible solutions. (When this approach is used, it is a good idea to regroup as a class to share "solutions" and "explanations" that have been developed.) As a recording device, some teachers prefer to use large sheets of butcher paper and felt marking pens to write down the "solutions" and "explanations." Still others favor writing these responses on clear acetate sheets and displaying them with an overhead projector. The method will vary according to teacher and student preferences, but clearly some planning must be done before the inquiry lesson begins.

Because there is an interest in getting a good many "solutions" and "explanations" put forward during this phase of the exercise, the teacher must guard against bringing the class to premature concensus. Preplanning in regard to this issue does not involve decisions relating to a choice of certain sorts of physical items (chalkboard versus butcher paper, for example) so much as it involves a simple self-admonition to "let the ideas flow." During the discussion, the teacher must be as nonjudgmental as possible when students suggest possible "solutions" and "explanations." This sort of teacher "openness" is essential if students are to feel free to make a contribution. The inquiry experience, particularly initially, probably will be somewhat threatening to some students. They find themselves in the unfamiliar role of producing information rather than simply recalling it from the security of a text. They need a good deal of teacher support as they grow toward a greater familiarity with the inquiry process.

TASKS FOR STEP 3 ("GATHERING EVIDENCE")

To maintain its momentum, the inquiry experience requires that evidence relating to the problem be available for students to use. Indeed, some evidence must be presented along with the introduction of the problem itself. Recall that the problem "must be clearly understood" by students as a preface to the remaining steps in the exercise. If a problem is introduced without some relevant accompanying information, students will not "clearly understand" the problem. Further, a discouragingly high number of the "solutions" and "explanations" they suggest during Step 2 may prove to be unsupportable when they do a broader survey of the supportive evidence during Step 3. Consequently, it is essential that the teacher identify sources of information that will be relevant to the selected problem.

It is absolutely insufficient to suggest to a group of students that they "go to the library and try to find something related to our possible 'solutions' and 'explanations.'" Students need guidance of a much more specific nature. If the library is to be used, students should be directed to some specific books and periodicals. Better yet, such materials might be brought into the classroom itself and made available for students to use. If such arrangements can be made, the teacher will need to plan some remarks directing students to certain titles and pages.

Of course, not all evidence will be found in printed materials. Indeed, for some problems, such materials may provide students with almost no relevant information. When other sources are needed, the teacher needs to plan for field experiences, film and filmstrip presentations, audiotapes, guest speakers, and other data sources that students might use in gathering information relevant to the problem.

In addition, some attention during the planning phase needs to be given to providing students with insights regarding qualitative differences among sources. If they have not already been exposed to such information, they need to be told differences among primary, secondary, and tertiary sources of information. They must recognize limitations of "eyewitness" accounts. They need to know something about the nature of the audiences various writers were addressing and how their remarks might have been shaped as a consequence. In short, the teacher must plan to give students some means for weighing the importance of evidence from source A as opposed to perhaps contradictory evidence from source B.

Tasks for Step 4 ("Evaluating Solutions")

During Step 4 of the exercise, students test the accuracy of the solutions or explanations they developed in Step 2. When the problem is clearly described and introduced with sufficient accompanying information, students ordinarily generate quite a number of solutions and explanations that prove to be supported after the extensive review of evidence that occurs in Step 3. Many students profit enormously from this experience. Finding they can suggest reasonably accurate explanations even given relatively little information, students grow in terms of their confidence in their abilities to make rational interpretations of unfamiliar events.

Preparation for Step 4 involves primarily decisions relating to (1) how student evidence will be presented and recorded and (2) what sorts of questions will be asked of students regarding how different pieces of evidence have been weighted. Some teachers find it convenient to deal with each solution or explanation suggested in Step 2 one at a time. One technique for doing this involves writing the solution or explanation on the chalkboard, on butcher paper, or on a transparency. Underneath the solution or explanation three columns are drawn. One of these is labeled *evidence supporting*, one is labeled *evidence opposing*, and one is labeled *evidence neutral*. If this scheme is used, a chalkboard might look something like the drawing in Figure 11–1.

During the discussion, the teacher or a student would write evidence relating to each solution or explanation under the appropriate category. When all evidence is in, then the class can decide whether to reject or accept the given explanation or solution. As this process goes forward, the teacher must be prepared to challenge students' interpretations of the worth of various items of evidence.

Explanation: The decrease in numbers of blacks lynched between 1890 and 1910 resulted because of the increased hostility toward foreign-born whites that took the place of hostility toward blacks.

Evidence Supporting	Evidence Not Supporting	Evidence Neutral
1. 1910—Foreign-born = 13.5 million; 1890—Foreign-born = 9.2 million.	1. 1910—27.3 per cent of all blacks in urban areas; 1890—19.4 per cent of all blacks in urban areas.	1. 1910—67 blacks lynched; 1890—107 blacks lynched.
2. 1910—45 per cent of all foreign-born in cities; 1890—32.9 per cent of all foreign-forn in cities.		
3. 1910—210 editorials about dangers of f.b. in city papers; 1890—91 editorials about dangers of f.b. in city newspapers.		

Figure 11–1. Example of a Format for Evaluating Suggested Solutions to a Problem During Step 4 of an Inquiry Exercise

TASKS FOR STEP 5 ("FORMULATING A CONCLUSION")

During final step, Step 5, students are encouraged to consider all available evidence and arrive at conclusions. Students should be encouraged to identify solutions and explanations that can best be justified by reference to available evidence. In helping students arrive at their conclusion, teachers must plan to provide students with guidelines for accomplishing the following tasks:

1. Categorizing information they have uncovered.
2. Evaluating the reliability of sources of information.

3. Interpreting and analyzing information.
4. Formulating conclusions supported by the "best" available information.

Much of this information may have been explained to students during previous phases of the inquiry exercise. But as the exercise winds down toward a conclusion in Step 5, techniques and procedures for dealing with information that has been gathered must be reemphasized.

Some teachers find that a good beginning to Step 5 involves encouraging students to place information they have gathered in categories. A scheme such as that suggested in Figure 11–1 might work well. Certainly, there are other possibilities that would be equally well suited to this task. When information relevant to a given point or issue is clustered together, students can begin to make some initial judgments regarding the amount of evidence uncovered with respect to given points. Further, the task of judging the quality of evidence is easier when evidence relating to common points or issues is presented in one place. In planning for Step 5, one should note that not all of the gathered evidence will be considered. It is quite possible that some evidence may have been eliminated from further consideration during Step 4. During Step 5, evaluation of evidence seeks not just to separate the "reliable evidence" from the "unreliable" (as in Step 4), but rather to identify the "best" of the reliable evidence.

In preparing to help students identify this "best" evidence, the teacher might prepare some focus questions in advance to prompt students to weigh presented evidence carefully. Questions such as the following might be considered:

1. What are the qualifications of the individual to whom you talked regarding this topic? (Assumes evidence gathered from an interview.)
2. What is the standing of this writer? Is he or she a professional historian? What else has he or she written? What do reviewers say?
3. This evidence comes from a personal diary. How close to the situation was the writer? Was the writer aware of the "big picture"? What other information is in the diary that might say something about the writer's observational abilities? How safe are we in generalizing from this material?
4. Was this newspaper article written on the basis of first-hand information? How do you know? Does the article have a reporter's by-line? If so, what is his or her professional standing? Does he or she have a well-known political point of view? How might this affect what has been written.
5. How were these statistics compiled? How accurate are they? What is the general reputation of the compiler?
   And so on.

Many teachers also find it productive to prepare some key questions in advance to be used in helping students interpret and analyze information that has been gathered. Some general questions of this type follow:

1. How do you explain the inconsistency between these statistics here and those statistics on the other board?
2. Why would the account of the wagonmaster (taken from his diary) be so different from that of Mary Larsen's diary?

3. What sense can you make of the rise in the numbers of blacks lynched between 1890 and 1900 and the fall in the numbers of blacks lynched between 1900 and 1910?
4. Why do you think the senator from Virginia was so opposed to opening up new lands in the Southwest?
5. What kinds of comparisons and contrasts can you make between the motivations of those opposing the issue and those favoring it? How would you explain these similarities and differences?
   And so on.

In preparing for the capstone exercise of the inquiry experience, some teachers like to write out a few focus questions. The intent of these questions is to keep students from coming to consensus too quickly. They are designed to push students to reconsider all of the important evidence. Some examples follow:

1. Tell me what evidence supports your conclusion. How do we know that evidence is reliable? Could that same evidence lead to any other conclusion?
2. What other interpretations are possible? How do you assess the evidence supporting those conclusions?
3. How do we know the evidence we have gathered is adequate? What other kinds of evidence might be useful? Where might we find it, and how might we proceed?
4. Are we failing to consider anything? Look again at the evidence? Now, do we want to make any changes?
5. How could we check further on the adequacy of our conclusion?
   And so on.

In working with a class during Step 5, the teacher must guard against students' tendency to conclude that their solutions or explanations are definitive. Even when large quantities of evidence are considered, *all* of the relevant information is never available. In addition to the issue of "gaps" in the evidence, students must be reminded that judgment has played a role in assessing the merit of the evidence that was available. Finally, they need to be reminded that new knowledge may add perspectives on the problem that may undermine the adequacy of their conclusions.

Certainly, students should be praised for their abilities to identify solutions and explanations that seem sound in the light of available evidence. But the point must be made that these answers are, at best, tentative approximations of "truth." An important lesson of inquiry is that there are no "final answers." Inquiry teaches a process that goes forward in the understanding that "truth" is something to be pursued rather than something to be found.

Teaching for Inquiry: An Abbreviated Example

In the following example, teacher and student comments for Steps 1 and 2 in an inquiry lesson will be included. More abbreviated comments will be provided for Steps 3, 4, and 5. Notice how the teacher emphasizes the problem and checks for student understanding of the problem. Notice, too, how the teacher tries to be nonjudgmental in accepting students' comments.

Step 1 ("The Problem")

As an opener, the teacher writes the information in Figure 11–2 on the chalkboard large enough for all students to see it easily.

Teacher: I would like you to look carefully at these statistics I've written on the board. They suggest a problem we are going to be looking at. Tell me what you see?
[Students begin to respond.]

Joanna: Well, in each of those years, more blacks than whites were lynched.

Teacher: Fine, Joanna. Now what else? Tim.

Tim: There were a few more total people lynched in 1900 than in 1890, but then, when you look at 1910, the number drops way down to seventy-six.

	Blacks	Whites	Total
1910	67	9	76
1900	106	9	115
1890	96	11	107

Figure 11–2. Numbers of Individuals Lynched by Race in 1890, 1900, and 1910. (Source: Adapted from U.S. Bureau of the Census, *Historical Statistics of the United States, Colonial Times to 1970,* Bicentennial Ed., Part I (Washington, D.C.: 1975), p. 422.)

Teacher: Are you saying that there was a more important change in the number of lynchings between 1900 and 1910 than between 1890 and 1900?

Tim: Well, I think so. From 1890 to 1900 there's only a difference of eight lynchings. But from 1900 to 1910 there is a difference of thirty-nine. That's almost five times as many.
[More exchanges between teacher and students follow.]

Teacher: From what we have said, we seem to have something of an unusual situation here. Who can tell me exactly what is puzzling about the information we have been working with? Nancy.

Nancy: Well, there seems to have been a change in the trend.

Teacher: What trend, Nancy? Go ahead and explain that a little more completely.

Nancy: Well, from 1890 to 1900 more blacks seem to have been lynched, but from 1900 to 1910 many fewer were lynched. Something must have happened. I mean, why would more be lynched in 1900 and 1890 and many fewer just ten years later.

Teacher: That's a bit of a problem, isn't it? We don't have enough information yet, but let's start thinking about the general question. Before we pursue it, though, let's be sure everybody knows what we are after. Burt, could you restate the problem or question we're looking at, and I'll write it here on the board.

Burt: Well, there seem to have been a lot more blacks lynched in 1890 and 1900 than in 1910, and we want to know why.

Teacher: All right, Burt, that's a good summary. Let me just write something on the board.
[On the chalkboard, the teacher writes: "In 1890 and 1900 more blacks were lynched than in 1910. Were there changes in conditions that could explain why there was such a reduction in lynching of blacks by 1910? If so, what were those changes?"]

Teacher: We'll leave this statement of the problem on the board as we continue our work.

Step 2 ("Possible Solutions")

Teacher: Now that we've identified our problem, let's think of some possible explanations. I am going to give each of you information that might be helpful as you begin thinking about your explanations. Look at all of the information first; then jot down some of your ideas on some scratch paper. Then we'll have a discussion and share some of our ideas.
(The teacher passes out to students duplicated copies of information presented here in Figures 11–3, 11–4, 11–5, 11–6, 11–7, and 11–8.)

Teacher: You've had a chance now to look over quite a little information. What might you suggest as some possible explanations for this rather puzzling situation we have noted here on the board? Who wants to begin? Ron.

Ron: Well, I'm not sure how relevant this is, but in all three years, 1890, 1900, and 1910, a lot more blacks lived outside of urban areas than whites.

Teacher: That's an interesting point, Ron. And what do you make of this difference?

	Blacks	Whites and Others	All Races
1910	27.3%	48.6%	46.3%
1900	22.4%	41.3%	39.1%
1890	19.4%	36.9%	34.8%

Figure 11–3. Percentages of Total Black Population and Total White and Other Races Population Resident in Urban Areas in 1890, 1900, and 1910. (Source: Adapted from U.S. Bureau of the Census, *Historical Statistics of the United States, Colonial Times to 1970,* Bicentennial Ed., Part I (Washington, D.C.: 1975), p. 12.)

Ron: This may be a bit shaky. We don't have much to go on here. But it seems to me the fact that more blacks than whites were lynched in all three years might have to do with their living in rural areas. I mean there might have been less police protection there.

Teacher: A good observation, Ron. I wonder, though, how you might tie in this point to the reduction in the number of blacks lynched in 1910?

Ron: Well, even though most blacks lived outside of urban areas even in 1910, there were a lot more living in cities in 1910 than h lived there in 1900 and 1890. Maybe these urban blacks had bette

	Blacks and Other Non-White Races	Native-born Whites	Foreign-born Whites
1890	56.8%	6.2%	13.1%
1900	44.5%	4.6%	12.9%
1910	30.7%	3.0%	12.7%

Figure 11–4. Percentage Illiterate in 1890, 1900, and 1910. (Source: Adapted from U.S. Bureau of the Census, *Historical Statistics of the United States, Colonial Times to 1970*, Bicentennial Ed., Part I (Washington, D.C.: 1975), p. 382.)

	Blacks and Other Non-Whites	Whites	Total
1910	44.8%	61.3%	59.2%
1900	31.1%	53.6%	50.5%
1890	32.9%	57.9%	54.3%

Figure 11–5. Percentage of School-aged Population by Race. (Source: Adapted from U.S. Bureau of the Census, *Historical Statistics of the United States, Colonial Times to 1970*, Bicentennial Ed., Part I (Washington, D.C.: 1975), p. 370.)

1910	13,515,886
1900	10,341,276
1890	9,249,547

Figure 11–6. Total Foreign-Born Population in 1890, 1900, and 1910. (Source: Adapted from U.S. Bureau of the Census, *Historical Statistics of the United States, Colonial Times to 1970*, Bicentennial Ed., Part I (Washington, D.C.: 1975), p. 14.)

police protection. That might account for the decrease in the number of lynchings.

Teacher: That is an interesting explanation. We'll want to check it out further a little later. All right, now how about some other possible explanations. Rachel.

Rachel: I was interested in the changes relating to education from 1890 to 1900 and then again from 1900 to 1910. It looks as if not much was done to improve educational opportunities for blacks between 1890 and 1900. The chart we received showed that there was even a drop in the percentage of black children in school in 1900 as compared to 1890. On the other hand, there was a big increase in this percentage by 1910. I think this might have had something to do with the lynching question.

Teacher: Good observations, Rachel. How, specifically, is this information possibly tied into the lynching issue?

Rachel: Two things. On the one hand, more blacks were educated by 1910. They might have been better able to put pressure on the government to stop lynching. Another thing is that the increased number of blacks in school might have meant an increasing tendency of whites to see blacks as legitimate human beings. If this were true, they might have been less inclined to lynch them than they had been ten and twenty years earlier.

Teacher: Certainly, those are possible explanations. We will want to follow up on them later.

1910	9,827,763
1900	8,833,994
1890	7,488,676

Figure 11–7. Total Number of Black Americans in 1890, 1900, and 1910. (Source: Adapted from U.S. Bureau of the Census, *Historical Statistics of the United States, Colonial Times to 1970*, Bicentennial Ed., Part I (Washington, D.C.: 1975), p. 14.)

	Percentage Increases in Black Population	Percentage Increases in White Population
1900 to 1910	up 11.25%	up 22.33%
1890 to 1900	up 17.96%	up 21.25%

Figure 11–8. Percentage Increases in Black and White Population Between 1900 and 1910 and Between 1890 and 1900. (Source: Adapted from U.S. Bureau of the Census, *Historical Statistics of the United States, Colonial Times to 1970*, Bicentennial Ed., Part I (Washington, D.C.: 1975), p. 14.)

Rachel: I'm a little uncomfortable about going out on a limb with so little to go on.

Teacher: Well, we all make judgments on the basis of incomplete information. In fact, we never have *all* the information. What we have to do is work with what we have and then try to learn more about the situation. We may later want to revise our decision, but sometimes we simply have to act on what is available at the moment. If you think your conclusions make sound logical sense given the limited information you had to work with, you've done as much as can be expected. All right?

Rachel: All right, but I'm still a bit uncomfortable.

Teacher: Carry, what would you like to suggest to us?

Carry: I'm intrigued by the differences in the percentage increases of the black population and the white population between 1890 and 1900 and 1900 and 1910. From 1890 to 1910 there wasn't much difference in the percentage increase of blacks and whites. But from 1900 to 1910 the white population increased almost twice as fast as the black population.

Teacher: A careful observation, Carry. Now, how do you tie this information to the question of lynching?

Carry: Well, I think because the increase in the white population from 1900 to 1910 was so much greater than that of the black population, the whites felt less threatened by the blacks. In a sense, you might say the blacks were getting lost in a sea of white faces.

Teacher: As I understand your point, you're saying the increase of the white population between 1900 and 1910 was so much greater than the increase of the black population that whites saw blacks as less of a "problem." Consequently, there were fewer lynchings in 1910 than in 1900.

Carry: That pretty well sums up my conclusion.

Teacher: We'll want to check that idea against some additional information later. Kevin, you've another point?

Kevin: I think we've been overlooking the issue of the foreign-born.

Teacher: All right, what do you think the foreign-born had to do with the question of lynching?

Kevin: Well, maybe quite a bit. I mean look at the increase in the number of foreign-born and the number of blacks between 1890 and 1900. Both groups up by a little more than a million, right. But then look what happened between 1900 and 1910. The number of foreign-born increased by more than three million. But there wasn't even a one million increase in the black population.

Teacher: Your figures seem to check out on our charts. But what is the connection to lynching?

Kevin: Well, I'm thinking lynching happens when a majority is very unhappy with a minority. Given this idea, isn't it possible that the native white majority by 1910 had become more fed up with foreign-born citizens than with blacks? Maybe the reduction in lynching of blacks resulted because many unhappy whites began to hate the foreign-born more than blacks.

Teacher: That certainly is a possibility we'll want to look at further.
[A few more comments ensue.]

Teacher: Now let me recall the explanations we've suggested. I'll write them on the side board. We'll keep them up as we continue working with this problem.
[Teacher writes the following suggestions on the chalkboard.]

1. A higher percentage of blacks lived in urban areas in 1910 than in 1900 and 1890. Because urban blacks may have had better police protection, this might account for the reduction in the number of blacks lynched in 1910.

2. Blacks in 1910 were better educated than in 1900 or 1890. Consequently, they were able to pressure governmental authorities to stop the practice of lynching.

3. Blacks in 1910 were better educated than in 1900 or 1890. This meant the entire community, whites included, was paying more money to educate blacks than was true in 1900 or 1890. From this, it can be concluded that a fundamental change of attitude toward blacks had occurred. Blacks in 1910 may have been regarded as more legitimate human beings by the white community than had been the case in 1900 or 1890.

4. Because the white population increased in size much faster than the black population between 1900 and 1910, the reduction in black lynchings in 1910 may have resulted because blacks were seen as a less threatening and less important minority.

5. With the great increase in the numbers of foreign-born between 1900 and 1910, many native-born whites may have transferred their hostility from blacks to foreign-born whites. This situation may have resulted in the reduction of the number of blacks lynched in 1910.

Teacher: Now we are going to see how good we have been in identifying explanations for the decline in the number of lynchings of blacks by 1910. I am going to divide the thirty of you into five teams of six students each. Each team will try to find additional information related to one of our five explanations. (Also, as you do your work, keep alert for information that might suggest other explanations that we failed to mention.)
I have some materials from the library—books, magazines, and pamphlets that you'll want to look at. Also, I have a list of several other teachers in the building who are good social historians whom you might wish to interview. On Friday, Mr. Smith of the Urban League will be here. You might ask him some questions. Don't be afraid to ask him about names of other people who might have something to say that might be useful. Finally, there is a television special Thursday night at 8 o'clock on Channel 6 about Black America at the turn of the century. You may be able to pick up some good information there. Of course, there are some other sources that would be just as good as those I've mentioned. If you've some other ideas, check with me.
As you gather information, take some notes. Organize your notes

so that you have three sets of information. One set will include all the evidence you find that "supports" your explanation. One set will include all the evidence you find that "does not support" your explanation. One set will include all the evidence that is "neutral" with regard to your explanation. Use either note cards or sheets of notebook paper. I will collect your notes next Monday; so keep them in a decent condition.

Names of students in each group and group coordinators are named on these sheets. I want each group to begin with a twenty-minute organizational meeting. Decide how to divide the work. Plan on being ready to present your information to the group on Tuesday. After I pass out the sheets with the group members named, move into your groups and begin planning. I'll handle any individual planning at this time.

[Teacher passes out group assignments, groups organize, teacher answers individual questions, and gathering of additional evidence begins.]

Step 3 ("Gathering Evidence")

In working with each group, the teacher reemphasizes points made in earlier lessons regarding weighing and evaluating the quality of evidence. Students are urged to consider not only what is said, but who says it and where it is said as well. There is an emphasis on helping students develop a feeling for the credibility of sources.

In general, the teacher serves as a resource person during this phase. The teacher might answer student's questions, suggest places they might look for further information, and ask individual students why they have decided to classify certain information as "supportive" of, "nonsupportive" of, or "neutral" with regard to a given explanation or solution.

Step 4 ("Evaluating Solutions")

Once evidence is in hand, the teacher begins by providing students with some specific instructions.

Teacher: I believe we have all finished gathering our evidence. I know I see a lot of note cards with writing. Incidentally, I appreciated the fine questions you asked Mr. Smith when he was here. I think he provided us with some good material.

Now what we need to do is get all of this information organized. Let's do it this way. I have some large sheets of butcher paper here. Let's have each group take one sheet. Someone from each group pick up one of these felt pens. On your sheet of butcher paper, write the possible solution you were investigating across the top. Then divide the sheet into three sections. In one of these, write in all of the evidence that *supports* the solution. In one write in all of the evidence that *does not support* the solution. And in the last section write in the evidence that is basically *neutral.*

[Students complete this task. This results in five pieces of butcher paper containing supporting, nonsupporting, and neutral evidence for each of the five proposed solutions that were investigated.]

Teacher: Let's deal with our proposed solutions one at a time. Let's start with the idea that reduction in lynching resulted because a larger percentage of blacks lived in cities in 1910 than in 1900 or 1890. Nancy's group looked into this possible solution or explanation to our problem. Will someone from that group tack the butcher paper on the board so we can see it?

[A student from this group places the butcher paper across a wall at the front of the room. The teacher leads a discussion focusing on the quality of evidence that has been gathered. Some sample teacher questions follow.]

Teacher: How reliable is this source? What is your reason for making this judgment?

Which pieces of evidence seem to be drawn from the most reliable sources? Do these pieces of evidence generally "support" or "not support" the proposed explanation? Or are they "neutral?"

Are there any pieces of evidence here that are so weak that they should not be considered? Why or why not?

And so on.

[This same procedure is followed until all groups have displayed their butcher paper and a discussion has ensued.]

Teacher: All right, now let's take a look at all of our evidence. Let's consider first of all the evidence that seems to have come from the most reliable sources. Let's gather it all together in a category we'll call "highly reliable."

Then let's look at some other evidence, not quite so reliable as that in our first category, but still reasonably sound. Let's place all of that evidence together in a category we'll call "generally reliable." For now, let's eliminate evidence from further consideration that we have decided to be "not reliable" during our discussion.

I would like Bob, Nancy, Burt, Sarah, and Joe to look over the sheets of butcher paper we worked with and help me recall what we decided about the quality of each piece of evidence. We'll group the good evidence into the two categories I mentioned, highly reliable and generally reliable. Tomorrow I'll have printed copies of evidence in each category for you to look at.

[Teacher and selected students arrange evidence in these categories. Teacher prepares lists of highly reliable evidence and generally reliable evidence to distribute to students in the class.]

Step 5 ("Formulating a Conclusion")

Teacher distributes to students copies of lists of evidence organized under the headings "highly reliable" and "generally reliable." A discussion ensues. Examples of kinds of questions the teacher might ask follow.

Teacher: You have to look at two things simultaneously now. First of all, you need to consider each of the five possible explanations of or solutions to the problem we identified. Second, you need to look at our list of highly reliable evidence and our list of generally reliable evidence. Looking at these lists, which of our explanations or solutions seem to have the most support? Are there several that seem well supported? Which are they? Why is their support better than that supporting other possible explanations?

Now, having considered all of this information, what do you think is the best explanation for the reduction in the number of blacks lynched in 1910 as compared to 1900 or 1890?

What kind of evidence would it take for you to change your position? How confident are you that your position is "correct"? Where could you go to find additional information to verify your conclusions?

Do you think people ten years from now might come to the same conclusion? Why or why not?

And so on.

The exercise concludes the students' developing final positions that they can defend with specific reference to reliable evidence. The teacher points out that even these conclusions may be subject to revision if evidence not presently considered or available were to come to light. Some teachers may wish to have students do a little additional work to verify further the accuracy of their conclusions.

This sample inquiry experience has been greatly compressed for purposes of illustration. It does, however, illustrate general steps followed in the inquiry process. The issue of time is an important one. Productive inquiry seeks to develop students' abilities to make decisions about issues that often are complex. Students do not master the processes of logical thinking quickly. These skills require adequate developmental time. Consequently, when a decision is made to organize instruction according to an inquiry mode, adequate time must be allowed if benefits of the approach are to accrue to students. If time is tight and "coverage of content" is the highest priority, an inquiry strategy probably does not represent a sound choice.

Finally, a point noted earlier bears repeating here. It is imperative that teachers do a thorough job of identifying specific sources of evidence students can use in an inquiry exercise. Little that is productive is gained when students, in effect, are told nothing more than "find it" and then left to their own devices. Many students will give up under these conditions. Those who do not will suffer needless frustration. Certainly, without some teacher direction in this area, many students probably will develop very negative attitudes toward inquiry-oriented instruction.

The Place of Inquiry Instruction

For the serious social studies teacher interested in using an inquiry-oriented approach, an important basic question has to be, How good is it? Certainly, the enthusiasms of some teachers for the approach are very genuine, and they have had great success with the inquiry teaching in their classrooms. Doubts of many others have also been expressed with force and candor. Beyond these sincere expressions of personal opinion on one side or the other of the issue, some insights regarding the effectiveness of inquiry-oriented instruction are to be found in the research literature. But, even here, no clear trend emerges with regard to the general effectiveness or ineffectiveness of the inquiry approach.

What the research does show is that few differences in student achievement seem directly related to the use of inductive or inquiry-based instruction or deductive instruction. It may be that whether instruction is organized inductively or deductively may not be so important as some other variables. For example, the issue of how students perceive social studies instruction might be a much more important factor affecting their learning in social studies classes. (See Celestino Fernandez, Grace Carroll Massey, and Sanford M. Dornbusch, "High School Students' Perceptions of Social Studies," *The Social Studies* (March/April 1976): 51–56.)

Another explanation that has been forwarded regarding the lack of consistent findings in studies investigating the impact of inductive and deductive approaches is that tests used to reveal differences have been inappropriate. The logic of this argument is that deductive and inductive approaches promote different kinds of learning. Consequently, the two instructional orientations cannot be compared by using a test designed to assess only a single kind of thinking. Particularly, the use of recall tests has been criticized to assess achievement of students who have been taught according to an inductive or inquiry mode. In this connection, Tanner has observed:

> Too many tests and studies have been limited to measuring and comparing the amount and rate of learning subject matter. Learning has many outcomes, and the multidimensionality of inquiry-discovery requires more sophisticated treatments.[1]

Given that there is some evidence that inductive or inquiry approaches and deductive approaches teach students different things, an implication for social studies teachers is that their instructional repertoire ought to include both inductive and deductive frameworks for organizing learning experiences. In determining whether an inquiry-oriented approach is to be preferred over a deductive approach in a given situation, the teacher must give consideration to the question of instructional purpose. Tanner and Tanner (1975) point out that, unless instructional purposes are identified as a preface to instructional planning, selection of an inductive or of a deductive approach cannot be made on a logical basis.

> The tendency of research on discovery . . . . is that one method is pitted against another without considering the goals, the objectives of education. Discussion regarding methods is meaningless when conducted outside the context of objectives, and uncomfortably similar to an attempt to compare walking, swimming, and taking a train; no conclusion is rationally possible until we know where we want to go and how long we have to get there.[2]

[1] Daniel Tanner, *Secondary Curriculum: Theory and Development* (New York: Macmillan Publishing Co., Inc., 1971), p. 35.

[2] Daniel Tanner and Laurel Tanner, *Curriculum Development: Theory and Practice* (New York: Macmillan Publishing Co., Inc., 1975), p. 359.

Though no generic claims of superiority can be claimed either for inductive or deductive instruction, there may be differences in the effectiveness of the two approaches related to instructional purposes. For objectives designed to promote students' decision-making skills, an inductive or inquiry approach may be the better choice. For objectives related to mastery of specific bodies of subject matter content, a case might be made for selecting a deductive approach. Again no solid body of research evidence offers overwhelming support in behalf of these suggestions. But logic does seem to commend them, and they might well be considered by social studies teachers in identifying purposes and selecting instructional techniques.

Summary

Inquiry approaches to teaching social studies classes have generated a good deal of interest in recent years. In general, these approaches organize instruction inductively. The basic purpose of inquiry-oriented instruction is to teach students the process of arriving at rational conclusions based on careful consideration of credible evidence. Inquiry is less useful as a way of organizing instruction to teach large quantities of specific content. The approach takes time. It requires careful planning and classroom organization. It places rigorous intellectual demands on students. But when planning has been careful, inquiry-oriented instruction has the potential for building an instructional bridge for students to the kind of problem-solving competencies that characterize thinking adults.

REFERENCES

DEWEY, JOHN. *How We Think*. Boston: Heath, 1910.

FERNANDEZ, CELESTINO; GRACE CARROLL MASSEY; and SANFORD M. DORNBUSCH. "High School Students' Perceptions of Social Studies." *The Social Studies* (March/April 1976): 51–56.

TANNER, DANIEL. *Secondary Curriculum: Theory and Development*. New York: Macmillan Publishing Co., Inc., 1971.

TANNER, DANIEL, and LAUREL TANNER. *Curriculum Development: Theory into Practice*. New York: Macmillan Publishing Co., Inc., 1975.

U.S. BUREAU OF THE CENSUS. *Historical Statistics of the United States, Colonial Times to 1970*. Bicentennial ed. Part I. Washington, D.C.: U.S. Government Printing Office, 1975.

Chapter 12

A BASIC PATTERN FOR

SEQUENCING INSTRUCTION

COMPREHENSIVE SOCIAL STUDIES PROGRAMS are characterized by instructional experiences organized both according to an inductive (inquiry) mode and a deductive mode. Both approaches have their individual strengths and weaknesses. For example, inductive approaches tend to be more time-consuming and hence potentially less attractive for teaching directed toward providing students with lower-level cognitive skills than are deductive approaches. On the other hand, when higher-level thinking skills are sought, the time required of an inductive approach may be justified because of the sophisticated nature of student thinking being developed.

In the planning of a sequence of instruction, ordinarily a variety of learning outcomes are sought. These will range from rather simple knowledge and comprehension skills to others in which students are asked to analyze, synthesize, and evaluate. Because most instructional units will be directed toward providing students with thinking competencies of varying degrees of sophistication, clearly decisions must be made regarding the kinds of learning experiences that might best help students to achieve all of the unit objectives. Further, once these experiences have been identified, they must be arranged in a logical order. For example, one would not want to put a group of students through an exercise demanding difficult analytical skills before they had a knowledge-level grasp of basic concepts involved. Ordering of instructional experiences is an important planning consideration.

A very workable scheme for organizing the sequence of instructional experience has been developed by the Northwest Regional Laboratory based on the work of Hilda Taba (Northam, 1972). The basic steps in this sequence are these:

1. Teach relevant concepts.
2. Provide students with opportunities to induce generalizations.
3. Provide students with opportunities to deduce predictions from those generalizations and to test those predictions.
4. Provide students with opportunities to induce revised generalizations based on results of prediction testing.
5. Provide students with opportunities to deduce predictions from revised generalizations and to test those predictions.
6. Provide students with opportunities to induce further revised generalizations based on results of prediction testing.
   (Steps 5 and 6 may be repeated, as appropriate, as students move closer toward validated "truth." The teacher makes the decision to terminate the cycle of making generalizations and testing predictions flowing from those generalizations against available evidence.)

Note that, though there are six steps listed in this process, only three distinct procedures are involved. The first of these centers on identifying and teaching relevant concepts. The second involves a sequence of events designed to help students develop generalizations inductively. The third requires students to make predictions flowing logically from those generalizations and to test those predictions against available evidence. Steps 4 and 6 are simply repetitions of the basic process involved in Step 2. Step 5 is a repetition of the basic process involved in Step 3.

Teaching Relevant Concepts

Before students can be expected to develop generalizations, they must understand concepts relevant to the basic topic of interest. For example, if a teacher were interested in teaching a unit focusing on European activities in Africa in the late 1800s, such concepts as "colonialism" would need to be understood clearly by students before they could be expected to engage in more sophisticated analyses leading to generalizations. A number of procedures for teaching relevant concepts are available. The program distributed by the Northwest Regional Laboratory, based on the work of Hilda Taba, describes one procedure known as "concept diagnosis" (Northam, 1972).

CONCEPT DIAGNOSIS

The "concept diagnosis" strategy has two purposes. On the one hand, the strategy can help the teacher identify any misunderstandings a student might have regarding an important concept. On the other hand, the strategy gives students an opportunity to learn a new concept inductively by exposing them to information they can use as they derive the defining characteristics of the new concept. There are three steps involved in the strategy of concept diagnosis. These are (1) listing, (2) grouping, and (3) labeling.

Listing. In implementing the listing step, the teacher ordinarily works either at a chalkboard or with a grease pencil and a blank transparency on an overhead projector or with a large sheet of butcher paper and a felt marker. The step begins when the teacher asks a broad general question intended to elicit student responses. The question is designed to bring forth information related to students' understanding of a concept that has been identified as relevant to a new topic of study. Some appropriate questions might include:

> What does the term *colonialism* mean to you?
> What comes to mind when you hear the word *socialism?*
> How would you describe an *immigrant?*
> What characterizes an *ethnic group?*

The teachers' role is to accept uncritically *all* student responses. Each response is written on the chalkboard (or on the transparency or butcher paper, as appropriate). At no point should the teacher evaluate either negatively or positively any of these student responses. The idea is to let the students freely express their own perceptions. A teacher remark or physical expression that is taken as judgmental may stifle students' willingness to make known their own views.

In using the concept diagnosis strategy, the teacher must decide whether the primary objective is to (1) determine present perceptions of students regarding a given concept or to (2) teach students an acceptable working definition of a given concept. When the purpose is to identify possible student misunderstandings of a concept, for example "socialism," it is sufficient to provide students with a stimulus question such as one of those listed earlier. Under such conditions, students rely on their present stores of information, whether accurate or inaccurate, as they volunteer responses to the teacher's question.

But when the purpose of the concept diagnosis strategy is to teach specific characteristics of a new concept, students must be provided with materials they can draw upon as they answer the teacher's questions. For example, if the focus concept was "socialism," the teacher might provide students with a series of short paragraphs illustrating the operation "socialism" in different settings, perhaps in the Soviet Union, in Yugoslavia, and in Sweden. Under these conditions, a classroom dialogue something like the following might ensue:

> *Teacher:* What comes to mind now when you think about how government affects people's lives in the Soviet Union?
> [Students respond, and teacher puts list of responses on chalkboard or transparency or sheet of butcher paper.]
> What comes to mind when you think about how government affects people's lives in Yugoslavia?
> [Students respond, and teacher puts list of responses on chalkboard or transparency or sheet of butcher paper.]

What comes to mind when you think about how government affects people's lives in Sweden?

[Students respond, and teacher puts list of responses on chalkboard or transparency or sheet of butcher paper.]

These responses all remain in full view of the students in the class. The teacher will have the students work with them during the "grouping" phase of the concept diagnosis exercise.

Grouping. Once the "listing" phase of the strategy has been completed, the teacher moves on to "grouping." This part of the exercise helps students develop their abilities to see relationships among isolated pieces of information. Additionally, they learn how to determine logical bases for organizing information. The teacher begins the grouping phase with a question such as, Are there some items on our lists that might be clustered together?

When students begin to respond, a coding scheme of some kind must be developed to keep track of which items are being grouped together. A simple system involves using letters of the alphabet. The letter *A* can denote items of one kind; the letter *B* items of another kind; and so forth. As many letters can be used as are needed to account for each cluster of items identified by students.

In managing the grouping exercise, the teacher needs to ask students to identify bases for grouping and to suggest an appropriate label for each group of items. For example:

Teacher: All right, let's look at our lists. Which items might go together?

Robert: I think government-owned gas companies, government-owned electric companies, and government-owned telephone companies might go together.

Teacher: Fine. Now what do they have in common?

Robert: Well, they are things people need to keep them comfortable at home and at work and to enable them to communicate. They all perform some kind of necessary and useful service. And they're all controlled by the government.

Teacher: Fine. Let's put a letter *A* before *government-owned gas companies, government-owned electric companies,* and *government-owned telephone companies* to indicate they form a category.

This procedure involves students in identifying some logical bases for organizing information. Further, the exercise provides insights to the teacher regarding the sort of rationale individual students are using to categorize information.

As the exercise goes forward, it is necessary to deal carefully with differences of opinion among students regarding how individual items should be grouped. Students should be encouraged to suggest different ways of grouping individual items. For example, one student might see a "ship" as belonging with a group of items having to do with "public transportation." Another might view "ship" as going more appropriately with a cluster of items relating to "maritime activities."

Both possibilities should be accepted. The "ship" can be included both as a one of the items clustered under the heading "public transportation" and as a one of the items clustered under the heading "maritime activities." This means that many items will have several codes beside them indicating their membership in a number of different categories.

Labeling. The third step in concept diagnosis is "labeling." Sometimes labeling occurs almost concurrently with the grouping process. The purpose of this phase of the exercise is to highlight the basis used to cluster a given group of items together by assigning a group name or "label" to the cluster. To help students develop a concept name or label, the teacher offers a series of debriefing questions. Lists developed during the grouping phase are left up for students to look at during the labeling debriefing.

> *Teacher:* Can anyone suggest a name for these things that we have clustered together and identified by the letter *A*?
>
> *Leona:* How about "government utilities"?
> (A discussion ensues, and the class accepts this label.)
>
> *Teacher:* All right, we seem to be agreed on the label "government utilities." Now who will define the term for us?
>
> *Peter:* Well, all the things we have mentioned are needed or useful to nearly everyone. Also they're all owned by the government. So I would say government utilities were things that were useful to nearly everyone and that were owned by the government.
> [A discussion follows, and the class accepts this definition.]

The concept diagnosis strategy is best used at the beginning of a unit of instruction. The strategy helps students pinpoint key concepts that will be important for them to understand as the unit unfolds. For the teacher, the strategy can provide useful information regarding which students begin the new unit burdened by a good deal of misinformation. (For example, if a given student clustered items such as "slow moving," "dirty houses," "tattered clothing" under a category he or she labeled "Mexican Americans," the teacher would know that subsequent instruction would need to account for this individual's unfortunate negative stereotyping.) By actively involving students in the process of concept learning, the concept diagnosis strategy can establish a highly motivating introduction for students to a new topic.

In terms of time, it is desirable that the entire strategy be accomplished within a given class period. The listing, grouping, and labeling procedures can become a tedious exercise if they become a persistent and a long-lasting feature of the instructional program. If the teacher feels students need some background materials before they can profit from the exercise, those should be provided in advance of the strategy's use. When concept diagnosis takes place during a concentrated period of highly involving classroom activity during a single class hour, the strategy provides a splendid entrée for the more time-consuming inductive and deductive strategies that will follow.

CONCEPT ATTAINMENT

"Concept attainment," as described by Tanck (1969), represents another approach to introducing students to a novel concept. The approach is considerably more direct than that characterizing concept diagnosis. There are six basic steps in the concept attainment strategy, as follows:[1]

1. Before working with students, the teacher identifies the concept, its defining characteristics, and both examples and nonexamples of the concept.
2. Both examples of the concept and nonexamples of the concept are presented to students.
3. Students are asked to name the defining characteristics of the concept.
4. Students are presented with additional nonexamples and examples without being told what they are. They are asked to identify the examples and the nonexamples. Students are asked to give reasons supporting their choices.
5. Students are asked to find and identify new examples on their own. (This step acts as a reinforcer of concept learning.)
6. The teacher assesses student learning by presenting students with examples and nonexamples and determining whether they can distinguish between them accurately.[1]

Suppose a teacher wished to use the concept attainment strategy to teach the concept "tie-in contract." The lesson might develop something like this:

Step 1

The teacher selects an appropriate definition of "tie-in contract." (A *tie-in contract* is an agreement made by a company to buy an amount of a product that (a) it may not really want in exchange for (b) the right to buy an amount of a product it does want at a satisfactory price.)

Step 2

The teacher presents the following examples and nonexamples of the concept to the class:

Teacher: I am going to read to you two short paragraphs that tell about a company placing an order for goods. Listen carefully. When I finish, I want you to tell me how the two situations differ.
(1) Amalgamated Lightning Rod placed an order for 800 lightning rods from Central States Metallics. Amalgamated Lightning Rod found that Central States Metallics would agree to sell the 800 lightning rods only if a contract were signed according to which Amal-

[1] Adapted from Marlin L. Tanck, "Teaching Concepts, Generalizations, and Constructs," in *Social Studies Curriculum Development: Prospects and Problems*, ed. Dorothy McClure Fraser, 39th Yearbook of the National Council for the Social Studies, 1969 (Washington, D.C.: NCSS, 1968), pp. 117–118. Reprinted with permission of the National Council for the Social Studies.

gamated Lightning Rod would also agree to buy 300 dozen boxes of brass bolts. Because Amalgamated wanted the lightning rods, it signed the contract and bought the bolts as well.

(2) Petrill Writing Papers offered to purchase 670 tons of paper pulp from Northern Michigan Sawdust. Northern Michigan was delighted to receive the order and drew up a contract offering to sell the pulp to Petrill at a very favorable price.

All right. Those are our two paragraphs. Now, how do they differ? [Teacher conducts discussion leading students to identify distinctions. As a conclusion, teacher identifies the name of the concept being illustrated in the first situation.]

Now, to put a name on the situation described in the first paragraph . . . . This is an example of something that is called a "tie-in contract." That is "tie-in contract."

Step 3

Teacher: All right, now that you have heard me read a paragraph containing an example of a tie-in paragraph, I wonder if you might be able to define the term for me?
[Teacher encourages the students to define term.]

Step 4

Now let's see whether your definition can help you to identify these paragraphs as examples or an nonexamples of a tie-in contract. I will pass out these sheets with the four paragraphs to you now. Raise your hands when you think you know which paragraphs are examples of "tie-in contracts" and which are not.

1. Smith School Desk wanted to order 50 new desk tops from Newcastle Wood Furniture. But before Newcastle would fill the order, that company insisted that Smith School desk sign a contract agreeing to buy 150 ink wells along with the new desk tops.

2. Halcyon Books recently signed two large contracts for the delivery of printing paper. Six thousand tons were ordered from Wisconsin Pulp Associates and 13,000 tons were ordered from West Coast Paper.

3. Armadillo Fireworks wanted to order 30,000 fuses from Southwest Powder. Southwest Powder agreed to fill the order but insisted that the purchase contract also commit Armadillo Fireworks to purchase 1,500 pounds of blasting powder.

4. Adams Ball Bearing wanted to purchase both ball bearings and bearing grease from Ft. Stockton Machinery Supply. But because of a shortage of grease, Ft. Stockton Machinery Supply agreed to allow Adams Ball Bearing to order only the ball bearings. Adams Ball Bearing reluctantly agreed to sign a contract calling for the delivery of the ball bearings but not the bearing grease.

Teacher debriefs students, pointing out that paragraphs 1 and 3 are examples and paragraphs 2 and 4 are nonexamples of "tie-in contracts."

Step 5

Teacher: Now, I would like each of you to take out a sheet of paper. On your paper, write a short paragraph similar to those you have seen in which you describe an example of a tie-in contract. Remember, now, I want an *example* of a tie-in contract, not a definition.
[Teacher gives students time to complete this task. Then students are asked to share their examples with the class; a discussion ensues.]

Step 6

On a quiz, teacher assesses students' grasp of the concept "tie-in contract" by presenting them with a series of paragraphs containing either examples or nonexamples of tie-in contracts. Students are asked to identify the examples and the nonexamples.

In this lesson, the teacher chose to use written materials to illustrate the examples and nonexamples of the new concept. Certainly, other kinds of materials would have been equally appropriate. Often, photographs, line drawings, paintings, or tangible objects can serve this purpose well. Care should be taken in the selection of examples to make sure that they highlight clearly the defining characteristics of the concept being taught. When these characteristics can be seen clearly, students soon develop a good facility in distinguishing between the examples and the nonexamples.

CONCEPT DEMONSTRATION

"Concept demonstration," another procedure described by Tanck (1969), differs from the concept attainment strategy primarily in that students are given the concept definition by the teacher. Further, the teacher presents students with examples of the new concept that he or she identifies as examples and with nonexamples of the new concept that he or she identifies as nonexamples. In short, the procedure develops according to a much more direct, deductive sort of approach than does the concept attainment strategy. The six basic steps of the concept demonstration strategy follows:[2]

1. Before working with students, the teacher selects the focus concept, identifies its defining characteristics, and prepares materials to serve both as examples and as nonexamples of the concept.
2. The teacher defines the concept for the class and carefully identifies its defining characteristics.
3. The teacher provides students with examples that are identified with examples and with nonexamples that are identified as nonexamples. The teacher points out how each example illustrates the defining characteristics of the concept.

---

[2] Adapted from Marlin L. Tanck, "Teaching Concepts, Generalizations, and Constructs," in *Social Studies Curriculum Development: Prospects and Problems*, ed. Dorothy McClure Fraser, 39th Yearbook of the National Council for the Social Studies, 1969 (Washington, D.C.: NCSS, 1968.) Reprinted with permission of the National Council for the Social Studies.

4. The teacher provides students with additional examples and nonexamples without identifying them. Students are asked to point out the examples and the nonexamples.
5. Assessment consists of the teacher's (a) asking students to construct new examples of the concept or (b) asking students to differentiate correctly between examples and nonexamples on a test or (c) asking students to respond correctly to questions related to the defining characteristics of the concept.
6. The teacher reinforces concept learning by periodically asking students to (a) distinguish between examples and nonexamples or (b) generate their own examples and nonexamples.

Suppose a teacher wished to teach the concept "progressive tax rate," using the concept demonstration strategy. The lesson might develop as follows:

Step 1

The teacher develops a workable definition of the focus concept. (A *progressive tax rate* is a tax rate characterized by (a) low rates on low incomes that increase incrementally toward (b) high rates on high incomes.)

Step 2

The teacher defines the concept for the class.

Teacher: Today, I want to begin with the term *progressive tax rate.* (Teacher points to term written on chalkboard.) A progressive tax rate is a tax rate in which rates are low on low incomes and increase to become high on high incomes. In other words, if you earn a low salary, you pay taxes at a lower rate than if you earn a high salary.

Step 3

Teacher: Now let's say that Mrs. Smeade, a beauty shop operator made $11,000 last year and paid 28 per cent of that money in taxes. And let's say that Mr. Rambo, an attorney, made $39,000 last year and paid 34 per cent of that total in taxes. Because the individual making more, Mr. Rambo, paid in a higher percentage of his income than the individual making less, we have here an example of a progressive tax rate.
On the other hand, suppose Mr. Rogers, a salesman, made $20,000 and Miss Stark, an architect, made $30,000 and both paid taxes amounting to 30 per cent of their incomes. In this case, there would be no progressive tax rate because the person earning the lower income and the person earning the higher income paid taxes at the same rate.

Step 4

Teacher: All right, now I am going to give you two examples. When I finish, I'll ask you to tell me which is the correct illustration of a progressive tax rate.

This is the first example. Mr. Fillmore, the contractor, made $70,000 last year. Dr. Stillwell, the dentist, made $36,000. Both Mr. Fillmore and Dr. Stillwell paid the government taxes totaling exactly $2,500. This is the second example. Mr. Norton, the used car salesman, earned $23,000 last year. Mr. Philips, the machinist, earned $17,000. Mr. Norton paid 23 per cent of his income in taxes, whereas Mr. Philips paid 17 per cent of his income in taxes.
Now, who can tell me which of these two examples illustrates a progressive tax rate?
[Teacher conducts debriefing discussion in which differences between the two situations are discussed and defining characteristics of *progressive tax rate* are reemphasized.]

Step 5

Teacher: For tomorrow, I want each of you to write down for me three examples illustrating the operation of a progressive tax rate and three other examples illustrating the operation of a tax rate system that does not meet the requirements of a progressive tax rate.

Step 6

From time to time, the teacher reinforces concept learning by presenting students with opportunities to distinguish between examples and nonexamples of the concept.

In the planning of sequences of instruction, it is important that the basic step of teaching relevant concepts not be overlooked. It is a mistake to assume that students can profit from learning experiences designed to engage them in higher-order thinking processes if they lack a basic understanding of these important concepts. The three concept learning strategies introduced here, "concept diagnosis," "concept attainment," and "concept demonstration," by no means represent an exhaustive overview of the available procedures for teaching concepts. They are presented as samples of systematic strategies for teaching concepts. Individuals interested in pursuing this general area in more detail are urged to look carefully at Peter H. Martorella's fine volume, *Concept Learning in the Social Studies: Models for Structuring Curriculum* (Scranton, Pennsylvania: International Textbook Company, 1971).

Inducing Generalizations: The Interpretation of Data Strategy

The "interpretation of data" strategy provides a systematic procedure for leading students to develop generalizations. In some instances, a teacher may have no particular generalization in mind and be primarily interested in providing creative thinking opportunities in which students develop explanatory generalizations that point out general patterns that might prove applicable to information beyond that which they are presented. More frequently, however, the teacher has some specific powerful generalizations in mind that students, he or she hopes, will come to grasp through a discovery or an inductive thinking process.

The interpretation of data strategy suggests a step-by-step sequence teachers can use to help their students develop to the point of being both willing and able to induce generalizations. (As noted previously, in most cases these are not "new" generalizations in the sense that they represent novel additions to knowledge. But though they may be selected by the teacher, these generalizations may be "new" to students who infer them from a process of investigating and analyzing specific items of information.) As a preface to the interpretation of data strategy, it is assumed (1) that the teacher has taken steps to assure that students are familiar with essential concepts, (2) that the teacher has made a decision either to identify appropriate guiding generalizations for the exercise or has made a decision to develop an unguided exercise directed toward the goal of developing students' creative thinking abilities, and (3) that specific facts and ideas have been identified along with procedures to present those facts and ideas to students that either illustrate the guiding generalization or are appropriate catalysts for a creative thinking exercise. Once these tasks have been accomplished, the interpretation of data strategy proceeds as follows:[3]

Step 1

Description of Specifics: In this step, students are asked by the teacher to recall specific information to which they have been exposed. This information may have been presented in a variety of ways, including readings from a textbook chapter, a film, periodical articles, photographs, paintings, and so on. The teacher asks questions that demand no interpretation, only simple recollection. (What happened? In what order did those events occur? Who did what? And so on.)

Step 2

Analysis of Relationships: In this step, students are asked to analyze relationships between and among specific facts and ideas. This step follows only after there has been a thorough airing of all of the "specifics" in step 1. Teacher questions seek comparisons and contrasts. (How was Hamilton's view different from Jefferson's? How did Germany's feelings toward reparations compare with England's? How would you compare Lincoln's first inaugural address with his second inaugural address?)

[3] Adapted from *Development of Higher Level Thinking Abilities-Participant Materials*, ed. Saralie B. Northam, (Portland, Oregon: Northwest Regional Laboratory 1972), pp. 319–320.

Development of Generalizations: In this step, students are urged to "go beyond the data" to develop explanatory generalizations. This is a psychologically "threatening" exercise for students because they must go beyond reference to specific information to develop explanations that demand an inferential leap. A student attempting to formulate a generalization can never proceed with the sense of security enjoyed by a student recalling a "fact" that rests comfortably available for checking in the pages of a textbook. The teacher needs to provide students with a good deal of encouragement and support during this phase of the strategy. Questions seek broad explanations of observed phenomena. (What conclusions might you draw from these observations? Why did these kinds of situations develop? What meaning does this have for you? What is the "big idea" the writer was trying to convey to us? And so on.)

In implementing this interpretation of data strategy, the teacher moves the level of discussion to successively higher steps through a skillful sequencing of questions. Note that in Step 1, questions ask students only to recall isolated pieces of information. These "what and who" questions pose little psychological threat in that they are tied directly to specifics presented in the learning material. Students tend to gain confidence and increase in their willingness to become active participants when the questioning sequence commences with questions of this type.

At Step 2, students are asked to begin engaging in comparisons and contrasts between specific items of information. This requires more self-confidence than the simple recall questions characterizing Step 1 of the strategy. But when students have had the Step 1 experience, they will likely have grown sufficiently in self-confidence to be willing to take "an interpretive plunge."

Finally, at Step 3 the teacher asks the students to move well beyond the specific information with which they have been presented to form a generalization or a broad conclusion. This step demands a good deal of courage on the part of the student because he or she is making a commitment to something that cannot be directly verified by reference to specific information in the learning materials. Certainly, the learning materials will have provided some basis for the generalization, but, by definition, a generalization will have applicability beyond this immediate situation. Consequently, students hesitate to "put themselves out on a limb" to formulate a broad-sweeping generalization unless the discussion has given them a good sense of personal security. When the teacher has used the interpretation of data strategy in proper sequence and systematically worked to build student confidence in Steps 1 and 2, then students will be psychologically as well as intellectually prepared to "take a chance" on describing a generalization that has broad explanatory power.

A mistake many new teachers make, who are unfamiliar with the sequential development of the interpretation of data strategy, is to *begin* a discussion with a question calling on students to make a broad, interpretive generalization. A question such as "What implications did you draw from the film for present

U.S. foreign policy in Middle East?" asked immediately after a class has viewed a documentary focusing on patterns of U.S. and Soviet aid to Israel and Egypt is almost certain to result in a long and embarrassing silence. The question poses a very high psychological threat in that it demands a broad interpretive generalization before students have had a chance to gain any measure of self-confidence in their abilities to respond correctly. Further, no preliminary questions have laid out for class consideration specific information that clearly must be taken into account before any such generalization can be drawn. The very same question can stimulate students to suggest some highly insightful generalizations *after* an appropriate information base has been developed in Step 1 and Step 2 of the interpretation of data strategy. But classroom discussions directed toward helping students to formulate generalizations will be disappointing if students are asked to generalize in the absence of preparatory questions designed to build an appropriate information base.

THE INFORMATION CATEGORIES CHART

In the implementing of the interpretation of data strategy, one of the problems students face is that of keeping track of large quantities of specific information. Frequently, learning materials contain so much detailed information that students have a very difficult time putting specific details together into any kind of a meaningful pattern. A procedure that can help students organize isolated information in a systematic way is the use of an "information categories chart."

An information categories chart is a matrix that along one axis ordinarily lists two or more major subjects or topics and along the other axis ordinarily lists two or more major concept headings. This matrix results in the creation of individual cells, each of which is described by a combination of a given topic and a given concept heading. In using the information categories chart, students (either individually or collectively) can write into the appropriate cell specific information relating to the major topic and major concept defining that cell. An example of an information categories chart is provided in Figure 12–1.

The information categories chart depicted in Figure 12–1 was used by a teacher who employed the "interpretation of data" exercise to help students grasp this generalization: "Industry in an area is largely dependent upon the availability of raw materials, transportation, and markets." Students were encouraged to identify information that could be classified into one of the twelve cells on the chart. (For example, "Raw materials in Venezuela.")

Use of an information categories chart is appropriate particularly when, after students have been exposed to basic learning materials, a teacher wishes to work with a class through all three steps of an interpretation of data strategy. Under such conditions, a very large information categories chart can be drawn on the chalkboard or on a large piece of butcher paper tacked or taped to a wall. Information can be written in appropriate categories either by the teacher or by students

	Industry	Raw Materials	Transportation	Markets
Western Venezuela				
Orinoco Valley				
Santa Catarina, Brazil				

Figure 12–1. An Example of an "Information Categories Chart." (Source: Adapted from Saralie B. Northam, ed, *Development of Higher Level Thinking Abilities: Participant Materials* (Portland, Oregon: Northwest Regional Laboratory, 1972), p. 457.)

appointed to take charge of this task. An appropriate set of teacher questions for an interpretation of data exercise might look something like the following:

Step 1

What kinds of industry did the materials indicate were found in Western Venezuela? In the Orinoco Valley? In Santa Catarina, Brazil?

Step 2

What raw materials are found in Western Venezuela? In the Orinoco Valley? In Santa Catarina, Brazil?

[The teacher follows the same format for the categories of "transportation" and "markets." As students identify pertinent information, this information is written in the appropriate cell on the information categories chart.]

What similarities do you see in the kinds of industry in the three areas? In the raw materials? In the transportation systems? In the nature of the markets?

What differences do you see in the kinds of industry in the three areas? In the raw materials? In the transportation systems? In the nature of the markets?

How would you compare Western Venezuela to the Orinoco Valley in terms of all of these things? How would you compare Western Venezuela to Santa Catarina, Brazil, in terms of all of these things? How would you compare the Orinoco Valley to Santa Catarina, Brazil, in terms of all of these things?

Step 3

What general conclusions can you draw about the kinds of industry one might expect to find in a given area? What led you to that conclusion? How might we check on the accuracy of that conclusion? And so on.

When an information categories chart is available for student use during an interpretation of data exercise, students have specific, detailed information immediately available to them. The availability of this information, organized into careful, systematic categories, helps them make the inferential "jump" from simple recall to generalizing. The information categories chart represents a highly useful tool for the social studies teacher interested in helping students develop higher-level thinking skills.

THE INTERPRETATION OF DATA STRATEGY: A RECAPITULATION

The "interpretation of data" strategy consists of a series of three steps designed to help students develop the ability to formulate generalizations. Inductive in its design, the procedure begins with a series of questions designed to elicit from students responses describing specific information, episodes, or incidents that have been introduced in learning materials to which they have been exposed. Next students are urged to compare and contrast specific items of information. Finally, they are asked to "go beyond" the "givens" to describe a generalization that will explain the information they have confronted as well as other situations in contexts not tied specifically to that information. The strategy seeks to give students a sense of intellectual power as they gain confidence in their ability to develop sound explanatory generalizations from a careful consideration of limited amounts of specific, known information.

Predicting from Generalizations: The Application of Knowledge Strategy

The "application of knowledge" strategy frequently is used toward the end of a unit of work after students have formulated generalizations as a consequence of their involvement in an interpretation of data strategy. In the application of knowledge exercise, students can be confronted with novel situations about which they are asked to make logical predictions that are consistent with the generalizations they have developed. This is a deductive procedure in that the specific predictions are made only after a consideration of the general "rule" contained in the generalization. The application of knowledge strategy proceeds according to the following steps:

Step 1: Predicting

The teacher asks students to make specific predictions about a situation in the light of generalizations they have formulated.

Step 2: Justifying

The teacher asks students to explain logical relationships between their predictions and the generalization(s) from which those predictions derive.

Step 3: Verifying

Students examine additional data to determine whether their predictions are supportable or in need of revision.

As an illustration of how an application of knowledge strategy might develop in a classroom, imagine that a teacher had concluded an extensive interpretation of data sequence and that, among others, students had formulated this generalization:

The terms a given people use to describe certain categories of individuals provide a good indication of the status accorded to those categories of individuals.

Given student development of this generalization, the teacher might provide students with the two following lists of adjectives. The first of these consists of adjectives used by a certain people to express approval of females. The second consists of adjectives used by this people to express approval of males. (In using

Words Used to Express Approval of Females	Words Used to Express Approval of Males
adorable	burly
beautiful	fire-eater
comely	hearty
dainty	hunk
delicate	husky
demure	muscle-bound
divine	rangy
dreamy	red-blooded
enchanting	rowdy
ethereal	rambunctious
heavenly	
lovely	
misty-eyed	
precious	

Adapted from Mary W. Matthews, "A Teacher's Guide to Sexist Words," *Social Education* (May 1977): 389–397; 395. Reprinted with permission of the National Council for the Social Studies.

such a list, the teacher should alert students to a possible bias on the part of the individual compiling the list.)

Some questions a teacher might ask students in using these data for an application of knowledge strategy at each step in the sequence follow:

Step 1

Teacher: All right, let's look again at one of the conclusions we developed at the end of yesterday's lesson. [Teacher points to the board where this generalization has been written: The terms a given people use to describe certain categories of individuals provide a good indication of the status accorded to those categories of individuals.]

I want you to think about that statement as I distribute these materials to you. [Teacher passes out sheets of paper containing lists of words used to express approval of females and words used to express approval of males in a certain society.]

Now, thinking about the statement on the board, look at both of your lists and make some predictions or suggestions about how people in this society regard women and how they regard men.

[Student responses ensue: "Women seem to be placed on sort of a pedestal." "Women are thought of as being physically weak." "Women are passive." "Women all work hard to achieve a certain standard of beauty." "Men are admired for their physical activity." "Men are seen as doers." "Men are viewed as active rather than passive." And so on. Predictions are written on the board.]

Step 2

Teacher: We have quite a number of predictions here. Let's look at each one of them independently. Louise, you suggested that in this society that women must be placed on some sort of a pedestal. What exactly do you mean by that? [Student responds.] How did you arrive at this conclusion from the lists of adjectives you looked at? Do some of you others agree with the logic behind Louise's prediction? Why or why not?

[Teacher pursues a similar pattern of questioning with respect to each of the remaining predictions.]

Step 3

Teacher: Let's look again at each of our predictions. How might we go about determining whether these predictions are accurate? [Discussion ensues. Teacher probes for student identification of appropriate information sources.]

[Following discussion, teacher arranges for students to work with additional data that might be appropriate to help determine the accuracy of their predictions. Given this situation, for example, materials relating to sex roles and sex role stereotyping in the United States would be appropriate.]

I would like you to look carefully at this additional information. [Teacher gives students an opportunity to work with appropriate materials.]

Now, let's consider our predictions, one by one. Which ones seem supported by the new information? Which ones seem a bit wide of the mark? How about those that seem to be accurate . . . can we assume that they are "true" predictions simply on the basis of this information, or do we have to look for still more information? [And so on.]

The final step in the application of knowledge strategy, verifying, leads students to consider additional isolated pieces of information. When this information does not confirm the prediction, the stage is set for the teacher to ask students whether there might be a need to reformulate the generalization from which the prediction was derived. This consideration of isolated information for the purposes of formulating a generalization, in essence, represents a repetition of the interpretation of data procedure; that is, isolated information is examined with regard to specifics and relationship, and, finally, a new or revised generalization results. Then new, hopefully more accurate predictions can be derived from the revised generalization according to procedures set forth in the application of knowledge procedure. The teacher can engage a group of students in an extended series of exercises, moving systematically from interpretation of data to application of knowledge until such time as students consistently develop generalizations that lead to predictions that have extensive logical support when additional data are examined.

Summary

Student growth is promoted when attention is given to sequencing instruction systematically. One scheme that has shown promise in this regard has been promoted by the Northwest Regional Laboratory (1972) and is based on work of the late Hilda Taba. This sequence commences with learning experiences designed to help students grasp basic and important concepts relevant to the topic under consideration. Once these concepts have been introduced and there is evidence that students understand them, a pattern of instruction is introduced according to which strategies leading students to formulate generalizations (interpretation of data) are alternated with strategies leading students to make and test predictions stemming from those generalizations (application of knowledge). The basic pattern, then, looks something like this:

1. Teach relevant concepts.
2. Interpretation of data strategy.
3. Application of knowledge strategy.

(Remaining elements are alternative repetitions of Steps 2 and 3, continuing so long as is appropriate in the professional judgment of the teacher.)

This pattern has merit in that it attempts to assure that students have the concepts critical to the understanding of a new area well in mind as they attempt learning challenges demanding higher-level thinking skills. Students are encouraged to make specific use of information with which they are presented as they attempt to formulate generalizations. Next they are encouraged to utilize these generalizations as reference points as they attempt to make predictions about new phenomena. By testing the accuracy of these predictions against additional data, students are provided with opportunities to revise their generalizations, make additional interpretations about other unfamiliar situations, and work toward a sharpened ability to move beyond given information to make sound, reasoned interpretations of the world around them. This basic pattern for sequencing instruction provides teachers with a viable framework for systematically and incrementally raising the level of students' sophistication as they work through new and unfamiliar topic emphases.

REFERENCES

MARTORELLA, PETER H. *Concept Learning in the Social Studies: Models for Structuring Curriculum.* Scranton, Pennsylvania: International Textbook Company, 1971.

MATTHEWS, MARY W. "A Teacher's Guide to Sexist Words." *Social Education* (May 1977): 389–397.

NORTHAM, SARALIE B., ed. *Development of Higher Level Thinking Abilities-Participant Materials.* Portland, Oregon: Northwest Regional Educational Laboratory, 1972.

TANCK, MARLIN L. "Teaching Concepts, Generalizations, and Constructs." In *Social Studies Curriculum Development: Prospects and Problems,* edited by Dorothy McClure Fraser, pp. 99–138. 39th Yearbook of the National Council for the Social Studies, 1969. Washington, D.C.: National Council for the Social Studies, 1968.

Chapter 13

SELECTING INSTRUCTIONAL TECHNIQUES

"INSTRUCTIONAL TECHNIQUES" ARE PROCEDURES teachers use on a daily basis to help students acquire understandings relevant to the social studies program. Instructional techniques are tactics the social studies teacher uses as elements within broader instructional strategies. These instructional techniques represent the smallest unit of planning for student-teacher interaction in the classroom.

Beginning social studies teachers occasionally make the mistake of asking questions such as, Are simulations good? Is it *ever* appropriate to use a lecture with ninth graders? Isn't brainstorming sure to lead to serious classroom control problems? Such questions are asked on the assumption that individual instructional techniques carry within them certain inherent qualitative features; that is, they are presumed to be either "good" or "bad" independent of the situation in which they are used. That presumption is untenable. Individual techniques' strengths and weaknesses cannot be discussed in absolute terms. The appropriateness of a given instructional technique is wrapped up in contextual features unique to the setting in which it is to be used. The question ought not to be, Is a lecture a good choice?, but rather, Under what *conditions* might a lecture be a good choice?

Considerations That Precede Selection of Instructional Techniques

A general principle that should undergird selection of instructional techniques is that a variety of approaches on a single day probably will prove to be more productive than the use of only one approach. Students even within a given classroom represent an incredible range of interests and abilities. Certainly, more of these individual characteristics are likely to be served when more than a single instructional technique is used. Additionally, there is a certain stimulation associated with a change in procedures that can serve as an important motivating function. A change to a new instructional technique frequently results in renewed student involvement in the day's lesson.

An important corollary of the "variety principle" is that, when possible, some instructional techniques selected for use each day should require active student participation of a verbal or physical nature. Many secondary school students attend six or more hours of classes a day. Some of these individuals, depending upon the courses in which they are enrolled, may be required to sit quietly for five or even six of those hours. University students complain vociferously when they are asked to register for three lecture courses on a given day of the week. Given the discomfiture of these older students, is there little to be wondered at difficulties some secondary students have in sitting quietly? Selection of instructional techniques that, at a minimum, allow students to participate verbally or, better yet, permit them to do a little moving about can provide a welcome relief from the very real discomfort of too much quiet sitting and can build enthusiasm for the social studies program.

Variety will not "just happen." Although certainly the teacher must be flexible and adjust instructional techniques to the ebb and flow of the lesson as it develops in the classroom, some advance planning can suggest some directions that might be taken at different times during the hour. When one plans for variety in selection of instructional techniques, it is a sound practice to think of the fifty-five- or sixty-minute period not as a single block of time, but rather as three blocks of about twenty minutes each that are clustered together to yield the total. Given this perspective, planning can be directed toward identifying instructional techniques to be used during each twenty-minute module of time. Certainly, some techniques may require more than one twenty-minute module (indeed, on some occasions, it may be necessary to identify one instructional technique to be used the entire period or for three concurrent twenty-minute modules).

Figure 13–1 illustrates one teacher's planning regarding the use of instructional techniques for a two-week period. This is probably about as long a time period as should be used for preplanning. Clearly, instruction must respond to students' development and reactions to the instructional program. This responsiveness is not well served when very elaborate, long-term preplanning seems to mandate a certain set of procedures that appear to suggest that, for example, a class to be conducted two months hence will open with a lecture regardless of what happens in the meantime. Day-by-day preplanning should not extend too far ahead of the ongoing instruction.

Another consideration for instructional technique selection is what might be called the typical "class activity profile." The *class activity profile* refers to the

```
                                      Week One

        Monday                      Tuesday                     Wednesday

    A.  Lecture                 A.  Team learning           A.  Lecture
    B.  In-class reading of     B.  Discussion              B.  Discussion
        materials              C.  Discussion              C.  Discussion
    C.  Team learning


        Thursday                    Friday

    A.  Simulation              A.  Simulation
    B.  Simulation              B.  Simulation
    C.  Simulation              C.  Discussion (Debriefing
                                   of Simulation)

--------------------------------------------------------------------------------

        Monday                      Tuesday                     Wednesday

    A.  Brainstorming           A.  Lecture                 A.  Lecture
    B.  In-class reading of     B.  Class debate            B.  Discussion
        materials              C.  Class debate            C.  Team learning
    C.  Questioning


        Thursday                    Friday

    A.  Discussion              A.  Discussion
    B.  Role playing            B.  Quiz
    C.  Role playing            C.  Quiz

--------------------------------------------------------------------------------

    Note:  Modules A, B, C, are of twenty-minutes' duration each.
```

Figure 13–1. An Example of a Teacher's Instructional Techniques' Planning Using 20-Minute Time Modules

tendency for most classrooms of students to be characterized by three distinct phases in terms of students' productive activity. During the first phase, the "settling in period," the teacher has completed taking the roll, attended to other administrative duties, and given students general directions about what they are to do. Students tend to ask clarification questions, to look for materials, to sharpen pencils, and to begin to "get on" with their responsibilities during this phase. During the second or "at task" phase, students generally have begun to follow the instructions given by the teacher during the first phase. Finally, toward the end of the period (particularly if either lunch or the end of the school day follow this instructional hour), students' activity tends to fall away from their assigned patterns of work. Some have finished their tasks. For others, it is simply a question of attention wandering in anticipation of a change of classes.

This class activity profile suggests that the instructional technique selected for use at the beginning of the period might be something that helps students get into a productive learning pattern. (For example, the teacher might greet students as they come in the door, present them with role descriptions printed on cards, and inform them that they had ten minutes to think through how they would play the role during a role-playing exercise to begin at precisely ten minutes after the hour.) The third phase of the class activity profile can become a fertile ground for discipline problems in the hands of an inexperienced teacher. As students finish their work (or simply stop working), there is a potential for difficulty. Selection of a highly involving instructional technique such as brainstorming at this time can often transform a potentially difficult situation into a productive learning experience for students.

Interests and other characteristics of students must be considered in selecting instructional techniques. Some students respond very well to role playing; others may not like it at all. Forcing a very shy student to make a public performance in front of a group of people with whom he or she may feel uncomfortable is needlessly humiliating. In identifying instructional techniques, the teacher must keep to the principle of keying those techniques to "where the learner is" and not to "where he or she ought to be." If the instructional technique does not "fit" the learner, there is scant promise that the content or process being taught through the use of that technique will be mastered.

Particular care needs to be exercised in selecting materials to support whichever instructional technique is selected. Because of variability among students, only rarely will a single textbook chapter, a single film, a single cartoon, or any other specific information source engage the attention, interest, and enthusiasm of all students in a class. As discussed elsewhere in this text, reading problems of students pose particular difficulties for social studies teachers. One response that has merit is to provide copies of a number of different textbooks focusing on the same general topic in the classroom. These texts should be selected to represent a broad range of reading difficulty levels.

Further, teacher-prepared materials, written in such a way that most students can read them (check these materials against the Fry formula described in the chapter on reading difficulties), can be provided as supplements to textbooks. Further, files of relevant periodical reprints can be made available to students. Finally, the rich array of media resources including newspapers, films, filmstrips, sound recordings, and videotapes can be surveyed to identify materials that can be used to support the selected instructional techniques.

Finally, instructional techniques and the learning materials selected to support them should be determined after a consideration of the purposes of the lesson. Some instructional techniques require teachers to play a role akin to that of a foreman as they give students directions, tell them what to do, and participate and guide students through experiences characterized by a high degree of teacher control. Other techniques require teachers to play a role akin to that of a creative design expert who provides individuals with some general guidelines and sits back to see what will unfold. Careful attention must be given to the specific learning outcomes sought before given instructional techniques are selected. A focus on the purposes of the lesson helps to assure a proper "fit" between the instructional techniques and the instructional ends to be served.

Individual Teaching Techniques and Intended Instructional Outcomes

Selection of a given instructional technique ought to go forward after a consideration of (1) the desired amount of direct teacher influence and (2) the purpose of the lesson to be taught. "Direct teacher influence" refers to the degree to which the teacher plays a dominant role. With regard to the issue of domination, Flanders (1963) has formulated a "rule of two thirds." According to the "rule of two thirds," during a given class session someone is talking about two thirds of the time. And during the time someone is talking, two thirds of that time that someone is the teacher. There is some evidence that students' attitudes and achievement tend to improve as the percentage of dominating teacher talk (direct teacher influence) decreases and the percentage of student talk increases. But as Flanders has noted (1967: p. 115), "in the control of classroom learning, there are times when direct influence is most appropriate and other times when indirect influence is most appropriate." The decision to select an instructional technique likely to result in a pattern of classroom interaction characterized either by direct influence or by indirect influence rests with the teacher.

In terms of the "purposes" sought in a given lesson, there are two general categories of concern. Some lessons are directed most clearly toward equipping students to acquire some specific information. This information might be thought of as the "product" emerging from the day's lesson. On the other hand, some lessons are directed not so much with a view to a specific product of learning as to helping students acquire the product. The "process" is viewed as a generalizable procedure that students might be able to apply in situations beyond the limits imposed by the lesson.

There are no instructional techniques that result only in instructional products. There are none that result only in instructional processes. Every lesson has, as an outcome, both products and process learning. But there are important differences regarding the degree to which individual instructional techniques promote product learning or process learning. Some tend to be more suitable when the purpose of the lesson is deemed to be primarily product learning. Others have strengths in the area of process learning.

In making a final selection of an instructional technique, the teacher must consider both the dimension of "teacher directedness" and the dimension of "product or process" learning. As a means of facilitating decision making, organization of potential instructional strategies into a matrix defined by these two dimensions is helpful. Figure 13–2 illustrates such a matrix. This figure lists ten instructional techniques within cells described by appropriate categories from each of the two dimensions. These instructional techniques are simply a small sample of the potentially much larger number of instructional techniques that might merit serious consideration.

Although these instructional techniques, as noted previously, do not represent an exhaustive listing of available options, they do constitute a good sample of possibilities that might be considered. General characteristics of instructional techniques that might be included within each cell of the matrix in Figure 13–2 are discussed in the following pages.

	More Interest in "Product" than in "Process" of Learning	Interest in Both "Product" and "Process" of Learning
More "Direct" Teacher Influence	Lecture	Discussion Team Learning
More "Indirect" Teacher Influence	Independent Study	Role Playing Simulation Class Debate Brainstorming

Figure 13–2. A Matrix Illustrating Characteristics of Selected Instructional Techniques in Terms of the Type of Teacher Influence Exerted and in Terms of the Major Learning Outcome Sought

CHARACTERISTICS OF INSTRUCTIONAL TECHNIQUES DISTINGUISHED BY (1) MORE "DIRECT" TEACHER INFLUENCE AND (2) MORE INTEREST IN "PRODUCT" THAN IN "PROCESS" OF LEARNING

Instructional techniques in this category tend to be characterized by clear teacher domination and control of classroom activities. This does not imply that teachers selecting these techniques are necessarily behaving in an insensitive manner toward their students. Domination is meant to imply simply that communication proceeds most frequently from teacher to student rather than from student to teacher or from student to student.

Further, instructional techniques of this type are designed with a view to transmitting specific content to students. There is a minimal interest in familiarizing students with the process according to which the information was packaged and delivered. For example, a teacher deciding to use a lecture as an instructional technique is concerned that students acquire information to be conveyed but probably is not at all committed to the idea that students should become proficient in the art of organizing and delivering lectures.

CHARACTERISTICS OF INSTRUCTIONAL TECHNIQUES DISTINGUISHED BY (1) MORE "INDIRECT" TEACHER INFLUENCE AND (2) MORE INTEREST IN "PRODUCT" THAN IN "PROCESS" OF LEARNING

Instructional techniques in this category are characterized by direct teacher participation only when the teacher acts to give students general operating instructions. The teacher establishes the ground rules but then largely removes himself or herself as the learning exercise goes forward. Techniques in this category are directed primarily toward having students acquire specific information. Independent study stands as a representative example of instructional techniques in this category.

CHARACTERISTICS OF INSTRUCTIONAL TECHNIQUES DISTINGUISHED BY (1) MORE "DIRECT" TEACHER INFLUENCE AND (2) INTEREST IN BOTH "PRODUCT" AND "PROCESS" OF LEARNING

The teacher plays a somewhat dominant mediating role when instructional techniques in this category are employed. The teacher's role goes beyond simple provision of instructions to include active monitoring of students' participation as the lesson unfolds. This monitoring may involve a central role for the teacher as a discussion moderator or as a questioner.

Instructional techniques in this category are directed both toward helping students acquire specific information and toward helping them to develop operational understandings of certain processes that can be used to generate logical conclusions. These processes are considered important because they have value as tools students can use to make sense out of fragmented information they will encounter in settings beyond the social studies classroom.

CHARACTERISTICS OF INSTRUCTIONAL TECHNIQUES DISTINGUISHED BY (1) MORE "INDIRECT" TEACHER INFLUENCE AND (2) INTEREST IN BOTH "PRODUCT" AND "PROCESS" OF LEARNING

Instructional techniques in this category involve the teacher primarily as a rule-maker. Once the teacher has provided guidelines for students, he or she tends to stand aside and let the activity go forward with a minimum of direct involvement. Certainly, he or she will be available for answering questions and settling disputes, but his or her role will not be central to the operation of the day's lesson. Most communication will be from student to student rather than from student to teacher or from teacher to student. Because these techniques are thought to have value in settings beyond the social studies classroom, there is interest in having students gain insight into the processes they are using to gain information as well as in acquiring that information itself.

Ten Selected Instructional Techniques and How to Use Them

The following instructional techniques by no means represent an exhaustive listing of those available for use in social studies classes. They do, however, constitute a reasonable sample of the kinds of instructional techniques that might be chosen to accomplish different instructional purposes. To identify more specifically the more general characteristics of each of these techniques, refer again to the matrix depicted in Figure 13–2.

LECTURE

Few instructional techniques have come in for so much criticism as has the lecture. Lectures have been accused of boring students, of ensuring that learners remain passive rather than active seekers after knowledge, and of generally assaulting students' sensibilities with too much information in too short a time. Proponents of inquiry-oriented learning particularly have been critical of the lecture.

It is true that the lecture has the potential to do all of the things for which it has been criticized. But these unfortunate consequences do not result from anything inherently weak, evil, or deficient in the lecture as an instructional technique. Rather, they have been the unhappy results when the lecture has been misused. Properly organized and incorporated into the social studies teacher's planning, the lecture can stimulate students thinking and can provide the motivational vehicle to stimulate their involvement into a serious inquiry into a new area of concern. These happy results will not result without careful attention to planning.

In preparing for a daily lesson in which a lecture will be used, the teacher should keep in mind a fundamental paradox with regard to the technique. The strength of the lecture as a vehicle permitting the teacher to present students with a great deal of information in a brief span of time is also its greatest weakness. So much material potentially can be delivered in a lecture that there is an ever-present danger of providing students with what might be termed "information overkill." Care must be taken to ensure that the rate at which new material is presented does not exceed students' capacity to absorb and relate to that material.

In making the decision concerning how much to cover, the teacher must regard as a primary consideration the individual group of students in the class. Frankly, lectures of any great length do not work well with very young secondary school students in middle schools and junior high schools. Many of these youngsters lack the necessary note-taking skills, the active vocabularies, and the ability to maintain attention on a lecturer's remarks over any very long period of time. (This is a very general statement. Certainly, some middle school and junior high school teachers will be blessed with students whose capabilities in these areas reflect a good deal more sophistication than is typical.)

Regardless of the group being served, the relative interest of students in the topic must be considered. Attention to the lecture will be much greater when a topic of high student interest provides the focus. This reality suggests the necessity of doing some diagnostic work to determine relatively strong areas of student interest before committing to the lecture as an instructional technique.

In planning for a lecture, teachers should observe the principle of brevity. When teachers do experience problems in using the lecture with secondary school students, a good deal of the difficulty frequently results because the lecture is too long. A short succinct fifteen- or twenty-minute presentation is much to be preferred over more loosely organized comments ranging over thirty or forty minutes. Lectures consuming an entire class period are almost never successful vehicles for communicating with secondary school students. This means, in general, that when a decision is made to present a lecture on a given day, decisions need to be made also regarding which other techniques will be used during the class hour.

In planning and organizing the substance of the lecture, one must take care to assure that students have already acquired information that the teacher assumes they know. If students lack such "base-line information," they will not profit from a lecture that seeks to expand their understanding of that information.

Point-by-point development must be clear. Inexperienced lecturers jump in almost random fashion from idea to idea without establishing the linkages for their audience. This kind of sloppy practice in the secondary classroom all but ensures that many students will lose the logical threads the teacher is trying to weave together. To avoid this possibility, the teacher will find it a good idea to build a careful lecture outline in advance. Development of such an outline and reference to it during the lecture can contribute greatly to the coherence of the presentation.

Beginning teachers, particularly, sometimes forget that many students have little understanding of some references that, to a teacher, seem very fundamental indeed. For example, many students have very shaky conceptions of geographic locations of places, and the teacher who delivers a lecture on the Civil War on the assumption that north-to-south alignments of the states are widely known will be disappointed. Because so much information is *not* known by students and because the lecture has the potential for presenting so much material in a short time span, it is sometimes helpful to provide students with a dittoed outline that they may follow as the lecture goes forward. Space should be provided for them to fill in details, as appropriate. An example of a workable outline might look something like the following:

TOPIC: CHANGES IN AMERICAN HOUSEHOLDS
FROM 1790 TO 1970

1.0 In 1790, 22 per cent of Americans lived in households with fewer than three individuals and 78 per cent lived in households with four or more individuals.
    1.1 Economic reasons favoring large households.
    1.2 Social reasons favoring large households.
    1.3 Political reasons favoring large households.
2.0 In 1890, 34 per cent of Americans lived in households with fewer than three individuals and 66 per cent lived in households with four or more individuals.
    2.1 Economic changes influencing diminished preferences for large households between 1790 and 1890.
    2.2 Social changes influencing diminished preferences for large households between 1790 and 1890.
    2.3 Political changes influencing diminished preferences for large households between 1790 and 1890.
3.0 In 1970, 63 per cent of Americans lived in households with fewer than three individuals and 37 per cent lived in households with four or more individuals.
    3.1 Economic changes influencing diminished preferences for large households between 1890 and 1970.
    3.2 Social changes influencing diminished preferences for large households between 1890 and 1970.
    3.3 Political changes influencing diminished preference for large households between 1890 and 1970.
4.0 From 1790 to 1970 there has been a consistent reduction in Americans' preference for living in households with four or more individuals and a consistent increase in their preference for living in households with three or fewer individuals.

Finally, during the actual presentation of the lecture, a variety of stimuli enhance the lecture's impact. Changes in rate of delivery, in volume, and in inflection stimulate attention. Use of physical gestures to support key points will help students identify important material from that which is of secondary importance. Finally, use of overhead transparencies, presentation of physical objects, and introduction of similar procedures that break the flow of words from the speaker enhance interest in the presentation.

In conclusion, there is nothing inherent within the lecture that makes it an inappropriate technique for use in secondary school classes. But the technique, when misused, can result in some lessons that are less than memorable (or worse yet, "memorable" for the wrong reasons). Despite potential pitfalls, the brief, well-organized, and clearly presented lecture belongs in the instructional techniques repertoire of the professional social studies teacher. The well-executed lecture provides students with an engaging and intellectually involving learning experience that acts as a stimulus to additional study.

INDEPENDENT STUDY

Independent study represents an instructional technique that, under most circumstances, is never appropriate for an entire classroom of students. Ordinarily, the student who responds well to independent study is highly motivated, mature, and able to follow general guidelines provided by the teacher with a minimum of direct supervision. Rarely will large numbers of individuals in a given class have the characteristics associated with success in an independent study program. But for individuals who are capable of profiting from independent work, such experience can be richly rewarding.

As a preparation for independent study, the teacher needs to do an especially thorough job of diagnosing students' interests and capabilities. Only those with reasonably high potentials for success should be selected. Once those individuals have been selected, specific tasks must be clearly identified. Basically, students must be given directions regarding the general tasks they are to perform, the amount of time they will have to complete these tasks, and the nature of any papers and projects they are to develop for the teacher to review.

Additionally, potentially useful learning materials must be identified. Though students are expected to complete their work with minimal teacher assistance, they cannot do so unless relevant materials are realistically available to them. Decisions must be made regarding which materials will be kept for the duration of the independent study exercise.

A decision must be made regarding whether students selected to participate are to do their independent study as an addition to their regular class work or as a substitution for regular class work. If they are to do their independent study as an addition to their regular class work, some system must be developed to reward them for their efforts. Even bright, highly motivated students will not stick to a task that places more demands and provides no additional compensations. On the other hand, if those students selected for participation are permitted to substitute their independent learning experience for regular class work, the teacher must develop responses to some logistical questions. For example, where will the independent learners be during regular class sessions? What is the teacher's legal situation with respect to liability for student actions when students are outside of the classroom area? What sorts of learning experiences can be provided for those not participating in the independent study experience? How can attitudes of learners not involved in the independent learning experience be dealt with?

Regardless of how the experience is organized, a decision to involve some students in independent learning will require additional teacher planning time. Compensation for this time must be measured in terms of the growth and enthusiasm of individuals involved in the independent learning experience. When these benefits appear to be significant, the decision to invest time in planning for an independent learning experience for some students can be defended. When such benefits are not apparent, efforts directed toward other sorts of instructional planning would represent a more defensible expenditure of the teacher's time.

DISCUSSION

Discussion is among the most frequently used instructional techniques in social studies classrooms. Properly monitored by the teacher, the discussion provides students with an opportunity for active participation and productive learning. To manage discussion professionally, the social studies teacher needs to become proficient in a number of important discussion skills. Six such skills have been identified by a project of the Northwest Regional Educational Laboratory (Northam, 1972):

1. Refocusing.
2. Clarifying.
3. Summarizing.
4. Mapping the conceptual field.
5. Accepting.
6. Substantiating.

Refocusing. The skill of refocusing is designed to keep a classroom discussion "on track." Without an occasional prompting comment from the teacher, there is a tendency for a discussion to bog down as issues peripheral to the central topic of concern are considered. When the teacher senses that the discussion is beginning to "drift," it is time to insert a comment to bring the group's attention back to the major focus topic. This needs to be done sensitively so that the last student speaker does not sense himself or herself to have been humiliated. For example, in a discussion centering on the threat of nuclear proliferation, the following exchange between teacher and student might have sufficed to reestablish a major emphasis on the focus topic:

> *Roger:* I read last night that some Italian scientists have figured out a way to use nuclear energy to dig canals.
>
> *Teacher:* That's very interesting, Roger. Lots of new technology is developing in the area of nuclear energy. I wonder whether you might comment on some possible connection between possible technological breakthroughs and our discussion of nuclear proliferation.

Clarifying. The skill of clarifying seeks to encourage students to state information clearly and logically. The teacher directs a question to a student who has just concluded his or her remarks. This question asks that individual to restate his or her position in such a way that points he or she has made are better understood by others in the class. For example:

> *Paula:* I think the government is interfering too much in our personal lives.
>
> *Teacher:* By "interfering in our lives" do you mean that there are too many rules businessmen must follow or that too much money is taken from us in taxes? Or did you have something entirely different in mind?
>
> *Paula:* Well, I hadn't thought too much about the things you mentioned, but I guess they are part of the problem, too. I was thinking more about this curfew business where we have to get off the streets by 11 o'clock on school nights.

Summarizing. The discussion skill of summarizing involves the teacher's working to pull together into a coherent whole a number of comments that are made during the course of a discussion. When the discussion has been of rather a short duration, a single summary at the end may well suffice. During longer discussions, several summaries might be made at logical points throughout the discussion. Most logically, summaries ought to be made when the discussion is about to move off in a new direction.

During the summary the teacher should attempt to take note of all student points. During the summary, students should be asked to contribute to assure that a comprehensive synthesis of what has been said results. For example:

> *Teacher:* Let's take stock of what has been said about the minimum wage this morning. One point was that raising the minimum wage will give employees at least enough annual income to stay above the federal poverty level. Somebody else pointed out that teen-agers might be hurt because employers may be unwilling to pay them more money. Let's see. What else? James.
>
> *James:* Rose said that some people might be thrown out of work. She said that some owners simply would not be able to pay the new rates and that we might get a few people earning more money, but that lots of others might be worse off than they were.
>
> *Teacher:* Yes, that was an interesting point. What else? Bob.
>
> *Bob:* Joe said that the industries with the big profits last year wouldn't be able to take unfair advantage of workers by paying them such a low wage. And I think Phil said that some more government agents might have to be hired to check up on enforcement.
>
> *Teacher:* Yes, all these are good points.

Mapping the Conceptual Field. The discussion skill of mapping the conceptual field is directed toward preventing students from jumping prematurely to conclusions based on limited evidence. This tendency is particularly notable among younger secondary students in middle and junior high schools who are a bit uneasy in dealing with unresolved issues and who are quick to grasp at an explanation that promises to end their uncertainty. In dealing with the tendency to close off discussion of alternative explanations too soon, the teacher needs to ask questions that encourage students to consider alternative possibilities. For example:

> *Nelda:* People are on welfare because they are just too lazy to get out and work.
>
> *Teacher:* That certainly may be one reason. Do you think that is the *only* reason people are on welfare? What other explanations might be logical? If you think about it, I'll bet you can give me at least six other plausible explanations for people going on welfare. Can you come up with more than six? Give it a try.
>
> *Nelda:* You're on! One, maybe they've been hurt and can't work. Two, maybe they have a skill that's outdated. Three, maybe they are mothers with lots of children who can't earn enough working to pay for sitters. Four, maybe they have some kind of chronic disease that

prevents them from working. Five, maybe they are just temporarily on welfare after a local factory shut down. Six, maybe there just aren't jobs available that match up their skills. Seven, maybe they have a severe alcohol or drug problem and no employer will hire them.

Accepting. The skill of accepting is very difficult for beginning teachers. It requires that the teacher welcome almost any student comment that has been voiced in good faith during a discussion. Frequently, students will make statements that represent either out-and-out misstatements of fact or statements that reveal very shaky logical underpinnings. There is a tendency for the teacher to want to "set things straight" with some comments of his or her own. This tendency should be suppressed. Students are more likely to join in a discussion willingly if they know their contributions will not be sharply contradicted by the teacher. Errors in fact and in judgment can be dealt with more effectively by using the discussion skill of substantiating than in rebuking a student contribution more directly.

Substantiating. Substantiating is the skill the teacher can use to deal with student comments that may be based on shaky logic (or, in some cases, on utter nonsense). When a student has concluded remarks in which he or she has staked out a given position, the teacher needs to do some probing with questions designed to elicit from the student some description of the evidence he or she has considered in arriving at that position. For example:

Jeffrey: After considering who all the major discoverers of the New World were, it seems to me that you'd have to argue that the English, Spanish, and Portuguese just about did it all. People in places like, say, France, must have not been very well educated at this time. I mean, they must not have known much about math and navigation and those sorts of things.

Teacher: You make the point that people in France at this time must have been somewhat backward compared to those in England, Spain, and Portugal. What can you tell me about education in France at this time?

Jeffrey: Well, not much.

Teacher: How about some other things. For example, what were the French really interested in during this time? How did they spend their money? Why did they spend their money this way?

Jeffrey: Well, if I had answers to some of those questions, I would probably be in a better condition to make a statement about the amount of French exploring as compared to the amount of English, Spanish, and Portuguese exploring. I think I'll hold off on my comment about the French being backward until I get some more information.

Teacher: See me after class, and I'll suggest a few places you might look for information.

Discussions conducted by teachers who are proficient in the use of these skills can provide valuable learning experiences for students. They can be actively engaged in processes requiring them to go beyond the "givens" to formulate supportable conclusions. This potential makes the discussion a particularly appropriate instructional technique when there is a desire to provide students with opportunities to develop their higher-level thinking skills.

TEAM LEARNING

Team learning is a technique that can be used effectively to introduce students to new material in a highly involving way. The technique takes advantage of both students' competitive instincts and their generally favorable attitude toward activities requiring them to work cooperatively with others.

As a first step, the teacher needs to identify a specific focus topic and learning materials relating to that topic that might be made available to "teams." Next a series of questions relating to the focus topic need to be distributed to each team involved in the exercise.

Next the teacher divides the class into four, five, or six teams. Four to six individuals are appointed to each team. Each team is instructed to appoint a student to play the role of "team recorder." Next sheets containing the questions relating to the focus topic are distributed. The last step in the preparation process involves directions regarding the availability of learning resources to be used as the exercise unfolds. In some situations, textbooks may be used. In others, special teacher-prepared materials can be distributed. The specific nature of the materials is not critical, but providing equal access to these materials by students in each group is imperative.

Dunn and Dunn (1972) suggest the following rules for the team learning exercise:[1]

> In attempting to answer the questions with which they have been provided, students in each group must adhere to these guidelines:
>
> 1. Any individual on a given team may help any other member on his or her own team, but he or she must not help anyone on another team.
> 2. Talking is permitted and encouraged, but it must be kept at a level low enough so it does not interfere with the work of students on other teams.
> 3. Each group attempts to answer each question of the list distributed by the teacher. Group members are encouraged to consult any available learning materials.
> 4. One student is selected to record responses of group members.
>
> Groups continue to work as the teacher moves throughout the room giving assistance where needed. The teacher lets the group activity continue until most groups have completed responses to all questions. Then the teacher calls the class to attention and begins debriefing as follows:

[1] This procedure has been adapted from Rita Dunn and Kenneth Dunn, *Practical Approaches to Individualizing Instruction* (West Nyack, New York: Parker, 1972), pp. 155–159. Copyright © 1972 by Parker Publishing Company, Inc.

1. One group's recorder is asked to read the first question and give his or her group's response.
2. The teacher asks for, and the class listens to, responses from other group recorders that are different from that given by the first group's recorder.
3. If there is disagreement, a discussion will ensue until the class and the teacher reach a consensus. Recorders for each group will mark responses to individual items made by their group as "right" or "wrong" in terms of how the group's responses compare to the consensus response.
4. This sequence is repeated until all questions have been considered.
5. As a conclusion, individual team scores can be computed. Count one correct for each question each group answered in a way consistent with the class consensus answer.
6. As a summary, the teacher can write consensus responses for each response on the chalkboard (or have some students do this). An alternative is to type this information and make copies for distribution to students the following day.

The team learning technique is particularly useful in situations requiring students to master a set of rather detailed information necessary or basic to the understanding of more sophisticated material to follow. For example, a teacher introducing students to a unit on Southeast Asia might wish to have students acquire information regarding river systems; mountain ranges; wind, rain, and ocean current patterns; and major agricultural regions as contextual background for a detailed study of that part of the world. The team learning technique would be an apt choice to help students acquire this important base-line information.

ROLE PLAYING

Role playing is an instructional technique particularly well suited to helping students better understand the perspectives of others. Many social studies students have a difficult time accepting the idea that their own particular conceptions of "good" and "evil" and of "right" and "wrong" are not universally regarded as definitive. The role-playing technique gives students an opportunity to gain insights into alternative views regarding these and other matters that can broaden the range of their concerns. Though no one can truly "get into another's head," the role-playing technique provides a reasonable approach toward the goal of sensitizing oneself to the world view of someone else.

In planning for a role-playing lesson, the teacher must begin by identifying roles that it might be logical for students to play. These roles may involve historical figures, or they may involve simply descriptions of fictitious individuals. Roles students are expected to assume should be selected with a view to giving them a specific perspective or frame of reference.

Once roles have been identified, the teacher needs to develop role descriptions for students. Role descriptions should include background information regarding the character to be portrayed, typical behaviors of this individual, his or her political preferences, his or her social views, and other information that can help the student come to terms with his or her personality. Role descriptions should be written as concisely as possible and distributed to the students who will be assuming the roles to be portrayed. If possible, these descriptions should be kept to two or fewer pages. The idea is to give the student enough information to represent the individual credibly without overwhelming him or her with so much background material that he or she fails to grasp the central characteristics of the personality he or she is going to attempt to assume.

Once role descriptions have been developed, the teacher must develop a scenario. The scenario describes the general situation the characters to be role-played find themselves in. Again, there should be sufficient detail to provide a legitimate context for the role players but not so much that they are overwhelmed by detail. Copies of the scenario should be distributed in advance of the role-playing exercise both to role players and to other students in the class.

After role players have had an opportunity to prepare their parts (perhaps after studying them overnight) and scenarios have been distributed, the stage is set for the exercise to unfold. Role playing is more effective when time limits are established so that the dialogue does not drift away from central concerns. Clearly, setting time limits has implications for the number of individuals that ought to be involved in a given role-playing exercise. Generally, players find it difficult to keep the dialogue moving forward productively when more than five or six individuals are participating at one time. If numbers of role players can be kept relatively small, twenty minutes time is ordinarily sufficient for the dialogue to have given individuals an opportunity to "flesh out" the character they have been portraying.

After the dialogue has concluded, the teacher begins the most important part of the role playing exercise—the debriefing session. The debriefing session involves role players and other class members in a discussion centering on what they observed during the dialogue phase of the exercise. Teacher questions such as the following can be used to guide discussion during this phase of the procedure:

1. Did individuals portray their people realistically? Why or why not?
2. Having seen Peter play the role of Lafayette in this exercise, what would you say were some of Lafayette's most notable personal characteristics? What do you base your opinion upon?
3. What values were held by the individual played by Jane? What is your basis for that judgment?
4. Would you have played any of these roles differently? What evidence do you have that your portrayal would have been "more true to life"?

The debriefing session provides a summarizing function for the exercise and helps students synthesize what they have observed into some defensible conclusions. Debriefing gives the teacher an opportunity to ask questions that probe the depths of understanding students have gained from observing and in participating in the role-playing exercise. It provides an important capstone to the activity.

When properly planned and executed, role playing provides students with a very stimulating learning experience. The technique has high potential for stimulating students' interest in their social studies classes as they deal very directly with the emotions, perspectives, and actions of potentially fascinating human beings.

SIMULATION

Long used by the military to approximate battlefield conditions as a training experience for new troops, simulations in recent years have been developed with a focus on situations of interest to secondary school social studies teachers. Simulations are designed to provide participants with an illusion of involvement in reality. This illusion seeks to provide participants with a sense of the essence of a simulated situation without exposing them directly to hazards that may be associated with that situation in the "real world."

Simulations provide an attractive vehicle for the secondary social studies teacher who, for example, wishes to give a class of students a taste of the political give-and-take that characterizes decision making in the United States Senate. Obviously, there is no way to provide such an experience for students directly. They cannot be "real" senators. But through the use of a simulation, they can experience some important elements of "reality" as it exists for individuals who are senators.

Simulations, in general, are well received by students. They typically have an apparent "relevancy" stemming from their focus on situations and circumstances that students recognize as valid. Further, simulations involve students in active, participatory learning. Decisions must be made, and outcomes are tied clearly to the nature of those commitments. In short, simulations provide students with opportunities to put basic information to use as they make decisions that are tested qualitatively against decisions undertaken by others and against certain standards built into the reward structure of the individual simulation.

Tremendous numbers of simulations are now available from commercial sources. Typical of the many that focus on a simulated replication of the legislative process is *Democracy* (copyright © 1969 by James S. Coleman); published by Western Publishing Company, Inc., New York, New York). *Democracy*, a series of eight possible games, gives students experiences designed to teach them about such issues as pressures legislators receive from constituents, the question of a legislator's personal conscience as it relates to wishes of his or her constituents, the committee structure in the legislature, the power of the floor leader, and taxation and public expenditure. Individual students portray legislators and respond according to rules described in the particular game being played.

Another favorite theme of developers of social studies simulations is international relations. Many commercial games are available that center on a presentation of a potentially dangerous situation, a frantic round of diplomatic activity, and the making of a decision designed to resolve the dispute short of armed conflict. *Crisis* (Western Behavioral Sciences Institute, La Jolla, California; copyright © 1969) is typical of simulations of this type. In *Crisis* a situation develops because of international rivalries seeking to control access to supplies of a critically important element. Participants form teams representing six fictitious nations. Negotiations go forward until some sort of a resolution of the situation occurs.

Social problems of various kinds represent another favorite concern of developers of social studies simulations. Representative of this *genre* is *Ghetto* (Western Publishing Company, Inc., New York, New York; copyright © 1969 by Dove Toll). *Ghetto* seeks to give students a feeling for the life of the urban poor by having them play roles of residents of inner-city neighborhoods. The game is structured in such a way that students develop a better understanding of the difficulties facing individuals trying to break out of the urban poverty cycle.

The number of social studies simulations available is so large now that even a rather exhaustive listing at the conclusion of the chapter would doubtless leave many unmentioned. The best reference for the social studies teacher interested in a comprehensive listing is a book devoted exclusively to providing just that information, Robert E. Horn's *The Guide to Simulation Games* (Cranford, New Jersey: Didactic Systems, 1976). Two books of especial interest to social studies teacher interested in using simulations are (1) Michael Inbar and Clarice Stoll, *Simulation and Gaming in Social Science* (New York: Free Press, 1972), and (2) Samuel A. Livingston, *Simulation Games: An Introduction for the Social Studies Teacher* (New York: Free Press, 1973).

If a simulation with a group of students is used, the following steps are involved:

1. Assignment of students to parts or roles.
2. Internalization by students of parts or roles.
3. Action phase of the simulation.
4. Debriefing.

The final step, debriefing, cannot be emphasized too heavily. Because simulations, by design, show only part of the "reality" they are attempting to convey to students, potentials exist for distortion. For example, a simulation designed to show how legislators do their work may emphasize the idea that, because legislators have more access to pertinent information than their constituents do, those legislators typically weigh constituents' letters rather lightly. Unless the teacher takes time during debriefing to explain that this bias was purposely built into the game by the developer to point out that, with respect to some issues, legislators rely heavily on their own convictions, students may leave with the false impression that it never makes any sense at all for a constituent to write a letter to his or her legislator. In short, the debriefing is designed with a view to filling in elements of the "reality" that may have been left out or may have been underemphasized during the simulated exercise.

When a simulation is found that focuses on an instructional topic central to the course, it can provide a very rich learning experience for students. Simulations have a high motivation capability. Indeed, some students who are apathetic at best during more conventional instructional approaches may perk up to become enthusiastic participants during simulations. When this kind of enthusiasm can be married to content that reflects the purposes of the course, simulation can serve as an instructional technique that is satisfying both to teacher and student.

Class Debate

The class debate varies considerably from the structure of the more familiar debate involving two contending parties. Alterations result from changes made to provide opportunities for larger numbers of individuals to be involved in debates on a given topic. A scheme that involves seven members in a group assigned to debate a topic works well. These seven are assigned responsibilities as follows:

> Three students are assigned to take a "pro" position.
> Three students are assigned to take a "con" position.
> One student is assigned to be a skeptical critic.

As with a traditional debate, the "pro" position's defenders attempt to marshal evidence in support of the proposition being debated. Those assigned to take a "con" position seek to find evidence and to develop a line of logic that oppose the proposition being debated. The individual assigned to be the "skeptical critic" seeks to find information that will be useful in attacking both arguments of the "pro" side and arguments of the "con" side.

Classroom debates work most effectively when topics that clearly are controversial are selected. Some examples follow:

> Resolved that the United States was morally wrong in dropping an atomic bomb on Hiroshima.
> Resolved that public education ought to be replaced by a system of privately financed schools.
> Resolved that California is the source region for most major innovations in American life.
> Resolved that all young people ought to spend two years of mandatory public service upon reaching the age of eighteen.
> Resolved that women ought to be assigned to combat duty in the armed forces of the United States.

The class debate follows according to the following general scheme of development. Times have been suggested as roughly appropriate for a fifty-minute exercise.

1. Each member of the pro team and each member of the con team speaks for two minutes. (Two minutes *each.*) The pro and con speakers alternate (pro, then con, then pro, and so on). Approximate time: Twelve minutes.
2. Each member of the pro team can cross-examine any member of the con team for two minutes. Each member of the con team can cross-examine any member of the pro team for two minutes. Approximate time: Twelve minutes.
3. Each member of the pro team and each member of the con team make final statements lasting no longer than one minute each. Approximate time: Six minutes.

4. The skeptical critic asks difficult probing questions of both pro team members and con team members. He or she may ask some questions of every team member, or may ask questions of only a few people. His or her function is to find fault with arguments of both pro team and con team members. Approximate time: Eight minutes.
5. Class votes to determine winner. Approximate time: Two minutes.
6. Teacher debriefs entire debate team and class.

The teacher debriefing is a critically important part of a classroom debate. During this phase of the exercise, the entire class can be involved in arguments and lines of logic developed during the debate. The teacher might ask questions such as the following:

What arguments impressed you?
Why were those arguments appealing?
What points would you have brought up had you been a member of the pro team? Of the con team?
Should the skeptical critic have asked some other kinds of questions? Give me some examples.

The classroom debate has high potential for generating active student involvement. A possible limitation is that such a debate cannot be completed in much less than an entire class hour. But when a need arises to consider controversial material and the time is available, the classroom debate represents a sound professional choice.

BRAINSTORMING

Rita Dunn and Kenneth Dunn (1972: pp. 192–195) have suggested a way of formatting a brainstorming approach that is particularly useful in social studies classes when students are considering some policy alternatives. Discussions of controversial issues frequently allude to several potential responses. Use of an analytic brainstorming approach can help students better grasp the implications of alternatives they may be considering.

In general, brainstorming proceeds according to the following rules:

1. The teacher provides the group with a dilemma, problem, or situation and asks members to call out possible solutions.
2. Students call out ideas as soon as they think of them. They are encouraged to call them out quickly, whenever an opening (of silence) occurs.
3. Students are admonished to shout or call out answers relating only to the dilemma, problem, or situation introduced by the teacher.
4. No editorializing on comments of others is permitted. All ideas are accepted.
5. Every idea is written down by the teacher (or by a designated recorder) as soon as it is called out.

Dunn and Dunn's (1972) "analytic brainstorming approach," systematically controls the kind of dilemma, problem, or situation posed by the teacher through five distinct phases. This process results in students' approaching a resolution of a policy problem with increasing precision with each succeeding step. The five steps are as follows:[2]

1. The teacher poses a problem in the form of a positive question or noncommittal statement about what an ideal resolution to a problem might be.

    The best solution to the problem of high unemployment among urban black males is . . .

2. The second teacher question asks students to describe what is preventing the ideal resolution from taking place. Responses to the first question should be visible to students as they begin responding to this question.

    What things are getting in the way of solutions you have suggested for dealing with high unemployment among black urban males?

3. The third teacher question asks students to describe what might be done to overcome obstacles cited in response to question 2. Question 2 responses should be visible to students as they begin responding to this question.

    How could we eliminate those things that are preventing us from resolving the problem of high unemployment among black urban males?

4. The fourth teacher question asks students to point out some possible difficulties in implementing ideas suggested in question 3. Question 3 responses should be visible to students as they begin responding to this question.

    What might prevent us from eliminating obstacles to implementing changes that might reduce the rate of unemployment among black urban males?

5. The fifth teacher question asks students to take the initiative in pointing out a specific "first step" that might lead to a resolution of the problem. Question 4 responses should be visible to students as they begin answering this question.

    Considering the problem and all the potential difficulties that have been mentioned, what should we take as our first steps in resolving this problem?

Use of this technique can generate a good deal of productive student involvement. The technique has the advantage of encouraging students to break away from the "conventional wisdom" to venture novel alternative solutions. As all student responses are welcome, there is no psychological threat of ridicule and a resultant dependence on shopworn responses. The number of solutions suggested during a brainstorming exercise is helpful in demonstrating to students that problems demanding policy decisions are complex and that many potential solutions may be viable.

Instructional techniques introduced here represent just a sampling of those available to the social studies teacher. In the selection of the appropriate technique, purpose of the given day's instruction must be kept in mind. As indicated in Figure 13–2, different instructional techniques have different characteristics relating to both the role of the teacher and their general function. Identification of the

[2] Adapted from Rita Dunn and Kenneth Dunn, *Practical Approaches to Individualizing Instruction* (West Nyack, New York: Parker Publishing Company, 1972). Copyright © 1972 by Parker Publishing Company, Inc.

preferred teacher role and the function to be served ought to precede selection of a given instructional technique. When this general procedure is followed, there is reason to believe that the selected instructional technique will be related logically to purposes going beyond a preference an individual teacher may have developed for working frequently with a given technique. Though personal preference is a concern, basing selection on priorities more clearly associated with purposes to be served by a lesson is a more professionally defensible criterion.

Summary

Instructional techniques vary both in terms of the role the teacher is to play and in terms of the kinds of learning outcome they best support. For example, teachers can play either a rather dominant leadership role, or they can exercise leadership more subtly and indirectly. Learning outcomes may vary in terms of placing highest priority on identifiable and specific information or on processes associated with learning information. A matrix was developed in Figure 13–2 suggesting how some techniques might best serve both different combinations of teacher roles and different priorities related to instructional outcomes.

A sample of techniques was selected for detailed explanation regarding specific steps to be followed in the social studies classroom. These techniques were described in terms of specific strengths, and, when appropriate, limitations on their use were discussed.

REFERENCES

ARMSTRONG, DAVID G.; JON J. DENTON; and TOM V. SAVAGE, JR. *Instructional Skills Handbook.* Englewood Cliffs, New Jersey: Educational Technology Publications, 1977.

DUNN, RITA, and KENNETH DUNN. *Practical Approaches to Individualizing Instruction: Contracts and Other Effective Teaching Strategies.* West Nyack, New York: Parker Publishing Co., Inc., 1972.

FLANDERS, NED A. "Intent, Action, and Feedback: A Preparation for Teaching." *Journal of Teacher Education* 14 (1963): 251–260.

———. "Teacher Influence in the Classroom." In *Research, and Application,* edited by Edmund J. Amidon and John B. Hough, pp. 103–116. Reading, Massachussetts: Addison-Wesley Publishing Company, Inc. 1967.

HORN, ROBERT E. *The Guide to Simulation Games.* Cranford, New Jersey: Didactic Systems, 1976.

INBAR, MICHAEL, and CLARICE STOLL. *Simulation and Gaming in Social Science.* New York: The Free Press, 1972.

LIVINGSTON, SAMUEL A. *Simulation Games: An Introduction for the Social Studies Teacher.* New York: The Free Press, 1973.

NORTHAM, SARALIE B., ed. *Participant Materials: Development of Higher Level Thinking Skills.* Portland, Oregon: Northwest Regional Educational Laboratory, 1972.

SUCHMAN, J. RICHARD. *Developing Inquiry.* Chicago: Science Research Associates, 1966.

Selected Themes

Chapter 14

DECISION MAKING

AND VALUES

THE ABILITY TO MAKE DECISIONS based on a clear understanding of relevant information and values is a hallmark of the competent adult. Mastery of the "decision-making" process does not come automatically. Clearly, it is more than a simple maturational matter. Given the concern of social studies educators for helping students grow toward active and responsible participation in public affairs, it is not surprising that lessons directed toward improving students' decision-making abilities have long been a feature of many social studies programs. Indeed, one distinguished social studies educator, Professor Shirley Engle (1960), has described "decision making" as the "heart of social studies instruction."

Instruction in decision making goes forward on the assumption that students do not derive lasting benefits from social studies programs requiring them to be only passive receptors of information. Rather, students' growth in decision-making abilities is thought to be promoted when they are confronted with unresolved problems and urged to formulate conclusions. As this process unfolds, students are encouraged to examine relevant evidence and personal and social values associated with a given issue. They are provided with guidelines designed to help them understand that evidence and values go together to provide bases for rational decision making.

Teachers bear a heavy responsibility as they help students master the processes of decision making. As students learn, they will make many mistakes. Some solutions to problems suggested by students may well be founded on misinformation, a shaky logical foundation, and socially destructive values. This suggests that the teacher needs to provide students with access to a wide array of sound informational sources, with an understanding of rational processes of analysis, and with techniques suitable for identifying both social and personal values.

The Informational Component of Decision Making

The "decision-making" process requires individuals to consider both information and values. In the social studies, some information ordinarily is drawn from history and the social sciences. These sources, however, reflect tradition rather than necessity. Certainly, information drawn from English, music, philosophy, and the arts or from combinations of disciplines can be utilitized. These academic subjects may serve as sources of evidence upon which rational decisions can be grounded. Evidence of this type has been described by Newmann (1970) as evidence of the "authority" variety. Establishing reliability of "authority" information requires consideration of questions such as the following:[1]

1. On what basis (bases) do the author or authors claim expertise in this area? Is this the *primary* area of expertise of the author or authors?
2. How close to the topic described was (were) the author(s)? Does this represent an account of an eye witness? Is it based on primary sources? On secondary sources?
3. What biases or preconceptions did the author(s) have in approaching this material? Is there evidence of irresponsible highlighting of some details and elimination of others because of the author's (authors') orientation?
4. Do conclusions suggested by the author(s) derive logically from the evidence? Are generalizations supported by extensive references to a wide range of specific data? Are conclusions presented after careful consideration of alternative explanations?

Newmann (1970) has described two additional varieties of evidence, "personal observation" and "common sense." In most situations, evidence derived from these sources is much less reliable than that derived from "authority."

The difficulty with common sense as a source of evidence is that what is common sense to one person frequently is not common sense to another. Consider, for example, the often conflicting folk sayings that have developed when common sense rendered different interpretations of a similar event. Should a young man take comfort when circumstances require him to move to a town 500 miles distant from his girl friend because "absence makes the heart grow fonder"? Or should he despair because of the common sense implied in the saying "out of sight,

---

[1] Adapted from Fred N. Newmann (with the assistance of Donald W. Oliver), *Clarifying Public Controversy: An Approach to Teaching Social Studies* (Boston: Little, Brown and Company, 1970), p. 59.

out of mind"? Common sense clearly has little to commend it as a basis for decision making.

Personal observation in a few restricted situations may have merit as a source of evidence. But biases of the individual doing the observing may affect his or her perception. Courtroom reports by witnesses to a common event provide abundant testimony to perceptual differences among individuals. Though personal observation may seem a perfectly reliable source of information to the person doing the observing, the selectivity of individual perception suggests that decisions made *only* on the basis of these observations may not be sound.

A further difficulty with relying on personal observation is that decisions need to be made about many issues that cannot be personally experienced by the decision-maker. How, for example, does every individual make a decision about the appropriateness of legalized abortion? Obviously, about half of the population, the males, could never have had a direct experience with this issue. Were personal experiences the only source of evidence upon which individuals could rely in making decisions, many decisions would be made capriciously. Clearly, the range of issues demanding decisions goes far beyond the limits of individuals' personal experiences.

The informational component of decision making in the social studies most appropriately rests on insights derived from disciplined knowledge. Sources of this information are not restricted necessarily to individual disciplines. For example, many appropriate social studies materials represent syntheses of information from a number of academic specializations. Whether organized as interdisciplinary efforts or as individual academic subjects, knowledge developed by scholars in the disciplines will likely have been tested against rigorous professional standards. Such knowledge provides reliable evidence for individuals to draw upon as they seek informational bases for decision making.

The Values Component of Decision Making

In addition to evidence drawn from informational sources, decision making involves a consideration of values. It is clear that people in coming to terms with day-to-day problems do not systematically process available information in the same way that a laboratory scientist works through a problem. Unlike the scientist who is "outside the problem looking in," most daily decisions require individuals to make decisions about problems "from the inside"; that is, people are personally and emotionally involved in situations demanding decisions. Consequently, personal values play a coequal role with available information as individuals attempt to make sound decisions.

The term *value* is a slippery one that demands definition before a productive discussion can proceed. Part of the definitional difficulty results because frequently in casual conversation such terms as *attitudes* and *values* are used interchangeably. Raths, Harmin, and Simon (1966) have provided a fairly rigorous definition of the term *value* that can help distinguish this concept from others. These individuals state that a value, by definition, must be[2]

1. Chosen freely from alternatives after careful consideration of the consequences.
2. Prized, cherished, and willingly affirmed in public by the person choosing it.
3. Acted upon repeatedly in some kind of recurring life patterns.

Attitudes do not meet all the requirements of this definition. They are simply "predispositions" to behave in a certain way but are not strong enough to be characterized as a value. For example, an individual may generally think highly of Republicans. He or she may from time to time say kindly things about that party to a close friend, but he or she may be unwilling to stand up in a large group and publicly affirm his or her belief. Consequently, his or her attitude of preference for Republicans falls short of the defining requisites of a value.

In helping students develop decision-making competencies, one needs to consider the issue of values at two levels. First of all, students need to recognize the values underlying decisions that have been made by others. A recognition that virtually every decision reflects a value orientation reduces the tendency of unsophisticated individuals to assume that a mechanistic, dispassionate system of weighing the evidence can point the way to a single "perfect" solution for every problem.

In addition to recognizing values undergirding decisions of others, students need to recognize values they hold and the relative importance they attach to each. When individuals recognize the hierarchies of values they have selected, they are better prepared to understand that a given decision may well support one value and contradict another. A value higher in an individual's hierarchy may well trigger a decision that is not consistent with a value lower in the hierarchy. For example, someone might value both quiet evenings and dogs as pets. If the value of quiet evenings is prized more highly than the value of dogs as pets, it is perfectly consistent for this person to sell his or her dog should the dog's evening barking become annoying. When individuals fail to recognize the hierarchical arrangement of values they hold, they may be disturbed by decisions that seem to put two deeply held values into conflict. Because of this possibility, social studies teachers have a responsibility to help students recognize the priorities they assign to the values they hold.

James Banks (1970) has suggested a useful model for helping students rationally identify and evaluate personally held values. Phases of the model provide a framework for sequencing teacher questions designed to help students clarify their values. A modified version of the Banks' Value Inquiry Model includes the following phases:[3]

---

[2] Adapted from Louis E. Raths, Merrill Harmin, Sidney B. Simon, *Values and Teaching* (Columbus, Ohio: Charles E. Merrill, 1966). Copyright 1966 by Louis E. Raths, Merrill Harmin, and Sidney B. Simon.

[3] Adapted from James A. Banks (with Ambrose A. Clegg, Jr.), *Teaching Strategies for the Social Studies: Inquiry, Valuing and Decision-Making* (Reading, Massachusetts: Addison-Wesley Publishing Company, Inc., 1977).

Phase 1: Recognizing value problems and value-relevant behaviors.
Phase 2: Pointing out values undergirding behaviors.
Phase 3: Identifying sources of personal values.
Phase 4: Naming alternative values and potential consequences of actions flowing from each.
Phase 5: Declaring and supporting value preferences.

Recognizing Value Problems and Value-Relevant Behaviors

The phase of the value inquiry model regarding recognizing value problems and value-relevant behaviors seeks to help youngsters identify values embedded in a given problem situation, determine the relative importance of each, and recall specific actions they have taken in the past when confronted with similar problems. The emphasis on past *behavior* is designed to bring to a conscious level personal value commitments. Recall that, by definition, a value must be a predisposition so strong that it has been *acted upon* with some regularity.

Questions such as the following typify those that are used to help students identify and establish priorities for values in a problem situation and reflect on past patterns of action:

1. You seem to be having difficulty in making up your mind. Can you explain the problem to me?
2. What are the advantages of solution A? Of solution B? Of solution C?
3. Which advantage is most important to you?
4. Have you ever had a problem like this in the past?
5. Can you tell me what specific things you did then?

Pointing Out Values Undergirding Behaviors

Questions to point out values undergirding behaviors seek to help students identify those values that prompted the decisions made to resolve problems identified in the preceding phase of the model. In addition to asking students to describe value bases for their actions, teachers encourage students to explain their reasons for believing these value commitments resulted in their decisions. The following questions exemplify those asked during this phase of the values inquiry process:

1. What do your past decisions tell us about what you think is important?
2. What was it about your decision that suggests these things are important to you?

Identifying Sources of Personal Values

During the next phase, identifying sources of personal values, students are encouraged to speculate about the sources of values they hold. Questions from the teacher seek to stimulate student thought about the reliability of these sources. The following are examples of questions designed to help students to begin evaluating the sources of their values:

1. When did you first come to believe that _____ was important to you?
2. Did anyone in particular give you that idea?
3. How do you know that your commitment to _____ came from that source?
4. Is that source a reliable one?
5. How do you know?

Naming Alternatives Values and Possible Consequences of Actions Flowing from Each

Once students have described a problem, identified past responses to similar situations, and named values and sources of values associated with those past responses, they should be encouraged to think about some alternative values that might suggest relevant problem solutions. Once such values have been identified, it is productive for students to consider potential consequences of problem solutions stemming from these alternative values. Questions such as the following typify those asked during this phase:

1. Now that we know the things you value most and where you got those values, let's think about some other possibilities. What sorts of things might be very important to someone other than yourself who was faced with this problem?
2. Suppose your primary value was _____. What kind of a decision would you make? Suppose it was _____. Then what would your decision be?
3. What good things might happen if your primary value was _____? What bad things might happen?
4. What would happen if you decided this problem on the basis of the same personal value according to which you decided similar problems in the past? What would the advantages be? The disadvantages?

Declaring and Supporting Value Preferences

The final phase of the process is designed to help students make a decision based upon a clear perception of alternative values and potential consequences of decisions made on the basis of each. The following questions exemplify those that might be asked at this time.

1. Now that you have considered a number of values that suggest different solutions to this problem, have you made a decision?
2. What do you think the likely consequences of this decision will be?
3. Does this solution say anything about the personal values that are most important to you at this time?

This value inquiry process, properly used, can greatly enhance students' self-confidence and general competence in arriving at sound decisions. The process demands a great deal of sensitivity and personal restraint from the classroom teacher. Students' answers to questions will not be a reliable guide to their true feelings in a classroom where they perceive the teacher to be taking a highly judgmental stance. As Banks (1977: p. 432) has noted, *"the teacher has to be very careful when asking questions like these so that he will not, in any way, abuse the student or punish him or her for freely expressing his or her beliefs."* When students *do* have confidence in their teacher's sensitivity, the value inquiry process can be a highly enriching experience for students. Surely, the approach belongs in the repertoire of all social studies teachers truly committed to developing personally secure and socially competent students.

Contexts of Rational Decision Making

Rational decision making requires a context of consensus regarding certain preeminent values or guiding ethical principles. For example, if there is no overriding conviction that human life is sacred, there exists no basis for discussion of values in a situation where a given decision might result in jeopardizing a life. Max Lerner (1957) used the phrase "cement of society" to describe the function of the broad-based principles from which other values derive their meaning.

Newmann (1970) suggests that values derived from Myrdal's American Creed (1944) are central to what he describes as "America's constitutional morality." Among values of the American Creed are

Inalienable right to life, liberty, property, and the pursuit of happiness.
Majority rule.
Due process of law.
Community and national welfare.
Rights to freedom of speech, press, religion, assembly, and private associations.

As Newmann (1970) points out, several of these core values have the potential for being mutually contradictory. For example, conflicts may develop between the value of "majority rule" and the value of the "worth and dignity of the individual" when a majority renders a decision that a minority feels it cannot accept. Many controversies stem from positions taken that, though congruent with one core value, may be inconsistent with another.

Although many issues arise because of conflicts arising as a result of conflicts between or among the values of the American Creed, these values themselves are not questioned. For whatever reason, they reflect commitments that our society has determined as fundamental, immutable, and axiomatic. They provide contexts for decision making that establish common objectives for contending parties. Two individuals may argue violently over whether a mandatory prison sentence for convicted "hit-and-run" drivers represents justice; they cannot argue logically about whether justice is important. This basic commitment must be assumed as a starting point for systematic argument and analysis.

Domains of Decision Making

Decision making in the social studies plays an important role in the areas of "intellectual education," "social education," and "personal education." In the intellectual education area, decision making focuses on subject matter content with a view to helping students identify informational and value components underlying conclusions of others. For example, the process might be used to help students understand the specific dimensions of historical problems, how those dimensions were viewed at the time, and what considerations went into the decision that was rendered. Then students can be encouraged to render a personal judgment of this decision in the light of information they have available and in light of their own values.

In the social education area, persistent present problems can provide a focus for decision making. Such issues rarely flow from the exclusive concerns of scholars within a given subject area. More frequently, the wide interest in these issues cuts such a wide swath that information pours forth from a bewildering array of sources. Clearly, some of these information sources have more merit than others. Students need help in making decisions relating to these issues that are based on both sound information and clear conceptions of the value underpinnings of alternative choices. Decisions that will need to be made in the years ahead in the area of energy utilization exemplify the vital need for providing students with decision-making experience in the social education area.

Bleak statistics relating to drug use among high school students and incidents of violence in secondary schools suggest the importance of developing students' decision-making abilities in the personal education area. It is illogical to presume that even the best intentioned and implemented programs can succeed if students are unable to come to terms with their own personal problems with a clear commitment to rational decision making. To nurture development of such a commitment, social studies programs ought to provide students with opportunities to enlarge their decision-making competencies in the personal education area.

In the following sections, recommendations will be introduced for organizing instructional practices supportive of student growth in decision-making competence in the intellectual education, social education, and personal education areas.

Decision Making and "Intellectual Education"

Decision making in the area of intellectual education seeks to help students analyze dilemmas introduced in subject matter content and to apply those insights to other settings. A model of this general process is presented in Figure 14–1.

The following short lesson built around the model in Figure 14–1 provides an example of a lesson directed toward building decision-making capabilities in the intellectual education area.[4]

---

[4] Adapted, with permission, from Tom V. Savage, Jr., "Roger Williams: A Case Study," Western Washington State College, unpublished paper, 1971.

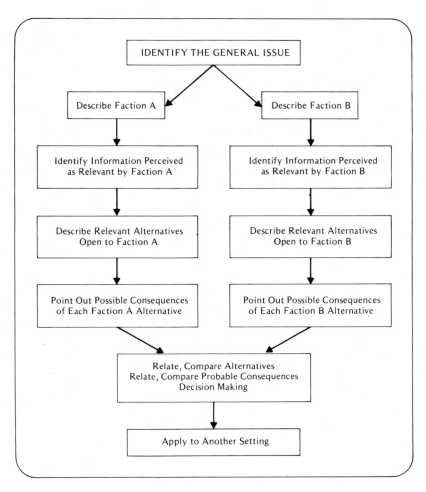

Figure 14–1. A Model for Decision Making in "Intellectual Education"

THE ISSUE:
SHOULD ROGER WILLIAMS BE ALLOWED
TO CONTINUE HIS TEACHING?

Describe Faction A (the Puritans)

The Puritans believed that the Church of England needed to be purified. By "purified" they meant that worship should be free from elaborate rituals. They feared that through the years the Church of England had adopted practices inconsistent with teachings of Early Christianity. The Puritans came to

America to save their children from "religious error" in England. They did not believe in religious freedom. Certain that their religious practices were "right," they had little tolerance for others who wished to worship in ways they "knew to be wrong."

The Puritans did not believe in equality. They had come to maturity in a society in which equality did not exist. True, they wished to be free from the rule of the king in England who supported the Church of England, but, in general, they were not greatly disturbed by the class structure of English society.

Puritans did not believe in democracy as we know it. They believed, for example, that only church members should be allowed to participate in the selection of political leaders.

The Puritans had left England with a serious purpose. They had left to create a kingdom they believed would please God. They felt they had an obligation to build a New Jerusalem in the New World. Because of this desire and because only church members selected political leaders, political opposition to the elected leadership tended to be seen as a threat to "correct" religion as well as a threat to political stability. The New England Puritan took pride in his tightly organized society inspired by "proper" service to God. This government provided a network of common commitment that, most Puritans believed, strengthened the ability of this relatively small number of people to survive in a forbidding New World.

Identify Information Relevant to Faction A (the Puritans)

Teacher questions:

What was most important to the Puritans?

What kind of a community did they want to build?

What was the relationship between the Puritan's religion and their government?

What did many Puritans consider to be the source of their strength, indeed, of their ability to survive in the New World?

Describe Faction B (Roger Williams and His Supporters)

The intense and intelligent young Puritan minister Roger Williams arrived in Massachusetts in 1631. Like the other Puritans, he had left England to find in the New World a life more in accord with God's will. As a minister in the town of Salem, Williams became the center of a controversy that became so heated that, in the end, he had to leave Massachusetts.

As Roger Williams reflected on God's will, he, in time, developed views that were at odds with those of the other Puritans. He came to believe that the Puritans should not seek to "purify" the Church of England but that they should break all ties to that Church. Most Puritans nurtured the hope that the model of religious practice they were establishing in the New World would be adopted ultimately by the Church of England. Therefore, they were extremely wary of breaking off official ties with that church.

Roger Williams also got into difficulty because of questions relating to land titles. He suggested that the Charter of the Massachusetts Bay Colony was a "public lie" because the King of England had no right to establish a colony on land that legally belonged to the Indians. To set matters morally straight,

Williams recommended that the Indians be compensated for their land. Most Puritans rejected this argument vehemently.

Most Puritans subscribed to the view that there was a single proper way to interpret God's "will." This "correct" interpretation was revealed to a certain "elect" few whom God had chosen for eternal life and through whom He made His desires known. Official church membership was restricted to these "elect." Roger Williams took issue with this point of view. He contended that God spoke to every man and that, consequently, every man had the right to worship God in accordance with how God spoke through his own conscience. He rejected the view that the Church should be restricted only to a few "elect" and that there was a single "proper" way of worship.

Identify Information Relevant to Faction B (Roger Williams and His Supporters)

What was most important to Roger Williams?
What kind of a community did he envision for New England?
What did Roger Williams believe about the Church of England?
What did Roger Williams believe about "proper" forms of worship?
What did Roger Williams believe about members of the elect as interpreters of God's will?

Describe Relevant Alternatives Open to Faction A (The Puritans)

Teacher question:
What options were open to the Puritans in the Roger Williams case?

Possible student responses:
They could have sent him back to England.
They could have executed him.
They could have made it illegal for anyone to listen to him.
They could have sent him away.

Describe Relevant Alternatives Open to Faction B (Roger Williams and His Supporters)

Teacher question:
What alternatives were open to Roger Williams?

Possible student responses:
He could have increased his public speaking activities to convince more Puritans that he was right.
He could have agreed to remain silent.
He could have gone back to England.
He could have left Massachusetts and established a colony for people who believed as he did.

Possible Consequences of Alternatives Open to Faction A (the Puritans)

Teacher question:
What might have happened if the Puritans had sent Roger Williams back to England?

Possible student responses:
He could have spoken out against the Puritans and tried to bring pressure on Parliament to make trouble for the Puritan leadership in New England.

Teacher question:
What might have happened if the Puritans had executed Roger Williams?

Possible student responses:
He might have become a "martyr" whose death made more dangerous those people who were opposed to the Puritan leadership.
People might have seen the folly of Williams's ways and all agreed that the Puritan view was best.

Teacher question:
What might have happened had the Puritans made it a crime for people to listen to Roger Williams?

Possible student responses:
A number of secret societies might have sprung up whose members were supporters of Williams.
Large numbers of Williams's supporters might have been arrested.
The government in England might have become increasingly interested in what was going on in New England.

Teacher question:
What might have happened if the Puritans had sent Roger Williams away?

Possible student responses:
He might have organized special agents to go into Massachusetts Bay to spread his message.
A number of his followers might have decided to go with him.
He might give up his cause.

Possible Consequences of Alternatives Open to Faction B (Roger Williams and His Supporters)

Teacher question:
What might have happened if Roger Williams had increased his public speaking activities in Massachusetts Bay to convince more Puritans that he was right?

Possible student responses:
He might have been arrested by the Puritan authorities as a threat to the Massachusetts Bay Colony.
He might have been secretly murdered.
He might have convinced so many people of the justice of his position that the Puritan leadership would have been forced to modify their views.

Teacher question:
What might have happened had Roger Williams agreed to remain silent?

Possible student responses:
Another one of his followers might have become a spokesperson for his cause.
Support for Williams's cause may have disappeared in time.

Teacher question:
What might have happened had Roger Williams gone back to England?

Possible student responses:

He might have set up a new church based on his beliefs.

He might have established a campaign to attack the Massachusetts Bay Puritans in the newspapers.

Support for Williams's views may have disappeared for a time in Massachusetts Bay.

Teacher question:

What might have happened had Roger Williams left Massachusetts Bay to establish his own colony?

Possible student responses:

Massachusetts Bay might have gone to war against this colony.

Massachusetts Bay might have petitioned Parliament to declare the new colony null and void.

Williams's new colony might have been successful.

Relate, Compare Alternatives and their Consequences

Teacher questions:

What similarities and differences do you see between alternatives open to the Puritan leaders and to Williams? How do you explain them?

Possible student responses:

Both could have gone to Parliament to get support for their respective positions.

Alternatives open to Williams basically required him to stop doing something. Those open to the Puritans required them to start to do something; that is, they had to take some new action to get Williams to stop spreading his ideas.

Alternatives open to Williams primarily involved just himself personally and perhaps a few followers. Those open to the Puritans were likely to set precedents involving the whole Massachusetts Bay Colony.

Teacher question:

How do you compare consequences of alternatives open to the Puritan leaders and those open to Roger Williams?

Possible student responses:

Those open to Williams held much more personal danger for him than those open to the Puritan leaders.

Some alternatives open to the Puritan leaders might have attracted unwanted additional attention from the government in England.

Alternatives open to Puritan leaders probably were easier for the leaders to decide upon than those open to Williams. This would have been true because probably a much higher proportion of the Massachusetts Bay Colony felt as the Puritan leaders did than supported Williams.

Decision Making

Teacher question:

Did Roger Williams have a right to challenge the authority of the Puritan leaders? Why or why not?

Possible student responses:

No, he did not. He understood the "rules" when he came. If he didn't like the arrangements, he should have stayed in England.

He had the right to think what he thought, but he didn't have the right to interfere with the stability of the colony by undermining the leaders.

Yes, he did. The Puritan leaders exceeded their proper authority when they claimed to rule because God had selected them.

Yes, Williams did have this right. English law protected property rights. Clearly, the Puritan leaders had made a mockery of this tradition in taking lands from the Indians.

Teacher question:

Did the Puritan leaders have a responsibility to oppose Roger Williams?

Possible student answers:

No, they did not. Roger Williams's followers were not numerous. He did not represent any real threat. In time, his ideas might well have been forgotten.

Yes, they did. Williams was a clear threat. He was a rotten apple in the barrel. In time, his followers could have made real trouble for the leadership of the colony. Without strong leadership, the colony may not have survived.

Teacher question:

What do you think should have happened in the Roger Williams's Case. Why do you have these feelings?

Possible student responses:

Williams should have been silenced as soon as he started suggesting a break with the Church of England. The church was tied to the government of the colony. As the colony was thinly populated and thousands of miles from the mother country, the primary concern should have been for security. Freedom of speech was a luxury the Massachusetts Bay Colony could not afford at this time. The danger to the colony's existence should have been nipped in the bud.

Williams should have been allowed to speak, and the Puritan leaders should have listened. Though the Puritans represented a majority in Massachusetts Bay, they did not represent a majority in England. By letting Williams speak his piece and perhaps attract some following, later relationships with England might have been smoother. Besides, compensating the Indians for their lands might have resulted in more positive relationships with them.

Williams should have been allowed to speak. The Puritan leaders did not have much faith in the logic of the position they were taking. If God had really wanted leadership to be exercised through an "elect" few, then open debate regarding the merit of that position surely would have resulted in a victory for supporters of that view. The Puritan leaders showed themselves to be somewhat weak-kneed and unconvinced of the merits of their own position when they took on Williams.

(Clearly, there are many many more possible student responses that might emerge at this point of the exercise.)

Application to Another Setting

Teacher questions:

How is the situation involving the Puritan leaders and Roger Williams similar to other instances in American history?

Are there similar conflicts involving group and individual responsibilities today? Which are they? How are these situations similar?

Should dissent be allowed? How should it be handled?

How would a person like Roger Williams be treated today?

How do you respond when you are pressured to do something you don't believe in? Are these situations similar to that faced by Roger Williams? How?

Organizing subject matter content to focus on specific dilemmas provides students with learning experiences that promote growth in their decision-making abilities. By emphasizing differences among value positions and alternative problem solutions, these lessons enliven content and help bridge the gap between school-based knowledge and a "real world" where social competence demands mature decision-making capabilities.

Decision Making, "Social Education," and "Personal Education"

The goal of social competence suggests that students be able to deal rationally with issues related to the areas of "social education" and "personal education" as well as with those related to "intellectual education." Certainly, one need look no farther than the headlines in the morning newspaper to discover the incredible diversity of social and personal dilemmas that must be faced by today's citizens.

The separation of social education and personal education issues into distinct categories is somewhat artificial. Certainly, every social problem, in one sense, is a conglomeration of personal problems. Too, personal problems that are experienced by large numbers of individuals soon become social problems as well. For the purpose of the discussion here, problems associated with the area of social education will be considered those so broad in scope that they impact simultaneously large numbers of people. Though these problems, viewed objectively, do impact large numbers of individuals, this does not mean that each individual senses these problems to be of overwhelming immediate importance. The relative importance attached to a given situation is related to differences in priorities attached to values relevant to the problem and to differences in evidence selected as relevant to the issue.

Problems in the area of personal education do not necessarily have to be so common in incidence that tremendous numbers of people are affected simultaneously (though, in some cases, they may be). In general, these problems are characterized by their having a large immediate importance to the individuals involved. For example, to a student with a relative on "death row," the issue of capital punishment is very likely to be a problem in the personal education area. For another student, the same issue may seem only a mildly interesting example of an issue that clearly is in the social education area.

Decision making in both the areas of social education and personal education demands consideration both of evidence from subject-matter sources and of personally held values. Consideration of this evidence in the light of value priorities

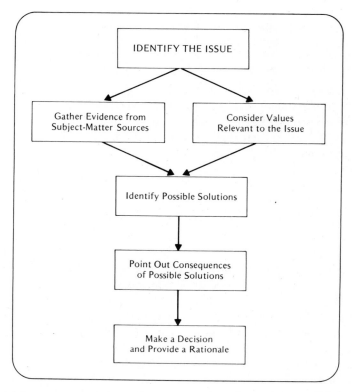

IDENTIFY THE ISSUE

Gather Evidence from
Subject-Matter Sources

Consider Values
Relevant to the Issue

Identify Possible Solutions

Point Out Consequences
of Possible Solutions

Make a Decision
and Provide a Rationale

Figure 14–2. A Model for Decision Making in "Social Education" and "Personal Education"

can help students to identify possible solutions, point out likely consequences of those solutions, and arrive at a supportable decision. A model for decision making in the areas of social education and personal education is provided in Figure 14–2.

The material that follows illustrates how this model might guide instruction designed to help students make decisions in the areas of social education and personal education.

AN EXAMPLE OF DECISION MAKING IN "SOCIAL EDUCATION"

Step 1: Identify the Issue

Recently, there has been a great deal of discussion centering on the ability of middle-class Americans to obtain access to certain kinds of professional services at a reasonable price. Much of the controversy has centered on the ability of people in this income bracket to secure adequate legal advice from lawyers when the need arises.

Those who suggest a need for change point out that the well-to-do have no problem in securing lawyers' services. Similarly, they note, poor and indigent citizens have access to publicly supported legal advisory services. But the middle class has neither the abundant funds of the well-to-do to pay for lawyer services nor the lack of funds, like the poor, to qualify for publicly sponsored legal aid services.

One reason lawyers' services are expensive, critics allege, is that there is no open competition. Laws prohibit, in most places, open advertising of rates. Further, lawyers' professional groups often view such advertising as unethical even when it is legal. Critics suggest that these conditions ought to be changed. Lawyers, they say, ought to be encouraged to compete in the free, unregulated market. Advertising of prices should be encouraged. Such a change, it is alleged, should bring fees down to the point that they are within the reach of middle class citizens.

In defense of present practices, many lawyers and lawyers' professional associations point out that advertising and open competition are unprofessional and will result in a deterioration of service. They point out that a "cheap" lawyer is not necessarily a "good" lawyer. Further, competitive rate setting might make earnings margins so narrow that lawyers would be extremely hesitant to take on long and time-consuming cases involving massive preparatory research. This situation might result in a net reduction in the total legal services available. Finally, some supporters of present prohibitions against advertising suggest that open competition would destroy the tradition of brotherhood of professionalism among lawyers. Though certainly this brotherhood does not mean that all lawyers take similar positions on all issues, still it implies a commonality of professional commitment to sound ethical practices. Given an openly competitive situation, this professional solidarity would be threatened. In the end, the quality of legal services might well be impaired.

The issue, then, reduces to this question: Should lawyers be permitted to compete openly for clients through the medium of advertising?

Step 2: Evidence from Subject-Matter Sources

(Information presented in this phase will vary in terms of the course being taught and the background of the individual teacher. The following questions exemplify those that might be used to guide efforts to obtain relevant information from several subject-matter areas, as indicated.)

History: What historical precedents led to the establishment of a noncompetitive guild system for setting prices for legal services?

Geography: What are present geographic distributional patterns across physical and social space? What changes might be expected in these patterns were lawyers to establish fees for services competitively?

Political Science: What authority structures seek to maintain the present noncompetitive system for establishing fees for lawyers' services? What changes would be likely should there be a change to establishing fees for these services competitively?

Economics: What effects does present noncompetitive establishment of lawyers' fees have on levels of those fees? What changes in levels
of fees might result from a change to a competitive fee structure?

Step 3: Consider Values Relevant to the Issue

What values are basic to the position of those favoring the establishment of
setting fees for lawyers' services competitively and encouraging advertising
for clients? How do you know?

What values are basic to the position of those favoring the retention of the
present system of noncompetitive fee setting and a prohibition of advertising?
How do you know?

Step 4: Identify Possible Solutions

(Clearly a number of possibilities may be suggested during an actual class
discussion. Several are suggested here as illustrations useful in demonstrating
techniques to be followed in the next step.)

What possible solutions can you suggest to this situation?

Possible Responses:

We can continue to maintain the present situation of no advertising and
noncompetitive rates.

We can insist that rates do become competitive and that lawyers be encouraged to advertise.

We can pass a law setting up a governmental agency to set lawyers fees
at an acceptable level.

Step 5: Point Out Possible Consequences of Possible Solutions

(Responses to the following questions are provided simply as illustrations. Students may come up with a much larger array of answers.)

What might happen if we make no changes in the present system?

Possible Responses:

The middle class will continue to have a hard time affording lawyers' services.

Young lawyers may go out of business unless they join a large, well-known
firm. People won't pay high fees to a beginner they don't know about.

There might be an inclination for too many young people to go into law
attracted by fees that remain artificially high because of the lack of competition.
Some may not be able to make a living as practicing lawyers because insufficient
numbers of people can pay those fees.

What might happen if rates do become competitive and lawyers compete
for clients through advertising?

Possible Responses:

Rates for lawyers' services may go down, making access to legal help available
to more people.

Large specialized firms may go out of business because they cannot compete successfully and maintain their heavy overhead expenses in an environment when fees are set competitively.

Lawyers may be reluctant to specialize in law school in important but infrequently demanded specializations. Too many may seek to become specialists in divorce law and in other areas where there is always a high public demand.

What might happen if a law were passed setting up a governmental authority to set rates for legal services?

Possible Responses:

Lawyers' fees could go down, and legal services could come within the reach of more people.

Lawyers' fees could go up, depending on the "official" schedule of rates set by the governmental agency.

Tremendous political battles could be developed as interest groups representing lawyers and consumers of legal services attempted to gain influence with the state authority.

Costs of state government could go up because of the need for new employees to monitor compliance with "official" legal fee rules.

Step 6: Make a Decision and Provide a Rationale

What should be the solution to this problem?

What evidence supports your conclusion?

What does your conclusion say about those things you believe to be most important?

Why do you believe those things to be most important?

AN EXAMPLE OF DECISION MAKING IN "PERSONAL EDUCATION"

Step 1: Identify the Issue

A particularly vexing problem for many students and adults is shyness. For those unafflicted with the difficulty, the problem may seem trivial; but for people who have it, coping with many of life's challenges is painfully difficult. Shyness can prevent talent from being fully developed. It can deny a community the needed insights of many competent people who just do not feel comfortable in speaking out in any kind of group setting.

Shyness, in some instances, results from cultural factors. For example, some girls may have been rewarded as small youngsters for "being such a quiet young lady." Early reinforcement of passive noninvolvement can be a contributor to social shyness in later years.

Other sufferers have experienced unpleasant consequences at some time during their lives when they have attempted to become an active participant in a social setting. For example, a given youngster may have been told his or her ideas were "dumb" so frequently by brothers, sisters, and playmates that he or she may have decided that he or she would do better to maintain silence rather than subject himself or herself to further humiliation.

However it is caused, shyness is a serious problem for large numbers of individuals. Because of problems associated with this condition, a number of authorities have directed their attention to procedures for helping shy people to build their self-confidence. Some of these individuals suggest that the problem is basically self-correcting; that is, unless people have serious emotional problems, the difficulty tends to disappear over time. This is particularly true of shyness in young people, these authorities allege, because shyness often results from different rates of physical maturation. For example, a young man may be much smaller than most of his age mates during his mid-teens. But by the time he is in his twenties, this difference may well have disappeared. Consequently, shyness associated with physical size may disappear as well.

Other authorities suggest that shyness ordinarily will not disappear automatically. They suggest that a person suffering from this problem needs to take specific steps to remedy it. One proponent of this view (Zimbardo, 1977) points out that shy people need to take specific actions based on a step-by-step plan of self-help. First, small realistic goals need to be set; that is, a shy person needs to identify a specific situation in which he or she will become an active social participant. Step-by-step actions need to be identified in advance, describing exactly how he or she intends to behave.

For example, a student wishing to participate actively in a student council meeting might write down what he or she intends to say in advance of the meeting. Additionally, he or she might write down possible answers to some questions he or she might get. The idea here is to provide conditions for success in a limited situation. The view of authorities recommending this procedure is that success in a limited area can build the sort of confidence that will encourage more active and more comfortable social participation in other areas.

This then is the issue: Should individuals follow what others suggest as a remedy for shyness, or should they wait and hope that the condition will cure itself?

Step 2: Evidence from Subject-Matter Sources

(Information presented in this phase will vary in terms of the course being taught and the background of the individual teacher. The following questions exemplify those that might be used to guide efforts to obtain relevant information from several subject-matter areas, as indicated.)

Psychology: What does developmental psychology say about shyness and maturation?

What does reinforcement theory say about the effect of social success on changes in behavior?

Sociology: What kinds of social conditioning might reinforce a pattern of shyness? A pattern of comfortable social participation?

Step 3: Consider Values Relevant to the Issue

What values are implied by the desire to make shy people more comfortable in social settings?

How do you know?

Step 4: Identify Possible Solutions

(Clearly a number of possibilities may be suggested during an actual class discussion. Several are suggested here as illustrations useful in demonstrating techniques to be followed in the next step.)

What do you think shy people should do about their condition?

Possible Responses:
They shouldn't do anything. The problem will probably go away in time.
They should develop a systematic plan of action. This should help them achieve small goals. These successes should build the confidence necessary for success in other situations.

Step 5: Point Out Possible Consequences of Possible Solutions

(Responses to the following questions are provided simply as illustrations. Students may come up with a much larger array of answers.)

What might happen if people suffering from shyness took no action directed toward changing that condition?

Possible Responses:
In time, these people might lose their shyness and become more comfortable as active participants in social situations.
Their shyness could remain at about the same level. This could deny others the benefit of their ideas.
Their shyness could grow much worse. In addition to denying others the benefit of their ideas, this situation could become so serious that their ability to function with others in *any* kind of a social situation could become seriously impaired.
What might happen if people suffering from shyness developed and put into operation a specific plan designed to help them overcome this condition?

Possible Responses:
In time these people might be able to develop enough self-confidence to enable them to function actively in a wide variety of social situations.
Their plans might not work. If not, these people could become more shy than ever.

Step 6: Make a Decision and Provide a Rationale

If you were a shy person, what do you think should be done about this problem?
What kind of evidence would you base your decision upon?
What would this decision tell people about what you think is important?
Why do you believe those things to be important?

The Scope of Decision Making

Decision making is a generic process that properly plays a role in all social studies classes, regardless of the subject-matter emphasis. Without rational decision-making abilities, students cannot be expected to deal with contents in the areas of "intellectual education," "social education," and "personal education" in any but a very superficial way. Activity and participation of any kind demand choice. If social studies courses are framed with a view to helping students go beyond the level of simple recall of content, these courses must provide opportunities for students to assume responsibility for actively manipulating content. Decision-making procedures described here can provide an opportunity for students to become social participants rather than passive observers of social phenomena. Given opportunities for participation of this type, youngsters are much more likely to develop the sorts of intelligent information-processing skills that characterize the socially competent individual.

Success in teaching decision-making procedures demands of teachers a sensitive attention to personal values of students that is coupled to a willingness to demand of students a rigorous attention to supplying evidence in support of positions. Balancing the concern for the worth and dignity of individual students' perceptions against the need for a rational organization of evidence in support of those perceptions is the hallmark of a professional social studies teacher. When an appropriate balance is struck between these two needs, students grow significantly in their abilities to deal systematically with the many dilemmas they must face now and in the future. This kind of rational self-confidence is fundamental to the social competence that is an overriding goal of social studies education programs.

Summary

Competent adults are characterized by their ability to confront problems and make rational decisions. Social studies programs can develop students' competencies in this area by providing programs calling upon them to make decisions in the light of evidence and personally held values. Learning experiences can be designed that focus respectively on intellectual education, social education, and personal education. The objective of instruction in each of these areas is to familiarize students not so much with academic content as with the process they use in arriving at conclusions.

References

BANKS, JAMES A. (with AMBROSE A. CLEGG, JR.). *Teaching Strategies for the Social Studies: Inquiry, Valuing and Decision-Making.* Reading, Massachusetts: Addison-Wesley Publishing Company, Inc., 1977.

ENGLE, SHIRLEY H. "Decision-Making: The Heart of Social Studies Instruction." *Social Education* (November 1960): 301–304, 306.

LERNER, MAX. *America as a Civilization.* New York: Simon and Schuster, 1957.

MYRDAL, GUNNAR. *An American Dilemma: The Negro Problem in Modern Democracy.* New York: Harper & Row, Publishers, 1955.

NATIONAL COUNCIL FOR THE SOCIAL STUDIES. *Social Studies Curriculum Guidelines.* Washington, D.C.: National Council for the Social Studies, 1971.

NEWMANN, FRED N. (with the assistance of DONALD W. OLIVER). *Clarifying Public Controversy: An Approach to Teaching Social Studies.* Boston: Little, Brown and Company, 1970.

RATHS, LOUIS E.; MERRILL HARMIN, and SIDNEY B. SIMON. *Values and Teaching.* Columbus, Ohio: Charles E. Merrill Publishing Co., 1966.

SAVAGE, TOM V., JR. "Roger Williams: A Case Study." Unpublished paper. Bellingham, Washington: Western Washington State College, 1971.

ZIMBARDO, PHILIP. *Shyness: What It Is, What to Do About It.* Reading, Massachusetts: Addison-Wesley Publishing Company, Inc., 1977.

Chapter 15

CULTURAL HERITAGE
STUDIES

NOT MANY YEARS AGO, the description of the United States as a "melting pot" of peoples and cultures was challenged only infrequently. Indeed, the statement was a feature of elementary and secondary social studies textbooks until very recent times. Today the view that ethnic differences are disappearing as groups gradually take on characteristics of a more general "American" culture is being challenged. There is increasing evidence that ethnic differences persist over generations even under conditions that may be far from ideal.

School programs promoting the "melting pot" view were undertaken in response to a need to deal with thousands of immigrant children entering public school classrooms in the late nineteenth and early twentieth centuries. Leaders of the day felt that the society could best preserve itself by quickly introducing the young to "the American way." By original intent, such programs sought to strengthen the social fabric by binding the new Americans to the old with threads of shared speech, attitudes, and values.

Although intentions of educators convinced of the merits of the "melting pot" view may have been innocent enough, often the consequences of practices stemming from this position were tragic for ethnic minority children. Many youngsters from ethnic minorities sensed that the school was making a special effort to ensure that they acquired certain attitudes and values that children from dominant ethnic groups seemed to acquire almost "automatically." To many ethnic minority youngsters, this situation suggested that there might be some problem with their ethnic group. Critics of educational programs stemming from the "melting pot" position have criticized this "deficit" view of ethnic minorities.

Button (1977) has pointed out that such programs seemed to suggest that there was "something wrong" with the child from a minority ethnic group when he or she came to school. Achievement problems frequently were blamed on resistance to "proper" change on the part of the minority group culture from which the child came. School programs, consistent as they were with the values of the dominant group, were viewed as "correct." Any adjustments or accommodations were to be made by the ethnic minority child. In other words, the child was obligated to bend to meet the needs of the school. But the school sensed little, if any, necessity to modify its practices to serve the special needs of the child from the minority ethnic group.

As educators (and the public at large) have become more sensitive to the persistence over time of differences among ethnic groups and less threatened by these differences, school practices have begun to respond more sensitively to special needs of members of all ethnic groups. As Button (1977) has noted, increasingly individuality and cultural differences are prized as enriching features of the American experience. Further, there is growing recognition that Americans live in a multicultural world. School programs have begun to respond to this reality as educational leaders have recognized that monocultural schools cannot serve adequately a multicultural nation and world. Among these responses have been new approaches in secondary school social studies departments directed toward multiethnic education.

Purposes of Multiethnic Instruction in the Social Studies

Multiethnic instruction in the social studies is directed toward two central objectives. On the one hand, these programs seek to develop the sense of personal worth and dignity of students from minority ethnic groups. On the other hand, these programs seek to sensitize *all* students to ethnic differences and to help them appreciate perspectives and contributions of ethnic groups other than the one to which they owe a primary psychological allegiance. In helping students grow in their understanding of ethnic differences, teachers will find it essential that students learn that there are valid and legitimate reasons for cultural differences. Without such understanding, too many will continue to see themselves as "normal" or "correct" and others as "strange," "not normal," or even "funny."

The eminent multiethnic education specialist Professor James A. Banks of the University of Washington (1975) has pointed out that too many schools fail to provide multiethnic programs because "we have no Blacks, no Native Americans, etc." and therefore perceive no need for such programs. Banks has commented:

> Perhaps unknowingly, educators who feel that ethnic minority content should only be studied by ethnic minorities and that minorities only need to study about their own cultures have a condescending attitude toward ethnic minority studies and do

not consider the ethnic minority experiences to be a significant part of American life.[1]

Modern life demands an understanding that crosses ethnic boundaries. Although individual members of majority and minority ethnic groups alike draw inspiration from unique perspectives of their groups, still, in a multiethnic world, they must learn how to get along with people having backgrounds widely divergent from their own.

Multiethnic education seeks to promote mutual understanding among members of different ethnic groups. Education reflecting only the perspectives of a single group has the potential to build walls rather than bridges between members of various ethnic groups. Thoughtful educators oppose strongly any move to allow multiethnic education programs to become a vehicle for resegregating schools along ethnic group lines.

Problems in Organizing a Multiethnic Education Program

Perhaps the single most vexing problem facing the teacher interested in instituting multiethnic education studies in the social studies is the inertia of tradition. Because so many materials have been developed from the traditional cultural perspective of the dominant white majority, frequently teachers experience great difficulty in perceiving alternative ways of viewing subject matter. This dilemma is particularly acute because most teachers are white and drawn from the middle class, the group most imbued with the perspectives of the dominant white culture. Because of their own backgrounds and their long exposure to viewing reality through the "eyes" of the dominant white majority, they often have difficulty accepting the legitimacy of alternative perspectives.

An example of how these "majority group" blinders affect instructional practices of many social studies teachers is the approach typically given in high school courses to the settlement of the United States. With few exceptions, this topic is treated as an east to west phenomenon. Textbook discussions proceed from the perspective of the European's gaining a tenuous foothold on the Atlantic Seaboard and working to "bring civilization" to the untamed West, increment by increment. Very sketchy treatment is given to countercultural flows from west to east (as a consequence of the interaction between Native Americans and Europeans) or from south to north (as a consequence of the interaction between Mexican-Americans and Europeans). For example, very little attention typically is accorded the profound influence of the Plains Indian cultures on military tactics later adopted as "standard" by the U.S. Army. The Army Signal Corps, at least in its early days, used manuals patterned almost directly on wigwag and other long distance signaling techniques developed by Native American groups on the western plains.

[1] James A. Banks, *Teaching Ethnic Studies* (Boston: Allyn and Bacon, Inc., 1975), p. 17.

The cultural flow of Spanish and Indian origin running from south to north has come in for even less attention than influences of Western Native Americans on European immigrants from the east. Reacting against the narrow east to west orientation of many United States history textbooks, Carlos Cortez has proposed a reorientation around what he calls the "Greater America Concept." Presented according to the Greater America Concept, United States history would introduce students to a much broader conception of the historical evolution of the nation. In this connection, Cortez has written:

> the social studies must be re-oriented on the basis that the Greater American heritage developed from the dual advance of societies from the Atlantic Coast west and from Mexico City north, as well as from the fusions and conflict between these advancing cultures and the already existent Southwestern Civilization.[2]

A program oriented around the Greater America Concept might include much information that gets overlooked in more traditional United States history courses. For example, contributions of Mexican mining technology might be highlighted, such as the migration northward of knowledge related to such practices as (1) the use of mercury to separate silver from silver-bearing ores, (2) the "dry-wash" method of extracting gold in areas with no available water, and (3) milling techniques for separating gold from quartz, all of which were essential to the success of mining enterprises in the West. Without the mass movement of people from mining regions of Mexico who carried their expertise to California, Arizona, Colorado, and other points in the West, development of valuable mineral resources would have been delayed for years.

Influences of this northward migration, of course, had an impact in many areas other than mining technology. Frontier English quickly accepted words of Mexican-Spanish origin, such as *mesquite, rodeo, bonanza,* and *mesa.* In states heavily influenced by the northward flow of immigrants from Spanish-speaking areas, "community property" laws governing property relationships between husband and wife were passed. Patterned on Mexican law, such legislation gave women a much firmer legal status with respect to property rights than the heavily male-oriented Anglo-Saxon law. With respect to agriculture, irrigation systems and management practices of large sheep and cattle operations were heavily influenced by traditions flowing north out of Mexico. There is no problem in finding sufficient content for courses oriented around a "Greater American Concept."

The Greater America Concept at bottom is a call for rearranging topical emphases in United States history courses to represent more adequately contributions of groups other than the white majority. But multiethnic education does not stop with a simple balancing of topics. If secondary students are to be provided with a truly multiethnic perspective, they must be introduced to the specific attitudes

---

[2] Carlos E. Cortez, "Teaching the Chicano Experience," in *Teaching Ethnic Studies: Concepts and Strategies,* ed. James A. Banks, 43rd Yearbook of the National Council for the Social Studies (Washington, D.C.: NCSS, 1973), p. 186.

and feelings that characterize individual ethnic groups. Without such understandings, a good deal of specific information that the teacher might present regarding actions of ethnic minorities won't "make sense" (make sense, that is, given the values of the dominant majority). Social studies teachers must acquaint themselves with values differences between and among various ethnic groups. Such differences may prove enormously helpful in developing students' appreciation for actions taken and words spoken by members of certain minority groups. To point out the great variation between Mexican-American and dominant white or Anglo-American values, Guinn (1977) has developed the following comparative scheme:

CULTURAL VALUE DIFFERENCES

Mexican-American	Anglo-American
1. Being rather than doing	1. Doing rather than being
2. Limited stress on material gain	2. Material well-being
3. Present-time orientation	3. Future-time orientation
4. Fatalism, accommodation to problems	4. Individual action and reaction
5. Tradition, reluctance to change	5. Change-directed

Adapted from Robert Guinn. "Value Clarification in the Bicultural Classroom," *Journal of Teacher Education* (January–February 1977): 46–47.

In addition to familiarizing themselves with value patterns of a number of ethnic groups, teachers in multiethnic education programs find themselves faced with a struggle to prevent their students from stereotyping members of various ethnic groups. Because much information about, for example, Mexican-Americans results from an examination of a great deal of information that is averaged to yield some sort of a "typical profile," students may well conclude that *all* Mexican-Americans fit this description. Exposed to Guinn's information about the "present-time orientation" of Mexican-Americans, some students might be highly surprised to learn that large numbers of Mexican-Americans are pursuing advanced degrees in American universities with a view to personal and financial rewards that lie well into the future. They might be perplexed, too, in learning that many inventions had been generated by Mexican-Americans, something that may seem incompatible with Guinn's finding that Mexican-Americans value "tradition" and do not prize "change."

The social studies teacher in multiethnic education must make clear to his or her students that there are enormous differences *within* individual ethnic groups. For example, Spanish-speaking Americans who trace their ancestry to Mexico are not even at consensus regarding what general term should be used in describing them. Some prefer *Chicano*. Others consider this to be a slanderous term. Some prefer *Mexican-American*. Others detest the term in the belief that any "hyphenated" American is viewed as less than a "real" American. In some sections of the country the terms *Hispano* and *Latino* are favored. In others, these terms can generate heated arguments.

In general, then, students need to learn that differences within ethnic groups are as profound as differences between and among ethnic groups. This understanding is absolutely essential if students are to avoid (unintentionally) insulting a member of a minority ethnic group by assuming that all members of that group share certain views or common experiences. An upper middle-class black person will likely think crass and insensitive an invitation to comment on "life in the ghetto." He or she knows no more about ghetto life, in all probability, than his or her rude questioner. In summary, students must understand that there are few, if any, characteristics of an individual ethnic group that apply universally to each member of that ethnic group.

Another difficulty social studies teachers interested in multiethnic education have relates to selection and delimitation of the minority ethnic groups to be studied. The number of such groups is so great that clearly not all can be treated. A balance must be struck between restricting the focus to too small a number and promoting hopeless instructional fragmentation by dealing with too many in a quick and superficial manner. Most programs focus on four to six groups. There is nothing magical about these numbers, but they do provide some rough guidelines.

Criteria for selection include (1) ethnic makeup of the school and community, (2) inclusion of white ethnic minority groups, (3) background and preparation of the teacher, and (4) interests of the students being served.

Ethnic makeup of the school. As noted previously, multiethnic education ought not to be restricted to schools having large minority ethnic groups represented in the student body. All students can profit from such courses. However, when schools do have large numbers of blacks, or American Indians, or Mexican-Americans, it is only logical that the multiethnic program include materials focusing on these groups. In a school and community where there are large numbers of blacks, black students and white students come into daily contact. Both groups can profit from a multiethnic program that includes some materials relating to blacks. (Every effort should be made to prevent such courses from becoming "segregated" offerings taken only by minority ethnic group students.)

Inclusion of some white ethnic minority groups. Many courses or programs within courses that purport to focus on multiethnic studies consider only nonwhite groups. This unfortunate practice reinforces a tendency for many white students to regard such programs as of interest only to nonwhite students. Including materials relating, for example, to Polish-Americans, Italian-Americans, Irish-Americans, or Norwegian-Americans promotes the view that the multiethnic program has something to offer all racial groups in the school. Certainly, every white student has an ethnic heritage that, to a degree at least, affects his or her perception of the world. Clearly, the multiethnic program has something to say to these students as well as to students from nonwhite groups.

Background and preparation of the teacher. In ethnic studies programs, as in other areas within the social studies, teachers should operate from their areas of strength when they have the option to do so. If, for example, a teacher has attended a summer institute on "Afro-American Studies," it would make good sense to include some material relating to blacks in his or her multiethnic education program. If the teacher does not have formal training relating to any specific minority ethnic group, then perhaps he or she has an interest in a self-study and self-development program with regard to one or more groups. If this is the case, then these groups can receive some attention as the multiethnic program unfolds. Of course, the criterion of "teacher preference" cannot override other important considerations. For example, if there are many Mexican-Americans in the community, information relating to Mexican-Americans cannot be slighted. If the school board has mandated inclusion of materials related to American Indians, they must be included. Additionally, a teacher with a compelling interest in a small ethnic group (for example, Americans of Luxembourgian extraction) cannot responsibly focus on that group at the expense of deleting learning experiences relating to larger minority groups such as blacks, American Indians, and Spanish-speaking Americans. (Of course, in a community where there was a large number of students (or adults) of Luxembourgian extraction, some consideration might well be given to spending some time on this group.)

Interests of the students. A key element in making any social studies program successful is student interest. Certainly no multiethnic program should be undertaken without making a systematic attempt to determine student interests in this area. When students play a role in identifying at least some of the groups that will be studied, they develop a sense of "ownership" in the course. Active participation in course design acts to heighten interest and personal commitment to the course. When there is any possibility at all that student preferences can be considered when minority groups to be studied are being selected, they should be weighed very seriously. Social studies teachers who follow this practice find that this joint planning pays off in terms of more intense student involvement and productive learning as the course develops.

A Framework for the Multiethnic Education Program

What is described here as a "multiethnic education program" does not necessarily imply the existence of a special course in multiethnic studies. Contents within existing courses, for example, United States History, can be organized to provide students with a multiethnic perspective. The multiethnic program implies only a commitment to provide students with a multiethnic perspective, regardless of whether the vehicle to accomplish this task is a course specifically designated "Multiethnic Studies" or is a traditional course reorganized to highlight perspectives of different ethnic groups.

In organizing multiethnic education programs, teachers must avoid fragmentation of content. This is a real danger that arises out of a temptation to deal with different ethnic groups, one at a time. This practice may reduce the preparation demands on the teacher who, under these circumstances, is required to deal with only one ethnic group at a time. But such programs can result in what might be described as compartmentalized learning; that is, students may develop certain understandings regarding blacks, others regarding American Indians, and still others regarding Puerto Ricans. Understandings about individual groups are kept separate and distinct. This approach highlights differences between and among ethnic groups, but it assumes there are no threads of common experience shared by different ethnic groups.

Organizationally, this sort of fragmented treatment is cumbersome. For one thing, there appears to be no logical limit to either the quantity or the kind of content that can be introduced with regard to each group. Further, this model cannot meet the needs of the teacher wishing to develop a multiethnic program within the context of a traditional secondary social studies course such as United States History.

A program that makes more logical sense and that provides a better framework for planning focuses simultaneously on features unique to individual ethnic groups and on common experiences of members of different ethnic groups. When common experiences can be identified, then shades of differences can be highlighted and comparisons and contrasts can be made between and among various ethnic groups. This approach has a great deal to commend it, particularly when the multiethnic program is provided within a given course.

Suppose, for example, a teacher wished to establish a multiethnic program in his or her United States History course. As a first step, major events in the course might be identified. Second, a number of ethnic groups would be selected (typically, four to six in number) for study according to criteria described previously. Using the major topics and the selected ethnic groups, the teacher can develop a data chart. The several ethnic groups are listed along one axis. The major topics are listed along the other axis. An example of such data chart is provided in Figure 15–1.

The data chart provides an opportunity for the teacher to identify kinds of information he or she will need to uncover in preparing learning experiences for his or her students. The chart can be used both as a vehicle for teacher planning and as a vehicle for helping the class to organize information as instruction unfolds.

THE DATA CHART AS A PLANNING VEHICLE

Look at the data chart illustrated in Figure 15–1. Notice that there are a total of twenty cells generated by the five ethnic groups listed along the vertical axis

Ethnic Groups	Major Events			
	The Civil War	Reconstruction	Restrictions on Immigration: 1890–1920	World War I
Blacks				
Native Americans				
Mexican-Americans				
Chinese-Americans				
Italian-Americans				

Figure 15–1. Data Chart for Organizing Instruction to Show Impact of Historical Events on Selected Ethnic Groups

and the four selected topics listed along the horizontal axis. Note that each of these cells is defined by a combination of one ethnic group and one topic. As one plans for instruction, use of the data chart suggests that specific information must be gathered with reference to the ethnic group and the topic suggested by each cell.

Specific sources of information in each of these areas need to be found both for use by the teacher and for use by students. Clearly, some of this information is going to be much harder to find than other information. Indeed, it is possible that little or nothing may be available for some of these major categories. For example, relatively few Italians had immigrated to the United States before the Civil War, and little information may be available regarding the Civil War and its impact on Italian-Americans.

Though the search may prove challenging, teachers who have tried this approach to organizing and preparing for instruction frequently are surprised at the amount of information that is available. For example, there was a considerable impact on Native Americans in Western territories during the Civil War. Because of the traditional emphasis on the war fronts of the East and South, little attention has been given to this aspect of the war. A multiethnic approach to this topic can provide students with rich new insights.

In using the data chart for planning, some teachers have found it convenient to lay out the chart on a large sheet of butcher paper. When this is done, specific materials to be used can be written directly on the paper in the cell to which they apply. Individual file folders can be prepared and labeled with the ethnic group and topic defining each cell. (For example, one file folder might be labeled "Blacks—World War I." These folders can be stored in a vertical file. Notes taken from source materials, clippings, and other relevant information can be stored for easy retrieval as instruction unfolds.

THE DATA CHART AS AN INSTRUCTIONAL AID

The data chart can play a helpful role as instruction goes forward. Assume a teacher had decided to organize his or her United States History course to include a multiethnic emphasis and had identified the sample topics indicated in Figure 15–1. A huge wall-sized version of the chart in Figure 15–1 might be prepared and hung either with tacks or masking tape.

From time to time, as learning experiences focusing on various ethnic groups and topics takes place, students can be asked to write some specific information in the appropriate cells of the chart with a wide-tipped felt marking pen. At the conclusion of these lessons, each cell in the chart will be filled with information. This completed chart provides an excellent focus for a culminating debriefing lesson. Such a lesson can help students review specifics, encourage them to make comparisons and contrasts between experiences of different ethnic groups, and provide a basis for making supportable generalizations. In conducting such a debriefing session, given a completed data chart based on categories included in Figure 15–1, the teacher might ask such questions as the following:

Phase 1

What specific comments can you make about how blacks fared during the Civil War? During Reconstruction? As a consequence of restrictions on immigration? During World War I? What conclusions can you draw about treatment of blacks during all of these periods? How do you account for this treatment? How do you feel about it?[At this stage, the teacher attempts to draw out student comments focusing on specific items of information. Beyond this objective, the teacher seeks to broaden students' understandings by asking them to generalize about patterns that recurred during several historical periods. This basic sequence is repeated for the other focus ethnic groups. In this case, a similar series of questions would be asked regarding Native Americans, Mexican-Americans, Chinese-Americans, and Italian-Americans. Students should be reminded to consider the information written on the large data chart in developing their answers.]

Phase 2

What similarities and differences do you see regarding experiences of blacks and Native Americans during the Civil War? Of blacks and Mexican-Americans? Of blacks and Chinese-Americans? Of blacks and Italian-Americans?

[This pattern is repeated for all combinations of ethnic group pairs. Questioning should be expanded to include comparisons and contrasts of how all ethnic groups experienced each historical period.]

Phase 3

Looking at all the information on the chart, can you now make some general comments about how these historical periods were experienced by these ethnic minorities? What are your conclusions? Think carefully. You will have to tell me your reasons for coming to your conclusions. [Questions in this phase of the debriefing exercise are directed toward helping students "put it all together." These questions provide a capstone for the activity.]

The data chart approach to planning and teaching in the multiethnic program has several important strengths. As noted previously, the data chart provides a framework that is helpful to the teacher in identifying relevant material in preparation for instruction. An even more important consideration is the impact such an organizational plan can have on students. Use of the chart (at least *proper* use of the approach) focuses on the commonality of human experiences as they cut across ethnic groups as well as on differences unique to individual ethnic groups. For Americans, there is a certain "glue of common experience" that binds people together as well as interesting differences that distinguish the many ethnic groups represented in the population. The multiethnic education program seeks to highlight the differential experiences of ethnic minorities as they have reacted and continue to react to events in light of their very special perspectives. The data chart can be a powerful tool in the hands of the teacher who seeks after this challenging goal.

Sources of Information

Materials of interest to teachers seeking to implement multiethnic education programs have proliferated at an astonishing rate over the past ten years. Predictably, there are enormous qualitative differences among these materials. Additionally, the increase in available materials has not been consistent with regard to all minority ethnic groups. As might be expected, tremendous numbers of book titles, special periodicals, tape-slide, and other multimedia offerings are available to the teacher interested in Black Studies. Abundant resources are available as well that focus on Native Americans and Mexican-Americans. Beyond these groups, though large numbers of materials are available, coverage tends to be a little less complete.

There is getting to be a considerable body of material focusing on Japanese-Americans, particularly with regard to the experiences of the Nisei during World War II. A reasonably good selection of items focusing on the Chinese is available, and a body of information focusing on Vietnamese-Americans is growing rapidly.

Yet certain other groups, long resident in the United States, are poorly represented in the available literature at the present time. Filipino-Americans, with a long history of U.S. Naval service and residence in the continental United States, are very much underrepresented in the available materials. Materials do exist, but they are few considering the size of the Filipino-American population. On the other hand, surprising quantities of information are available regarding groups such as, for example, Samoan-Americans.

In general, the teacher who is willing to look will have little difficulty in identifying sources of information. Some books in the list that follows may provide a logical starting point. Clearly, these are only representative items. These lists make no claims to comprehensiveness. But still these titles do represent an appropriate beginning point for teachers interested in developing a multiethnic education program.

SPECIFIC INFORMATION ABOUT SELECTED ETHNIC GROUPS

1. *Blacks*
   BIRMINGHAM, STEPHEN. *Certain People*. Boston: Little, Brown and Company, 1977. (A study of the black upper classes in urban America.)
   BLASSINGAME, JOHN W. *The Slave Community*. New York: Oxford University Press, 1972. (Deals with the institution of slavery as it was viewed by the slaves themselves.)
   CLARK, JOHN HENRIK, ed. (Assisted by Amy Jacques Garvey). *Marcus Garvey and the Vision of Africa*. New York: Vintage Books, 1974. (A collection of materials relating to the life, work, and thought of Marcus Garvey.)
   DRIMMER, MELVIN, ed. *Black History*. Garden City, New York: Doubleday & Company, Inc., 1969. (A well-known and very readable account of the black experience in America.)
   FRANKLIN, JOHN HOPE. *From Slavery to Freedom: A History of Negro Americans*. New York: Vintage Books, 1969. (A distinguished account of the history of blacks in the United States.)
   MEIER, AUGUST, and ELLIOTT RUDWICK. *From Plantation to Ghetto*. Revised. New York: Hill and Wang, 1970. (A history of blacks that underscores influences they have exercised as conditions have changed through time.)
   STAMPP, KENNETH M. *The Peculiar Institution*. New York: Vintage Books, 1956. (A classic interpretation that undermines traditional stereotypic views of slavery.)
   WILKERSON, DORIS Y., and RONALD L. TAYLOR, eds. *The Black Male in America: Perspectives on His Status in Contemporary Society*. Chicago: Nelson-Hall, 1977. (A somewhat demanding work that provides a number of perspectives regarding the nature of the roles played by black males in American society.)
   WILSON, WALTER, ed. *The Selected Writings of W. E. B. Du Bois*. New York: Mentor Books, 1970. (A broad selection of writings from the works of Du Bois.)
2. *Mexican-Americans*
   ACUÑA, RODOLFO. *Occupied America: The Chicano's Struggle Toward Liberation*. San Francisco: Canfield Press, 1972. (A furiously heated account of Mexican-American history viewed through the eyes of an intense Chicano partisan.)
   McWILLIAMS, CAREY. *North from Mexico: The Spanish-Speaking People of the United*

States. Philadelphia: J. B. Lipincott Co., 1949. (A solid basic resource for teachers interested in Mexican-Americans.)

MEIER, MATT S., and FELICIANO RIVERA. *The Chicanos: A History of Mexican Americans*. New York: Hill and Wang, 1972. (A very readable overview of Mexican-American history.)

MEINIG, DONALD W. *Southwest: Three Peoples in Geographic Change. 1600–1970*. New York: Oxford University Press, 1971. (Interactions of Mexican-Americans, Native Americans, and white ethnics viewed through the perspective of a well-known cultural geographer.)

MOQUINN, WAYNE, with CHARLES VAN DOREN, eds. *A Documentary History of the Mexican-Americans*. New York: Praeger Publishers, Inc., 1971. (A fine collection of basic documents and other basic resource materials.)

ROBINSON, CECIL. *With the Ears of Strangers: The Mexican in American Literature*. Tucson: University of Arizona Press, 1963. (A compelling analysis of the treatment of Mexican-Americans in American literature.)

STEINER, STAN. *La Raza: The Mexican Americans*. New York: Harper & Row Publishers, 1969. (A broad overview of the Chicano movement.)

3. *Native Americans*

BRANDON, WILLIAM. *The American Heritage Book of Indians*. New York: Dell Publishing Co., Inc., 1961. (Provides an overview to a large number of Indian cultures. Very readable.)

DELORIA, VINE, JR. *Custer Died for Your Sins*. (A strong statement of the dilemma of the Native American in contemporary American society.)

FORBES, JACK D., ed. *The Indian in America's Past*. Englewood Cliffs, New Jersey: Prentice-Hall, Inc., 1965. (A collection of articles that detail interesting episodes involving relationships between Native Americans and other groups.)

JOSEPHY, ALVIN M., JR. *The Indian Heritage of America*. New York: Bantam Books, 1968. (A rich history of Native Americans in both North and South America.)

MCLUHAN, T. C., ed. *Touch the Earth: A Self-Portrait of Indian Existence*. New York: Pocket Books, 1971. (Contains a powerful array of statements by leading native Americans on a number of important issues.)

MOMADAY, N. SCOTT. *House Made of Dawn*. New York: Harper & Row, Publishers, 1966. (A novelist's treatment of cultural conflict between Native Americans and whites.)

SPICER, EDWARD H. *A Short History of the Indians of the United States*. New York: Van Nostrand Reinhold Company, 1969. (A history of Native Americans that is rendered particularly useful by the inclusion of a number of basic documents.)

STEINER, STAN. *The New Indians*. New York: Harper & Row, Publishers, 1968. (A discussion of major political movements among Native American groups.)

4. *Puerto Rican-Americans*

CORDASCO, FRANCESCO, and EUGENE BUCCHIONI, eds. *Puerto Rican Children on the Mainland: A Sourcebook for Teachers*. Metuchen, N.J.: Scarecrow Press, 1968. (Materials that focus on special difficulties Puerto Rican children experience as they confront life on the mainland.)

CORDASCO, FRANCESCO. *The Puerto Ricans, 1493–1973: A Chronology and Fact Book*. Dobbs Ferry, New York: Oceana Publications, 1973. (A rich source of basic information about this group.)

FITZPATRICK, JOSEPH P. *Puerto Rican Americans: The Meaning of Migration to the*

Mainland. Englewood Cliffs, N.J.: Prentice-Hall, Inc., 1971. (A well-written interpretive account of the Puerto Rican migration experience.)

LEWIS, OSCAR. *La Vida: A Puerto Rican Family in the Culture of Poverty—San Juan and New York.* New York: Random House, Inc., 1966. (A case study approach focusing on members of an extended Puerto Rican family in New York and in San Juan.)

WAGGENHEIM, KAL, and O. J. DE WAGGENHEIM, eds. *The Puerto Ricans: A Documentary History.* New York: Praeger Publishers, Inc., 1970. (An excellent profile of Puerto Rican life. Extraordinarily rich details.)

5. *Asian Heritage Americans* (selected groups)

Chinese-Americans

BARTH, GUNTHER. *Bitter Strength: A History of the Chinese in the United States, 1850–1970.* Cambridge: Harvard University Press, 1964. (A study of Chinese life on the West Coast of the United States during the mid-nineteenth century.)

BRETT, VICTOR G., and DEBARRY NEE, eds. *Longtime California: A Documentary Study of an American Chinatown.* New York: Pantheon, 1972. (A focus on the Chinese culture in San Francisco's Chinatown.)

ISAACS, HAROLD. *Scratches on Our Minds.* New York: The John Day Company, Inc., 1958. (A fine, detailed examination of changing American perceptions of the Chinese at various times in our history.)

LYMAN, STANFORD M. *Chinese Americans.* New York: Random House, Inc., 1974. (An overview of cultural patterns of Chinese-Americans.)

MILLER, STUART C. *The Unwelcomed Immigrant: The American Image of the Chinese, 1785–1882.* Berkeley and Los Angeles: University of California Press, 1969. (A careful analysis of the gradual development of anti-Chinese sentiment during the historical period covered.)

Japanese-Americans

BOSWORTH, ALAN. *America's Concentration Camps.* New York: W. W. Norton & Company, Inc., 1967. (A discussion of the World War II internment of Japanese citizens.)

DANIELS, ROGER. *Concentration Camps U.S.A.: Japanese-Americans and World War II.* New York: Holt, Rinehart and Winston, 1971. (A highly readable account of World War II internment of U.S. citizens of Japanese ancestry.)

ICHIHASHI, YAMATO. *Japanese in the United States.* New York: Arno Press and *The New York Times,* 1969 (first published in 1932). (An excellent and thorough treatment of Japanese immigration to the United States.)

KITANO, HARRY H. L. *Japanese-Americans: The Evolution of a Subculture.* Englewood Cliffs, N.J.: Prentice-Hall, Inc., 1969. (A general study of history and cultural characteristics of Japanese-Americans.)

6. *European Heritage Americans* (selected groups)

Irish-Americans

GREELEY, ANDREW M. *That Most Distressful Nation: The Taming of the American Irish.* Chicago: Quadrangle Books, 1972. (A highly readable account of life among the Irish-Americans.)

Italian-Americans

GAMBINO, RICHARD. *Blood of My Blood: the Dilemma of the Italian-Americans.* New York, Doubleday & Company, Inc., 1974. (An insightful account of problems faced by the Italian-American in the context of the larger American culture.)

LOPREATO, JOSEPH. *Italian-Americans.* New York: Random House, Inc., 1970. (A very general treatment of Italian immigration, settlement, and adjustment to life in the United States.)

MOQUIN, WAYNE, with CHARLES VAN DOREN, eds. *A Documentary History of the Italian Americans*. New York: Praeger Publishers, Inc., 1974. (Documentary history containing many useful selections for the teacher interested in this group.)

Jewish-Americans

GOLDSTEIN, SIDNEY, and CALVIN GOLDSCHIEDER. *Jewish Americans: Three Generations in a Jewish Community*. Englewood Cliffs, N.J. Prentice-Hall, Inc., 1968. (A very enjoyable account of the American Jewish cultural landscape.)

SKLARE, MARSHALL. *America's Jews*. New York: Random House, Inc., 1971. (An excellent introduction to Jewish life.)

General Works

FRIEDMAN, MURRAY, ed. *Overcoming Middleclass Rage*. Philadelphia: The Westminster Press, 1971. (Focuses on special problems of less affluent white ethnics in urban areas.)

GLAZER, NATHAN, and DANIEL PATRICK MOYNIHAN. *Beyond the Melting Pot*. Cambridge, Massachusetts: The M.I.T. Press, 1970. (Focuses on white ethnic groups in the city of New York.)

GREELEY, ANDREW. *Why Can't They Be Like Us?* New York: American Jewish Committee Institute of Human Relations Press, 1969. (Deals with identity problems and prospects of white ethnic groups.)

HANDLIN, OSCAR. *The Uprooted: The Epic Story of the Great Migrations That Made the American People*. Revised Edition. New York: Grosset & Dunlap, Inc., 1973. (A classic account of the European migration to the United States. Richly detailed and eminently readable.)

LITT, EDGAR. *Ethnic Politics in America*. Glenview, Illinois: Scott, Foresman and Company, 1970. (A discussion of ethnic influences on voting and other political behavior.)

NOVAK, MICHAEL. *The Rise of the Unmeltable Ethics*. New York: Macmillan Publishing Co., Inc., 1972. (A provocative case for white minority ethnic group assertiveness against the white Anglo-Saxon majority.)

SOWELL, THOMAS. *Race and Economics*. New York: David McKay Co., Inc., 1975. (A superlative overview of minorities and the American experience. "Must" reading.)

As noted at the beginning of this section, these titles represent only a sampling of those available. Because of space limitations, it was impossible to include titles of books focusing on groups such as Cuban-Americans, Hawaiian-Americans, Portuguese-Americans, and others that a social studies teachers might wish to include in his or her multiethnic studies program. Books are available dealing with these and many other ethnic groups. More specific information with regard to teaching materials focusing on a wide variety of ethnic groups can be found in issues of the leading social studies professional magazines, *Social Education* and *The Social Studies*, which from time to time publish excellent articles on multiethnic education programs. In addition to these sources, a number of excellent resource books are available for social studies teachers in the general area of teaching multiethnic program. Typically, these materials describe a wide variety of specific resource materials. Some of the better "how to teach multiethnic studies" materials are listed in the following section.

Professional Materials for Teachers

Banks, James A. *Teaching the Black Experience: Methods and Materials*. Belmont, California: Fearon Publishers, 1970. (A short, highly readable little book that provides a fine assortment of specific suggestions for teaching about blacks in American life.)

Banks, James A., ed. *Teaching Ethnic Studies: Concepts and Strategies*. 43rd Yearbook of the National Council for the Social Studies. Washington, D.C.: NCSS, 1973. (An excellent compendium of articles focusing on general problems associated with multiethnic education and specific sections on selected ethnic groups. Excellent teaching suggestions follow many of the selections.)

Banks, James A. *Teaching Strategies for Ethnic Studies*. Boston: Allyn and Bacon, Inc., 1975. (The most comprehensive source of information relating to multiethnic studies programs. Includes advice relating to curriculum planning, teaching strategies, and resources for teachers and students. A well-balanced treatment including sections on African, Asian, European, Native American, and other ethnic groups.)

Banks, James A., and William W. Joyce, eds. *Teaching Social Studies to Culturally Different Children*. Reading, Massachusetts: Addison-Wesley Publishing Company, Inc., 1971. (An excellent selection of materials. Focuses heavily on special needs of culturally different students.)

Cortez, Carlos E.; Fay Metcalf; and Sharryl Hawke. *Understanding You and Them: Tips for Teaching About Ethnicity*. Boulder, Colorado: ERIC Clearinghouse for Social Studies/Social Science Education Consortium, 1976. (A collection of practical ideas for teachers.)

NCSS Task Force on Ethnic Studies Curriculum Guidelines. *Curriculum Guidelines for Multi-ethnic Education*. Arlington, Virginia: National Council for the Social Studies, 1976. (A framework for organizing a professional multiethnic studies program. Available from The National Council for the Social Studies, Suite 400, 2030 M Street N.W., Washington, D.C. 20036.)

The Individual Student in Multiethnic Education Programs

Attention to the sensitivities of individual students is a must for the successful multiethnic studies program. Dangers that classroom discussions of ethnic "differences" can slip over into discussions of perceived ethnic "deficiencies" are very real. The teacher must work diligently to deal honestly with differences while, at the same time, helping students to avoid a tendency some may have to make negative value judgments about members of another ethnic group. As James Banks has noted (1975), "almost no one considers his culture deprived and his home a ghetto" (p. 65). The multiethnic program seeks to help students, regardless of their ethnic background, to cherish and understand the perspectives of their own group and to be sensitive to the perspectives of other group. The twin pillars of self-understanding and tolerance of others support the entire multiethnic program. The social studies teacher must encourage open and sensitive communication among students if these fundamental aims are to be met.

A special problem encountered by many teachers in multiethnic programs is that many white students do not perceive themselves as having any ethnic background. Large numbers assume the term *ethnic* applies only to others. Though many are quite willing to learn about other groups, the task sometimes is undertaken with a lack of the sort of personal intensity that is associated with subject matter that seems more clearly relevant. To overcome this tendency, teachers need to develop an immediate focus on the "Where did I come from?" question. That Irish-Americans, Swedish-Americans, German-Americans, and other white ethnic groups have certain unique perspectives needs to be emphasized. Many youngsters have a very mixed ethnic heritage. They may be interested in learning the special ways of viewing the world that characterize the several ethnic groups of their ancestral forebears. The multiethnic program needs to stress that all people, including the ethnic majority groups, have been and continue to be conditioned to see the world through the special perspectives of the ethnic groups of which they are a part. When students understand this fundamental condition of society, their interest in and commitment to the multiethnic program will grow stronger.

The multiethnic program can expand students' concerns for others. As they learn to understand the unique perspectives of ethnic groups other than their own, barriers of communication between and among members of different ethnic groups come down. Given a world in which technical advances bring widely divergent ethnic groups into more frequent direct contact, students have a need to tolerate, appreciate, and understand the perspectives of those who are "different." In a polycultural world, sensitive understandings of others is an imperative for survival. Though certainly the multiethnic program cannot bear the entire burden of expanding students' sense of humanity and interpersonal concern, certainly it has the potential for exerting a very positive force in this direction.

Summary

Multiethnic education programs promote students' understanding of their own ethnic heritages. Equally important, these programs help students to comprehend and tolerate the perspectives of other ethnic group members. The multiethnic program may be framed within a special course. Alternatively, the program may be included within a more traditional secondary school offering.

There is a danger of fragmentation within multiethnic programs. This results when no attempt is made to deal simultaneously with more than one ethnic group. If a one-group-at-a-time approach is taken in the course, students may learn isolated bits of information with regard, for example, to blacks, Puerto Rican–Americans, Native Americans, and Irish-Americans. Such programs fail to provide students with insights regarding commonalities among groups as well as differences. Organizing the multiethnic program around common issues and how individual groups have reacted to those issues is a response that can overcome the threat of fragmentation. A data chart used as an organizational vehicle can lead to instruction calling for students to compare and contrast perspectives of a number of ethnic groups. This organizational scheme promotes the view that, though differences exist, all ethnic groups have had to face certain common problems.

Inclusion of some white ethnic groups in the multiethnic education program is essential. When this practice has not been followed, there has been a tendency for white students to view multiethnic programs as directed only toward blacks, Mexican-Americans, Puerto Rican-Americans, or other minority ethnic groups represented in the school population. The multiethnic education program should be directed toward all students. Inclusion of materials relating to some white ethnic groups encourages white students as well as minority ethnic students to enroll. If the program is to encourage both self-understanding and tolerance of others, it is essential that a broad spectrum of the student population be represented in courses with a multiethnic focus.

A growing body of resource materials is available to serve the needs of teachers wishing to prepare themselves for teaching a multiethnic education program. In addition to books and articles focusing on specific groups, professional social studies periodicals and several texts are available for teachers interested in instituting a multiethnic education program in their school. Given the availability of materials and the need to promote intergroup understanding, the prognosis for expanding multiethnic education program in the secondary schools appears favorable.

REFERENCES

BANKS, JAMES A. *Teaching Strategies for Ethnic Studies*. Boston: Allyn and Bacon, Inc., 1975.
BUTTON, CHRISTINE BENNET. "Teaching for Individual and Cultural Differences." *Educational Leadership* (March 1977): 435–438.
CORTEZ, CARLOS E. "Teaching the Chicano Experience." In *Teaching Ethnic Studies: Concepts and Strategies*, edited by James A. Banks, pp. 180–199. 43rd Yearbook of the National Council for the Social Studies. Washington, D.C.: NCSS, 1973.
DICKLEMAN, MILDRED. "Teaching Cultural Pluralism." In *Teaching Ethnic Studies: Concepts and Strategies*, edited by James A. Banks, pp. 4–25. 43rd Yearbook of the National Council for the Social Studies. Washington, D.C.: NCSS. 1973.
GUINN, ROBERT. "Value Clarification in the Bicultural Classroom." *Journal of Teacher Education* (January-February 1977): 46–47.

Chapter 16

LAW-FOCUSED STUDIES

L AW-FOCUSED STUDIES IN the social studies have emerged from a concern of the professional legal community that students ought to understand better the legal context within which their lives unfold. As a result of this interest, a number of programs, sponsored by national, state, and local bar associations, have been established. These have resulted in the development of courses of study, learning materials, and instructional techniques suitable for use in school classrooms.

These programs have been premised on three basic assumptions. First, law-focused studies have been promoted because law touches all aspects of human life (Gross, 1977). Second, much traditional instruction on topics related to the legal system has not been well done. Arid memorization tasks associated with a study of the U.S. Constitution have been cited as examples of bankrupt instructional practices in this area. Finally, there has been concern that too many students (and adults) believe themselves to be helpless victims of a legal system that is beyond any kind of personal control. Law-focused studies seek to promote the view that the law deals with issues about which men disagree and that the clash of ideas results in a constant reshaping of the legal environment of the society. In simpler terms, individuals can shape the legal system, but they need sharp intellectual tools to exert an influence that is meaningful. Law-focused studies have been described by some as providing a vehicle for sharpening students' wits so that they can become more effective contenders in the public policy arena.

The Need for Special Law-focused Studies Programs

There is evidence that students have little grasp of the fundamental legal system that serves as a kind of "umpire" for life in this society. Many students, for example, are unfamiliar with the substance of even something so basic as the Bill of Rights of the U.S. Constitution. Pittenger (1973), in a speech before a group of lawyers and educators interested in law-focused programs, made the following observation:

> A group of students, somewhere in the Midwest, I believe, did a sidewalk survey for a government course a few years ago and found that many people not only did not recognize the Bill of Rights, but, without the benefit of its title, described it as "Communist Propaganda." A government which takes pride in being based on laws, not men, is in serious trouble when that kind of public ignorance exists [p. 5].

The problem, however, involves much more than a lack of familiarity with basic public documents. The essence of a democratic system is a public debate on divisive policy issues. Supporters of law-focused studies programs suggest that these programs can teach students to recognize quickly the basic issues that are in dispute. In this connection, Pittenger (1973) has noted:

> I have often been exasperated . . . by having to listen to people making arguments that were essentially irrelevant to the question before us. The ability to grasp what facts and what arguments do indeed bear on the central issue: that quality, more than anything else, seems to me to distinguish lawyers from laymen [p. 6].

This interest in students' abilities to think through issues suggests an emphasis on an instructional program presenting opportunities for this kind of analysis. Partisans of law-focused studies suggest that traditional social studies programs have presented too few opportunities for productive analyses of alternative positions. Instead of promoting analysis, too many teachers have relied upon the "exhortation model." These teachers have simply told students how to act. There is evidence that teacher exhortation has marginal impact on students' behavior. Essays on "What It Means to be an American" and "Justice in America" are thinly disguised teacher exhortation exercises. Students prepare responses in terms of what they believe to be "ideal standards." Rarely do such exercises result in careful analysis of difficult alternatives.

To counter the teacher exhortation model, proponents of law-focused studies suggest a need to inject into social studies classes some instruction modeled on practices in law schools. Students should be taught ". . . by rubbing their noses in the dirt of reality: by making them read about real people and real cases" (Pittenger, 1973: p. 6). Given this kind of training, students can become more careful analysts of divisive policy issues. As they grow in their analytical abilities, they will tend to develop increasing confidence in this ability to influence the legal world within which they live. When citizens recognize that their system is a responsive one, they become both more active in their attempts to shape the system and more appreciative of the system that affords them this opportunity.

Emphasis of the Law-focused Studies Program

Joel F. Henning, in his capacity as staff director of the American Bar Association's Special Committee on Youth Education for Citizenship, has suggested that law-focused programs properly ought to include four basic emphases. These (Henning, 1973: p. 10) are an emphasis on

1. Basic legal concepts.
2. Fundamental principles of American law.
3. The scope and limits of law.
4. How institutions of law really work.

BASIC LEGAL CONCEPTS

As Henning (1973) has noted, certain common threads are found in the legal systems of nearly every rational society. Ideals such as fairness, responsibility, and honesty are almost universally reflected. These basic concepts are fundamental to formal legal systems. It is from the interpretation of these ideals as they apply in different sets of circumstances that legal systems evolve. As this is the case, law-focused programs need to spend some time helping students to identify and discuss these basic legal concepts in the light of their own experiences. (What does responsibility mean? How does it affect your life? What things have you done that you would consider responsible? Irresponsible? How do you judge when something is responsible or irresponsible? Do others make the same kinds of judgments? Why or why not? And so on.)

FUNDAMENTAL PRINCIPLES OF AMERICAN LAW

There has been much ritual in social studies classroom concerning the Bill of Rights, the Declaration of Independence, the Constitution and other famous public documents. For example, students sometimes have been praised for being able to cite the first ten amendments in order or to get up in front of a group and deliver a flawless rendition of the Preamble to the Constitution. Such exercises are largely cosmetic. They involve recitations of words that are supposed to imply understanding. But when the emphasis has been only on performance, students may well become little more than "parrots" able to reproduce sounds pleasing to the teacher (or to their parents) but unable to grasp the meanings of the famous words they are delivering.

Law-focused programs seek to help students move beyond verbalism to genuine understanding. Understanding requires that conflicts within the Bill of Rights, for example, be brought forward for systematic classroom investigation. The language of the Constitution must take a back seat to the fundamental ideas of the document. In general, in teaching the fundamental principles of American law, teachers of law-focused programs seek to focus on issues of substance that can help students grasp and appreciate the complexities and the subtleties of our system.

THE SCOPE AND LIMITS OF LAW

For many students, the law has no limitations in terms of its extent. This misperception has become increasingly widespread in recent years as courts have moved into areas that for years seemed beyond the jurisdiction of the legal system. Who, for example, thirty years ago would have imagined courts taking an interest in issues such as schools' rights to impose certain standards of dress on members of the student body? Because there has been an increase in the range of court concerns, some students (and their parents, too) believe that the law is all-powerful. Clearly, every problem does *not* have a legal solution. Students need to be alerted to the limitations of the law as well as to those areas where it is an appropriate regulator of behavior.

The Way in Which Institutions of Law Really Work

In law-focused studies programs, students must have opportunities to learn how institutions of law really work. Too frequently, students, with minimal preparation, have been loaded on buses and taken to the county courthouse for a tour. The building, the names on the doors, and other features of the physical edifice have an intrinsic interest; but they shed little light on how the legal system functions. Students must become acquainted with the heated arguments that go on within the courthouse as the slow process of accommodating different interpretations of social and legal standards goes forward. Confrontation with this give-and-take ought to be the emphasis. The courthouse, itself, provides just one public forum for debate on these divisive issues. Focus on the forum must not be allowed to overshadow consideration of the issues.

What all this means is that students must be helped to understand that there are serious discrepancies in the "real world" between the "ideal" and the "actual." Henning (1973) has suggested that law-focused studies programs can help students to compare and contrast the fundamental principles upon which our legal system is based and situations they observe in their daily living. How, for example, does "due process" work in a school setting? How do observed practices conform to the "ideal" of due process? Why are there some discrepancies?

In addition to promoting analysis of observed situations as they compare to basic legal principles, law-focused studies programs hope to help students see that movement toward achieving these ideals in practice demands active involvement by concerned citizens. A long-term objective of student analysis of how institutions of law really work is the development of responsible and involved citizens. Activities in law-focused programs that demand analysis of the actual operation of standards, rules, and regulations can help students learn that the legal system is constantly being redefined in response to "signals" it receives from interested and involved citizens.

Law-focused Studies in the Classroom

A number of very productive approaches to teaching law-focused materials have been developed. In general, these approaches center on involving students in activities relating to disputes that the legal system has been called upon to adjudicate. Frequently, actual court cases provide the focus. Because courts consider such a wide variety of issues, the teacher has a real possibility to select something that students see as having some immediate personal relevance. For examples, numerous cases have considered issues such as the right of school authorities to conduct locker searches without permission, the right of school authorities to regulate hair length of male students, and the right of school authorities to regulate student publications. Many such issues are of compelling interest to students. Properly selected, law-focused programs based on court cases can be highly motivating learning experiences.

Because many students have never considered the impact the legal system has on their daily lives, some attention must be devoted to introducing law-focused lessons. Once the importance and relevance of law-related information has been established, instruction can be provided with a view to confronting students with some of the very difficult issues with which our society has had to grapple. The "mock trial" has proved to be an excellent vehicle for involving students in clear and careful analysis of many difficult issues. In the next sections, a familiarization exercise will be introduced and a sample mock trial-based lesson will be described.

FAMILIARIZATION EXERCISE: MINDWALK

David T. Naylor (1977) has described an excellent exercise for helping students appreciate the impact the legal system has on their lives. He calls this exercise a "mindwalk." An example of a mindwalk lesson follows:[1]

[1] David T. Naylor, "Law Studies in the Schools: A Compendium of Instructional Strategies," *Social Education* (March 1977): 170–171. Reprinted with permission of the National Council for the Social Studies and David T. Naylor.

A DAY IN THE LIFE OF TOM PHILLIPS

Tom Phillips is *thirteen years old.* He lives at *2893 Sycamore Street, Sweet Gum, Ohio* with his *family,* a *mother* and *father,* a *brother,* and a *dog.* Today was a *school day,* so Tom got up when his mother called him at *7:00 A.M.* He washed his face with *Dial soap,* brushed his teeth with *Crest toothpaste,* and then got *dressed* for *school.*

Soon Tom came to the kitchen. He turned on the *radio* and sat down to eat a breakfast of *orange juice,* a *bowl* of *Cheerios, toast,* and a *quart* of *milk.* When he finished eating, Tom attached a *leash* to his dog's *collar* and took the dog for a walk around the *block.*

Returning to his *house,* Tom heard the sound of the school bus. He grabbed his books and ran to meet the bus which had stopped in front of his house, its *red lights flashing.* Tom boarded the bus and greeted the bus *driver* with a friendly smile. Another day of school was about to begin.

Classroom Procedures

1. Distribute copies of the story to each student. Read the story aloud.
2. Ask students to re-read the story, this time underlining each instance in which a law is involved in the story. (Note: For purposes of illustration, such instances are italicized above.)
3. Cite the following example: " 'Tom Phillips' should be underlined. Your name is your identity in society. It is given to you at birth and recorded on a birth certificate, a legal document. It determines, to a large extent, all of your legal rights and responsibilities."
4. Discuss each of the situations identified by the students, using them as springboards to illustrate how much law impacts upon the daily lives of students. Examples include:
   address (zoning, taxes, schools, local ordinances, etc.)
   family (name, inheritance, marriage, divorce, etc.)
   dog (type and treatment of pet, innoculations, leash laws, potential liability, etc.)
5. When students have completed the lesson, ask them to make a collage illustrating the various ways law affects their lives. Display the collage in a prominent place in the classroom.

A MOCK TRIAL[2]

Mock trials in secondary social studies afford an opportunity for students to analyze, synthesize, and evaluate information. Though many teaching techniques purport to develop these higher-level thinking skills, few attend so well as the mock trial to providing students with a solid base of relevant information before decision

---

[2] A much abbreviated version of this mock trial appeared in David G. Armstrong, "Thermal Pollution: Background Material for a Mock Trial," *Law in American Society* (February 1977): 27–30.

making begins. In the mock trial, student lawyers, like their adult counterparts, work hard to lay out all pertinent information before the jury or panel of judges is asked to make a decision.

Mock trials help students understand that divisive issues tend to be complex. They help them understand that really important questions seldom have simple answers. Further, because of their complexity, answers made in the public arena rarely are completely satisfying to partisans of different points of view. The mock trial can help students learn that our jurisprudential system functions not as an absolute arbiter of "right" and "wrong," but rather as a thoughtful blender and evaluator of contending positions.

Planning the mock trial. A mock trial has four phases. These include (1) preplanning, (2) role assignment and internalization, (3) the simulated trial experience, and (4) debriefing. The first of these phases places primary, but not necessarily exclusive, responsibility on the teacher.

During preplanning, the most important task to be accomplished is the identification of the case to be used as the trial focus. Though it is possible to invent a completely fictional case, there are two important advantages of developing the mock trial around a real case. First of all, selection of a real case assures that the trial will focus on an issue that has stimulated fairly heated debate; otherwise, no litigation would have occurred. Second, the record of the real trial includes the decision and the line of logic used by the court in arriving at the decision. This information can be used to good effect during the debriefing session at the conclusion of the trial simulation phase.

A number of sources for appropriate cases are available. In a subsequent section of this chapter, a number of organizations and groups will be identified with interests in law-focused studies. Many of these groups have prepared casebooks with highlights of interesting trials that can be readily adapted for classroom use. Many books and periodicals are available in libraries that summarize trials. For example, teachers interested in developing a mock trial around some of the witchcraft trials in early New England might find fascinating *Narratives of the Witchcraft Cases 1648–1706*, edited by George Lincoln Curr (New York: Charles Scribner's Sons, 1914). Teachers with a more contemporary interest might find suitable materials in a number of journals that summarize cases within a certain category. For example, issues relating to the environment are regularly reported in the *Environmental Law Reporter,* available in most larger libraries. (The case selected for illustration here was reported in this publication.)

Once a case has been selected, the teacher must prepare a *case overview.* Typically, the case overview will be from two to three pages in length, but these are simply guidelines, not strict limitations. The case overview should include (1) a general background concerning the case, (2) the basic issues in contention, (3) the positions of the disputants, and (4) the court's decision and the logic supporting that decision.

Assume, for example, that a decision had been made to build a mock trial around the case of *Department of Environmental Protection v. Jersey Central Power and Light Company,* No. A-218-73 (Superior Ct. N.J. App. Div., March 21, 1975). The case overview might look something like the following:

Case Overview

A. Background. The Jersey Central Power & Light Company operates a nuclear-powered electrical generating plant in Ocean County, New Jersey. The plant is situated between the south branch of the Forked River and Oyster Creek. Oyster Creek is a stream that empties into the Atlantic Ocean and that is subject to tidal flow. When the power plant was built, a canal was constructed linking the Forked River and Oyster Creek. The plant itself was built alongside this canal between Forked River and Oyster Creek. Where the canal passes by the power plant, a dike was built. Water flows from the Forked River to the dike. At this point, four pumps take the cold water from the Forked River side of the dike and circulate it through the plant to cool the condensers under the generators. After passing through the plant, the water is emptied back into the canal on the Oyster Creek side of the dike. Because the water becomes heated in passing through the plant, the water emptying into the canal on the Oyster Creek side of the dike is much hotter than that coming into the plant from the Forked River side of the dike. Indeed, at the point where water from the canal enters into Oyster Creek, Oyster Creek itself is some 25 degrees warmer than it would be without infusion of the water flowing down the canal from the nuclear plant.

The heating of the water in Oyster Creek at the outflow of the canal has attracted large numbers of a commercially important fish called menhaden into Oyster Creek; a commercially important fishing industry became established in the area.

On January 28, 1972, the Jersey Central Power & Light Company plant was shut down because of some Atomic Energy Commission standards relating to safety. Some unexplained leakage of water within the plant had been observed. Though the plant generators were shut down, three of the four pumps carrying cold water from the Forked River side of the dike continued to bring water in to circulate around the condensers and flow out to the Oyster Creek side of the dike. As the reactor was shut down, the water pumped through the plant was not heated. Consequently, water flowing back into the canal on the Oyster Creek side of the dike was no warmer than that being pumped into the plant from the Forked River side of the dike. As a result of this situation, the water temperature in Oyster Creek near the outflow of the canal dropped 13 degrees in twenty-four hours. Shortly thereafter upwards of 500,000 dead menhaden were found in and along the banks of Oyster Creek. State inspectors found no toxic matter in the fish. Death was attributed to the thermal shock brought about by the sudden drop in water temperature.

The Department of Environmental Protection of New Jersey brought suit against the Jersey Central Power and Light Company for violating N.J.S.A. 23: 5–28. This statute, reads, in part, as follows:

> No person shall put or place into, turn into, drain into or place where it can run, flow, wash or be emptied into, or where it can find its way

into any of the fresh or tidal waters within the jurisdiction of this State any petroleum products, debris, hazardous, deleterious, destructive or poisonous substances of any kind; . . . In case of said waters by any substances injurious to fish, birds, or mammals, it shall not be necessary to show that the substances have actually caused the death of any of these organisms . . .

This law includes a penalty not to exceed a fine of $6,000. An original decision found the Jersey Central Power & Light Company guilty of violating the statute. The case was appealed.

B. The Issues. The company stated that had the legislature intended thermal pollution in the form of hot or cold water to be included among those substances whose introduction into New Jersey waters was prohibited, explicit language to that effect would have been written into the statute. Further, the company argued, can water—a substance not in and of itself "deleterious"—be forbidden, considering that sometimes hot water may be dangerous and sometimes not and that sometimes cold water may be dangerous and sometimes not?

Among basic questions at issue in the case were these:

1. Did unavoidable necessity cause the plant to shut down?
2. Was the damage to the fish clearly attributable to actions taken by the company to be in compliance with Atomic Energy Commission standards?
3. If the company did have to shut down, was it necessary for the pumps to keep operating?
4. Did the company recognize in advance that it might be acting in violation of the statute?

C. The Positions of the Disputants. The *company* suggested that the language of the regulation does not specifically mention thermal pollution. The shutdown was necessitated because of a mandate of the Atomic Energy Commission, a federal regulatory agency. Holding the company responsible under the statute represents a violation of due process.

The State Environmental Protection Agency noted that the language of the law speaks of the introduction of ". . . hazardous, deleterious, destructive substances of any kind . . ." Clearly, water, under conditions when it is "hazardous, deleterious, or destructive" meets the intent of the regulation.

D. The Court's Decision. The Appeals Court upheld the company's conviction. The fine of $6,000 was upheld, and the award of $935 to the State of New Jersey as compensatory damage for the destruction of public resources (the fish) was affirmed. The court rejected the company's contention that a lack of specific mention of thermal pollution in the statute indicated that such pollution could not be prosecuted according to the terms of the law. The court interpreted legislative intent to include the prohibition of *any* substance that would be hazardous, deleterious, or poisonous to life. As the introduction of the cold water resulted in the destruction of the menhaden, in this instance the cold water was a "hazardous and deleterious substance" as those terms are used in the statute.

The court rejected the company's contention that there had been a denial of "due process of law." The company had suggested that as water, either hot or cold, was sometimes hazardous and sometimes not, the finding of violation of the basis of cold water in this instance denied the company of due process. This was true, the company alleged, because there was no way of knowing, in advance, whether an action resulting in a discharge of cold water would be considered a violation or whether it would not. The court rejected the view that any substance, to be considered a pollutant, must be considered hazardous under all sets of conditions. The court pointed out that the company was aware that the fish and the commercial fishery had been attracted as a result of the heating of the waters of Oyster Creek near the discharge point of the canal. Given this knowledge, the court ruled, the company surely knew that a sudden drop in temperature would harm the fish. Such a deleterious effect, in the view of the court, was clearly a violation of the statute.

The court pointed out, further, that the company's own representatives had testified that it was possible to shut down the water pumps when the reactors were not in operation. Thus, the court rejected the company's contention that the introduction of the cold water and the subsequent death of the fish resulted because of an "unavoidable necessity."

The completed "case overview" provides the basic information from which the teacher plans the remainder of the mock trial exercise. Once this material has been completed, the next step is that of *role assignment and internalization*. This phase begins with a consideration of the roles to be filled during the simulated trial experience.

Some basic roles are involved in all mock trials. For example, nearly all will require a judge. If the case is one taken from an appelate jurisdiction, a panel of judges may be selected. Plaintiff, plaintiff's attorneys, plaintiff's witnesses, defendant, defendant's attorneys, defendant's witnesses, and jury members are among basic roles for the simulation. Many teachers embellish the cast of players by adding such roles as that of the bailiff, the clerk of court, and the court reporter. Numbers of individuals assigned to each role may vary, depending on the case selected. Some cases require many witnesses; others, only a few. Although twelve is a number frequently associated with juries, the number of jurors selected for a mock trial experience may be expanded to include all students not having other assigned roles. In a trial based on an appellate proceeding where the actual decision will be made by a panel of judges, students not playing other roles may serve as observers of the process who can be polled at the conclusion to determine whether their decision would have been the same as that of the panel of judges.

Once roles have been identified, background information about the case needs to be provided for individuals representing the contending parties' interests. For example, information needs to be provided to plaintiff's attorneys, plaintiff's witnesses, defendant's attorneys, and defendant's witnesses. The teacher needs to prepare sheets with special information that can be supplied to these individuals a day or two before the trial. Students playing these roles need to be encouraged to become as familiar as possible with the information. They should be warned, too, about divulging any information to others in the class. (It is particularly important that members of the jury and the judge or judges not be introduced to this material in advance of the actual trial simulation.) By way of explanation, students can be told that all relevant information will emerge during the trial and that prior disclosure might prejudice the thinking of those people who will be trying to make a decision.

Assuming that a mock trial experience was being planned based on the appellate case involving the Jersey Central Power & Light Company and the New Jersey Department of Environmental Protection, background sheets such as the following might be provided to (1) the plaintiff's attorneys, (2) the plaintiff's witness, (3) the defendant's attorneys, and (4) the defendant's witness:

Background for Plaintiff's Attorneys

1. Your suit is against the Jersey Central Power & Light Company for violation of N.J.S.A. 23: 5–28. In part, that statute states: "No person shall put or place into . . . any of the fresh or tidal waters of this state any petroleum products, debris, hazardous, deleterious, destructive, or poisonous substances of any kind . . ."
2. The Jersey Central Power & Light Company operates a nuclear-powered electrical generating plant under a license from the Atomic Energy Commission.
3. The reactors in this plant are cooled by cold water brought from the Forked River. This cold water is pumped around condensers in the plant, then out again into a canal flowing into Oyster Creek. The circulating water is heated as it cools the condensers. This heated water has raised the temperature of Oyster Creek near the point of outflow of water from the plant. This heating of Oyster Creek has attracted thousands of menhaden, a commercially valuable fish, to swim into Oyster Creek from the Atlantic. It can be shown that these facts were known to the defendant, who also knew that shutting down the reactors would cause Oyster Creek to cool down rapidly. This cooling would occur exceptionally rapidly if, in the event of a reactor shutdown, pumps drawing in cold water from the Forked River, through the plant, and out into Oyster Creek were not shut down at the same time.
4. On January 28, 1972, the Jersey Central Power & Light Company shut down its reactors because of a problem. Pumps continued to carry water from the Forked River to Oyster Creek. The pumps were kept running only as a convenience, not out of necessity; rust and scale are less of a problem when water is kept flowing through the system. Because the water was no longer heated by the reactors and because the Forked River is naturally cold, the temperature of Oyster Creek dropped thirteen degrees in twenty-four hours.
5. More than 500,000 menhaden were found by state inspectors to have died because of the sudden drop in temperature. You, the Department of Environmental Protection, have sued the Jersey Central Power & Light Company under the authority of N.J.S.A. 23: 5–28 (See no. 1.)

Background for Witness for the Plaintiff

1. You are a state inspector for the New Jersey Department of Environmental Protection.
2. When nuclear reactors at the Jersey Central Power & Light Company were shut down on January 28, 1972, there occurred massive deaths of menhaden (over half a million) in Oyster Creek.
3. It was apparent that the plant shutdown was accompanied by a sudden drop in the temperature of Oyster Creek (thirteen degrees in twenty-four hours).
4. Investigations of the menhaden carcasses revealed that the deaths had not resulted from exposure to poisonous substances. It was concluded that the sudden drop in temperature was the sole cause of death.

Background for Defendant's Attorneys

1. You represent the Jersey Central Power & Light Company, which, under a provisional operating license from the Atomic Energy Commission, runs a nuclear-powered electrical plant cooled by waters pumped from the Forked River, around condensers underneath the reactors, and into an outflow canal emptying into Oyster Creek (a stream flowing into the Atlantic).
2. When unaccounted-for leakage of radioactively contaminated water reaches a specified level, Atomic Energy Commission regulations require a shutdown of reactors for inspection. Because of this AEC regulation, reactors were shut down for four days beginning on January 28, 1972.
3. During this shutdown, pumps continued to carry cold Forked River water into Oyster Creek. As the reactors were shut down, the water did not take on heat from the condensers. As a result, the water was not warmed, and it was quite cold when it emptied into Oyster Creek. This meant that the water in Oyster Creek dropped thirteen degrees in twenty-four hours. State inspectors reported that over half a million menhaden—a commercially important fish—died because of thermal shock.
4. The menhaden had never existed in large numbers in Oyster Creek before the nuclear plant was built. They were attracted to that stream only after the plant opened and the temperature of the water was raised as a result of the outflow of water from the plant. A commercial fishery established itself only after the plant had been opened and the menhaden attracted to swim into Oyster Creek from the Atlantic.
5. Because of the deaths of the menhaden, the New Jersey Department of Environmental Protection sued your company under authority of N.J.S.A. 23: 5–28. This statute, in part, states: "No person shall put or place into . . . any of the fresh or tidal waters . . . of this

stateany petroleum products, debris, hazardous, deleterious, destructive, or poisonous substances of any kind."

Background for Witness for the Defendant

1. You are a representative of the Federal Atomic Energy Commission.
2. The Atomic Energy Commission, as a condition of licensing, places strict operating guidelines on nuclear-powered electrical plants such as the one operated by the Jersey Central Power & Light Company. One of these regulations mandates a shutdown when unaccounted-for coolant leakage around the reactors reaches a specified level. Federal AEC safety regulations take precedence over state statutes.
3. The shutdown of the reactors by the Jersey Central Power & Light Company on January 28, 1972, was consistent with AEC regulations because leakage was approaching the specified level.
4. The shutdown on January 28, 1972, and the subsequent inspections of the facility could have been accomplished without continuing to pump cold water from the Forked River. But maintenance is greatly simplified if the plant engineers continue to run the pumps when the reactor is not in operation.

Once these role background materials have been prepared and distributed to students selected to play the several parts in the simulated trial experience, students need to be given sufficient time to learn well the background material with which they have been provided. Ordinarily, if students are selected and assigned to roles, they can "internalize" or learn thoroughly the basic information in a day or two. Given this preparation, the actual trial experience can go forward.

Assume that, given the case that has been described, the teacher has decided to have a panel of three judges (remember that this a case from an appellate jurisdiction), two attorneys for the plaintiff, two attorneys for the defendant, one witness for the plaintiff and one witness for the defendant. Students have been assigned to roles, and they have had time to familiarize themselves with the background material provided them. They are ready to engage in the *simulated trial experience*. For this part of the exercises to be productive, some procedural guidelines are required.

In leading students through the simulated trial experience, beginning teachers are tempted to try to replicate every feature of a "real" courtroom procedure. Such an effort is likely to result in tedious discussions of procedural points that detract from the proper emphasis of the exercise. The simulated trial experience has as a primary goal the careful examination of contending views on an important issue. The structure of the trial should keep this focus in mind. Actual roles of procedure may vary widely provided that opportunities are provided for contending parties to air opposing views, introduce and question the quality and the reliability of evidence, and provide time for the judge(s) to reach a decision. An example of a set of "rules" that meet these basic criteria follow:

Simulated Trial—Procedures

1. Five-minute opening argument by the defendant's attorneys. Time may be divided as agreed upon by defendant's attorneys. (During this phase, the issue in question must be clearly explained to the panel of judges) (time: five minutes)
2. Five-minute opening argument by the plaintiff's attorneys. Time may be divided as agreed upon by plaintiff's attorneys. (time: five minutes)
3. Plaintiff's attorneys call witness. Plaintiff's witness is examined by plaintiff's attorneys. (time: five minutes)
4. Plaintiff's witness is cross-examined by defendant's attorneys. (time: five minutes)
5. Defendant's attorneys call witness. Defendant's attorneys examine defendant's witness. (time: five minutes)
6. Defendant's witness cross-examined by plaintiff's attorneys. (time: five minutes)
7. Final argument by plaintiff's attorneys. Time may be divided as agreed upon by plaintiff's attorneys. (time: five minutes)
8. Rejoinder by defendant's attorneys. [Defendant's attorneys attempt to respond to and comment on points made by plaintiff's attorneys in their final argument.] (time: three minutes)
9. Final argument by defendant's attorneys. Time may be divided as agreed by defendant's attorneys. (time: five minutes)
10. Rejoinder by plaintiff's attorneys. Plaintiff's attorneys attempt to respond to and comment on points made by defendant's attorneys in their final argument. (time: three minutes)
11. Judges retire and return with decision. (time: varies)
12. Debriefing.

This set of procedures is simply an example. Clearly, many other schemes would be as good or better. The exact set of procedures adopted must be selected by the teacher in the light of his or her own set of conditions. For example, are instructional periods fifty, sixty, or seventy minutes long? Should the simulated trial experience last more than a single classroom period? What is the attention span of students? These kinds of questions must be answered as a preparation for planning the actual procedures to be followed during the simulated trial experience.

The final phase of the simulated trial exercise, *debriefing,* is very important. During this part of the experience, the teacher helps students to "put it all together," to develop some insights with regard to what has taken place. The debriefing exercise has two major components. The first of these involves a discussion of the actual information that came out during the simulated trial in the classroom. The second centers on a discussion of the decision made in the actual case upon which the simulation was based and how that decision compares to the one reached by the student judges in the simulation exercises. Careful planning of this debriefing phase is essential for the success of the entire simulated trial experience.

Among questions that can be asked during that part of the debriefing focusing on what actually took place during the classroom exercise are the following:

1. What basic issue was in dispute?
2. What position was taken by the plaintiff?
3. What evidence supported the plaintiff's view?
4. What position was taken by the defendant?
5. What evidence supported the defendant's case?
6. What did the plaintiff's attorneys do to present evidence supporting the plaintiff's case and to raise questions about the defendant's evidence? What did the plaintiff's attorneys do that particularly impressed you? What might they have done better?
7. What did the defendant's attorneys do to present the defendant's evidence in the best light and to raise questions about the plaintiff's evidence. What did the defendant's attorneys do that particularly impressed you? What might they have done better?
8. *To the judges:* Tell us the line of thinking you used in arriving at your decision. What evidence especially impressed you? What would it have taken for you to change your mind?

After these questions have been asked and students have had a chance to discuss what occurred in the classroom simulation, the teacher, as a culminating activity, tells the class what actually happened in the trial upon which the case was based. Refer to the case overview for details relating to the actual disposition of this case. Once students have been familiarized with this information, a final set of debriefing questions can be asked. The focus, this time, is on a comparison and contrast of the student judges' decision and that of the "real" judges. Questions such as the following might be asked:

1. What arguments apparently impressed the real judges that did not impress our student judges?
2. How was the logic used by our student judges similar to that of judges in the real case?
3. How might you account for any differences between our student judges' decision and the decision made in the real case?
4. Now that you have seen how this case turned out both in our classroom trial and in the actual trial setting, what personal reactions do you have? What do you individually feel the most "just" solution would have been? Upon what logic are your feelings based? What strong personal values are suggested by your feelings about this situation? And so on.

This capstone discussion is designed to help students derive some personal meaning from the case they have seen introduced during the simulated trial. This discussion helps to tie together the entire simulated trial experience into a meaningful whole. Students, at the point the actual trial simulation phase concludes, may have picked up some impressions that are not accurate. Because of this possibility, it is essential that this final debriefing not be overlooked. A few key questions, such as those suggested earlier, ought to be prepared in advance to serve as guides to direct the general direction of the discussion. Thought about the entire debriefing portion of the exercise ought to demand at least as much time during the preparation phase as that devoted to selection of the case and preparation of the role descriptions. Given attention to preparation of all components of the exercise, the simulated trial experience has high potential for engaging students in an exciting and productive learning activity.

Contributions of Law-focused Studies Exercises

Only rarely are entire courses built around law-focused studies. A much more common pattern is to include some law-focused exercises or lessons as components of other social studies courses. For example, U.S. history courses sometimes are organized to include mock trial simulations of some key decisions that helped define the appropriate relationship between federal and state authorities. Simulations of important civil rights cases have also enjoyed some popularity. In social studies courses drawing heavily upon contents from the behavioral sciences, simulation of cases having to do with conflicts between the individual and the social group of which he or she is a part have been featured with some regularity. Given the range of available cases and the multitude of topics that provide a focus for social studies instruction, it is not difficult to identify relevant material for law-focused instruction presented via a mock trial or some other appropriate format. Certainly, law-focused studies have great potential for reinforcing learnings in a number of kinds of social studies classes.

Yet primary contributions of law-focused studies in the social studies classes do not relate to specific information students might acquire as a result of their participation in a "mindwalk," a "simulated trial," or in other law-focused learning exercises. One significant objective of law-focused programs is to help students understand the legal process. Familiarity with essentials of this process can help students become more sophisticated consumers of legal services when the need arises. In addition to teaching legal processes, law-focused programs in a more general sense help students to (1) identify key issues in a dispute, (2) compare and contrast logical support of positions on opposing sides of a dispute, and (3) make decisions in the light of the best evidence and after consideration of relevant personal and social values.

Law-focused studies programs help students to see beyond peripheral issues to the fundamental unresolved question. The entire process provides students with a laboratory for decision making. They learn that difficult questions have no easy solutions. They learn that decisions rarely satisfy all the needs of contending parties. With the possibility for providing students with these important insights, law-focused studies programs deserve consideration as a component of courses in the secondary social studies curriculum.

Sources of Information

A large number of groups presently are engaged in the production of classroom materials and practical ideas for presenting law-focused learning experiences to secondary school students. Typically, these materials have resulted from joint efforts of educators and lawyers interested in public education. For information relating to available materials and procedures related to law-focused learning programs, write to one or more of the following:

American Bar Association Special Committee on Youth Education for Citizenship
1155 East 60 Street
Chicago, Illinois 60637

Correctional Service of Minnesota
Educational Division
1427 Washington Avenue South
Minneapolis, Minnesota 55404

Institute for Political/Legal Education
Box 426, Glassboro-Woodbury Road
Pittman, New Jersey 08071

Law, Education and Participation
6310 San Vincente Boulevard
Los Angeles, California 90048

Law in a Free Society
606 Wilshire Boulevard, Suite 600
Santa Monica, California 90401

Law in American Society Foundation
33 North La Salle Street
Chicago, Illinois 60602

National Organization on Legal Problems in Education
5401 Southwest Seventh Avenue
Topeka, Kansas 66606

National Street Law Institute
412 Fifth Street, N.W.
Washington, D.C. 20001

Lawyers' professional associations in a number of states have joined together with educators to develop law-focused studies programs. These programs are too numerous to list here. For those interested, there is a directory of these state efforts. It is entitled *Directory of Law-Related Educational Activities,* and it is available from the Special Committee on Youth Education for Citizenship, American Bar Association, American Bar Center, 1155 East 60 Street, Chicago, Illinois 60637.

An additional excellent discussion of information sources for law-focused studies programs is presented in Susan E. Davison's "Curriculum Materials and Resources for Law-Related Education" (*Social Education*, March 1977: 184–193). This entire issue of *Social Education* is centered on law-focused education, and other articles provide additional insights related to organizing and managing such programs.

Finally, local bar associations in many areas have an education committee interested in law-focused studies programs. Certainly, a teacher interested in this area would do well to make a contact with the local lawyers' group. He or she might find that some groundwork has already been done and, as importantly, make some contact with individuals who might be willing to come and work with students when law-focused studies lessons were being presented.

There is no shortage of materials for the teacher interested in this area. Given this situation and the potential contribution they can make in developing students' decision-making capabilities, law-focused studies lessons increasingly are becoming features of secondary social studies programs.

Summary

Concern for students' lack of grasp of fundamental democratic legal principles has stimulated the professional legal community to consider ways of helping students grasp the essentials of our jurisprudential system. Out of these concerns, a number of programs have emerged, developed jointly by lawyers and educators. These programs seek an active engagement between students and difficult issues. Frequently, a simulated trial has been used as a vehicle for helping students work through the logic supporting contending positions. To raise the level of student interest, one can place emphasis on featuring cases of interest to secondary students, for example, those relating to restriction on students' behavior (distribution of student newspapers, regulation of hair length, due process related to dismissal, and so forth).

Few schools have developed entire courses devoted to law-focused education. But significant numbers include some law-focused study programs within existing courses. Because of the range of jurisprudential concerns and the diverse nature of topics featured in social studies classes, it has not proved difficult to identify material for law-focused lessons that is relevant to the course in which such lessons are presented. A number of organizations around the country have emerged that have developed many excellent materials for use in secondary school classrooms.

A major strength of law-focused studies programs, as they relate to social studies education, is their potential for developing students' decision-making capabilities. Law-focused studies programs help students to identify, think about, and make decisions about difficult questions. This experience, to a degree at least, parallels the kind of decision-making dilemmas faced by thoughtful adults throughout their lives.

REFERENCES

ARMSTRONG, DAVID G. "Thermal Pollution: Background Material for a Mock Trial." *Law in American Society* (February 1977): 27–30.

GROSS, NORMAN. "Teaching About the Law: Perceptions and Implications." *Social Education* (March 1977): 168–169.

HENNING, JOEL F. "Law Related Education: What Works and What Doesn't." In *Reflections on Law-Related Education*, edited by Susan Davison, pp. 9–11. Philadelphia, Pennsylvania—May 21–22, 1973, Working Notes No. 3. Chicago: Committee on Youth Education for Citizenship, American Bar Association, 1973.

NAYLOR, DAVID T. "Law Studies in the Schools: A Compendium of Instructional Strategies." *Social Education* (March 1977): 170–178.

PITTENGER, JOHN C. "The Spirit of Liberty and the Classrooms of Pennsylvania." In *Reflections on Law-Related Education*, edited by Susan Davison, pp. 5–8. Philadelphia, Pennsylvania—May 21–22, 1973, Working Notes No. 3. Chicago: Special Committee on Youth Education for Citizenship, American Bar Association, 1973.

Chapter 17

MORAL EDUCATION

O UR BROAD AND DIVERSE SOCIETY encourages the flowering of a vast array of individual talents. Curiously, this allegiance to the broad goal of individual development can occur only under conditions of widespread respect for certain shared principles. Nurturing the individual is clearly associated with commitment to the social value of tolerance. Even as social studies educators seek to promote individual development, they must seek as well to promote a certain conformity to the value of tolerance.

Social studies education is interested in individual development within a social context; that is, individual development is encouraged so long as it is not clearly destructive of the social order within which this development takes place. Though limits in this society are among the least restrictive that have been devised by social groups throughout history, still there are limits that define "appropriate" individual behavior. Because these limits do exist, social studies educators have had a long interest in the issue of moral education.

In general, moral education is directed toward preserving the "social glue" that binds the society together and defines the limits of appropriate behavior. Several approaches to moral education have been taken in social studies classes over the years. For years some teachers simply told their students that x was "right" and y was "wrong." An implication of this approach was that "bad" or "immoral" behavior is never rewarded. There are too many counterexamples in the "real world" to this somewhat simplistic equation, and there is evidence that moral education programs characterized by telling students what was "good" or "bad" have had minimal impacts on students' behavior.

A second approach that has enjoyed some currency in recent years has been termed "values clarification" or "values education." Based on work by Raths, Harmin, and Simon (1966), the values clarification approach scrupulously avoids any attempt by the teacher to impose a "correct" set of values. Rather, the objective is for students to bring the set of values they individually hold into clearer focus so that these values can be identified and ordered in terms of their importance. Values clarification desires to help students realize that some values they hold conflict and that they should not be upset when they take actions congruent with some personal values and at odds with others. Individuals prize some of their values more highly than others. When there is a conflict, action will likely be guided by the more highly prized value. (For example, a person might like both operas and football games. On a given Saturday afternoon, that individual might have to choose between an opera and a game. If the opera were selected, that simply would imply that the "love of opera" value was more strongly held than the "love of football" value.)

A great strength of the values clarification approach is its emphasis on the individual. As noted, every effort is made to avoid imposing values of others. The approach has been criticized, however, for failing to consider that some personally held values may be more supportive of or more destructive of the social order of others. Critics have alleged that the values clarification approach is so nonjudgmental in its orientation that even very socially destructive values come in for no condemnation. For example, someone who had chosen freely from among alternatives the value of genocide for the Jews would not necessarily come in for comment any more than an individual who had chosen freely from alternatives the value of universal human love and tolerance. Although the benefits of identifying and assigning priorities to individual values have been recognized widely, supporters of value clarification have been consistently questioned about the approach's seeming acceptance of all individually held values, even those that may be destructive of the social order.

Another approach that has been receiving a good deal of attention centers around a moral values education program based on the work of Lawrence Kohlberg. Critics of both the "teacher as teller of 'right' and 'wrong'" approach and the "values clarification" approach are attracted to Kohlbergian programs for two basic reasons. First, moral values must be developed by the individual student and not imposed by the teacher. Second, some moral values are viewed as more desirable than other moral values.

Kohlberg's Six Stages of Moral Development

Lawrence Kohlberg has identified six basic moral stages. These moral stages are distinguished from one another, not by the nature of a response an individual might make to a given situation, but rather by the conception of justice the individual has in making his or her decision. In other words, it makes a difference and says something about an individual's relative moral development if he or she decides to go to an opera (1) because he or she will be punished if a contrary decision is made or (2) because "nice" people go to operas and enjoy being seen there. The actual decision (to go to the opera) is the same, but the logic (or the conception of justice) used in arriving at the decision is different. In the first case, the decision is seen as just because of a primary allegiance to raw power. In the second, the decision is seen as just because it conforms with what the community approves. Kohlberg would view the logic of the second reason as reflecting a higher moral stage than that of the first. An understanding of each of Kohlberg's stages will provide a background for understanding moral education programs based on his work.

Preconventional Level
   Stage 1. *Punishment and Obedience Orientation.* The consequences of a decision in physical terms are the primary bases for judgment. Decisions reflect an unquestioning respect for raw power. No consideration is given for a broad human meaning of a decision,
   ("I have decided to empty the garbage so daddy won't spank me when he gets home.")
   Stage 2. *Instrumental Relativism.* The decision is made based on a clear conception of what it will do to further the personal interests of the decision-maker. Interactions with others are viewed in terms of how some personal "pay off" might be arranged.
   ("I'll do your math homework, if you'll do my chemistry homework.)

Conventional Level
   Stage 3. *Interpersonal Concordance.* The decision is made with a view to pleasing others in the group. Sometimes this is referred to as the "good girl" stage. Decisions reflect perceptions of how "ideal" individuals in the group might respond in similar situations.
   ("Sure I'll give to the Red Cross Drive. Our homeroom always gives 100 per cent to all the charity campaigns.")
   Stage 4. *Law and Order Orientation.* The decision is made out of a respect and esteem for established rules, regulations, and entrenched social practices. Duty, tradition, and formal authority are respected.
   ("No one in our family has ever had a ticket. And if the governor wants me to drive fifty-five, well it's fifty-five I'll drive.")

Postconventional Level
   Stage 5. *Social-Contract Legalistic Orientation.* The decision results from a consideration of formal rules and guidelines established by the entire society and by personal values and opinion. Where society has not provided a guideline, there is a reliance on personal insights. There is an emphasis on the individual's ability to influence and change formal rules and guidelines of the society.
   ("I am going to take the IRS to court to challenge their claim that I cannot deduct my convention travel as a legitimate business expense.")

Stage 6. *Universal Ethical-Principle Orientation.* The decision is made based on the dictates of the individual conscience. The individual looks for guidance to universal principles such as human love and dignity rather than to formalized rules and regulations or traditional guidelines. These universal principles are chosen by the individual decision-maker and not imposed or suggested by others.

("I realize that this may be considered stealing, but I shall not be swayed by any petty laws or regulations in the fight for justice. The food is there in the warehouse, and the poor are there in their rat-infested hovels. Tonight, I shall go, take the food, and give it to the people. My arrest will be a symbol to those who see the corruption of a system that provides too much to the few and too little to the many.")

Kohlberg is a developmentalist. That means that individuals do not arrive at a given moral stage by any random pattern. Rather, individuals pass systematically from stage 1 through stage 2 and so forth. Individuals' levels of moral development stop at different stages. Very very few reach stage 6. Indeed only about 10 per cent of the American population reasons at any stage beyond stage 4. (Kohlberg, 1975).

In a given situation, an individual may make a decision based on the logic of the highest moral stage he or she has achieved or any lower moral stage. For example, someone at stage 4 may make decisions based on the logic of stage 4, 3, 2, and 1. In general, a high percentage of decisions will reflect the highest moral stage achieved. For example, someone at stage 2 cannot be expected to give 10 per cent of his or her income to the church because "that's what the membership rules say, and we certainly want to abide by them." (That logic would reflect stage 4—moral thinking.) Of course, he or she might well give the money (remember it's the *logic* supporting the decision, not the decision itself that distinguishes between moral stages) because "if I give 10 per cent, then my name will be included in the list of sustaining contributors" (a stage 2 justification for the action).

In general, there is an increase with each ascending stage of moral development in a person's concern for others. Decisions at stage 1, for example, tend to be based only on a concern for the retribution or reward likely to come to the individual as a consequence of the decision. Stage 2, as well, is characterized by a logic of "what's in it for me." On the other hand, individuals at higher stages of moral development base decisions on a much deeper concern for the thoughts, actions, dilemmas, and beliefs of others. Stage 5 moral thinking reflects a concern for the general rules of the society, and decisions mirror a sense of justice that goes beyond self-interest to encompass broad consideration for others. At stage 6, nearly all decisions are undertaken in a belief that they are promoting broad human values. Self-interest plays almost no role at this stage of moral decision making.

As Fenton (1976) has pointed out, decisions made by individuals at higher stages of moral development are likely to be better than decisions made by individuals at lower stages of moral development. This results because these decisions will likely consider the impact of alternative courses of action on other people. Desirable as it is for people to function at high stages of moral development, relatively few people, in fact, develop into natural stage 5 or stage 6 decision-makers. Indeed, many adults never move beyond stages 1 and 2. However, as Fenton (1976) notes, well-designed school programs can help students move to higher moral stages. For social studies teachers, with their interest in helping students enlarge their concern for others, there is a particular interest in promoting this kind of moral development. In the next section, some specific contributions of a moral education component in the social studies program will be introduced.

Moral Education in Social Studies Classes

Teachers may use Kohlberg's six stages of moral development in two basic ways. First, the system can be used to diagnose students' present level of moral reasoning. This information is useful to the teacher because it can suggest the kind of logic that might be used in dealing with an individual student. For example, if a teacher learns that a student is operating at stage 2, a discussion with a given student about a possible decision he or she has made or is about to make should not depend on logic characteristic of moral development above stage 3. People can understand arguments at or below their own stage. But if a teacher were to use stage 4 logic ("We should obey the school rules") with a student operating at stage 2 ("How will I benefit, if I do what you want?"), the student has little likelihood of identifying with the teacher's logic.

A second use of Kohlberg's system of moral stages can occur in a formal classroom program designed to raise students' sensitivity to others by raising the stage at which they make moral decisions. Programs of this type feature systematic presentations of moral dilemmas to students with a view to providing them opportunities to reorganize their patterns of thinking with a hope that new patterns will reflect higher stages of moral development. Specifics of moral development programs will be introduced in a subsequent session.

Moral Development for Individual Counseling

Proponents of Kohlberg's system point out that a teacher's responses are most effective when they are keyed to the moral stage of the student with whom he or she is working. Properly, the teacher pegs his or her response at either the same moral stage at which the student is operating or one moral stage higher. Consider the following two teacher responses to the same situation:

Scenario 1

John: Well, yes I did cheat on the test. Not me personally, you understand, but I did give Paul a little help.

Teacher: A little help? Tell me exactly what happened.

  John: Well, Paul's a genius in chemistry. He said if I slipped a couple of answers to him on your history quiz, he'd help me work out some of these weird valence problems.

Teacher: John I'm concerned about your reputation. Do you realize that, regardless of your good intentions, by helping Paul you might have everybody thinking about you as a cheater? Do you want people to think of you in this way?

Scenario 2

  John: Well, yes I did cheat on the test. Not me personally, you understand, but I did give Paul a little help.

Teacher: A little help? Tell me exactly what happened.

  John: Well, Paul's a genius in chemistry. He said if I slipped a couple of answers to him on your history quiz, he'd help me work out some of those weird valence problems.

Teacher: John, I am going to read you a section from student handbook. Listen carefully. "Any student, either receiving or giving aid on an examination may be subjected to disciplinary action that may include (a) detention, (b) suspension, or (c) other appropriate punishment." John, it is simply essential for us to follow the school rules. Do you understand that?

In both scenarios, John's responses indicate a stage 2 level of moral development. His explanation is a classic example of the "you scratch my back, then I'll scratch yours" that characterizes the moral basis of decisions of individuals operating at this level. In scenario 1, the teacher responds with a comment reflecting a stage 3 level of moral functioning. The teacher appeals to John by suggesting that "good" students in the school do not behave as he behaved. This stage 3 response is pegged only a single stage above John's stage 2 logic. It is quite possible that John will be able to identify with this logic and decide to change his pattern of behavior.

In scenario 2, the teacher makes the mistake of pegging his or her response at a moral level that is inappropriately high. Though John's logic clearly stems from stage 2 moral functioning, the teacher's response reflects stage 4 moral functioning. John is not very likely to identify with the law and order argument being made by the teacher. He may hear the teacher's words, but he probably cannot follow the logic. The teacher has violated the principle of keeping the response to the student at a level no higher than one stage above the level at which the student appears to be operating.

This principle is a very important one for social studies teachers. Beginning teachers frequently are disturbed at students' failure to identify with the plight of other less fortunate people. But when teachers understand that students' level of moral development may not be beyond stage 1 or 2, their lack of identification with issues requiring a broader human sensitivity become more understandable.

A student who operates from a "What can I personally gain if I do this for someone else?" perspective (stage 2) cannot be expected to be outraged at the acts of international terrorists whose actions are perceived as having no personal relevance at all. In order to help students broaden their interpersonal concerns, efforts can be undertaken in the classroom that are designed to raise students to a higher moral stage. Guidelines for such a program are provided in the section that follows.

RAISING STUDENTS' LEVELS OF MORAL REASONING

A teacher interested in developing a classroom program designed to raise students' levels of moral understanding and reasoning must begin by ascertaining the moral stage each student has attained at the time the program commences. Ordinarily, this is achieved by presenting students with several moral dilemmas (frequently presented in a paragraph or two). Students are asked how they would act if confronted with this situation and how they would justify their actions. These student responses are reviewed by the teacher. Answers are evaluated in terms of the stage of moral thinking reflected. Students are considered to be at the moral stage implied by the logic they use in explaining their decision. An example of a moral dilemma follows:

> You are one of eight people huddled together in a log cabin during a bitter cold winter storm that has raged outside for days. You have no electricity. You have no way of communicating with the outside world. The nearest town is ninety miles away. All food has been gone for four days.
>
> At the end of the day, one man dies. The group makes a decision that anyone who wishes to do so may eat the remains. What do you do?
>
> Examples of responses indicating different stages of moral thinking:
>
> *Stage 1 response:* Yes, I shall eat the human flesh. The only thing that really counts in life is my personal survival. If I refused to eat, I would in effect be committing suicide. God would surely punish me if I took my own life in this way. Therefore, I shall eat.
>
> *Stage 2 response:* Yes, I shall eat. I have a responsibility to take care of myself. No one will do this for me. I have done for this old man what I could during his life. Now, it seems only natural that he will do something for me.
>
> *Stage 3 response:* Yes, I shall eat the human flesh. The group has decided that anyone who wants to may eat. Because the group has made this decision, eating human flesh is considered appropriate behavior in the group of which I am presently a member. As I wish to behave consistent with the group's intentions, I shall eat the human flesh.
>
> *Stage 4 response:* Yes, I shall eat the human flesh. Cut off as we are from other human beings, we now constitute a society all of our own. Our society, like any other, has certain rules that govern our behavior. Even in our little group, our individual behavior must be within the limits of these rules. It is my belief that I have a duty to uphold and live within these limits. As our group has decided that it is all right to eat human flesh, I am well within

the limits of our rules by eating to survive. For this reason, I shall eat the human flesh as a demonstration of my loyalty to the rule of law governing our little group.

Stage 5 response: Yes, I shall eat the human flesh. Though laws and regulations in our society as well as long-standing tradition abhor the consumption of human flesh, I as a human being have a right to exercise my own will. These laws and traditions have been designed to serve the needs of normal times. These are not normal times, and by eating human flesh and perhaps having to answer later for my actions in a court of law, I can move the common law into a more humane and broader understanding that places limits on individual behavior only after a special consideration for prevalent conditions. I shall eat the flesh as a first step in seeking a more appropriate shaping of the legal and social system under which we live.

Stage 6 response: Yes, I shall eat the human flesh. The choice here is one of not eating human flesh and all dying or eating human flesh and permitting some to live. No laws have the right to interfere with the fundamental right to life. The same goes for traditions or broadly accepted social practices. I care not for what some individuals may think of my action. For me, preservation of life is a celebration of the human spirit. I eat this flesh not for myself, but as a testament to life itself.

Note that the decision in each case is the same. In deciding at which stage a student is operating at a given time, one must examine the rationale or logic he or she uses in defending whatever choice is made. Of course, many other responses might have been made to this dilemma. Those given here are meant only to indicate the sorts of student statements of logic that might be categorized appropriately at each of Kohlberg's stages.

After several moral dilemmas have been introduced for students for purposes of diagnosing students' entry-level stages of moral development, a systematic program of instruction can be undertaken with a view to raising individual students' stages of moral development. The assumption of such programs is that students tend to move to the next higher moral stage when they are presented with fairly frequent opportunities to reason about moral issues. To achieve this objective, a program of "moral discussions" can be organized. Beyer (1976) describes a "moral discussion" as a "purposeful conversation about moral issues" (p. 194).

"Moral discussions" involve a systematic consideration of moral dilemmas. Beyer (1976) suggests a five-step format for such lessons:[1]

Step 1. Introduction of the dilemma.
Step 2. Recommend tentative responses to the dilemma.
Step 3. Discuss reasoning in small groups.
Step 4. Examine reasoning as a class.
Step 5. Reflect on reasoning and draw tentative conclusions.

Introduction of the dilemma. In selecting a moral dilemma, one ought to select something that (1) is real to the experience of the students and (2) has the complex-

---

[1] Adapted from Barry K. Beyer, "Conducting Moral Discussion in the Classroom," *Social Education* (April 1976): 194–202; 196–197.

ity of issues they will face as adults in the "real world." Students can identify much more closely with issues that they do not perceive as contrived merely for the purposes of having a classroom discussion. The dilemmas can be presented in written form (they should be kept short; a few paragraphs will do), on audiotape, on videotape, or in almost any other medium that seems appropriate for the group. The following are two examples of moral dilemmas that might be used:

Moral Dilemma 1

Mrs. Smith's husband has suffered an industrial accident. The family is in desperate financial straits. Workmen's compensation benefits have run out. Savings have nearly been exhausted. Buying food for the family of four is becoming a real problem.

While shopping in the grocery store, Mrs. Smith observes twenty-five dollars' worth of food stamps fall to the floor from the open purse of a careless shopper. Mrs. Smith walks to the place where the food stamps have fallen. No one is looking. She picks up the stamps. Should she keep them, or should she return them to the person who dropped them?

Moral Dilemma 2

James works as Coach Smith's student basketball trainer. James has given this job his best effort because he admires Coach Smith very much. Coach Smith appreciates James's work very much. At the basketball assembly last week he stood before the entire student body and said, "Without having somebody like James to count on, we just couldn't get our job done. He's our 'Mr. Reliable' down at the gym."

Last Wednesday at the end of practice, Coach Smith asked James whether he might take a load of equipment across town for the game with Center City High that evening. James, realizing that his own car was too small to hold the equipment, thought he could borrow his father's station wagon. So, he said, "Sure, Coach, you can depend on me."

When James got home, he and his father got into an argument about some grade problems. "James," his father said, "you're spending too much time with that basketball team and not enough with your books. I want you to stay home for the rest of the week. Give me your car keys." After a heated argument, James turned over his keys to his father.

After dinner, James's father was picked up by another member of his Wednesday evening bowling league and taken to the alleys for the evening. James noticed that the keys to the family station wagon were on the table. Should he take the car and deliver the equipment to Coach Smith or should he do as his father wished and stay home?

Recommendation of tentative responses to the dilemma. Once members of the class have been introduced to the dilemma, each student should be asked to write down what he or she personally would do in the situation described. Next the students should be asked to write down as complete an explanation as possible for their decision. Students might be told to write their answers as though they were going to have to defend their choices to someone who disagreed with their intended course of action.

After students have completed these tasks, the teacher should ask for a show of hands of students favoring alternative A and alternative B. This information will reveal the extent of the division of opinion with regard to the appropriate response to the moral dilemma and can serve as a basis for organizing students into groups. When students have indicated their feelings about which alternative they prefer, the class should be divided into five or six groups, consisting of five or six students each. The teacher should take care to make sure that some people in each group favor alternative A and some alternative B. Discussion within groups tends to be much more spirited when different positions are represented.

Discussion of reasoning in small groups.   Once groups have been established, students are instructed to discuss the reasoning behind their choices. There will be an initial tendency for some students to emphasize "what" they decided rather than to explain "why" they decided it. It will be necessary for the teacher to point out that the conclusion itself is not the key point of the discussion. Rather, reasons why individuals chose a given alternative should be the basic focus of the discussion.

In a small group, there is an excellent chance that students operating at several of Kohlberg's stages will be present. This situation is likely to result in a good number of students being exposed to logic reflecting a level of moral development one stage above their own. Exposure to this kind of logic in a discussion setting can help raise the level of moral reasoning of some individuals.

These discussions should be allowed to continue only so long as participation remains at a high level of intensity. Five to ten minutes is often sufficient. At the end of this period, the teacher might ask each group to select a spokesperson. This individual will write down all the reasons given for the alternative positions represented in the group.

Examination of reasoning as a class.   After small group discussions have concluded and spokespersons for each group have written down all reasons given, the class can be reassembled into a single large group. To facilitate this phase of the lesson, the teacher can tape two large pieces of butcher paper across the front wall. One of these can be reserved for reasons associated with alternative A; and the other, for reasons associated with alternative B. Spokespersons from each group can be invited to write reasons given by members of their groups on the appropriate sheet of butcher paper. A felt-tipped marker works well for this purpose.

After all reasons have been recorded, the teacher can lead a general discussion about the alternative lines of reasoning. The teacher must be accepting of student opinions and nonjudgmental during this discussion. As the discussion unfolds, the teacher must listen carefully for individual student comments. Whenever possible, the teacher should attempt to identify the moral stages being reflected in the comments of individual students. If, for example, the teacher listens to one student speaking and realizes that he or she is making an argument reflecting a stage 2 level of moral reasoning, the teacher can call for a response from another student known to have made previous comments reflecting a stage 3 level of moral reasoning. To the extent that it is possible, efforts are made to expose students to expressions of moral reasoning one stage higher than that at which they are presently operating.

Reflection of reasoning and development of tentative conclusions. After students have had an opportunity to explore all reasons listed on the sheets of butcher paper and to suggest additional ones, the activity moves toward a conclusion. Beyer (1976) suggests that the teacher at this time ask each student to take a piece of paper and write down all the reasons supporting the alternative he or she does *not* support. This exercise demands a final careful consideration of logic other than his or her own. Having done this, students then can be asked to write down their own decision and the most compelling reason or reasons they can think of supporting their decision. Students should be told in advance of this final activity that they will not be required to turn in their final papers. However, the teacher should make clear that, should some students wish to share their preferred course of action and supporting logic with the teacher during a private conference, appropriate arrangements can be made.

IMPORTANT CONSIDERATIONS FOR THE MORAL EDUCATION PROGRAM

In the planning for a moral education program, careful consideration must be given to (1) program goals, (2) diagnosis of students' entry-level stages of moral reasoning, (3) program length, and (4) specific moral dilemmas selected. Attention to these details is related very closely to the likelihood a given program will succeed.

Program goals. There is a tendency for some teachers to set goals too high. It is necessary to remember that only 10 per cent of the entire adult population reasons at stages 5 and 6 (Kohlberg 1975). Given this reality, it makes little sense to set out to turn every student into a stage 5 moral reasoner. Practically speaking, if several students can be moved from stage 2 to stage 3 or from stage 3 to stage 4, the program should be judged a success. Many students may well remain at the stage of moral development that characterized them at the very beginning of the program. However, the program may well have provided them with experiences that will help them to move to a higher stage of moral reasoning some time after the conclusion of the program. There is good reason to suppose that this transition may be speeded up by their exposure to the moral dilemmas and discussions presented during the moral development lessons.

Diagnosis of students' entry level stages of moral development. The moral development program has slight chances for success unless careful attention is given to determining entry-level moral reasoning stages of students. Recall that individuals cannot understand the logic of decisions based on moral reasoning more than one stage above their own stage of development. This situation makes imperative a careful assessment of students' entry-level moral reasoning stages.

As noted previously, students ordinarily are presented with several moral dilemmas to which they are asked to react as part of the diagnostic phase of the program. Students give their responses and lay out the logic upon which their responses are based. In an effort to establish that the pattern of responses consistently reflects thinking characterizing a single stage of moral reasoning, students should react to more than a single moral dilemma. Fenton (1976) suggests that students might be introduced to three dilemmas. Use of several dilemmas reduces the possibility that a single set of responses might be unique to the situation introduced in a particular dilemma.

Program length. The moral development program typically consists of a series of individual, group, and entire class exercises focusing on different moral dilemmas. Clearly, students will grow tired of and bored with classroom activities that include nothing but a wearisome consideration of new moral dilemmas day after day. Moral development programs ought not to be regarded as entire courses of instruction or as components within existing courses that tie up six, nine, or twelve weeks of instructional time. Rather, the programs ought to be relatively brief in duration and "salt-and-peppered" periodically throughout other courses. By keeping length of such programs relatively short and by interspersing programs occasionally throughout other courses, the teachers can keep motivation at a high level. Certainly, student interest will be very hard to hold when moral development programs are allowed to run on too long.

Regrettably, there is no magic figure that prescribes the "ideal length" of such a program. The teacher must observe how the instruction is being received by his or her students. When interest begins to flag and negative comments begin to surface, the time has come to shift to another activity. A return at a latter date to some moral development lessons will usually prove to be more productive than pushing students to maintain an interest in something that has begun to bore them.

Specific moral dilemmas selected. Careful attention needs to be given to the selection of the moral dilemmas used as a focus for classroom discussions. As noted previously, dilemmas work best that have some "reality" for the student. If situations introduced are so fanciful that students cannot imagine themselves ever having to face them, then there is reason to doubt that the logic they use in defending their intended course of action is a true representation of their highest stage of moral reasoning. Every effort should be made to select situations with which students have a real possibility of becoming personally involved.

Fraenkel (1976) has suggested more attention might be given to sequencing moral dilemmas. One possibility that might be considered would involve presenting dilemmas sequentially in such a way that each succeeding dilemma would be characterized by a higher level of complexity than that which preceded it. Dilemmas in the "real world" are not simple. By the systematic increase of the complexity of dilemmas to which students are asked to respond, a closer approximation of the difficult choices students will face in life might be achieved. Certainly, Fraenkel's suggestion merits serious consideration.

CRITICISMS OF PRACTICES STEMMING FROM KOHLBERG'S STAGES OF MORAL REASONING

Although there has been a great deal of support and interest in Kohlbergian moral reasoning programs, such programs have not been without their critics. Rest (1974) questions the practicality of a teacher's actually being able to conduct a group discussion in such a way that every student was able to hear some logic derived from a stage of moral reasoning one stage above his or her own. For example, a teacher is supposed to (1) listen to what a student says, (2) simultaneously understand the content of the student's statement and identify the moral stage reflected in the student's reasoning, and (3) immediately provide a comment back to the student that reflects logic at a moral stage precisely one stage above that of the student. It has been suggested that teachers simply cannot do all of these things during a rapid-fire classroom discussion. Individual student contributions simply come too fast for the teacher to identify correctly and respond to students in the light of the moral reasoning stages implied by their comments.

Fraenkel (1976) points out that Kohlberg himself has indicated that only 10 per cent of the American adult population reason at moral levels above stage 4. This means that large numbers of teachers reason at levels 4, 3, 2, or even 1. If this is the case, critics wonder, how can teachers be expected to provide responses to students that, in every case, reflect logic associated with a moral stage higher than those of the students? As individuals cannot even understand, much less express, logic reflecting a moral stage more than one stage higher than their own, it is difficult to understand how, for example, a stage 3 teacher could provide a stage 5 argument to help a stage 4 student. Critics allege that the programs stemming from the work of Kohlberg erroneously assume that every classroom teacher is either a stage 5 or a stage 6 moral reasoner.

Another criticism that has been suggested rests on the kind of evidence that is used to determine the particular moral stage at which a given individual is said to be functioning. Recall that Kohlberg's moral stages do not focus on the decision itself, but rather on the logic that is used to defend the decision. Some critics have suggested that a more proper focus is the decision itself. They point out that a decision may be socially irresponsible even though the logic the individual uses to support it may reflect a moderately high level of moral reasoning (as measured by Kohlberg's stages.) For example, suppose a country passed a series of laws declaring Jews to be "nonpersons." Given such a situation, an individual might kill a Jew and rationalize his or her action as follows: "Our laws declare the Jews to be nonpersons. Therefore, I have not committed murder. I am a law-abiding person, and my action was well within the limits of the law." Some might regard this as stage 4 reasoning. But few would support the conclusion that the act represented sensitive, humane, and socially desirable behavior.

Moral reasoning programs have also been questioned because of their assumption that, in discussions of moral dilemmas occurring in groups representing students at different moral reasoning stages, logic reflecting various stages of moral reasoning will come out. Merely because a cross section of individuals is in a group does not assure that all will participate. Indeed, there is evidence that some strong-willed students (perhaps stage 1 or stage 2 moral reasoners) may dominate group discussions. In such cases, it is likely that the amount of time devoted to airing logic of stage 3, 4, and 5 students will be strictly limited, if not, in fact, eliminated altogether. Certainly, teachers can do much to assure that this situation does not develop, but it is a problem that demands careful teacher attention.

Conclusion

Though teachers need to be aware of their limitations, practices derived from the work of Kohlberg do have a contribution to make to the social studies program. It is true that some partisans of Kohlberg's work may have misjudged a teacher's practical ability to respond quickly during large-group discussions with logic keyed one moral stage above that represented in a given student's comment. Yet there *are* occasions when the teacher can respond in such a fashion, even though it may be impossible to do so during every teacher-student interchange. There is evidence that even a limited exposure of students to a logic reflecting a moral stage one higher than their own can have positive results. Certainly, this limited exposure is better than none at all.

Kohlberg's work appears to have considerable application in situations when teachers are working with students individually. Kohlberg's system provides a logical referent that can be used to assess and react to the particular rationale used by a given student. If a student's logic reflects stage 2 thinking, then the teacher can respond with a stage 3 response. The system, though certainly not perfect, provides a guideline for much more specific kinds of responses to students' logic.

In general, Kohlberg promotes the view that people ought to be helped to grow toward higher levels of moral reasoning. These higher levels tend to be characterized by a logic that reflects a much greater sensitivity to needs and concerns of other human beings than do lower levels. Because the social studies seeks to help students develop individually in the light of an appreciation of the social world of which they are a part, social studies teachers have a stake in helping students reflect on issues from the perspectives of higher stages of moral reasoning.

Though Kohlberg's scheme is far from perfect, it represents a beginning from which professionals can build with profit.

Summary

Lawrence Kohlberg has proposed that individuals pass sequentially through a series of stages of moral reasoning. Six stages of moral reasoning have been identified. Stages are distinguished from one another by the logic the individual uses in arriving at a given decision. Individuals at different stages may reach a similar conclusion, but they will justify their decision in different ways.

Individuals do not automatically progress through all six stages. Indeed, the vast majority of people never get beyond stage 4. Kohlberg and his associates have found that individuals tend to move to a higher stage of moral reasoning when they are presented with opportunities to discuss moral dilemmas with individuals whose logic represents moral thinking at one stage above their own; that is, if one is at stage 2, there is a good chance he or she will develop into a stage 3 moral reasoner if he or she is presented with opportunities to interact with individuals who can offer logic reflecting stage 3 moral reasoning.

People are said to be able to understand logic reflecting moral reasoning at their own stage, at all lower stages, and at one stage higher than their own. They cannot understand the logic of moral arguments reflecting moral reasoning stages two or more stages higher than their own. An implication of this reality is that students' stages of moral reasoning need to be determined by teachers. When teachers have this information, they can attempt to prepare arguments for use with individual students that do not reflect an inappropriately high level of moral reasoning.

Classroom discussions of moral dilemmas in the social studies can help raise stages of moral reasoning of individual students. This is a desirable outcome because higher levels of moral reasoning tend to be more associated with logic reflecting a concern for others than lower levels.

REFERENCES

BEYER, BARRY K. "Conducting Moral Discussion in the Classroom." *Social Education* (April 1976): 194–202.

FENTON, EDWIN. "Moral Education: The Research Findings." *Social Education* (April 1976: 188–193.

FRAENKEL, JACK R. "The Kohlberg Bandwagon: Some Reservations." *Social Education* (April 1976): 216–222.

KOHLBERG, LAWRENCE. "The Cognitive-Developmental Approach to Moral Education." *Phi Delta Kappan* (June 1975): 670–677.

RATHS, LOUIS E.; MERRILL HARMIN; and SIDNEY B. SIMON. *Values and Teaching: Working with Values in the Classroom.* Columbus, Ohio: Charles E. Merrill Publishing Co., 1966.

REST, JAMES. "Developmental Psychology as a Guide to Value Education: A Review of Kohlbergian Programs." *Review of Educational Research* (Spring 1974): 241–59.

Chapter 18

UTILIZING THE LOCAL

COMMUNITY.

F OR MANY STUDENTS, social studies classes seem overly concerned with people, places, and events that appear little connected to their own lives. Although sophisticated adults can grasp the links that join people together over time and space, students often have difficulty in seeing the personal importance of learning experiences centering on the study of unfamiliar people and places. Because many of the thinking skills social studies teachers seek to develop are by no means tied to exotic content ("exotic," at least, in the minds of students), a case can be made for devoting some time in social studies classes to developing these skills by focusing on content that does appear more "real" and "relevant" to students. Studies of the local community have proved motivating for many students. Such programs have real potential for building students' interest in the social studies that can carry over to topics that are more psychologically remote from their own experience.

The local community might be thought of as a "laboratory" for the social studies. In this laboratory, students learn to seek out information, analyze information, develop tentative conclusions, test those conclusions, and revise conclusions in the light of all information available. In short, the local community can help build students' decision-making skills. The local community provides a particularly appropriate setting for such exercises because there is an element of "believability" about the local community that cannot be matched by textbook treatments of distant places and peoples. Certainly, this does not suggest that all social studies instruction should be based on the local community. Rather, such studies should be viewed as a mechanism for stimulating student interest in topics and ways of arriving at conclusions that can be applied to studies of less proximate times, regions, and peoples.

The community laboratory stimulates students' interest in the social studies because, in the local community, students function both as *observers* and as *participants*. This represents an important difference, for example, from the roles student play in courses such as American history, where they can function only as observers. The added element of personal participation in local community studies represents a powerful stimulus to motivating students involved in such programs.

A common problem teachers experience in establishing community studies programs is finding a framework for organizing all planned learning experiences. There is no shortage of information regarding specific kinds of lessons that might be taught as part of a local community study program, but specific guidelines for integrating these lessons to assure comprehensiveness are hard to find. One approach, suggested by Armstrong and Savage, Jr. (1976), advocates planning programs that consider (1) stimulus experiences and (2) anticipated student learnings.

Stimulus Experiences

In general, stimulus experiences are artifacts, materials, events, and other phenomena to which students are exposed during a local community study program. Stimulus experiences can be subdivided into the three general categories of (1) historical residues, (2) present interactional processes, and (3) likely future patterns.

Historical residues. Historical residues are reminders of the past history of the community that have survived through time. They include such things as old documents, records, photographs, historic buildings, and other physical evidences of life in the community in years gone by. Local community studies should include some lessons that use historical residues as a starting point. For example, the teacher might have found a copy of an old jailer's register on a dusty shelf in the city hall. A copy of a page such as the following might be distributed to students:

Date	Name	Charge and Comments
2/6/91	Smith, Elroy D.	Negro out after sundown. Cell 5
2/6/91	Heming, T. D.	Negro, drunk in public. Cell 5
2/6/91	Steptoe, C. (Red Eye)	Indian, drunk. Cell 7
2/6/91	Peterson, Pete	Public nuisance (panhandling). Cell 8
2/6/91	James, Jimmy	Negro. Cut his woman (again). Cell 5
2/6/91	Pauley, R. C.	Cut bartender. Drunk. Cell 8
2/6/91	Norton, D. C.	Negro. Drunk in public. Cell 5
2/6/91	Philpot, Pauley	Negro. Out after sundown. Cell 5

Students might be asked to look over the information on this copied page from the jailer's log as a first step in the lesson. Next the teacher might take them through a series of discussion questions such as the following:

> What kinds of people tended to be arrested most frequently?
> What were the most common complaints against them?
> How were member of different groups (blacks, Indians, whites, and so on) treated by the jailer?
> What charges would you consider unusual today? Why?
> What would you say people at this time feared? Why? What evidence is there to support this view?

Following this discussion, students might be asked to write a short historical account on the topic "What the Public Expected of Lawmen in 1891." After students had completed this assignment, copies of additional pages from the jailer's log could be provided to everyone in the class. Students might then be asked to look at what they had written and then go through the additional pages to find information that (1) tended to support their conclusions and (2) tended to refute their conclusions. As a final activity, members of the class might comment upon the kinds of changes they would make if called upon to rewrite their papers. The entire "jailer's log" exercise is an example of how lessons focusing on historical residues can help students learn certain basic tools of historical research while focusing on topics relevant to a better understanding of their own community.

Another possibility many teachers have found attractive involves students' locating and developing a historic site within the local community. The site itself may be of many types. An old building may be suitable or, perhaps, a physical location in the local community where something notable took place. As a class exercise students can gather information about the site and, with teacher help, develop background material for individuals who can act as guides for individuals interested in learning about the site. Students in the class might invite community leaders or parents to tour the site under the helpful direction of one or more youngsters selected to serve as official class guides. Such exercises tend to generate a tremendous amount of student enthusiasm. Additionally, they can result in some very favorable publicity for the social studies program. Certainly, such efforts deserve encouragement.

The number of options available under the general "historical residues" heading is limited only by the teacher's imagination. History fairs, student-managed local history museums, old-time cornhusking bees, and evenings of traditional games and dances represent only a few possibilities. All, when properly managed, can be highly productive learning experiences for students.

Present interactions. Lessons focusing on present interactions seek to help students understand that life in communities is characterized by a high degree of interdependency. Many secondary students imagine themselves to be rugged independent figures of the romantic early nineteenth-century frontiers type. They tend to under-estimate the degree to which their patterns of living depend on other people. (In a class taught by the author, one assertive young sixteen-year-old, who fantasized about being quite free of any dependency on others, backed off considerably from this position when a fellow student challenged him to state the chemical formula used in making the plastic buttons keeping his pants closed.) Lessons emphasizing interdependence of various community functions help point out a fundamental reality of life in social groups.

"Community use logs" represent one approach to helping students see that interactions do occur between individuals and different functions and services provided by people in the local community. The "community use log" exercise involves the following steps:[1]

1. Students keep accurate personal records or logs for one week that indicate every location visited by a family member. (Consider only locations in the local community.)
2. Students are provided with an outline map of the local community (one map for each student).
3. Each student marks an *X* on the map at each location visited by a family member. If there were several trips to the same location, then several *X*'s will appear. An *X* should be marked for each different day of the week someone in the family visited that location (for example, if one member of the family went to the bank every day of the week, there should be five *X*'s marked at the location of the bank on the map).
4. When individual student maps have been completed, each student should be asked to place *X*'s from his or her map onto a large master outline of the map (preferable wall-sized). When every student has completed this task, the large master outline map will include a large collection of *X*'s clustered in various patterns. These *X*'s provide the bases for a culminating inquiry discussion.
5. Culminating inquiry discussion:
   What places on the map seem to have been visited most?
   What happens at those places?
   What places in the community were visited by only a few people?
   What takes place in those parts of the community?
   Were there any parts of the community that were visited by no one?
   What goes on at those places?

The "community use logs" exercise helps students understand that intensity of interactions between people and places within a community are not uniform; that is, some parts of the local community are used much more heavily by the population than others. For example, people tend to be heavy users of parks. On the other hand, relatively few people regularly visit warehouses in the industrial district.

---

[1] Adapted from David G. Armstrong and Tom V. Savage, Jr., "A Framework for Using the Local Community in Grades 4 to 6," *Social Education* (March 1976): 164–167.

The several community services and functions that might be identified during a discussion in "community use logs" lesson are not distributed randomly. There tend to be patterns of distribution of individual services and functions that remain pretty much the same from community to community. To highlight this point, the teacher will find the "yellow pages" exercise, based on the use of the local telephone book, useful.

The following steps are involved in implementing the "yellow pages" exercise:

1. Divide the class into about six groups (approximately five students in each.)
2. Provide each group with an outline map of the local community and with several telephone books (or, if the community is large enough to print separate volumes of white pages and yellow pages, the yellow pages alone). Be sure that the maps list street names and have a system for locating individual streets.
3. Assign members of each group to look up, in the yellow pages, addresses of all examples of one function or service provided by the local community. For example, one group might look up service stations; another, physicians; another, drug stores; another, churches; another, jewelry stores; and another, used car dealers.
4. Members of each group should be asked to mark the location of each address found on their map with a small X.
5. When all groups have completed work on their maps, place a large, preferably wall-sized community map at the front of the room. Ask a representative from each group to come up and place X's from the group map on the large map. Give each group representative a different colored marking pen for this purpose. For example, the service stations might be marked in red X's, the physicians in blue X's, and so forth.
6. Conduct a debriefing session:
   Why are churches and car dealers distributed differently?
   What is the pattern of distribution of service stations and used car dealers?
   Where are jewelry stores located? How would you describe their arrangement? Scattered? In straight lines along certain streets? Clustered?
   How do you explain the different patterns of distributions you see?

The "yellow pages" exercise helps students recognize that there is some order to the distribution of services and functions found in the local community. The debriefing discussion can highlight reasons for the typically linear arrangement of service stations, used car dealerships, and other automobile services along major thoroughfares. The tight clustering pattern of jewelry stores at corners of the busiest parts of the central business districts or at the busiest corners in shopping centers can be explained. (Rents at these locations, on a per square foot basis, tend to be the highest in the city. To survive, a business must be capable of displaying very valuable merchandise in a relatively small area. Jewelry stores can display thousands of dollars of merchandise in a very limited area. A car dealership does not have this capability. Consequently, it must locate where rents are lower.)

In addition to identifying patterns of individual services and functions, students are also helped to recognize associations between different services and functions by the "yellow pages" exercise. As noted earlier, automotive services tend to have a predictable spatial relationship in most communities. Another that is frequently seen is between locations of hospitals and locations of physicians offices. Whereas physicians offices are located at various points throughout the community, particularly in larger communities there tends to be a clustering of these offices in areas reasonably close to hospitals. Many other associations will suggest themselves, depending upon which services and functions have been selected for examination during the exercise.

Many other kinds of lessons can be devised to emphasize interactions occurring within local communities. Interactions between people in the local community and those living elsewhere might be emphasized with a focus on personal ties between students and their families and relatives living in other areas. Transportation networks within the local community can be examined in terms of how they provide easy access to some community services and how they might make access to some other services more difficult (as in the case of a residential neighborhood cut off from a shopping center by a freeway right-of-way). Study of distribution patterns of goods going from major warehouses to retail outlet offers another possibility for emphasizing the interactive nature of community life. With a little imagination, a host of productive learning experiences can be devised.

Likely future patterns. Stimulus experiences focusing on likely future changes in the community ought to be included in a comprehensive local community studies program. Such lessons prepare students for the reality that change is one of life's few constants. Recognizing that "things won't remain the same," students may become more inclined to examine forces leading to change more critically with a view to determining whether specific changes will be desirable or undesirable. One vehicle for involving students in a serious consideration of likely future patterns is a program that might be called a "Community Futures Day" (Armstrong and Savage, Jr., 1976). A "Community Futures Day" is nothing more than a symposium organized by students and featuring presentations by prominent community figures. The steps in organizing such a program are as follows:

1. As a class, identify various segments of the local community population who ought to be represented. For example, a class might decide that there should be representatives from government, from medicine, from education, from law enforcement, from the legal profession, from organized labor, and from local business.
2. A group of students should be appointed as an organizing committee responsible for identifying a representative for each community segment to be represented; that is, there should be an *ad hoc* committee on "government," an *ad hoc* committee on "medicine," and so forth.
3. Each group, with appropriate help from the teacher, should identify a speaker from the community segment to which they have been assigned. A representative from the group should be instructed to contact the speaker. The speaker should be provided with the time and place of the "Community Futures Day Presentation," asked to prepare about a ten-minute talk on changes he or she would

foresee in his or her segment of the community (law, government, and so on) over the next fifty to one hundred years, and requested to key remarks to a level appropriate for secondary students. Speakers should also be asked to leave time for student questions.

4. A chairman should be appointed from the class to serve as a moderator of the symposium. Basically, the moderator should introduce speakers and work to assure smooth transitions from one speaker to another.

5. During the "Community Futures Day" presentations, members of the class should take notes on comments made by each speaker.

6. On the day following the presentations, a large piece of butcher paper can be taped along one wall of the classroom. At the top of the paper, names of various community segments represented at the "Community Futures Day" presentations can be written (government, education, and so on). Students can be asked to write in specific changes speakers expect to see in the future under the appropriate headings on the chart.

7. A final debriefing discussion can help students compare and contrast projected changes in each area:
   What changes in government are anticipated?
   Do these changes have any possible impact on education? What is that impact?
   What things will change the most? The least? What accounts for the differences?
   Which changes seem most attractive to you? Least attractive?
   What kinds of things might be done to promote changes you favor and to oppose changes you do not favor?

8. Another possibility for a culminating event might be the production by class members (or at least by some of them) of a model of the community as it might look twenty-five or fifty years in the future. This model might be explained by certain student "experts" to parents on visitation nights or to various community groups to which students might be invited.

Involvement in lessons focusing on "likely future patterns" are designed to help students understand that the future will not "just happen," but that it will be shaped by actions of human beings. By highlighting alternative possibilities, lessons focusing on the future encourage students to become involved to work for desirable changes and against undesirable changes. In summary, exercises such as the "Community Futures Day" promote the idea that "good" citizenship demands active participation in the decision-making process.

Anticipated Student Learnings

Stimulus experiences introduce students to certain phenomena that have characterized the local community in the past, continue to characterize it now, or seem likely to characterize it in the future. These experiences can be systematized and presented to students according to a variety of approaches. Several alternatives, including the "jailer's log exercise," the "community use log," and the "Community Futures Day" were described in the preceding section. Each of these learning experiences is provided with a view to helping students learn something. "Antici-pated student learnings" need to be considered carefully in planning the local community studies program.

Anticipated student learnings can be divided into three major subcategories (Armstrong and Savage, 1976). There are learnings associated with student abilities in the areas of (1) making grounded generalizations, (2) examining values, and (3) making decisions. In the comprehensive community studies program, there is an effort to provide learnings in each of the three areas for every stimulus experience provided. That is to say, for example, that when historical residues are considered, they should be studied with a view to helping students (1) make generalizations, (2) examine values, and (3) make decisions.

Organizing the Total Local Community Study Program

In selecting learning experiences for a comprehensive local community studies program, the teacher can consider a series of questions. These questions relate both to the particular stimulus experience being considered and an associated learning outcome. Some suggested questions follow with stimulus experiences and anticipated student learnings as indicated.[2]

Historical Residues

Making grounded generalizations
  What has been left?
  What do these residues tell us about what life used to be like here?
  Why did you reach these conclusions?
  How might you check the accuracy of these conclusions?

Examining values
  What values of people who lived in this community in the past are suggested by
    remaining residues?
  How do you feel about life in the past in this community as suggested by remaining
    residues?

Making decisions
  What do you think life in the community was really like in the past? Why?
  What features of life deriving from this community's past should continue to be
    emphasized? Why?
  Were there some things that happened in the past that set undesirable precedents
    for the present and for the future? Which ones, and why?

Present Interactional Processes

Making grounded generalizations
  What is made here and sent out? What is brought in?

[2] Adapted from David G. Armstrong and Tom V. Savage, Jr., "A Framework for Utilizing the Community for Social Learning in Grades 4 to 6," *Social Education* (March 1976): 164–167. Copyright © 1976.

Where do people live and where do they work in the community? How do they get back and forth? How do you know?

How do you account for any changes you see? How might you check the accuracy of your explanation?

Examining values

What values, priorities are associated with present ways of life in this community?

How do you feel about values, priorities reflected in present ways of life in this community?

Making decisions

What aspects of present life in this community most appeal to you? Why?

What aspects of present life in this community do you find most distressing? Why?

What aspects of life in this community are most in need of change? Why?

How might you begin working with others to bring about changes you desire?

Likely Future Patterns

Making grounded generalizations

What is life here going to be like in ten years? In fifty years?

What specific things happening now lead you to predict what life will be like in the future?

What changes that have not yet occurred must take place before your predicted future can occur.

Examining values

What values are reflected in the likely future of this community?

How do you feel about values reflected in the likely future of this community?

Making decisions

What kind of a community would you like to live in? Why?

What are the differences between the kind of a community you would like to live in and this community?

How might you begin to work with others to bring about the type of community you would most like to live in?

Consideration of the questions listed under each of the categories when learning experiences are being planned will reduce the likelihood of developing a sequence of lessons that are too narrow in scope. These questions and the stimulus experience and anticipated student learning categories to which they are related can be depicted graphically in the form of a matrix. This matrix provides a visual framework that can be used as local community studies programs are being planned. The matrix is depicted in Figure 18–1.

Identifying Resources for Local Community Study Lessons

A local community study program requires a teacher who is well acquainted with the total range of resources available in the local community. Additionally, the teacher needs to have readily available a good deal of specific "factual information" about the community. As a beginning, a "community survey" needs to be undertaken.

Many teachers find it convenient to gather information together on file cards regarding different sources of information about the local community. These cards can be organized under several major headings. For example, a teacher might

	As Stimulus Materials Students Look At		
	Historical Residues	Present Interactional Processes	Likely Future Patterns
Make Grounded Generalizations	What has been left? What do residues tell us about life used to be like here? How could we check on the accuracy of these conclusions?	What is made here and sent out? What is brought into the community? What is your evidence? Where do people live and where do they work in the community? How do they get back and forth? How do you know? How do you account for any changes you see? How might we check on the accuracy of your explanation?	What is life in the community going to be like in ten years? In fifty years? What specific things are happening now that lead you to predict what life will be like in the future? What changes that have not yet been observed must take place before your predicted future for the community can occur?
Examine Values	*Community values:* What values of people who lived in this community in the past are suggested by remaining residues? *Personal values:* How do you feel about life in the past in this community as it is suggested by remaining residues?	*Community values:* What values, priorities are associated with present ways of life in this community? *Personal values:* How do you feel about values, priorities reflected in present ways of life in this community?	*Community values:* What values are reflected in the likely future of this community? *Personal values:* How do you feel about values reflected in the likely future of this community?
Make Decisions	What do you think life in the community was really like in the past? Why did you reach that conclusion? What features of life deriving from this community's past should continue to be emphasized? Why? Were there some things that happened in the past that set undesirable precedents for the present and the future? Which ones, and why?	What aspects of present life in this community most appeal to you? Why? What aspects of present life in this community do you find most distressing? Why? What aspects of life in this community are most in need of change? Why? How might you begin working with others to bring about changes you desire?	What kind of a community would you like to live in? Why? What are the differences between the kind of community you would like to live in and this community? How might you begin to work with others to bring about the type of community here you would most like to live in?

Figure 18–1. A Framework for Organizing a Local Community Study Program. (Source: Reprinted by permission from David G. Armstrong and Tom V. Savage, Jr., "A Framework for Utilizing the Community for Social Learning in Grades 4 to 6," *Social Education* (March 1976): 164–67. Copyright © 1976.)

decide to gather information under the headings "community history," "community businesses," "community government," "community professional organizations." These are simply representative of categories that might be selected. Some teachers may want to include many more. Others may be satisfied with a smaller number. For purposes of illustrating how a community survey might proceed, assume that a teacher had decided to gather information under the several headings suggested earlier. Card files would be started for each category, and the teacher would begin to develop a series of questions for which he or she would attempt to secure answers.

Questions that might be generated to prompt gathering of information about community history could include the following:

Community History

1. What has happened to the community's population over the past twenty years? Numbers up or down? Any shifts in ethnic composition? How about average age?
2. Who are longtime residents who have knowledge of the community's past? What specifically do they know? Will they come to school to speak to students?
3. What historical museums, sites, monuments, and other points of interest are there in the local community? Is it possible for classes of students to visit these places? Under what conditions?
4. Are there people or groups who would be willing to loan old photos, diaries, artifacts, and other interesting materials about the local community that might be suitable for use in the classroom? What are the sources of these items? Under what conditions can they be had for classroom use?
5. Are there any clues to unusual historical events provided by the headstones at the local cemetery? Evidence of devasting epidemics? Lots of foreign-born? Other mysteries?
6. Does the local newspaper have a file of old issues that can be reviewed? Are these available to students as well as to the teacher?
7. Where did street names come from?

Community Businesses

1. What kind of speakers are available through the chamber of commerce and other business groups? Will these people speak to audiences of secondary students? On what topics?
2. Which firms have individuals who can supply speakers for social studies classes?
3. Are there businesses who would welcome a visit by a class of students? What specifically might students be able to learn from such an experience? What kind of arrangements must be made? Who are the contact people?

Community Government

1. What governmental agencies hold meetings open to the public? Would it be possible for an entire class of students to attend? What might they be expected to learn? What kind of arrangements must be made?
2. Are there government officials who will come to school to speak to students? On what topics? Necessary arrangements?
3. Are there government officials who might be willing to have limited numbers of students serve as unpaid interns? What kind of duties would be involved? What might a student be expected to learn? What kind of selection criteria would be appropriate?

Community Professional Organizations

1. Is there a local unit of the American Medical Association, the American Dental Association, the American Bar Association, and other professional groups?
2. Which professional associations have individuals who would be willing to speak to social studies students? On which topics? Arrangements?
3. Are there special times of the year when professional organizations themselves make a concerted effort to communicate with students? (For example, Law Day, May 1, is a traditional time for lawyers to make presentations in schools in many parts of the country.) If so, is it convenient and appropriate to invite them to participate in the community study program at this time?
4. Are there professionals who would be willing to have limited numbers of students visit and observe them at work? Under which conditions? Nature of potential student learning? Arrangements?

These four categories, as noted previously, represent simply a sampling of those an individual teacher might select. The questions, too, are provided only as examples of those that a teacher might wish to have answered in planning for community study lessons. Whether these categories and questions or others are selected is not the important issue for program planning. The key point is that *some* categories and *some* questions ought to be developed by the teacher to guide information gathering before specific lesson planning goes forward. Given access to solid information about resource people in the community, the possibility for developing a program that brings students face-to-face with leading adults in the community is enhanced. This kind of person-to-person learning can add an exciting dimension to lessons that might seem dreary at best to students when organized around texts and other printed material. A fired-up representative from the American Medical Association presenting that group's view on problems associated with medicare and medicaid can generate levels of student interest that cannot be matched by accounts prepared by individuals less directly concerned about the issue.

Though, as noted previously, many general categories might be selected to guide preparation of card files with local community information, there ought to be a general attempt to identify a fairly broad range of information. When categories are too narrow in scope, students may derive impressions that result in a distorted view of the community. H. H. Gross (1959) in his classic *The Home Community* identified five major constituent elements of a community. Thorough preparation for a local community studies program might well consider gathering information relating to (1) physical elements, (2) spatial elements, (3) human elements, (4) cultural elements, and (5) social elements (Gross, 1959).

Physical elements. Physical elements of the local community include all natural phenomena found in the area. In preparation for community studies lessons, a teacher might undertake to learn all he or she could regarding such things as local topography; local climatic conditions; the nature of soils, plants, and animals found in the area; and mineral resources of the local community region. Intensity of study with regard to each of these topics would vary according to the nature of the individual community and according to the background of the teacher and potential interest of the students.

Spatial elements. Among other things, spatial elements of the local community take into consideration such factors as size, physical shape of the community (for example, what barriers force growth patterns in certain directions), and location of the community. A teacher might wish to add to his or her own understanding of such points as latitude and longitude coordinates pinpointing the community on the surface of the earth, the economic region within which the community is located, and the particular vegetation belt that surrounds the community.

Human elements. Human elements of the local community relate to all important characteristics of the resident population. For example, a teacher might be interested in determining such things as the population density in the area, the average educational attainment level, the economic situation of the residents, racial and ethnic compositions of the population, and patterns of professional and recreational group membership. Gathering information about human characteristics of a local community presents a challenge because of the tremendous volume of data available. Practically speaking, it is not possible for a given teacher ever to know "all there is to know" about the human elements in the local community. The teacher must make a decision to focus on a limited number of human characteristics selected out of a consideration for the needs of his or her own students' needs and interests.

Cultural elements. Cultural elements include structures, institutions, and other features that reflect the way in which residents of the community have organized their lives to meet needs they have identified as important. Types of residences, nature and locations of recreational facilities, medical establishments, industrial facilities, and governmental installations of all kinds are representative cultural elements of the local community. In planning the local community studies program, the teacher needs to give some consideration to these important features of community life.

Social thought. Patterns of social thought in a local community are reflected in a number of ways. For example, letters to the editor in the local newspaper reflect issues that are important to community members. Patterns of family and group living also reflect what individuals view as "appropriate" behavior. The extent to which historical landmarks and monuments have been preserved reflects upon the relative importance the community places on its historical roots. In preparing for lessons focusing on the local community, the teacher must be alert for important indicators of social thought. Such information can result in planning lessons that highlight prevalent local patterns and compare and contrast them with those in vogue in other areas.

Planning the Local Community Field Trip

Local community study programs frequently feature field trips. Though most students look forward to such excursions (perhaps only as an "escape" from the routine of the classroom), the excursions must be well planned if the learning that occurs is to measure up to initial student enthusiasms for the experience. In planning for a field trip, the teacher must pay attention to several very important considerations.

First of all, many beginning teachers are unprepared for the legal implications of taking students out of the school for a visit to some place in the community. Suits in recent years have made school officials very wary about exposing themselves to a situation of any kind that might result in liability charges being filed. Consequently, restrictions on student movement to off-school sites are quite severe in many districts. Generally, for example, there is reluctance to allow students to drive their own cars to attend a museum or to visit some other place in the community. This means that teachers must frequently make arrangements for busing students on district-owned vehicles. This requires a good deal of advance planning with administrative officials. Frequently, too, some release-from-liability forms will have to be signed in advance by students' parents. Because of these requirements, a field trip must involve close cooperation between the teacher and the school administrative officials.

Once administrative arrangements have been made, it is necessary to consider organization of the field trip experience itself. A productive field trip requires more of students than simple exposure to a particular setting within the community. Specific tasks for students to accomplish on the field trip need to be identified in advance. Frequently, teachers have had success in dividing their class into four or five groups. When this is done, students in each group can work together on a common task.

As a means of prompting careful observation, some sort of student "product" may be required that focuses on information acquired from the field trip experience. This might be a short paper, a brief talk, a poster, a model, or some other kind of evidence that some learning has taken place. These student "products" may well be turned in several days after the conclusion of the field trip experience.

Finally, a debriefing experience to pull together all the information gathered during the field trip should be provided. This debriefing lesson presents students from each group with an opportunity to listen to information gathered by others. Some teachers find it useful to have representatives from each group note major points on a large piece of butcher paper with a felt marker. This helps to reinforce learning by having a visual representative from each group note major points on a large piece of butcher paper with a felt marker. This helps to reinforce learning by having a visual representation of key points available as the discussion unfolds. It may be profitable, too, to take the time to type up major points and make dittoed copies for distribution to students. Students can retain this information for possible review on examinations that might involve some expectation of familiarity with the field trip experience.

In summation, the steps involved in planning a field trip experience are as follows:

1. Work with administrators to attend to details associated with legal requirements, especially as they relate to transportation.
2. Make special arrangements with people at the site to be visited, as appropriate.
3. Establish specific tasks for individual students or groups of students to accomplish.
4. Assign students to develop "products" that focus on learning derived from the field trip experience. Describe nature of acceptable "products" and establish a time line for their completion.
5. Conduct a debriefing session. Consider the possibility of providing students with printed summations of key points that come out during the debriefing.

Summary

Learning experiences focusing on the local community have a high potential for engaging students' interest. This results because the local community setting appears to students to have genuine relevance for their own lives. Social learning occurring as a result of a focus on the local community may transfer to an increased interest in social studies lessons focused on topics and areas that students sense to be more psychologically remote.

Through the years, many kinds of community-based lessons have been suggested. Much less attention, though, has been given to the issue of designing a comprehensive community studies program. To remedy this situation, the author has suggested a program-planning matrix. Using this matrix, teachers can organize lessons that respond to questions suggested by categories defined by interactions between the three headings of (1) historical residues, (2) present interactional processes, and (3) likely future patterns and the three processes of (1) making grounded generalizations, (3) examining values, and (3) making decisions.

Productive community studies programs require careful teacher planning. It is particularly important that content be selected in such a way that students do not get a distorted impression of community life. Guidelines have been provided that teachers might use in considering kinds of content to select to ensure adequate breadth of coverage. Given attention to this breadth and a commitment to the planning process, the community studies program has great promise of increasing students' interest in the entire social studies curriculum.

REFERENCES

ARMSTRONG, DAVID G., and TOM V. SAVAGE, JR. "A Framework for Utilizing the Community for Social Learning in Grades 4 to 6." *Social Education* (March 1976): 164–167.
GROSS, HERBERT H. *The Home Community.* Normal, Illinois: National Council for Geographic Education, 1959.

Source Disciplines

Chapter 19

HISTORY AND GEOGRAPHY

A s ELSEWHERE, tradition is a powerful force operating on the social studies curriculum. For generations, courses in history and geography have been standard features of the secondary school program. Though there has been some slippage, particularly with respect to geography, still courses organized around these disciplines predominate in secondary school social studies departments (Jarolimek, 1977).

In terms of their undergraduate training, more teachers have strong academic backgrounds in history than in other social and behavioral sciences. Though many are required to teach geography, or at least courses including a good measure of geography-oriented content, not many bring substantial academic training in geography to their initial teaching positions. Though teachers' preparation tends to be less thorough in geography than in history, content derived from geography continues to play a very important role in many social studies programs.

The National Council for the Social Studies has argued for broadening the content base of the social studies. But there has been no great ground swell of support for such a change from teachers in the classroom. As Dante has noted, where content from disciplines other than history and geography has been introduced into the social studies program, it has been done "more by infiltration of existing courses than by securing separate courses . . ." (Dante 1974: p. 109).

Certainly, few deny that history and geography can provide students with valuable perspectives as they grow toward personal and social maturity. But there are other kinds of knowledge that are important, too. Insights from anthropology, economics, political science, psychology, sociology, and other disciplines can play an important role in

349

the social studies program. Indeed, even when course titles for whatever reason reflect a clear tie to the disciplines of history and geography, large numbers of professional social studies teachers draw on perspectives from a wide variety of disciplines as they seek to provide students with knowledge and thinking skills they will need to understand themselves and the world they live in.

From a political point of view, there is a certain "respectability" associated with courses having titles indicating their connection to history or geography. Long familiar to parents, such courses frequently are defended on the grounds they have met and passed the "test of time." A special burden of proof is placed on any proposed substitute courses because the adequacy of history and geography courses is regarded widely as a "given." Considering this situation, courses with strong links to history and geography will likely be features of many social studies programs for years to come.

History: Important Background Issues

A number of persistent problems are associated with teaching history. Some of these stem from the nature of the college and university training received by history teachers. Others have to do with student interests and motivations. Still others are related to conceptual problems encountered by secondary school students in history classes. Each of these issues merits some special consideration.

ACADEMIC PREPARATION OF HISTORY TEACHERS

Many of the newer secondary school programs in history are designed with a view to having students "do something" with historical content; that is, students are expected to identify problems, analyze information, and draw supportable conclusions. In short, they are expected to act much as professional historians might act in considering historical issues and rendering judgments about these issues. Regrettably, few social studies teachers encounter this approach to teaching history in their college and university classes.

Frequently, college and university courses focus not on significant historical problems and interesting methods historians have used to develop understandings of these problems, but rather on rather general descriptions of historical findings. All too often these findings are introduced in large lecture hall settings in which the professor introduces information in a narrative form. It is true that many history professors are skilled, dynamic presenters who excite and motivate audiences of undergraduates. But, interesting as these presentations may be, they do not usually expose students to the sophisticated analytical skills used by professional historians as they work toward conclusions. Because many university courses do not demand that undergraduates master such techniques, many secondary school social studies teachers are unfamiliar with their use. Little is to be wondered, then, at the disinclination of large numbers of secondary social studies teachers to engage their own students in serious historical analysis.

As a consequence of the nature of their undergraduate training in history, many secondary school social studies teachers (notably beginners) try to present material to their junior and senior high school students as it was introduced to them by their university professors. Not only might such an approach seem logical given the nature of the undergraduate program in history, it is, as Dante has suggested, ". . . easier to tell a story and to be expository than to raise analytical questions . . ." (Dante, 1974: p. 110).

Clearly, the tendency to follow the practice of the university professor by relying heavily on the formal lecture when dealing with classes of junior and senior high school youngsters has pitfalls. In addition to the issue of maturity, students in secondary school classrooms represent a much broader range of abilities than is found in the typical college or university lecture hall. Many will lack the background and skills necessary to profit from a heavy dose of expository presentations. At the other end of the spectrum, bright or talented students, held responsible for manipulating, analyzing, and evaluating information in science and mathematics classes, may conclude that there is something "soft" or "superficial" about history when the subject is developed simply as a narrative tale to be learned, but not analyzed. Given the range of students in a secondary school classroom, there may be a few who may profit from and enjoy a course organized exclusively around a "listen and take notes" model, but many others (probably a majority) will be less receptive to such an approach. A heavy reliance on the presentation style favored by many college and university history professors may result in a deterioration of student interest to the point that classroom control becomes a problem.

The Question of Students' Interests

Many beginning social studies teachers report disappointment at their students' apparent disinterest in historical topics. Several explanations for the lack of concern for history noted in many secondary students have been suggested. Part of the attitude is explained by a cultural tendency to look toward the present and to value information that is perceived as having some relatively short-term "personal pay-off." This point of view by no means is unique to the young. It is a simple reflection of the larger society of which they are a part.

For example, many secondary school students subscribe, at least covertly, to the idea that the "young" and the "new" are in nearly every case to be preferred over the "old." These convictions reflect changes in the perceptions of the entire population over the past half century. A comparison of human models in Sears, Roebuck, and Company catalogs printed in the 1920s and those of today reflect this trend. Models in the 1920s catalogs are middle-aged; those in today's version are young. This reflects an attitude of many secondary students that the things in life that are really valuable are of fairly recent vintage.

The present American romance with nostalgia may herald a shift away from this attitude. Certainly, worries about environmental pollution, frustrating shortages of materials necessary for the functioning of complex equipment, and a general feeling that "life is just becoming too complicated" have stimulated a yearning for what is perceived to have been a "simpler time." It remains to be seen whether the nostalgia fad will spawn a serious interest in historical study or will result in a highly romanticized "fantasy history" that bears little evidence of a concern for historical truth. Consider, for example, the new interest in wearing clothing fashioned from denim. Many who wear denim do so out of a wish to identify with a past time when allegedly simpler men wore clothing crafted from inelegant materials. Yet the cut of denim clothing worn today, in order to sell, must reflect the styles of the late 1970s and early 1980s. If this reflects a concern for history, it is a history fashioned with a dramatically contemporary flair. Clearly, it is possible that the nostalgia fad may be just a rather unusual example of Americans' concern for keeping "up-to-date."

Motivating students' interest in history demands organization and presentation of material in such a way that clear linkages are established between the past and present concerns of students. Many students come into their history courses with little feel for the flow of time and its influence on their lives. They sense little connection, for example, between the popular pressures that brought down the monarchy during the French Revolution and the citizen protests in this country during the Vietnam War. Those social studies teachers who are successful in engaging students' interests in history place a heavy emphasis on relating historical problems to present circumstances. When students begin to feel that history has some value as a tool for understanding and managing their own lives, then one begins to observe the kind of emotional commitment to the subject that signals its transformation from an arid concern of teachers to a relevant source of insight for today's world.

History: Engaging Students' Interest

Good instruction in history begins with a careful analysis of students' interests and concerns. With this information in hand, the teacher can organize his or her program with a view to relating historical content to these interests and concerns. Students must see that history has some personal value before they can be expected to development a strong commitment to the subject. A teacher who expects students as a "given" will have some appreciation for the study of history as an intellectual exercise will be disappointed. Unless they can see some personal value in the subject, many students will begin (and end) their history program in a condition that can be described as, at best, apathetic.

Many beginning social studies teachers are astonished to learn that large numbers of their students have interests running little beyond the limits of their own direct experience. Consequently, instructional programs that seek to incorporate historical evidence that is available locally have much to commend them. Using local materials to supplement more traditional learning resources such as textbooks and films places heavy responsibilities on the teacher. Generally, the teacher must do much of the legwork by himself or herself, and only occasionally have such materials been organized by others in such a way that a beginning teacher can accommodate them easily into the instructional program. But when teachers are willing to commit the time to support their instruction with locally available evidence, prospects for enhancing student interests are excellent. For example, older houses near the school might support lessons focusing on the Victorian Age. Even something as prosaic as a shirt button might provide a focus for a lesson on technological innovations. Clearly, there is a need to move beyond the pages of the textbook to identify manifestations of historical phenomena that are close at hand.

A study of history that involves students in productive learning going well beyond listening to a teacher's exposition of "the facts" demands analytical skills. Students must be able to develop hypotheses, weigh evidence, and draw conclusions. Many beginning teachers who would like their students to engage in analytical activities make the erroneous assumption that students, even before the course begins, arrive at conclusions through a systematic process of defining a problem, developing speculative solutions, and testing these solutions against evidence. In fact, many students develop conclusions through little understood processes that are only marginally logical. It is necessary, then, for the teacher to determine how each student really does come to believe what he or she sees as "truth" and to provide specific instruction in the rational processes of thinking.

Finally, the social studies teacher must strike a balance between two potentially conflicting aims. On the one hand, schools are expected to be agencies that implant and nurture a certain commitment to core values of the culture. Outcomes of schooling and, more particularly, social studies instruction frequently are said to include such things as appreciation of democratic decision making, respect for the rights of others, and an appreciation of the legal system. On the other hand, there is an expectation that social studies teachers will help students develop their critical and their analytical abilities. The fundamental dilemma reduces to one of teaching critical analysis in such a way that analysis does not result in total rejection of basic cultural values. Each social studies teacher bears the burden of adjusting his or her instruction in the light of the characteristics of the students to strike a compromise between unthinking chauvinism and total rejection of the cultural milieu within which the students must live their lives.

As has been noted, a theme running through all difficulties faced by secondary school social studies teachers as they draw on content from history is the lesson that the substance of lessons must be thought of in terms of its relationship to students. Justifications for teaching history that fail to consider student variables may be convincing to logicians. But they are unconvincing to unsophisticated junior and senior high school students. If history is really a door opening the way to broader personal and social understanding, social studies teachers have an obligation to prepare learning experiences that will make students want to cross the threshold and go through the door. To accomplish this end, teachers need to give specific attention to several key issues. These include (1) designing instructional experiences that help the teacher to "personalize" history, (2) developing students' abilities to determine "historical truth," and (3) helping students to acquire a meaningful time perspective.

PERSONALIZING HISTORY

Traditionally, the textbook has served as the primary information source for secondary students of history. Although exceptions exist, many (if not most) textbooks present a reality very different from that experienced by most students. Human beings, in particular, tend to be portrayed in dull, two-dimensional terms. To avoid offending potential purchasers, textbooks sometimes attempt to "sanitize" certain historical figures by excising any negative references. In other cases, critical comments are couched in very vague language that obscures meaning for all but the handful of students willing to pursue their interest by digging into alternative sources of information. In the sections that follow, a number of alternatives to relying on the textbook will be introduced that might prove useful in a program designed with a view to making history more meaningful to individual students.

Original source materials. One approach that has been taken to make learning materials more "real" for students has been the use of original source materials. A number of commercial publishers of learning resources for the social studies have produced reproductions of public documents, letters, newspapers, and other items of historical interest. When teachers use these materials, students are asked to review them and, with teacher help, to draw their own conclusions.

All collections of original source materials or reproductions of original source materials are not equally suitable for student use. Many original documents include language that students find very difficult. These documents may include outdated usages and be written in a style that is perplexing to many students, particularly those who are not good readers. Fortunately, numbers of reproductions of original source materials are available today from commercial publishers that have been carefully edited for school use. These edited versions take into account possible reading difficulties many students will experience, and suggestions are provided to the teacher regarding how the materials might best be used. Certainly when these well-edited materials are available, the use of original source materials to bring students closer to historical reality has much to commend it.

Media resources. Analysis of historical events demands that, to some extent, students move outside of themselves to take on the perspectives of historical characters. Television productions, plays, commercial films, documentary films, and audio recordings afford opportunities for students to gain such insights. Such resources are particularly well suited for students who are not proficient readers.

Many possibilities exist for introducing students to these nonprinted materials. For example, Hal Holbrook's impersonations on television of Mark Twain and James Whitmore's impersonations of Harry Truman and Will Rogers provide insightful glimpses into the perspectives of the individuals portrayed. Jean Shephard's television play "The Phantom of the Open Hearth" is a rich and evocative reprise of coming of age in middle America in the late 1940s and early 1950s. "Upstairs, Downstairs," "A Family at War," and other television series suggest a flavor of the past that tends to engage interest to a degree that far surpasses the impact of textbook treatment of similar times and circumstances. Exposure to a wide array of media resources can help teachers to assist students in recognizing important linkages between their own lives and historical characters and events.

The history exposition. Student interest in history tends to grow when active rather than passive learning characterizes the program. This implies that learning activities ought to demand more of students than simply reading or listening and that something ought to be done with information once it is in hand. A history exposition represents a possibility for encouraging intense student involvement both during the learning process and with the information resulting from the learning process.

Basically, the history exposition represents an opportunity for the social studies program to "go public." Science educators with their science fairs, physical educators with their competitive sports schedules, and music educators with their music festivals have long recognized the benefits of "going public." Students and teachers in these areas both have benefited from these opportunities to display the results of instruction in a public setting. The history exposition represents a similar opportunity for teachers of history-oriented content and their students to build enthusiasm for their program by planning to display the results of instruction in a public forum.

The history exposition basically is an opportunity for students to demonstrate what they have learned and for the public to become better acquainted with part of the social studies program. The exposition can be grandiose in its scope, perhaps being housed in a large exhibit hall with invitations being tendered to an entire community. On the other hand, small-scale efforts, perhaps directed toward an audience of parents and teachers in a given building, can be worthwhile undertakings as well. Though they vary in terms of their planning and format, history expositions tend to share the following characteristics:

1. A single focusing theme is selected.
2. Students are actively involved both in the planning of the exposition and in the gathering of information to be disseminated.
3. Students take an active part in introducing information to visitors during the exposition.

4. Members of the community other than other students and teachers are invited to play an active part in the exposition.
5. Invitations are extended to community members to attend.

Suppose, for example, a class had decided to set up a modest historical exhibition as part of an evening Parent-Teacher Association meeting. The five steps might evolve as follows:

1. *Selection of the theme.* After a class discussion, the teacher and the students might agree on a theme of "Early Settlers in Smithville: Where They Came From and How They Enjoyed Themselves."

2. *Planning and gathering information.* The class might decide to set up the exhibition in the cafeteria. Six different locations could be identified to be major points of interest. They might be (a) a demonstration of Easter egg dyeing, using nineteenth-century onionskin techniques; (b) a demonstration of making root beer, using special root extracts available from a local supplier (from a nineteenth-century recipe); (c) a collection of rubbings from graves of early day settlers in Smithville (to include interesting epitaphs and information about where these people lived before moving to Smithville); (d) an Edison phonograph and cylindrical recordings of early day "hits"; (e) a "wish book" center with reproductions of children's toys offered for sale in late nineteenth-century catalogs and magazines. Seven class committees are organized. One of these is a steering committee to oversee planning of the entire exhibition. Each of the remaining six committees is given responsibility for planning events at one of the six interest points.

3. *Role of students.* Committees planning for presentations, demonstrations, or displays at each point of interest need to decide specifically which students will be involved and what they will do. For example, selected students might be identified actually to do the demonstration of the onionskin technique for dyeing Easter eggs. Where decisions have been made to feature certain community members doing a given demonstration (perhaps making root beer from root extract), certain students might be identified to stand by and describe what is going on (or at least assist in the explanation). Members of the steering committee will need to consider how students might be assigned to manage the flow of traffic through the exhibit. For example, a system of guides might be devised to take visitors through in groups of five or six.

4. *Selecting community participants.* Committee members might select members of the community to participate as demonstrators or presenters at some of the interest centers. For example, someone with a large collection of old Edison recordings might be asked to tell visitors about the recordings and play them at the center, focusing on "hit" music of the past. Others might be involved demonstrating how root beer was made, using old recipes. In every case, some

consideration should be given to having some students work with these adults in each center.

5. *Inviting visitors.* The class and the teacher will need to identify procedures for extending invitations to the people who will be invited to visit the exhibition. A notice might be included in the Parent-Teacher Association bulletin. The school newspaper represents another possible outlet. Special invitations to parents might be sent home to parents. Generally, it is wise to use several methods of communicating with potential visitors. If they do not get the message from one source, then there is a possibility they might get it from another.

Planning for the history exhibition needs to be related in a meaningful way to topics that are being considered in the classroom. The exhibition just described, for example, would fit in nicely with a unit focusing on the theme of social and technological change. Where some parallelism can be maintained between the orientation of the history exhibition and the major historical contents of a course, student understandings can be enriched by promoting active and personal involvement with key and central issues. Given this possibility along with the opportunity to involve the community in the social studies program, the history exhibition represents an extraordinarily rich motivational opportunity.

Oral history. Oral history represents an excellent approach for increasing students' interest in history. Basically, oral history involves students in face-to-face conversations with individuals who have experienced personally important historical events. Clearly, this restricts the focus to relatively recent times. But interest prompted by this experience has good potential for carrying over and promoting a more generalized student interest in historical topics.

In the preparation of oral history, a number of frameworks are possible. The following steps are typical of those ordinarily used to guide development of a class oral history project:

1. *Selection of a topic.* The topic must be relevant to content being treated in the course; otherwise, possible reinforcement value is lost. Also, the topic must be one for which individuals can be found to serve as "subjects" for student interviewers. (For example, there are many more World War II veterans than World War I or Spanish-American War veterans in most communities.)

2. *Identification of individuals to be interviewed.* Suppose a class had decided to undertake an oral history project focusing on "immigration." A community survey would have to be undertaken to identify people who (1) had been immigrants and (2) would be willing to be interviewed.

3. *Preparation of questions.* To get the most out of interviews, students need to prepare sets of guiding questions. Because most history texts shy away from much treatment of emotional reactions of individuals to the historical events described, questions asking for personal atti-

tudes and feelings can enrich students' understanding of episodes reported by individuals they interview. Certainly, some questions should be prepared asking for personal reactions and observations of the interviewees. Students should be cautioned to use the prepared questions as guidelines during the actual interview and not allow them to prevent a discussion of other interesting material that might come forth during the interview itself.

4. *Arrangements for interviews.* Students with help from the teacher must make arrangements for interviews. Where are they to occur? When are they to occur? Will a tape recorder be used? How long will the interview last? Questions such as these must be answered during the preplanning phase.

5. *Organization of material from interviews.* Decisions must be made about processing information. If interviews are not too long, students can be asked to provide word-for-word transcripts. Where longer interviews occurred, they can be asked to provide word-for-word transcripts only of segments they consider to be important. (Where no tape recorder was used, they will have to paraphrase what was said from notes.) Sometimes it might be desirable for students to write short paragraphs of explanatory material to connect word-for-word transcriptions of the remarks of the individual interviewed.

6. *Debriefing students.* An effort needs to be made by the teacher to help students bring all of the information together into some kind of a coherent whole. Some teachers begin this process by having the class produce a "book" consisting of dittoed or mimeographed copies of each interview. This enables each student to have access to all gathered information. Whether this is done or not, a series of debriefing questions is essential to help students make sense out of the material. Some examples follow:

Where did these people come from?

Why did they leave?

What did they expect to find here?

Were they surprised at what they saw?

What things were most difficult for them?

How did people here react to them?

In general, what were their feelings about their experience?

Do you think you would have felt the same way? Why?

If people were to do this today, would they feel the same way or different? Why, or why not?

The following is an example of how one student's oral history interview might be prepared. Note the choice of a different typeface when the student is writing his own explanatory remarks and when the word-for-word remarks of the interviewee are reported:

Topic: Immigration   *Interviewer:* Jerry P. Phinney
Date: 9/6/79   *Person Interviewed:* Mr. Paul Stone
[Note: Mr. Stone's remarks were transcribed from a tape recording of the interview.]

In December 1920, Mr. Stone, then aged fourteen, left England for the United States. The family of six sailed from Liverpool bound for New York. They had traveled to Liverpool from their home at Whitehaven in northwest England.

> The trip across took nine days. It was cold . . . cold all the time. We couldn't see much. It was foggy. The water was rough and some of us were sick . . . not us so much as ma and my dad. We traveled as cheap as we could go, I don't remember anything about what class it was, but dad was trying to save money to get started over here. When we got to New York harbor, they let the high paying passengers out at Ellis Island. I remember being impressed at the time, but I heard later that that place was not exactly a resort hotel. Anyway, the rest of us had to stay on the ship for a couple of more days. Finally, they sailed us over to New Jersey and let us get out. So I did get to see the big buildings in New York, but I never got there. We had to get on the train right away.

Mr. Stone and his family caught a train in New Jersey and headed west. They were going to Great Falls, Montana, where they had relatives who had come over from England earlier. They went to Chicago first. Then they caught the Great Northern train to Montana.

> We got to Great Falls sometime in January. It was dark and was it cold! The wind was howling, and the temperature was down below zero. Our relatives met us, and we had to walk three miles across the prairie to a house they'd found for us over on the west side. When I woke up in the morning and looked out the window, all I could see was white. The wind was still blowing, and there was snow all over the place. I couldn't believe that any place could be so cold. You know in England we almost never got any snow, and we *never* had any of this below zero stuff. I thought my dad had moved us all to the North Pole. It wouldn't have taken much to get me on the train headed the other direction, I'll tell you. But, of course, I didn't have that choice.

Mr. Stone reported that Great Falls seemed like a very strange place at first. He mentioned that he even had trouble understanding some of the language for a while. Other things were different, too.

> About a week after we arrived, my dad took me downtown. I still remember how shocked I was in going into my first dime store. There were people, right where they could be seen through the front window of the store, jammed up on stools and *eating*. Where we came from, eating was a private affair. It was a time for privacy. Even restaurants were set up so people weren't jammed up against one another. It took me quite a while before I could sit at a counter stool and eat a hamburger with someone sitting next to me. To tell you the truth, I still don't like to eat that way.

This represents just a fragment of a much more extensive interview. It does however suggest how a student might organize material he or she has gathered. When material is presented in such a fashion, the teacher can easily generate appropriate debriefing questions. The practice has merit, too, as a vehicle for developing students organizing and writing skills.

Some very elaborate programs coming out of the oral tradition have received national attention. The work of Eliot Wigginton in Georgia has resulted in the publication of the *Foxfire* books (Anchor Books). This series of books features transcripts of interviews that are accompanied by excellent photographs. There is a heavy emphasis on topics relating to traditional life-survival skills. For example, *Foxfire 2* includes chapters on such activities as beekeeping, on making a tub wheel, and on washing clothes in an iron pot. Students involved in the *Foxfire* program interview people having traditional life-survival skills, take photographs, and participate in editing the articles that eventually are gathered together and published in books. The motivational potential of the Foxfire approach has stimulated numbers of schools across the country to initiate similar programs of their own. (For example, *Dovetail* magazine is a result of such a project undertaken by a small Montana high school. Write *Dovetail Magazine*, Ronan High School, Ronan, Montana.) Teachers interested in the approach developed initially by Wigginton are directed to the several books in the *Foxfire* series.

Determining "Historical Truth"

A good many secondary school students (and adults, too) develop conceptions of reality that conflict with conclusions clearly supported by reliable evidence. Sometimes these misconceptions result because processes that are basically logical are applied to inaccurate understandings of fundamental information. For example, a student in one of the author's classes, when asked to describe what a "feudal society" might be like, responded that in such place people "just fight all the time." Clearly, this individual had assumed mistakenly that the word *feudal* was a derivative of the word *feud*.

On other occasions, surprising conclusions result when students rely too heavily on a single source of information. For example, a student might argue that "my uncle was at Pork Chop Hill in Korea, and he says it wasn't *anything* like the book says." Overgeneralization is a common problem.

Still another source of confusion results from students' lack of skills associated with rational problem analysis. A good number of beginning social studies teachers assume that their students follow a systematic process in arriving at conclusions. In fact, large numbers of students have not acquired systematic thinking skills (though they may have been exposed to them). Consequently, there is merit in taking class time to familiarize students with logical processes used by historians as they work toward defensible conclusions. Specific instruction might well focus on such issues as determining (1) external validity, (2) internal validity, and (3) biases of the individual historians.

External validity. It is doubtful that many secondary school classes can be actively involved in the sophisticated tests used by professionals to establish external validity. But students should be made aware of what external validity is. External validity basically is concerned with the issue of authenticity.

Consider a historian interested in a document that appears to have been written in Florence in 1630. He or she needs to have tests run to provide assurances that the document indeed does date from that time and place. Examinations of vocabulary might be undertaken to determine whether words used are consistent with those prevalent in documents of the time. Samples of paper might be analyzed to determine whether it was manufactured according to processes known to be in use in 1630. Chemical analysis of the ink might be undertaken to establish that the formula represented one known to have been available in 1630. In general, tests to establish external validity seek to unmask forgeries. A host of techniques are available to assist scholars in establishing the authenticity of their source materials.

Occasionally, new technology makes possible a reconsideration of sources long regarded as authentic. Secondary school social studies students might find interesting the exposure of the so-called Piltdown man as a fraud. Until this revelation, decades of students were taught that the Piltdown Man was an important "link" in man's evolution.

Internal validity. In addition to the issue of external validity, students should be introduced to internal validity, which focuses on the reliability of a given source of information. They must understand that it is not simply enough to establish the authenticity of, for example, a document. It is necessary also to establish the accuracy of the information reported in the document.

It is well to introduce students to some general questions historians ask in attempting to establish the internal validity of a source. For instance, when the source involves a written document, historians must determine whether the individual who wrote it (1) was capable of writing it and (2) was interested in writing accurately at the time it was written. It is not enough to "let the words speak for themselves." The same words may carry several messages. For example, consider a letter, intended by the writer to reflect sarcasm, that included the sentence "He is sure to be a great favorite of the frontline troops." A careless historian who read these words too quickly and failed to appreciate the context within which they were written might draw a totally inappropriate conclusion.

Importance of internal criticism (the search for internal validity) was revealed during the famous *"Pueblo* Incident" of the late 1960s. The U.S.S. *Pueblo,* a United States vessel equipped with sophisticated electronic intelligence gathering gear, was captured by North Korean forces and brought into the port of Wonsan in North Korea. Crew members were taken prisoner. Shortly thereafter, a "confession" from the commander of the vessel was released by the North Korean authorities. In part, the "confession" stated: "The U.S. Central Intelligence Agency promised me that if this task would be done a lot of dollars would be offered to the whole crew members of my ship . . ." (*Newsweek,* February 5, 1968, p. 16).

The stilted, unnatural phrasing of this statement led authorities to conclude that the "confession" did not reflect either the true feelings or the personal words of the commander of the *Pueblo*. The language used in the text released by the North Korean authorities led U.S. officials to suspect that the commander had been forced to issue a statement prepared for him by his captors.

When reading statements by historical figures, students should be encouraged to look for consistencies and inconsistencies with other statements made by the same individuals. When a statement appears highly inconsistent with others, students should be encouraged to consider (1) the context of the remarks, (2) whether possible qualifying remarks might have been deleted when the statement was published, and (3) and other issues that might lead a reasonable observer to question the accuracy of the reported statement.

Personal bias or perspective. Historical accounts are prepared by human beings. Consequently, they reflect, to some degree at least, biases and perspectives of the individual historian. Because the sheer volume of information makes inclusion of "everything" impossible, each historian engages in a process of selection. Certain criteria are established that the historian uses as bases for including some information and excluding other information. There is nothing at all insidious about this process. But students need to know how it operates. They need to look for differences between accounts of similar events written by different individuals with a view to pinpointing differences in perspective.

Students find particularly interesting accounts of historical events written by individuals coming out of different cultural orientations. For example, many textbooks printed in Great Britain place great emphases on events that occurred in Canada in their treatment of events in North America in the eighteenth century. The victory of Wolfe over Montcalm at the Battle of Quebec comes in for very heavy attention. On the other hand, many of these same writers give very sketchy coverage to the American Revolution as compared to texts prepared by American writers.

French writers covering the American Revolution not too surprisingly pay particular attention to the French involvement in the naval aspects of the war, the contributions of the Marquis de Lafayette, and the influences of the American experience on the French Revolution of 1789. Contrasting views of a single historical event or epoch help students understand that history represents not a simple recitation of past events but rather *thought* about these events. Because thought is involved, the particular frame of mind of the individual historian cannot be ignored.

Developing a Time Perspective

Secondary school students have a difficult time understanding chronological relationships. Generally, there is a tendency for them to compress time and assume that nearly everything of "any real importance" is of very recent origin. A scheme

1885	1895	1905	1915	1925	1935	1945	1955	1965	1975	
	grandfathers (father's side) Jensen	grandfathers (father's side) Arams Cole Fogg Bentz	grandfathers (father's side) Denny Ender Gear Howar Islip		fathers Arams Bentz Cole Denny Ender Fogg Gear Howar Jensen Islip	fathers Bentz Denny Ender Gear Howar Islip		Our Class A. Arams B. Bentz C. Cole D. Denny E. Ender F. Fogg G. Gear H. Howar I. Islip J. Jensen and so on.		
	grandfathers (mother's side) Bentz	grandfathers (mother's side) Arams Cole Jensen	grandfathers (mother's side) Denny Ender Fogg Gear Howar Islip		mothers Arams Bentz Cole Ender Fogg Gear Howar Islip Jensen	mothers Arams Denny Ender Fogg Gear Howar Islip Jensen				
		grandmothers (father's side) Cole Fogg Jensen	grandmothers (father's side) Arams Bentz Denny Ender Gear Howar Islip							Birthdays of our class parents and grandparents
		grandmothers (mother's side) Arams Cole Jensen Bentz	grandmothers (mother's side) Denny Ender Fogg Gear Howar Islip							
ballpoint pen 1888	diesel engine 1895	electric vacuum cleaner 1907	automatic toaster 1918	television 1927 electric razor 1931	parking meter 1935; helicopter 1939	long-playing records 1948; transistor 1947				Inventions
										Kinds of schools
										Games children played
										Clothes people wore
										Kinds of houses or other shelters people lived in
										Wars
										Transportation: how people got from place to place
										Miscellaneous items
1894	1904	1914	1924	1934	1944	1954	1964	1974	1984	

Figure 19–1. An Example of a Relative and Time Chart

that has worked well with younger secondary students to improve their sense of time and chronology is the "relative and time chart." The relative and time chart is premised on the assumption that time can be better understood when the concept is introduced in a way that conveys personal meaning to the student. The relative and time chart accomplishes this by including specific references to the date of birth of students' mothers, fathers, grandmothers, and grandfathers.

In laying out the chart, the teacher selects a large sheet of butcher paper. At about twenty-four-inch intervals, vertical lines are drawn on the paper. Space between each pair of lines represents a ten-year span of time. At the top of each space, the first year of the ten-year span is indicated, for example, 1885. At the bottom of the space, the tenth year is indicated, for example, 1894. The space between the pair of lines farthest to the right includes the most recent ten-year span. Each space to the left represents a span of time ten years earlier than the space to its immediate right. An example of a "relative and time chart" is depicted in Figure 19–1.

Once the basic chart has been made, students are asked to determine the birth dates of their mother, father, grandmothers, and grandfathers. If an exact date cannot be found, an approximation will do. Once all students have had an opportunity to acquire this information (perhaps in two or three days' time), information is written on the chart. Students' relatives are identified and listed according to the ten-year time spans within which they were born. This procedure results in a chart that helps students see the flow of chronological time and note its personal implications for them.

A variety of other information can be included, depending upon what the class is studying and the interests of individual groups of students. Relevant information can be added to the chart in the appropriate ten-year time spaces. In Figure 19–1, a decision has been made to include information relating to such issues as inventions, housing, wars, and children's games. Certainly, other categories would serve equally well.

Use of relative and time charts helps personalize time for students. They provide an excellent beginning point for classroom discussions designed to engage students in analyses of changes over time. Their use, then, can facilitate both a growth in students' grasp of time and chronology and in their ability to think analytically.

Geography: Background Issues

One of the overriding difficulties experienced by teachers of geography is the widespread feeling that the subject lacks sophistication. In many schools, courses in geography have been set aside for students lacking the talent to do well in social studies courses drawing content from allegedly "more rigorous" academic disciplines. Even in schools where some geography is required for all students, there is a tendency to regard the subject as something of a "lightweight."

Several factors contribute to this misconception. First of all, many adults received very poor geographic instruction in school. Many seem to remember little about their geography courses other than that they had to memorize the capitals of all the states in the fifth grade. A second difficulty is that too many geography courses are taught by teachers with very little academic preparation in the subject. This regrettable situation is perpetuated by a logic (or more properly an illogic) that holds that geography, a "simple subject," can be taught by anyone. As Preston James (1969) has noted, even many of the instructional materials in geography frequently have been prepared by people with little or no training in the field. Fortunately, this situation has begun to improve in recent years.

Professional involvement by highly skilled geographers has made available to secondary school teachers truly excellent materials during the past few years. Materials growing out of the High School Geography Project, funded by the National Science Foundation, exemplify the kinds of fine new materials now available for use in junior and senior high school classrooms. Today teachers have materials that can support instruction in geography across its full range of elegance and sophistication. Geographically oriented content can provide a basis for challenging and interesting learning experiences for students.

Geography: Traditional Emphases

William Pattison (1964) noted that geographers have devoted their professional attention to four central themes or traditions. These are (1) the spatial tradition, (2) the area studies tradition, (3) the earth science tradition, and (4) the man-land tradition.

Geographers interested in the "spatial tradition" have been concerned with the spatial aspects of our world. They have investigated relationships associated with patterns of movement across space. Studies of movements of goods, ideas, and people between and among settlements of different sizes are within geography's spatial tradition.

Investigations of the nature of specific regions have concerned geographers working within the "area studies tradition." The area studies tradition has had a long history of emphasis within the school social studies program. For years many elementary and secondary geography textbooks devoted sections to "The New England States," "The Middle Atlantic States," "The Southeastern States," "The Southwestern States," "The Rocky Mountain States," and "The Pacific States."

The third geographic emphasis, the "earth science tradition," plays a less important role in most secondary social studies programs today than it did in years past. The earth science tradition focuses heavily on physical terrain features. Because of increasing academic specialization, much content of this type today is introduced by geologists at the university level rather than by geographers. In secondary schools, much content of this nature has been taken over by courses within the science curriculum.

The "man-land tradition" focuses on the human race and its interaction with physical and cultural environments. The leading association for educators interested in geography, the National Council for Geographic Education, tends to promote this emphasis in its publications. Many of the newer materials available for use by social studies teachers interested in geographical content also reflect this orientation.

Geography: An Organizational Framework for the Secondary Program

Taafe (1970) identified a number of subtheses falling generally within the man-land tradition. These subthemes can provide a useful framework for secondary social studies teachers interested in organizing programs featuring geographic content. The six subthemes are

1. Spational distributions and interrelationships.
2. Circulation.
3. Regionalization.
4. Central place systems.
5. Diffusion.
6. Environmental perception.

SPATIAL DISTRIBUTIONS AND INTERRELATIONSHIPS

The particular interest of geography in spatial distributions and interrelationships is the impact on people of varying patterns of distribution. Urban geographers, for example, have long been fascinated by the relationships between land values, densities of population, and distance from the central core of the city. This particular interest can be translated without too much difficulty to the secondary school classroom.

For example, a teacher might do something like the following:

1. Obtain a large city street map that can be tacked on the wall (one that can be written on).
2. With a felt pen draw a circle around the "100 per cent Corner." (The place in the center of the business district where vehicular and pedestrian traffic is at its maximum. Ask the police department or the chamber of commerce to provide you with this location if you don't know it.)
3. With a felt marker, make marks on the map at the following points:
   ½ mile north of the 100 per cent Corner
   1 mile north of the 100 per cent Corner
   1½ miles north of the 100 per cent Corner
   2 miles north of the 100 per cent Corner
   3 miles north of the 100 per cent Corner

½ mile south of the 100 per cent Corner
1 mile south of the 100 per cent Corner
1½ miles south of the 100 per cent Corner
2 miles south of the 100 per cent Corner
3 miles south of the 100 per cent Corner
(If desired, similar marks can be made at points east and west of the 100 per cent Corner. Also, distances can be varied, depending on the size of the community.)

4. Next identify names of streets immediately adjacent (or as close by as possible) to each of the preceding marks. Select one street name for each mark. Draw a circle around one block of this street at a point close to the felt mark. Identify general address of this block (1000 block of Glade Street, and so on). The following street blocks might be selected for each of the points noted with the felt marker:
100 block of Ash Street (½ mile north of 100 per cent Corner)
1300 block of Nye Street (1 mile north of 100 per cent Corner)
1900 block of Adams Street (1½ miles north of 100 per cent Corner)
2700 block of Stevens Street (2 miles north of 100 per cent Corner)
3900 block of Jeremiah Street (3 miles north of 100 per cent Corner)

200 block of Paul Street (½ mile south of 100 per cent Corner)
1200 block of Neah Way (1 mile south of 100 per cent Corner)
1800 block of Smith Street (1½ miles south of 100 per cent Corner)
2600 block of Jones Street (2 miles south of 100 per cent Corner)
3800 block of 41 Avenue (3 miles south of 100 per cent Corner)

5. Provide students with data for each of the identified blocks and with data for one of the blocks at the 100 per cent Corner. For each of these locations, the following information is needed:
a. Density of residential population per block.
b. Assessed value of all the property on the block (both sides of the street).
(Note: Some teachers prefer to have students gather this information. Committees might be formed to contact planning commissions, tax offices, real estate offices, and other governmental agencies and private sector firms. Some, for example, might have the special phone books that organize numbers by street address rather than by last name. These could be used to count population densities in each block.)

6. When students have the necessary information, a debriefing discussion can be used to help students focus on varying patterns that seem to be influenced by spatial relationships. Some examples:
Where is the property that has the highest assessed value located? The next highest? The next?
How do you account for these differences?
Would we have found the same thing had we chosen east and west rather than north and south distances from the 100 per cent Corner.
Where is population density the highest. Next highest? Next? And so on.

Why do you suppose there are differences?

Would we find these same general patterns somewhere else? Why or why not?

What kinds of businesses would you expect to find at the 100 per cent Corner? Why? What kinds of businesses would you expect to find at these other locations?

Would you say that there is some pattern to the organization of our community? How would you describe this pattern? What forces tend to maintain it? Change it?

An exercise such as the one just described can lead into productive discussions of other important geographic concepts that might be illustrated in the local community. For example, a discussion might focus on the extent to which patterns in the local community parallel what might be predicted from the "distance-decay" principle (basically, the notion that land values would be expected to go down as population density thins out at increasing distances from the 100 per cent Corner).

CIRCULATION

Circulation studies center on flows. Flows include movement of elements of transportation systems, movement of commodities from one place to another, communication of information along networks of various kinds, and other situations involving a movement of some phenomenon, tangible or intangible, from one location to another. A good deal of attention has been focused on the question of what happens when established flow patterns are broken. Studies of this type can be adapted productively for use with secondary school social studies students.

For example, a decision to build an urban freeway through the center of an existing neighborhood may create a severe disruption of traditional driving and visiting patterns with residences on opposite sides of the new highway. Students might consider how a hypothetical freeway through an established neighborhood might influence such things as church attendance patterns, business at neighborhood shopping centers, numbers of people using parks, and school attendance boundaries. Such information might be balanced through a consideration of possibly improved access to other churches, parks, shopping areas, and schools once the highway was completed.

An important outcome of lessons focusing on circulation is the understanding that flows from point to point are not random. Their restriction to certain established routes (for example, arterial streets) has implications for certain life activities. To highlight this point, students might be provided with copies of the yellow pages of the telephone book. It is not necessary that a current book be used. Students might be asked to bring old books to school shortly after new ones have been issued. Students can be provided with instructions such as the following in doing this exercise:

1. For this exercise, you will need to use the city map, the yellow pages in your phone book, and a set of five colored pens or pencils.
2. Open your yellow pages. Look for addresses of individuals, firms, churches, and so forth listed under these five headings:
    a. Service stations.
    b. Churches.
    c. Shopping centers.
    d. Physicians.
    e. Jewelry stores.
3. On your maps mark a colored point for each address listed. Use a different colored pen or pencil for each category as follows:
    a. Service stations—make *red* marks.
    b. Churches—make *blue* marks.
    c. Shopping centers—make *green* marks.
    d. Physicians—make *black* marks.
    e. Jewelry stores—make *orange* marks.
4. Raise your hand when you are finished, and I will check your work. Are there questions?

When students have completed these tasks, they will each have maps with sets of colored dots representing addresses of service stations, churches, shopping centers, physicians, and jewelry stores. Because of the color coding, it will be possible to note some patterns of distributions. For example, red dots will suggest the locational pattern of service stations. When students have these completed maps before them, the teacher can engage the class in a discussion. Questions such as the following might be used:

1. What general pattern characterizes the distribution of service stations? Churches? Shopping centers? Jewelry stores? Physicians' offices?
2. Do some of the distribution patterns appear to be similar? Which ones, and why?
3. What factors might explain patterns of distribution of service stations? Churches? Shopping centers? Jewelry stores? Physicians' offices?
4. Would we find similar distributions elsewhere? How could we find out? (To check whether patterns found locally are typical, the teacher might bring in yellow pages from a phone book in a distant city. A committee of students might be provided with a map of this city and be asked to plot addresses much as was done with the telephone books from the local community. This map can be compared with those of the local community, and a comparison of patterns in the two communities can be made.)

This exercise has good potential for pointing out to students that patterns of distribution of key community services tend to be quite predictable. This information can sharpen students' observational powers as they become keener observers of the system and order characterizing civilized life as it goes forward in the community setting.

REGIONALIZATION

Formerly, regional studies frequently focused on isolated characteristics of a given area. When a study of one place was considered, students moved on to look at another area. Little attempt was made to engage students in activities requiring them to compare and contrast features of different regions. Learning the world one region at a time was a tedious undertaking at best. Today geographic educators are more interested in helping students identify patterns that exist across regions.

Regions may be compared with respect to a wide number of characteristics. One interesting comparison might be the influence of one region on other regions. For example, to what extent do designers of leisure time clothing in Southern California influence trends outside of that area? What are the "boundaries of appeal" of Portland and Seattle as migration centers attracting farm and small-town youth in the Pacific Northwest? If some service is to be established in one region that is to be used by people in that region as well as by people in another, where is the best place to put it?

There are a number of adaptations of regionalization studies that can be incorporated into the secondary social studies program. For example, the student council may be considering placing new bulletin boards in the school to supplement the one presently available just outside the main office. If two new bulletin boards are to be provided, where are the two best places to locate them? A decision might be made to position them in locations reflecting the shortest average foot travel time from the "most distant" points. Of course, the "most distant" points will vary, depending upon where they are located.

In deciding where to put them, students might consider such things as density of hall traffic, physical distances from one place to another, placement of stairwells, and other points before making a decision. Once the new boards are up, additional information could be gathered to see whether the locational decisions were good ones. For example, has the very act of providing the new boards resulted in an unanticipated change in hall traffic patterns? This exercise can help students develop an appreciation for the great difficulties community planners experience in making policy changes that might result in altered patterns of community use of selected community facilities.

CENTRAL PLACE SYSTEMS

Lessons focusing on "central place systems" seek to help students appreciate that every community does not provide every service used by its residents. According to central place theory, communities exist in a hierarchical relationship to one another. This means that tiny communities are incapable of providing all services of towns, towns are incapable of providing all services of cities, and cities are incapable of providing all services of giant metropolitan areas. Individual communities, then, provide services that vary according to (1) the size of the community,

(2) the distance between the community and other communities, (3) the services provided in those other communities, and (4) the other communities that depend on the individual community for support services.

It is difficult (and even somewhat disappointing) for some secondary students to learn that in some respects their community is subordinate to other communities. But they can take some solace that, except for the tiniest of settlements, most communities serve other smaller communities that play clearly subordinate roles. For example, many towns of 30,000 close to major metropolitan areas have very small local newspapers. These local newspapers give very sketchy coverage to regional, state, and national affairs. Most residents depend on newspapers from the major metropolitan area for news of this type. In terms of regional, state, and national news, then, such communities clearly are subordinate to the major metropolitan area.

On the other hand, shopping centers in towns of 30,000 or so residents may well attract large numbers of customers from smaller communities and from rural areas. Surely, they will serve the vast majority of the needs of local citizens. This illustrates the point that the service of providing general consumer goods is not nearly so highly centralized as is the service of providing news. Lessons can be developed to help students appreciate that different kinds of services vary in terms of the size of a town or city that logically might be expected to provide them.

For example, students might survey a cross section of local business people to identify those cities most frequently called on long-distance lines for business purposes. When such information is gathered together, students should be able to identify major wholesaling and merchandising centers serving the local community.

Another lesson or set of lessons might be built around a consideration of airline schedules. A number of communities in the local area or within the state can be examined to determine how many stops a traveler boarding a plane at each identified place would have to make before reaching such major national centers as Los Angeles, Chicago, and New York. In general, those places having flights to these places requiring fewer stops might be regarded as more important transportation hubs. (Clearly, there are exceptions. For example, a relatively unimportant town or city might be located very close to one of these major metropolitan areas. In such a situation, the existence of a nonstop flight has little significance. Class discussions should highlight these special situations.)

DIFFUSION

"Diffusion" studies ordinarily center on examinations of how things, tangible or intangible, are disseminated. Many investigations, for example, have focused on patterns of adoption of innovations and inventions. Many who have not thought seriously about this issue have assumed that adoption of any change spreads out in an unbroken wave from the source of the innovation. In fact, professional students of diffusion have found that frequently there is a "jump" over hundreds of miles from the source of an innovation to an adopter of an innovation. A classic example is the six-shooter. The six-shooter was invented and manufactured in New England, but it was first embraced by residents of the Western frontier.

Social phenomena as well as inventions have been studied. Investigators have found some evidence, for example, that student activism of the 1960s "jumped" thousands of miles from a site of origin in the San Francisco Bay area to Eastern campuses before gradually spreading out through the rest of the country. Building on knowledge gathered from serious students of diffusion, a leading operator of schools for high school cheerleaders builds new routines around what is found to be popular with high school students in Southern California. He has found that tastes of high school youngsters in this part of the country set a pattern that, in time, diffuses to other sections of the nation.

There are a number of possibilities for introducing lessons focusing on diffusion into the secondary social studies program. Many teachers have experienced success with a simple technique centering on the "flow" of a new joke through the student body. The activity develops as follows:

1. The teacher finds a new joke (one believed to be new to the school at least) and tells it to five students. Each student is asked to tell it to one friend. (The teacher should check in a day or two to see that this has taken place.)
2. After two weeks or three weeks have gone by, the teacher tells the joke to the entire class. As an assignment students are asked to interview as many of their fellow students as possible. People interviewed are to be asked (1) whether they have heard the joke, (2) from whom they heard (if they have, in fact, heard it), and (3) when they heard it.
3. When students return with data from these interviews, a debriefing discussion can ensue directed at plotting the route of the joke through the student body. Some possible questions:
    a. Did certain kinds of people hear the joke before others? If yes, which kinds? (athletes, student council members, chess club members.)
    b. Did physical location of students homerooms make a difference? Did people in some areas hear the joke first? Why?
    c. Did eleventh and tenth graders hear the joke before ninth and tenth graders? Other way around? Why?

Building on this rather simple example, teachers might design additional lessons on diffusion to survey dissemination of innovations in the community. For example, which people bought video television games first? Forty channel CB's? Video-cassette players? Diesel-powered automobiles?

ENVIRONMENTAL PERCEPTION

In recent years, interest in "environmental perception" has increased. Geographers specializing in this area suggest that a good deal of human behavior is explained not by the nature of the environment as "it is," but rather the nature of the environment as "it is perceived." Studies have revealed that an individual's perception tends to be influenced by his or her own personal experiences. For example, individuals who are backpackers and who have covered miles of trails in a national forest tend to see a much smaller proportion of the national forest as "wilderness" than individuals who see the national forest only as they drive through in their cars.

Environmental perception studies can serve as the basis for some very productive social studies lessons. For example, students might be assigned to describe the "ideal public park." They might be asked to identify its location, estimate its size, and describe the amenities available to users. Once students have accomplished these tasks, a debriefing discussion can highlight personal experiences of individual students and how these influenced the design of the several "ideal public parks." This exercise can give students an appreciation for difficulties encountered by planners in attempting to design public facilities that respond to many tastes.

Some teachers have drawn upon friendships with social studies teachers in other parts of the country in designing environmental perception lessons. Students in both sets of classes are asked to respond to a common set of questions. Each teacher keeps a copy of the responses of his or her own students and sends a second copy to his or her friend. When both teachers have copies of both sets of answers, interesting discussions can develop focusing on intriguing perceptual differences of students in the two places. There are many possibilities for questions that students might be asked. Some examples follow:

1. If you were told to move to San Francisco, how would you feel and why?
2. Is it farther from Boston to New York or from San Francisco to Los Angeles?
3. If you wanted to have some fun outdoors, what would be the best time of year to visit Minneapolis?
4. How would you describe the state of Texas to a foreign visitor?

In leading a discussion centering on responses to such questions, the teacher might ask for responses to questions similar to the following:

1. What differences do you notice in the patterns of responses of students in the two areas?
2. What misconceptions are revealed in these answers?
3. How do you explain these misconceptions?

The imaginative teacher can devise many other kinds of lessons to bring home to students the important point that reality does not exist independent of how people view it. When students understand this, they grow toward a more sophisticated understanding that the facts almost never "speak for themselves." Rather, they are shaped by how they are seen and interpreted by individual human beings.

Summary

History and geography have a long association with social studies instruction in this country. Indeed, when attempts have been made to introduce content derived from the behavioral sciences and other social sciences, very frequently this content has been introduced through courses drawing most of their content from history and geography. Given a widely held perception that some of the curricular innovations of the 1960s and early 1970s resulted in academically "soft" instructional programs, it seems likely that traditional history and geography courses will be in the secondary social studies program for some time to come.

When teachers introduce content derived from history and geography, interests of the individual student must be the starting point. Few secondary school students are impressed by arguments that history or geography are "necessary for good citizenship" or "enriching." Many youngsters in the schools come to their social studies classes with very limited academic interests. This does not suggest, however, that these interests cannot be extended. It does imply a need to begin "where students are" rather than to begin with the assumption that students come to their classes sharing the concerns of the professional social studies teacher with interests in history and geography.

REFERENCES

DANTE, HARRIS L. "Status of History in Modern Social Studies." *National Association of Secondary Schools Bulletin* (November 1974): 107–113.

GILL, CLARK C. "Interpretations of Indefinite Expressions of Time." *Social Education* (December 1962): 454–456.

JAMES, PRESTON E. "The Significance of Geography in American Education." *The Journal of Geography* (November 1969): 473–483.

JAROLIMEK, JOHN. "The Status of Social Studies Education: Six Case Studies." *Social Education* (November–December 1977): 574–579.

Newsweek. February 5, 1968, p. 16.

PATTISON, WILLIAM D. "The Four Traditions of Geography." *Journal of Geography* (May 1964): 211–16.

TAAFE, EDWARD J., ed. *Geography.* Englewood Cliffs, New Jersey: Prentice-Hall, Inc., 1970.

Chapter 20

POLITICAL SCIENCE AND ECONOMICS

C ourses in political science and in economics are features of the social studies program in most secondary schools. Indeed, in many school systems, students must enroll in such courses to qualify for graduation.

In secondary schools, courses in political science and economics appear under a variety of titles. With respect to political science, very frequently encountered course titles are civics, government, and public affairs. Courses drawing content from economics may be labeled variously consumer education, personal finance management, and free enterprise education, among other options.

Though courses based upon the disciplines of political science and economics are found in nearly every secondary school social studies program, their relative influence on the total social studies curriculum in middle schools, junior high schools, and senior high schools tends to be less than that of courses based primarily on history and geography. A basic explanation for this situation is that more history and geography courses are required for high school graduation. Further, most traditional history courses and many geography courses are designed to fill an entire year's instructional time. On the other hand, many courses that draw upon political science and economics are designed for only one semester's instructional time (a traditional semester lasts one half of an instructional year). Many students graduate from high school with exposure to no more than one-half year of instruction in content related to political science and no more than one-half year of instruction in content related to economics.

A fundamental problem, then, facing many teachers of courses related to political science and economics is the restriction of instructional time. Responsible treatment of topics related to these subjects demands careful consideration of concepts that are both subtle and difficult. Such consideration takes time. Given a course lasting only a semester, the teacher must make very difficult decisions about restricting content coverage to permit adequate time for students to deal meaningfully with topics and information that might be introduced in such courses. This process of selection causes responsible social studies teachers no little agony.

In the sections that follow, present practices in courses related to both political science and economics will be detailed. Special difficulties associated with each will be outlined. Finally, some suggestions for improving instruction in courses drawing upon contents from these academic disciplines will be introduced.

Political Science

Courses relating to political science have been a feature of social studies programs for many years. Special interest in introducing content derived from political science in formal school courses was stimulated by a concern for "Americanizing" immigrants in the nineteenth century. Gradually, this notion came to be formalized as a concern for "citizenship education." Responding to this concern, the National Education Association's Committee on Citizenship in 1915 recommended the inclusion of a special course in citizenship education in the mandatory secondary school social studies program. Typically labeled "civics," courses of this type came to be installed in most secondary social studies programs.

Interest in citizenship education persists in social studies programs today. The vast majority of states have legal requirements calling upon schools to provide students with instruction in "citizenship." Though the wording of such statutes varies, generally the attempt seems to be one of encouraging the schools to inculcate respect for and commitment to rather generalized patriotic values. This legal context has had implications for the nature of instructional experiences provided students in many courses drawing contents from political science.

WIDESPREAD INSTRUCTIONAL PRACTICES

There is evidence that many secondary school courses in government and civics continue to be heavily oriented toward promoting reverence for the *status quo.* This view is reflected in the heavy emphasis in texts for these courses on the legalistic structure of government and on formal operating procedures. Entire chapters are devoted to topics such as "amending the Constitution" and "how a bill becomes a law." Yet there is little or no discussion of the merits of the assumptions upon which these procedures are based. Nor, typically, is a great deal of attention directed toward increasing students' understanding of the processes of political decision making. There is an apparent presumption that a student (1) needs to know the steps a bill goes through to become a law in a legislative session but that he or she (2) must be protected from gaining insights into the nature of the political give-and-take that resulted in the final form of that bill.

In an indictment of many of the instructional materials used in civics and government classes, Zeigler (1970) has observed:

> Classes are easier to manage if the authority structure is not challenged. Engaging in controversy presents a challenge to the authority structure and is therefore avoided. Avoidance of controversy is reinforced by the content of texts which, for better or worse, establish the nature of the content of a course of instruction. A brief survey of the validity of public school texts in history, government, civics, and so on indicates the Victorian attitude toward politics which is typical of American education. The main object of most texts is, apparently, to protect the minds of youth rather than to inform them.[1]

In his examination of the civics curriculum, Zeigler (1970) pointed out that loyalty appears to be the major goal of instruction in this area. He noted a repetitive emphasis on symbolic indicators of loyalty in such courses. A difficulty with such an orientation is that (1) it probably is unnecessary as most secondary school students already are committed to a strong belief in the basic values of their country (Easton and Hess, 1962) and (2) it fails to provide students with an opportunity to examine carefully policy alternatives and values undergirding each. In reflecting on the poverty of instruction in government and civics courses that emphasize only existing institutional arrangements, Freeman (1973) has noted that "what is forgotten in all these arrangements is that there is a difference between dogma and practice" (p. 196).

In addition to difficulties associated with texts and courses of instruction, there is evidence that many teachers are reluctant to move from rather sterile considerations of institutional arrangements to considerations of policy alternatives that reflect different value priorities. Zeigler (1967) found that, of 803 secondary school teachers surveyed, a large majority did not feel the classroom was an appropriate setting for the teacher to express an opinion of a controversial nature.

Reflecting on this situation, Zeigler (1970) suggested that the adult population tends to agree with ideals in the abstract and to shy away from applying them to specific, concrete situations. If such a tendency characterizes adults, it may be only natural for high school students to do little more than give unthinking approval to these generalized values and to avoid thinking about implications of their application to specific policy decisions. Surely, secondary school students seem little likely to discuss, pinpoint, and question values associated with policy decisions in the absence of instructional programs designed to promote such behavior. Regrettably, many courses in government and civics fail to provide them with such an opportunity.

[1] Harmon Zeigler, "Education and the Status Quo," *Comparative Education* 6 (March 1970): 19–36.

In a consideration of contributions of courses derived from political science offered to secondary school students, it is necessary to examine (1) information and misinformation students may bring with them to such courses and (2) potentials for such courses to effect a change in students' understandings and attitudes. After years of exposure to family, friends, the media, and other sources of influence, secondary students begin work in government and civics classes with some fairly fixed notions about the "reality" of the world they live in. Smith (1970) has written that his students come to class with a full complement of what might be styled ". . . aberrant knowledge, and [that] is nearly as firmly implanted as the tenacious conviction in the minds of many journalists that an American invented the bath tub" (p. 243).

Smith (1970) found the following misconceptions to be common among secondary school students:

1. The United States is the world's largest democracy.
2. The United States has intimate, personal, and minisized congressional districts. (Actually each district represents nearly half a million people.)
3. The United States is the world's most populous country.
4. The United States has had the largest number of continuous peaceful transfers of power from one government to another. (Untrue. The United Kingdom holds this record.)
5. The Colonial Epoch was very short compared to our time as a constitutional republic. (Untrue. The duration of the Colonial Epoch was almost equal in length to our time as a constitutional republic.)

Sources for misinformation of this sort are many and varied. Given the breadth of information, both accurate and inaccurate, to which students have been exposed even before they reach their secondary school years, it is hardly surprising that many bring a great many mistaken conceptions to their civics and government courses. Indeed, a large number of adults probably have many of the misconceptions Smith (1970) noted in secondary students.

The problem is a serious one even for students (and adults, too) who are sophisticated enough to identify sources of information that are reliable and distinguish them clearly from other sources that cannot be trusted. In a fascinating study, Hovland and Weiss (1951) exposed one half of a group of intelligent adults to an article taking a strong position on a debatable public issue that was identified as being written by a source most in the group believed not to be reliable. The other half of the group read an article taking an identical position on the issue that was identified as being written by a source most in the group believed to be highly reliable. In a test given immediately after both halves had read their respective articles, those individuals who had read the article from the source believed to be unreliable were much less swayed in terms of their opinions regarding the issue than those who had read the article from the source believed to be highly reliable. But when a similar test was given four weeks later, there was no difference in the amount of opinion change of individuals who read the "unreliable" as opposed to those who read the "reliable" source.

Apparently what happens is that, over time, sources of information become confused. One remembers only that he or she "read something or heard something 'somewhere.' " Because individual sources cannot be recalled, the information from those sources cannot be sorted easily into "reliable information" and "unreliable information." Given this situation, it is only natural that many secondary students will come to their government and civics classes (and to other classes, too) with some rather farfetched "understandings."

In addition to the problem of aberrant knowledge, secondary school teachers in government and civics classes find themselves faced with students who are at an age when many basic political values and beliefs have already been established. As Easton and Hess (1962) reported, "the truly formative years of the maturing member of a political system would seem to be the years between the ages of three and thirteen."

These attitudes tend to be influenced very early by what the young child sees and hears in his or her home. Cleary (1971) has pointed out that, because of the very early age at which basic political orientations are established, "the secondary school and college are more likely to be concerned with developing or re-ordering existing orientations than they are with helping to develop new orientations where none previously existed" (p. 67). Even with regard to "developing" or "re-ordering" political value orientations of students, influences of formal classes in government and civics may be limited.

Coleman (1961) found that members of the general adolescent culture, not teachers or parents, were the primary figures to whom secondary school students look for support. Political opinions of the adolescent peer group seem to carry much more weight with students than insights derived from formal course work.

Cleary (1971) pointed out that a number of studies reveal that the community in which a student resides has a great deal to do with his or her willingness to modify a basic political orientation. Secondary students have been found to reject the major political party of their parents more frequently in communities where a sizable majority supports the other major party.

Students' preconceptions and evidence that many basic political values have been well established before students reach secondary schools suggest that teachers of civics and government classes face a most difficult instructional task. On the one hand, little is to be gained by orienting a course to promote traditional values that most students will already have acquired during their elementary school years (and even earlier). On the other hand, a considerable body of evidence suggests that students' attitudes and basic perspectives are somewhat fixed by the time they begin middle, junior high, and senior high school.

These limitations, however, do not suggest that nothing can be done. Rather, this information can be used as a basis for planning instructional experiences in courses derived from political science. For example, knowing that views of the adolescent peer group have a great influence on secondary students, some diagnostic work by the teacher is in order to determine just what the dominant views of the students in the school are. What seems to be the source of these views? On what logic are they based? Further investigation can reveal basic community orientations and how they might be affecting student perceptions. The logic of this entire process is to begin "where the students are" and build from that point. Attempts to move students away from even a position that has no logic to support it will have scant chance for success unless instruction begins with a sensitivity to students' present orientations and the milieu from which those orientations sprang and continue to be supported. This process is not an easy one. It involves careful instructional planning with a view to developing students' abilities to pinpoint issues, recognize values undergirding options, and to make decisions that, in many instances, they would rather avoid making.

Considerations for Responsible Political Education

As an alternative to civics and government courses that seem narrowly directed toward the goal of promotion of "loyalty," Cleary (1971) has suggested that

> school programs of this nature might center on an understanding of man's role in the polity—that is, on how an individual interacts with his political environment and how he might control it, rather than on a conscious attempt to instill an instinctive feeling of national loyalty in the student.[2]

At bottom, political life requires individuals to make difficult choices that pertain to core values. These core values, in the abstract, are almost universally accepted by Americans. The difficulty comes when they are applied to specific situations demanding political decisions. What one man, for example, sees as a decision clearly designed to expand upon the principle of "freedom" may be seen by another as a threat to that very same principle of "freedom." Even more frequently, political decisions are required that place certain core values in conflict. For example, a proposed nationwide limitation on maximum driving speeds may be perfectly consistent with a core value emphasizing order and conformity and equally at odds with a core value emphasizing individual freedom.

The necessity for choice demands responsibility. This suggests a need for (1) pinpointing specific issues that are in need of resolution, (2) identifying potential solutions and values associated with each, (3) assigning priorities to values that are associated with alternative solutions, and (4) making decisions in full knowledge of the values choices that have been selected.

Cleary (1971) has suggested the following core value strands in American life:

---

[2] Robert E. Cleary, *Political Education in the American Democracy* (Scranton, Pennsylvania: Intext Educational Publishers, 1971), p. 3.

1. An emphasis on freedom, equality, and dignity of the individual.
2. A stress on achievement and material well-being.
3. An emphasis on order and conformity.

Courses in civics and government need to provide students with opportunities to consider issues in the light of how possible decisions might reflect one or more of these core value strands. Responsibility is promoted when students are taught to analyze problems rationally with a recognition that every decision has some limitations. This requires alternative positions, even unpopular ones, to be brought forward for reasoned discussion. Students need to be encouraged to take positions on a problem, state a rationale for doing so, and state the value priorities that they have established in making their decisions.

Instruction of this sort places heavy demands on the teacher. He or she must be willing to deal with positions that may be controversial. Further, the teacher, too, must not shy away from personal participation in the same sort of analysis demanded of the students. As Cleary (1971) has noted:

> If a student gains the impression that the teacher does not ever consider it important to personally take a position on a problem examined in class, explaining his reasons for the stance he is taking, students may gradually become more disposed to avoid difficult choices in problem situations themselves.[3]

Selecting an instructional focus. As noted earlier in the chapter, students come to courses in government and political science with many basic political values already established. Further, what adjustments do occur are quite likely to occur from influences of other students and the community in general rather than from formal classroom instruction. An implication of this situation is that instruction must proceed from the interests and basic orientation of the students. This does not mean that this orientation is necessarily "good" or logically supportable, but it does provide a logical entry point for instruction. For example, if the adolescent peer group is a significant influence, then it makes sense to consider issues that have meaning for young people of this age. Certainly, those interests can be broadened, but the connection can be made easier when, as a beginning, adolescents' more immediate and parochial concerns are considered.

One response that a number of teachers have found to be successful focuses initial attention on issues faced by student government. Questions relating to topics such as dress and deportment codes, conflicts between organizations seeking authorization to sponsor dances on important weekends, drug law enforcement procedures, and others may provide a useful entrée leading to analysis of political decision making in other forums. If a decision to focus on local student government is taken, the teacher must not shirk from reasoned analysis of student questions concerning limitations on the powers of such bodies as compared to city and county councils, state legislatures, and the U.S. Congress.

---

[3] *ibid.*, p. 117.

Local and community issues offer opportunities for students to gain insights into the political decision-making process. Issues concerning zoning regulations are especially likely to generate heated debate and offer splendid opportunities for students to observe firsthand the difficulty of resolving disputes when basic core values conflict.

In addition to utilizing issues of interest to the local community to introduce students to the political decision-making process, some teachers have arranged for their students to become even more directly involved. Borrowing from a model long in use in business education courses where students have been provided with work-study experiences, teachers have made arrangements to place certain students as aides and assistants with local officials. Such programs cannot involve large numbers of youngsters, but those who do participate gain insights into "how government works" that simply cannot be replicated in the classroom. Though arrangements for such experiences take time, probably social studies teachers in civics and government classes could be doing more in this area.

Political parties at the local level welcome involvement of older secondary school students. Participation in a political campaign and active involvement in party affairs can be broadening learning experiences for students.

Though it makes sense to involve students with more locally focused political decision making initially, certainly every effort should be made to expand the dimensions of students' concern to issues of state, national, and international significance. Many students will have such interests even from the beginning. Television, newspapers, and other information resources provide students with at least some familiarity with issues being debated even in distant forums. Given instruction in basic processes of rational analysis and some direct experience with processes of political decision making at the local level, students at the secondary level certainly have the capability of dealing with broader issues.

A Framework for Analyzing Political Decision Making

Regardless of whether the issue is narrow or broad in scope, a common set of questions can be used to guide rational analysis of political decisions. These three basic questions are

1. What is the influence of broad-based social values on decisions?
2. Who are the decision-makers, and what are their roles?
3. What are the sources of influence on the decision-makers?

Broad-based values. In investigating political decisions, students might use Cleary's (1971) core value strands as referents as they attempt to discern the most logical value underpinnings of a given decision. Recall that these value strands involve

1. An emphasis on freedom, equality, and dignity of the individual.
2. A stress on achievement and material well-being.
3. An emphasis on order and conformity.

For example, a discussion of a court decision upholding a school's regulation concerning male hair length might lead to a conclusion that the decision reflected a higher value for "order and conformity" than for "freedom, equality, and dignity of the individual."

Discussions related to the question of broad-based social values also might be directed toward helping students understand that these values assist people to accept decisions that are made. For example, in athletics, the emphasis on "sportsmanship" (a variant of the core value strand emphasizing "order and conformity") generally results in a crowd's accepting the results even when the home team loses. Certainly, there will be a few expletives from very partisan followers, but rarely does this displeasure become transformed to hostile physical action. The importance of broad acceptance of the basic commitment to sportsmanship has been obvious on those few occasions when passions have run so high that the commitment to this value has been forgotten and people have been hurt and even killed (as in some soccer matches, for example).

The importance of a focus on broad-based social values is clear. Without these values, the social fabric within which political decisions are made would not hold. These values help to explain the kinds of decisions that will be made and why people will accept them.

The decision-makers and their roles. A second general question students might probe in studying political decisions relates to the roles of decision-makers. A very basic issue here is simply, "Who makes the decisions?" Beyond this, selection of these decision-makers becomes a logical focus topic for class discussion. Students might be interested in the social and economic backgrounds of key decision-makers. Do decision-makers represent a broad cross section of the community, or do most represent a privileged elite? How do decision-makers maintain their ability to win positions of control?

As important as the issue of selection and personal characteristics of decision-makers is the question of the deliberative processes these individuals use in arriving at decisions. Students might inquire into how decision-makers formulate and clarify a problem. How is evidence gathered? What is the nature of that evidence? Is the source of evidence as important as the nature of the evidence? Which sorts of arguments to these decision-makers find most compelling?

Sources of influence on decision-makers. In an examination of political decisions, there is merit in encouraging students to deal with the basic issue of "Where does the real power lie?" "Group theory" suggests that *ad hoc* clusters of individuals form in support of and in opposition to specific issues. Members of these interest groups may share little in common other than a common view of a given issue. Conflicts between contesting groups are thought to result ultimately in decisions. Power, then, flows as a result of the influence of this group conflict.

Students might also consider "class theory," a perspective that holds that certain social and economic classes tend to have common interests that bind members together and lead them to take a position on a variety of issues in terms of their class. It is an interesting exercise for students to look at political decisions with a view to determining whether a given social or economic class consistently seems to be the primary beneficiary of these decisions. If so, does this situation result from a conscious effort on the part of this social or economic class, or can it be explained by chance factors?

Still another source of influence students might look for is an "extralegal" influence. Are decisions really being made by an individual or individuals outside of the formally constituted political apparatus? In some totalitarian countries, for example, the real power is wielded by a single political party. Decisions of this party, in reality, are simply echoed by the government. This occurs, even though the trappings of a legitimate deliberative body are there. Students need to be sensitized to differences between governments where decisions, though they may be influenced by outsiders, really are made by those inside the government and others where decisions that, in fact, are made by outsiders are simply rubber-stamped by those inside the government.

Economics

The study of contents derived from the formal academic discipline of economics occurs in two general ways in secondary schools. On the one hand, there are courses titled variously Economics, Free Enterprise, Personal Finance, Consumer Economics, among other options, that organize instruction directly around contents derived from economics. On the other hand, many other social studies courses, for example, U.S. History and World History, include much economics-related material even though economics is not the primary discipline from which content is drawn.

A number of difficulties are associated with instruction in economics regardless of the nature of the course within which the content is included. One of these difficulties relates to teacher training in economics. Very few social studies teachers major in economics. Indeed, very few with majors in history and other social science have even two or more courses in economics. In part, this lack of trained teachers can be explained by the unique status of economics as a social studies discipline whose graduates find their services in high demand by the private sector and by governmental agencies outside of public education. Put simply, salaries offered to social studies teachers cannot compete, in many instances, with those offered to individuals trained in economics by other potential employers. Consequently, many required courses in economics are taught by individuals with little formal training in the area.

Another difficulty relates to text and other printed materials designed for use in secondary economics classes. A review of tables of contents of many texts reveals that little distinguishes them from books used in introductory college economics courses. The range of contents is simply enormous. The attempt to cover such a quantity of difficult content within a course that in many schools lasts only a semester has high potential for frustrating students.

Texts, too, suffer from severe readability problems in many cases. Because many high schools offer semester-long economics courses during the senior year, many publishers have paid less attention to reading difficulty levels than has been the case with texts directed toward audiences of younger students. Consequently, many students simply cannot handle the reading in course texts. Compounding this difficulty is the specialized use in economics of many terms that have a common "street use" that is known to students. Because vocabularies of most secondary students probably will include such terms as *scarcity, market,* and *capital,* they frequently imagine themselves to "already know" what the textbook author is attempting to describe. A failure of students to attend carefully to specific definitions of these terms as they are used by economics presents secondary economics teachers with a frustrating challenge.

Another textbook-associated difficulty relates to the heavy reliance on graphs and other visual representations of data. Few students will have encountered social studies materials requiring such sophisticated levels of visual literacy before they take economics. Many students are frustrated, if not downright baffled, by charts and graphs that involve the simultaneous manipulation of several variables as in the case of supply and demand schedules.

When economics content is embedded within courses in history and other social studies courses, problems associated with inadequate teacher preparation and text-book content are compounded. Because of their lack of training in economics, large numbers of teachers, for example, are not able to deal with economic motives associated with the search for gold and minerals in the West during the last half of the nineteenth century. To make the problem even more difficult, many secondary school texts, when they do make some mention of economic factors, provide erroneous information (O'Neill and Newton, 1975). For example, O'Neill and Newton (1975) found that some U.S. history texts perpetuated the idea that inflation results whenever each paper dollar is not backed by an equivalent amount of gold, a view that is discounted by the vast majority of professional economists.

There is an illusion of simplicity to economics that curriculum planners find appealing. This results because, as compared to history and the other social sciences, it tends to have a broader agreement with respect to which concepts are central to the discipline. There is much less diversity among economics texts in terms of topics covered than among texts in other disciplines from which social studies courses draw contents. This agreement provides a framework for course design that curriculum makers find appealing. But the ease of design does little to ameliorate difficulties associated with content difficulty, textbook deficiencies, and problems related to undertrained instructional staffs. As O'Neill and Newton have observed, "The highly structured nature of the discipline makes curricula design relatively easy, while its attendant complexity makes it a difficult subject to teach well" (1975: p. 274).

RESPONSES TO THE TEACHER PREPARATION ISSUE

The charge that "Americans are economic illiterates" has been made repeatedly over the years and has resulted in some specific actions designed to remediate this situation. A difficulty pervading economic education is that "economic truth," to some extent at least, must be viewed in an appreciation of the political context within which it is provided. What is "economic literacy" to Ralph Nader or to the AFL/CIO may be "economic illiteracy" to the U.S. Chamber of Commerce or the National Federation of Independent Businessmen. Because social goals may be assigned different priorities by large and important groups in our society, it is not surprising that their concepts of "economic truth" vary as well.

In an attempt to provide a clearinghouse for economic education information of a sort that various groups could live with, the *Joint Council on Economic Education* was established in 1949. The Joint Council is an independent, nonprofit, nonpartisan organization dedicated to the improvement of economic education. Its financial support comes from foundations, business, organized labor, farm groups, and interested individuals. The Joint Council has sponsored the development of useful curriculum guides for freestanding economics courses, procedures for infusing economics content into other courses, and general instructional materials for class-room teachers. Additionally, the Joint Council has sponsored large numbers of training programs for in-service teachers. Information about the Joint Council and a list of materials and information relating to other services are available for the asking from:

Joint Council on Economic Education
1212 Avenue of the Americas
New York, New York 10036
(212) 582–5150

In addition to the efforts of the Joint Council, many other programs have been established to provide program outlines and teacher materials for economics courses. Chambers of commerce, for example, in many cities have programs and materials that are available to secondary school teachers. Large corporations frequently have large educational services divisions. Some materials available from these corporate sources are outstanding. (The five "American Enterprise" films, produced by a grant from the Phillips Petroleum Company, represent a commend-able addition to the resources available to classroom economics teachers. For information regarding how these free-loan films can be scheduled, write to Modern Talking Picture Service, 2323 New Hyde Park Road, New Hyde Park, New York 11040.) Organized labor organizations also make programs and materials available. Finally, a number of colleges and universities have established economics education centers with a special orientation or focus. One of these is the Center for Education and Research in Free Enterprise at Texas A & M University. (For information regarding available teacher materials, write to Center for Education and Research in Free Enterprise, Texas A & M University, College Station, TX 77843.)

Interestingly, the thrust of most of these teacher training and service programs is in-service education. There is a realization that, if economics education is to be upgraded, skills of the career teacher need to be upgraded. Because of this realization, large numbers of special summer training programs are offered each summer across the country. Many of these provide participants with at least partial reimbursement (in some cases, all expenses are paid) for tuition, housing, and travel. For beginning social studies teachers interested in adding to their expertise in economics, these programs represent excellent opportunities for professional development.

DELIMITING CONTENT IN ECONOMICS COURSES

Efforts to delimit content in courses related to the discipline of economics have been of two general types. One response to this problem has been to create courses restricted to content that has been thought to respond to a pressing student interest or need. Courses such as consumer economics and personal finance, for example, have been established largely because they have been thought to provide students with some necessary "survival skills."

Critics of such courses, though not denying the necessity of providing students with useful information, question the narrow focus on consumerism or on personal financial management. Understandings accruing to students from such courses may not provide them with the background necessary to make reasoned decisions on policy questions that can have significant long-term economic consequences. As an alternative, courses focusing on how the economy works as a *system* have been posed as a way of delimiting content. This response to the delimitation problem is premised on the belief that, given instruction in characteristics of a limited number of elements of the economic system, students will become more sophisticated in their assessment of governmental policy alternatives. A growing number of economic educators believe that understanding the economy as a system is a prerequisite for economic literacy.

A number of proposals have been put forward to identify contents that might be included in courses attempting to build understanding of an economy as a system. Becker and Reinke (1974) suggested the following topics as appropriate:

    I. Resources (human, natural, capital, time).
    II. Scarcity and opportunity cost.
    III. Incentives (pecuniary, material, psychic).
    IV. Economic efficiency.
    V. The market (demand, supply, market equilibrium).
    VI. Market imperfections.

VII. Externalities.
VIII. Real vs. nominal values.
  IX. Aggregate flow of economic activity.
  X. Economic growth and income distribution.

The Becker and Reinke scheme and others like it do delimit topics but, by themselves, do not provide guidelines for teachers in dealing with content. They do, however, represent a commendable "paring down" of the much broader array of contents found in many textbooks.

Another scheme—and one that suggests more clearly how instruction might proceed—has been developed by Allen (Allen, 1977; Allen and Armstrong, 1978). This scheme suggests that instruction should be organized around two central ideas. The first of these is the idea that all societies attempt to meet certain broad social goals. Second, ways these goals are assigned priorities at a given point in time can be seen by comparing a given economic decision to what that decision would have been if the United States had a "pure market economy." Discussion and lessons then proceed from instruction in the elements of a "pure market economy" system. Elements of this system are used as common referents as economic decisions are compared to determine their inconsistency or consistency with the "pure market system." Findings of both consistency and inconsistency provide opportunities for discussing social goal priorities that appear to underlie these decisions.

Social goals that all economic systems attempt to serve include

1. Economic growth.
2. Economic efficiency.
3. Security.
4. Stability.
5. Equity.
6. Freedom.

Clearly, several of these goals are in conflict. For example, the goal of security may well result in policy decisions that restrict freedom, another goal. Further, policies leading to economic efficiency may be so oppressive that they threaten the social order and, thus, undermine the goal of stability. Students need to understand that economic policy decisions always are characterized by some prioritization of these goals. A given decision never can serve all of these goals equally well.

Allen and Armstrong (1978) have suggested five hallmarks of a "pure market economy." Commitment to a pure market economy reflects a very heavy commitment to the social goals of economic growth, economic efficiency, and freedom and a much diminished commitment to security, stability, and equity. The five hallmarks of a pure market economy are these:

1. Private property.
2. Economic freedom.
3. Incentives.
4. Decentralized decision making.
5. A limited role for government.

Provided with basic instruction relating to the six basic social goals and the five hallmarks of a pure market economy, students are in a position to engage in rational analysis of current economic problems. Suppose, for example, the following article appeared in the morning newspaper:

> *Washington, D.C.* Senate and House conferees today are expected to reach agreement on a proposal that will require employers to pay that portion of the social security tax now paid by their employees. Passage of this measure would result in an increase in take-home pay for many workers of as much as $100 per month. Employers would find their monthly income reduced by an amount equivalent to the total social security taxes paid each month by their employees. When the compromise measure returns to the floor of the House and the Senate, intense debate is expected.

In debriefing a class of students familiar with both the social goals and the hallmarks of the pure market economy, a teacher might proceed as follows:

> *Teacher:* What social goals seem to be the primary objective of this measure? How do you think somebody favoring this bill would prioritize the basic social goals?
> [Students respond.]

> *Teacher:* What consistencies and inconsistencies with our pure market economy do you see in this measure?
> [Students respond.]

> *Teacher:* How do *you* feel about this idea?
> [Students respond.]

> *Teacher:* What deviations are you willing to accept away from our pure market economy in this instance? What does your answer say about how you assign priorities to individual social goals? What implications for our economic system do you see if this measure is adopted?
> [Students respond.]

This discussion, of course, is much abbreviated. The purpose is simply to illustrate how an emphasis on a current economic issue can be tied back to a concern for getting students to look at the economic system as a system. When issues are viewed not as isolated phenomena but rather as questions having implications for the functioning of our economic system, then real economic understanding begins to take root. This sort of analytical understanding is a major objective of secondary programs in the area of economics.

Summary

Secondary school courses drawing content from both political science and economics present social studies teachers with some real difficulties. First of all, many such courses last no longer than a single school semester. Because of restricted instructional time, important and difficult decisions must be made in selecting content to be emphasized. In addition to these general difficulties, there are some peculiarities associated with contents from each discipline.

With respect to political science courses, there is evidence that many students come to their classes with some firmly entrenched spurious knowledge that stand in the way of genuine understanding. Further, political attitudes of many are well established before they begin secondary education programs, and attitudes may not be heavily influenced by classroom instruction. Finally, many such programs have been too heavily oriented toward promoting "patriotism" and "loyalty," qualities the vast majority of students have before entering junior and senior high school, and too little oriented toward examining the processes and values associated with political decision making.

Economics-oriented courses frequently are considered very difficult by students. This situation, in part, results because many social studies teachers have an inadequate background in economics. Additionally, many texts attempt to present too much content for secondary students to absorb. Readability difficulties associated with many printed materials in this area further contribute to student problems. The need for improvement of instruction in economics has been widely recognized, and excellent work is being done by the Joint Council on Economic Education and other groups.

REFERENCES

ALLEN, JOHN W. "An Introduction to the American Free Enterprise System." Monograph. Texas A & M University, College Station, Texas: Center for Education and Research in Free Enterprise, 1977.

———— and DAVID G. ARMSTRONG. "Hallmarks of a Free Enterprise System." Monograph. Texas A & M University, College Station, Texas: Center for Education and Research in Free Enterprise, 1978.

BECKER, WILLIAM E., JR., and ROBERT W. REINKE. "What Economics Should the Educator Know?" *The Social Studies* (September/October 1974): 195–204.

CLEARY, ROBERT E. *Political Education in the American Democracy.* Scranton, Pennsylvania: Intext Educational Publishers, 1971.

COLEMAN, JAMES S. *The Adolescent Society: The Social Life of the Teenager and Its Impact on Education.* New York: The Free Press, 1961.

EASTON, DAVID, and ROBERT D. HESS. "The Child's Political World." *Midwest Journal of Political Science.* (August 1962): 235–236.

FREEMAN, JOSEPH F. "Learning Politics." *The Social Studies* (October 1973): 195–202.

HOVLAND, CARL I., and WALTER WEISS. "The Influence of Source Credibility on Communication Effectiveness." *Public Opinion Quarterly* (Winter 1951): 635–650.

O'NEILL, JAMES B., and RICHARD NEWTON. "Economics—Forgotten Social Science in Today's U.S. History Books." *High School Journal* (March 1975): 274–283.

SMITH, JOWN W. "They Don't Come to Me Tabula Rasa." *The Social Studies* (November 1970): 243–248.

ZEIGLER, HARMON. "Education and the Status Quo." *Comparative Education* (March 1970): 19–36.

————. *The Political Life of American Teachers.* Englewood Cliffs, New Jersey: Prentice-Hall, Inc., 1967.

Chapter 21

| SOCIOLOGY, PSYCHOLOGY, AND ANTHROPOLOGY |

THOUGH THREADS OF CONTENT FROM sociology, psychology, and anthropology are found throughout the secondary social studies curriculum, courses focusing exclusively on contents from these disciplines are relatively few in number. History and geography courses continue to be required in the vast majority of school districts. In many parts of the country, these requirements result in several years of required courses drawing contents from these two disciplines. Political science and economics courses, though typically only a semester in length, continue to be required for graduation in many areas. But, with few exceptions, courses drawing primary content from sociology, psychology, and anthropology are elective offerings.

Elective courses, generally, do not begin to enroll students in the same large numbers as required courses. Nearly every secondary student in the country takes a course in U.S. history during his high school program, whether he or she is interested or not. Given a free choice in the matter, numbers enrolling in the course would be greatly diminished from present levels. Even though contents of courses oriented around sociology, psychology, and anthropology are interesting to large numbers of young people, still there are many others who prefer to earn elective credits in other areas of the curriculum. So long as courses drawing central content from sociology, psychology, and anthropology tend to remain elective rather than required, the frequency of such offerings will be low as compared to required courses focusing on history, geography, political science, and economics.

For the present, there seems little likelihood that courses drawing heavily from sociology, psychology, and anthropology will be required for all students. Relatively small numbers of social studies teachers major in these disciplines or even have large numbers of credits in these areas. Most social studies teachers tend to be heavily oriented toward history, geography, and political science in terms of their undergraduate preparation. They feel more comfortable in dealing with contents derived from these major subject areas than with contents from the behavioral sciences. Additionally, the heavy force of tradition restrains attempts to substitute required courses in sociology, psychology, and anthropology for the more familiar offerings in history, geography, and government.

Finally, until relatively recent times, materials derived from the behavioral sciences suitable for use with secondary school students were not widely available. Today, thanks to the efforts of professional educators, sociologists, psychologists, and anthropologists, outstanding materials are available for secondary school students. But because many of these items are of relatively recent vintage, many practicing social studies teachers are not familiar with them. Further, many of them have been fashioned on the assumption that teachers would take readily to programs and materials requiring a preponderance of inductive modes of instruction. Large numbers of teachers, untrained in inductive approaches, have experienced difficulty in incorporating many of the new programs and materials into their traditional patterns of interacting with students. Teachers who have been fortunate enough to attend special summer training institutes where programs and instructional procedures for the behavioral sciences have been offered have become enthusiastic partisans of courses drawing heavily from sociology, psychology, and anthropology. Regrettably, such summer opportunities have touched only a small fraction of secondary social studies teachers. For the majority, content from the behavioral sciences remains an interesting adjunct but certainly not a central core of the secondary program.

Despite the relatively low profile courses emphasizing behavioral science-oriented content enjoy today, there is a possibility that the influence of such courses may be on the upswing. First of all, with their emphasis on human beings and what they do, courses emphasizing content from sociology, psychology, and anthropology may seem more clearly relevant to secondary school students than courses in history, geography, political science, and economics. There is evidence that such courses have increased in popularity since the early 1960s. Further, social studies teachers being prepared today typically take more undergraduate courses in the behavioral sciences than did teachers trained ten and fifteen years ago. Given exposure to sociology, psychology, and anthropology in their college and university programs, such individuals may well feel more comfortable in teaching secondary school courses with a behavioral science orientation than their older colleagues.

In the next three sections, specific concerns relating to sociology, psychology, and anthropology will be introduced. Common threads bind together all three disciplines, but the fabric of each reflects its own special texture.

Sociology

Sociology seeks to explain human behavior in groups. Though individuals retain identifiable personal characteristics, much of their behavior can be explained in terms of their interaction with other human beings organized in groups. In explaining the function of sociology, Robert Perucci (1966) has written:

> Society is found to abound with social forces which were not willed into existence, and man's behavior is found to modify social forces quite independently of his intentions. It is the task of sociology to seek an understanding of the laws governing man's social behavior, and in so doing to better understand the workings of society.[1]

An implication of Perucci's (1966) statement is that there is a certain pattern to organized human behavior that professional sociology can unveil. Stated another way, sociology is a normative science that seeks to make supportable generalizations about human behavior by examining behavioral data from large numbers of individuals. Professional sociology does not take a position with regard to the desirability of these patterns. Rather, sociology seeks only to point out "what is there."

One stream of thought associated with incorporating sociology-oriented programs into the secondary social studies curriculum has been premised on the belief that such programs should emphasize sociology as a science; that is, instruction should seek to provide students with the tools for gathering and analyzing sociological data there are used by the professional sociologist. Phillips (1969), in his discussion of a leading secondary school sociology program, points out that one of its central objectives is to teach students scientific methods of inquiry that can be used to produce verifiable knowledge about social groups. Clearly, this intent is consistent with the view of secondary sociology as a crucible for training tough-minded, objective, and analytical students capable of making decisions with little or no interference from personally held values.

The "sociology as science" position has come under attack for several reasons. First of all, the approach seems to be based on the assumption that the secondary school student, at the conclusion of his or her course, ought to possess many skills of the professional sociologist. This outcome, critics allege, may have some merit for individuals who may truly have aspirations of becoming professionals in this area. But numbers of students with such a vision are few. Consider, for example, that less than 5 per cent of the undergraduate college population majors in sociology. Of the small number who do major in sociology, fewer than one in twenty go on to graduate study in the discipline. Given such numbers, secondary school sociology as vocational preparation seems to have little logical support.

In addition to supply-demand problems associated with training students for a career in professional sociology, a heavy emphasis on the analytical tools of the

---

[1] Robert Perucci, "Sociology" (Publication 101 of the Social Science Education Consortium, Boulder: University of Colorado, 1966), p. 1.

highly trained sociologist may result in a decline in interest of secondary school students in sociology. Analysis of data to arrive at generalizations requires some statistical manipulation. Fraser and Switzer (1970), in commenting on student reactions to portions of a sociology course in which there was an emphasis on statistical processing of information, noted a good deal of student resistance to this phase of the course. They noted that

> students, who may raise no objection to statistics in their physical science classes, seem reluctant to apply them to the analysis of social questions. This dislike may be the result of previous experience more than anything—students are used to making lightweight exchanges of opinion in their social studies classes.[2]

As Fraser and Switzer note, negative student reaction to manipulation of data may be a result of little experience and thus be a remediable condition. Yet the finding does suggest that, initially at least, such an approach may dampen students' enthusism for the course.

As an alternative to organizing programs designed to equip students with the more technical skills of the professional sociologist, it has been suggested that a more proper objective might be to provide them with what has been described as as "sociological perspective." This sociological perspective reflects how the sociologist looks at the world, the kinds of problems he or she sees as important, and the kinds of basic questions he or she asks. Courses directed toward provision of a sociological perspective may introduce students to much of the fascinating content of sociology without burdening them with too heavy a dose of specialized analytical techniques.

But sociology-oriented programs directed toward fostering a sociological perspective are not without their pitfalls. Even when stripped, for example, of much emphasis on quantitative data processing, the sociological perspective requires students to examine reality dispassionately and analytically. The concern is with *what is* as opposed to *what ought to be*. Many students find it difficult to accept the merit of analysis in the absence of values considerations. Additionally, the tendency of sociologists to look at groups rather than individuals and to speak in terms of central tendencies or averages is disconcerting to a good many students. In this regard, Fraser and Switzer (1970) noted that

> Some students contend that the uniqueness of the individual should not be obscured by categories and statistics . . . They find it disconcerting to view the world from a sociological perspective.[3]

Fraser and Switzer (1970) undertook a massive survey of student attitudes toward Inquires in Sociology, a one-semester high school course developed by Sociological

---

[2] Graeme S. Fraser and Thomas J. Switzer, "Inquiries in Sociology: Responses by Teachers and Students," *Social Education* (December 1970): 924.

[3] Graeme S. Fraser and Thomas J. Switzer, "Inquiries in Sociology: Responses by Teachers and Students," *Social Education* (December 1970): 925.

Resources for the Social Studies, a curriculum project sponsored by the American Sociological Association. The course is organized around these key themes:

1. Socialization.
2. Institutions.
3. Stratification.
4. Social change.

Frazer and Switzer (1970) found highest student ratings for course material related to "socialization." Lowest ratings were for "institutions" and "stratification." The investigators postulated that students were more interested in those parts of the course that seemed of immediate personal concern. By this criterion, the issue of stratification was apparently viewed as more abstract and impersonal than the issue of socialization. Students tended to prefer case studies and biographies over surveys and data table analysis.

A thread running through the Frazer and Switzer (1970) report is the connection between students' interest and students' personal concerns. Where course materials related directly to these personal interests, motivation was high. When they did not do so, students were less enthusiastic. An implication of this finding is that some trade-off may be necessary between the objective of producing students who can assess issues dispassionately from a "sociological perspective" and the objective of maintaining interest in the course by keying some instruction toward special interests and values reflected by individual students in the class. It seems clear that sociology-oriented courses directed exclusively toward an examination of *what is* cannot expect to have the emotive appeal of those that, in part at least, focus attention on the motivating question of *what ought to be*. The social studies teacher must strike a responsible balance between the need for motivation and the need for students to move outside of themselves to make reasoned and supportable decisions about the social world within which they live.

FUNDAMENTAL IDEAS OF SOCIOLOGY

Senesh (1967) has identified the following three statements as summing up the basic position of sociology as a discipline:

1. Values and norms are the main sources of energy to individuals and society (Senesh, 1967: p. 32).
2. Societies' values and norms shape social institutions, which are embodied in organizations and groups where people occupy positions and roles (Senesh, 1967: p. 32).
3. People's positions and roles affect their attitudes toward society's values and norms and result either in support of the existing values and norms or in demands for modification of them, and the circle starts again (Senesh, 1967: p. 32).

Values and norms along with beliefs are things in which individuals commit to in an emotional sense. Though individuals vary in terms of the relative emphases they give to certain values and norms, still patterns are discernible across large numbers of people. For example, Perucci (1966) has pointed out that most Americans subscribe to the following fundamental values:

1. Achievement and success.
2. Education.
3. Material comfort.
4. Judaeo-Christian morality.
5. Equality.
6. Freedom.
7. Science and rationality.
8. Group superiority themes.

These core values shape our social institutions, organizations, and groups. In turn, those social institutions, organizations, and groups to an extent shape the behavior of the individuals within the institutions, organizations, and groups. Positions individuals play within these large clusters of individuals result in social roles determined in part by the nature of the position itself and in part by how a given individual interprets that position. Because of variations between individuals, basic social values and norms are continually under review. Some are satisfied with the *status quo*. Others seek change. Sociologists study the fascinating dynamic that occurs in the interaction between individuals (and their clusters of values and norms) and groups (and their clusters of values and norms).

Robert Perucci has reduced this process to a schematic reflecting the fundamental structure of sociology. The schematic is reproduced in Figure 21–1.

SOCIOLOGY-ORIENTED INSTRUCTION IN THE CLASSROOM

Many opportunities occur in social studies classroom to draw upon content from sociology. For example, the social structure of the school might be examined to illustrate some basic concepts. Instruction might focus on such questions as the following:

1. What values and norms are reflected in the school?
   What maintains those values and norms?
   What forces seek to modify them?
   How are supporters and opponents of those values and norms organized?
2. What are the goals of organizations in the school?
   What kinds of requirements led to the establishment of these organizations?
   How do these organizations shape members behavior?
   How do members influence these organizations?
3. What groups exist in the school that are not formal organizations?
   How do such groups differ from formal organizations?
   What are their purposes?
   How do they influence members?
   How do members influence them?

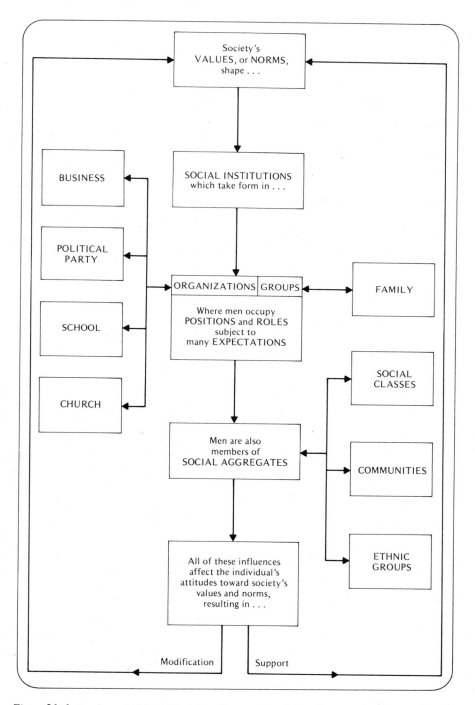

Figure 21–1. Fundamental Ideas of Sociology. (Source: From Robert Perucci, "Sociology." Publication 101 of the Social Science Education Consortium (Boulder, Colorado: University of Colorado, 1966), p. 31. Reprinted with permission of Social Science Education Consortium, Inc., Boulder, Colorado 80302.)

4. What social roles are played by people in the school?
   How do individuals interpret their social roles differently?
   What are the relationships between and among individuals occupying different social roles?

There is no need, of course, to focus only on the immediate school environment. As Fraser and Switzer (1970) pointed out, the key is providing instruction centered on topics students perceive to be of some immediate personal importance. Although for some students lessons built around an examinations of issues associated with the school might meet that criterion, for others such lessons might fall well short of the mark.

Certainly, today's adolescents have interests ranging well beyond the immediate school environment. Many hold jobs and are interested in issues associated with conditions of employment. For others, analyses of such issues as male-female relationships, drugs and alienation, women's rights, medical ethics, and other topics might be appropriate. Regardless of the issue, contents derived from sociology with their potential for providing insights regarding the age-old dilemma of establishing a proper relationship between the individual and the group and the group and the individual have much to offer the secondary social studies teacher.

Psychology

Courses in psychology in the secondary schools typically are one-semester, elective courses. There seems to be an increased interest in teaching psychology as a separate course. Zunino (1974) reported that 90 per cent of school administrators surveyed favored teaching a course in psychology in high school. The same investigator reported that, at present, the course tends to be offered more frequently in large than in small high schools and to be taken more frequently by juniors and seniors than by freshmen and sophomores. Many students who enroll in such courses are academically talented youngsters who intend to attend colleges and universities.

There has been some discussion about which department should control instruction in psychology in secondary schools. Generally, this issue has been resolved by placing psychology instructors in social studies departments. Zunino (1974) found that about two thirds of psychology courses in high schools were taught by social studies departments. When the courses are not offered by social studies departments, most typically they are offered by science departments.

That the preponderance of secondary school instruction in psychology is offered by social studies departments suggests that, for the present at least, there is a broader commitment to the view that the course should be directed toward students' "self-understanding" rather than toward understanding of "basic scientific principles of psychology." The debate between these two fundamental positions has raged for some time. In general, professional psychologists have favored a heavier emphasis on grounded scientific principles of behavior. Secondary school teachers of psychology, in general, have been more inclined to emphasize personal adjustment and development of students. Reflecting this division of opinion, high school psychology textbooks, as compared to textbooks used in college psychology courses, devote less space to biological foundations of behavior, learning, and statistics. They devote more space to the study of personality, personal problems, and mental health (Zunino 1974).

Very few high school teachers of psychology have had extensive academic training in the subject. Zunino (1974) reported that a large number of such teachers have had only a single college course in psychology. Given the paucity of their professional training in the field, perhaps it is not surprising that many secondary school psychology teachers do not feel particularly comfortable with a scientific approach to psychology that emphasizes biological, statistical, and experimental aspects of the subject. Ross (1972) has suggested that many students come to their psychology class with certain preconceptions about what the focus of the course should be. Generally, students believe that self-understanding ought to be the central purpose of the course. Ross (1972) pointed out that given (1) teachers' lack of professional preparation in psychology and (2) the pattern of student expectations, it is not surprising that many teachers adopt a self-development or a mental health orientation toward the teaching of psychology. This trend, however, does not mean that *only* self-development is taught. Rather, it indicates a relatively heavy emphasis on this dimension and a relatively light emphasis on scientific psychology. In this connection Zunino has written:

> Thus, an understanding of psychological theory and an objective approach to studying behavior is still important and is still taught. However, there seems to be more emphasis now on a classroom objective of applying the findings of psychological research to a better understanding by students of the dynamics of personal and social behavior—including their own.[4]

Course Patterns in Psychology

Unlike sociology and anthropology, disciplines whose major professional associations have sponsored the development of large-scale curriculum projects for secondary schools, curricula in psychology have not benefited from an intensive national developmental effort. Excellent programs and materials do exist. But the whole issue of curriculum and materials development for the secondary schools has not been as broadly attacked in the area of psychology as in some of the other behavioral sciences. Some beginnings in this direction have been taken, however. A committee of the American Psychological Association prepared an excellent monograph entitled "Program on the Teaching of Psychology in the Secondary School" (American Psychological Association, 1970). The monograph includes reviews of materials;

---

[4] Natalia Zunino, "The Teaching of Psychology in American High Schools: What's Happening?" *Social Education* (March 1974): 258.

lists psychological journals; suggests titles of novels, case studies, and other books potentially useful in psychology courses; points out some student-involving teaching techniques; and provides some very general guidelines for organizing a course of instruction. Material in this monograph can be useful to the social studies teacher interested in drawing upon content from psychology. Much of the "nuts and bolts" of an actual course design, however, remains to be accomplished by the individual teacher.

Given that relatively little concentrated attention has been devoted toward developing large-scale curriculum projects in psychology, there tends to be considerable variation in how psychology courses are organized in secondary schools. Though, as noted previously, there tends to be a concensus of interest on topics related to self-development of students, individual instructors have developed a variety of emphases in helping their students to arrive at the self-knowledge objective. Reporting on a survey of topic emphases in western New York State, Zunino (1974) found the following topics to be most commonly taught in high school courses in psychology:

1. Emotion.
2. Addiction.
3. Principles of human development.
4. Mental health and illness.
5. Personality and personality development.

Still consistent with the view that the psychology course ought to be oriented toward the objective of promoting students' self-understanding, Langhorst and Sullivan (1968) suggested the following topics for a high school course in psychology:[5]

1. Maleness and femaleness.
2. Conformity versus autonomy.
3. The alienation of youth.
4. Problems in child rearing.
5. Personality disturbances.
6. Coping with the modern world.

Though topics are different in the Zunino and the Langhorst and Sullivan lists, still the concern for students' development is clear.

PSYCHOLOGY AND THE SOCIAL STUDIES TEACHER

For the social studies teacher, the fundamental problem with respect to psychology parallels to a considerable degree the problem with sociology. On the one hand, students come to classes in psychology (or in other courses drawing heavily on contents from psychology) with the expectation that the course will solve many of their personal problems. Their motivation for the course, in many cases, is

---

[5] H. Walter Langhorst and John L. Sullivan, " 'Hey That's Me!'—A Relevant Course," *The Clearing House* (December 1968): 204.

tied up with this expectation. On the other hand, professional psychologists, or at least a good many of them, tend to look at normative data; that is, at information gleaned from examining and averaging hundreds and even thousands of cases. From such investigations, these professionals have attempted to formulate certain predictive laws of behavior. These laws, however, are not stated as absolutes as, for example, the law of gravity in physics. Rather, they are stated as probabilities— that is to say that something may be true *most of the time* but not necessarily *all of the time*.

Given that these laws are strong probabilities, not absolutes, the social studies teacher cannot answer a question from a student that in effect says, "What about me?" The law may be true in the general case. But there is no way of knowing whether an individual student will be one of the exceptions. (For example, even if psychology establishes that something happens ninety-nine out of one hundred times, when a student asks whether it will happen to him or her, the question cannot be answered. Is that student one of the ninety-nine, or is he or she the one hundredth student that is the exception to the general rule? There is no way of knowing.)

The task of the social studies teacher, then, is one of striking an instructional balance between students' desire to have answers to personal problems and the limitations of scientific psychology when applied to individual cases. The motivation of the student must be maintained. Yet there is an obligation, too, to impress students with psychology's limitations as well as its potentials. Given the difficulty of the task, success does not come easy. But for teachers who make an accommodation between the sometimes conflicting demands of students of psychology and the discipline of psychology, rewards can be very high. There is a level of intense involvement and commitment to social studies courses drawing content from psychology that can make them a showcase for the secondary school social studies department.

Anthropology

Courses titled Anthropology and courses drawing heavily on anthropological content are relative newcomers to the secondary school curriculum. In many areas of the country such course content is centered almost entirely within "elective" offerings. But, in some areas at least, contents derived from anthropology are increasingly finding their way into the "required" social studies curriculum. For example, in New York State, certain required courses, including those emphasizing the study of Asia and Africa, emphasize the cultural approach.

The key concept of anthropology is "culture." Pelto (1965: p. 3) defines *culture* as "socially learned patterns of behavior based on symbolic processes." The culture concept can provide a powerful basis for organizing social studies instruction. By focusing attention on common patterns or themes as they are shaped in different cultural milieux, teachers can help students examine the motivations underlying their own behaviors and those of others.

Interest in teaching anthropologically oriented content was not widespread before 1960. (Dynneson, 1975). In 1962 the National Science Foundation funded the Anthropology Curriculum Study Project. About the same time the U.S. Office of Education initiated support for the Georgia Anthropology Curriculum Study Project and Project Social Studies at the University of Minnesota (both heavily oriented toward anthropology). These curriculum development projects produced some outstanding instructional materials.

The Anthropology Curriculum Study Project developed a one-semester high school course entitled Patterns of Human History and two junior high school units. The high school course includes four units requiring three to four weeks of instructional time each. These Patterns of Human History units are

1. Studying societies.
2. Origins of humanness.
3. Emergence of complex societies.
4. Modernization and traditional societies.

The design of Patterns of History allows for great flexibility of use of the program. All four units may be clustered together in a semester-long course. But each unit is also sufficiently independent of the others that it may be infused as a special topic within other courses in the social studies program.

Each Pattern of Human History unit is packaged as a multimedia kit. The kits include (1) books of student readings, (2) teaching plans, and (3) instructional support materials including records, filmstrips, simulated artifacts, and blackline masters for spirit duplicating machines. Course developers have provided teachers with commendably detailed and specific guidelines for using the material.

The junior high school materials developed by the Anthropology Curriculum Study Project include two units. These units are (1) The Great Tree and the Long House: The Culture of the Iroquois and (2) Kiowa Years: A Study in Culture Impact. These units have been designed to be taught as components of longer courses taught in the junior high school social studies curriculum.

PURPOSES OF INSTRUCTION IN ANTHROPOLOGY

Proponents of an increased role for anthropology in the social studies program suggest that contents from this discipline provide a perspective that is not well served by history and other social and behavioral sciences. In this connection, Bohannon has written that

> Anthropology finds the theories and methods of all the other social sciences more or less inadequate, principally because of the ethnocentrism inherent in most explanations of human situations that are not cross cultural.[6]

[6] Paul Bohannon, "Anthropology" (Publication 106 of the Social Science Education Consortium, Boulder: University of Colorado, 1966), p. 4.

The great goal, then of anthropologically oriented instruction is to provide students with a truly cross-cultural perspective. Certainly, well before the recent interest into infusing content from anthropology into the secondary social studies curriculum, social studies teachers did study other peoples and other places. But, according to Kalso,

> In the past, when we have studied other peoples or cultures, we have too often done so in a superficial manner. We have tended merely to point out the customs that were unique, or novel, from our point of view, without really learning the reasons for the customs, or the value of them.[7]

More contemporary programs tend to downplay the emphasis on the bizarre (from our perspective) patterns of behavior of certain peoples of the world. Rather, anthropology is viewed as a mechanism that can highlight the common threads that run through the world's disparate cultures. When students come to recognize that, though responses of different peoples may differ, these responses are directed toward shared and relatively constant dilemmas, their sense of humanity is extended.

The analytical potential of the anthropological perspective makes perhaps the best case for including anthropologically oriented content in the social studies program. This perspective helps students understand that all cultures have had to deal with certain basic questions such as the following:

1. How should economic institutions be organized?
2. How should families be structured?
3. How should property be transferred from generation to generation?
4. What personality characteristics shall be prized?
5. How can prized values be artistically expressed? And so on.

By identifying shared dilemmas and pinpointing responses to these dilemmas of different cultural groups, students will have their appreciation and tolerance for individuals in different culture groups enhanced. Instruction directed toward these understandings promotes Kluckhohn's view that anthropology properly is a "science of human similarities and differences" (Kluckhohn, 1949: p. 2). Such programs can provide students with a much better understanding of their own culture as it is defined in terms of its unique cluster of responses to fundamental human problems.

ANTHROPOLOGY AND THE SOCIAL STUDIES TEACHER

Though evidence exists of an increasing interest in anthropology, still anthropology-oriented programs face some difficulties in gaining acceptance in the social studies program in many districts. A fundamental difficulty is that very few social studies teachers major in anthropology. This has created problems when teachers have

---

[7] Milton R. Kalso, "Contributions from Anthropology to Elementary Social Studies Curricula," *The Social Studies* (November 1973): 254–257.

been asked to deal with content derived from anthropology. As Dynneson (1975) noted, many teachers were not disposed to think well of Patterns of History when it was first presented to them as a pure anthropology course, but they were more receptive when later it was described as special kind of a history course. This situation suggests that those favoring a strong emphasis on cultural studies must be prepared to work carefully to make teachers comfortable with a perspective and with materials that they may well never have encountered previously.

For teachers who are interested in introducing anthropologically oriented content, a number of excellent materials are available. In addition to materials noted previously, teachers might well investigate programs developed by Interculture Associates (address: Quaddick Road, P.O. Box 277, Thompson, CT 06277) and American Universities Field Staff, Inc. (address: P.O. Box 150, Hanover, NH 03755).

Many teachers have reported positive student reactions to some of the anthropology-oriented simulations that are available, including "Dig," "Culture Contact," and "Potlatch Package." "Dig" (available from Interact, Box 262, Lakeside, CA 92040) puts students to work at various tasks, including (1) creating an imaginary culture, (2) developing artifacts reflecting characteristics of this culture, (3) burying these artifacts in places unknown to most class members, (4) using archaeological excavation techniques to locate and unearth these artifacts, and (5) making inferences about the nature of an imaginary culture based on examinations of artifacts.

The game of "Culture Contact" (available from Abt Associates, 55 Wheeler Street, Boston, MA 02138) emphasizes the difficulties of communicating under conditions of cultural stress. Members of the class divide into two cultural groups. Members of each group attempt to learn perspectives of the other group. The objective of the exercise is to help students resolve cultural conflicts.

The "Potlatch Package" (available from Abt Associates, 55 Wheeler Street, Boston, MA 02138) tries to give students a feel for the essentials of a culture very different from their own, that of the Kwakiutl Indians, who once occupied much of Vancouver Island off the coast of British Columbia, Canada. The exercise requires about two weeks of class time. During most of this period, students learn about the Kwakiutl culture. The exercise culminates in the Potlatch Game, in which students compete for status, a la Kwakiutl, by giving away material goods.

A number of excellent books are available to teachers interested in cross-cultural studies. A fine introduction to the approach is provided in Corinne Brown's *Understanding Other Cultures* (Englewood Cliffs, New Jersey: Prentice-Hall, Inc., 1963). Three titles provide fascinating descriptions of cross-cultural studies that could be replicated relatively easily by secondary school students are (1) Edward T. Hall's *The Hidden Dimension* (Garden City, New York: Doubleday & Company, Inc., 1966), (2) Edward T. Hall's *The Silent Language* (Garden City, New York: Doubleday & Company, Inc., 1959), and (3) Robert Sommer's *Personal Space: The Behavioral Basis of Design* (Englewood Cliffs, New Jersey: Prentice-Hall, Inc., 1969). Certainly, too, many of Margaret Mead's books would be appropriate for use with secondary school students. Indeed, the number of titles in this area is so large that the teacher is faced with a real problem of winnowing those available down to a manageable figure.

Teachers who develop a serious interest in anthropology may be interested in using the Human Relations Area Files (HRAF) available at major universities. These files are a collection of primary source materials on selected cultures in all areas of the world. They are organized in a way to provide quick access to information on a given topic as it pertains to a large number of cultures. For example, under the three-number code 593 (family relationships), a researcher can find references to findings of investigators with respect to family relationships on dozens of world cultures. The actual references themselves are available in microform. The system provides an extraordinarily rich resource for teachers interested in developing instructional materials of their own design. For additional information, write for this booklet: "Nature and Use of the HRAF Files: A Research and Teaching Guide," HRAF Manuals, Human Relations Area Files, Inc., P.O. Box 2015 Y.S., New Haven, CT 06520.

Another source of general information for the secondary school teacher interested in anthropology is the Council on Anthropology and Education. Write to the Council on Anthropology and Education at 1703 New Hampshire Avenue, N.W., Washington, D.C. 20009.

Though anthropology seems unlikely ever to dominate the secondary social studies program in the way history and geography have dominated it for decades, contents from the discipline have much to offer students as our world grows smaller and contact with people from other cultural traditions becomes more frequent. Perhaps packaged and distributed to teachers as a "new kind of history," anthropologically oriented programs have a defensible place in a secondary school program directed toward sensitizing students to perspectives of others. Given an increasing public awareness that peoples of the world are increasingly interconnected, there are good prospects that there will be a continued infusion of content from anthropology into the social studies curriculum.

Summary

Sociology, psychology, and anthropology, when the three disciplines are represented by separate courses in the social studies curriculum, tend to be elective courses rather than required courses. Most frequently such courses are designed as one-semester offerings.

Few teachers bring substantial college-level course work to their social studies positions in sociology, psychology, or anthropology. Most continue to be heavily oriented toward history, geography, and political science. An implication of this situation is that when contents from the behavioral sciences are presented for infusion into the existing curriculum, they must be presented in a way that appears palatable to teachers oriented toward history, geography, and political science.

College and university specialists in the behavioral sciences and public school teachers of the behavioral sciences have not always seen the same purposes for secondary school instruction in sociology, psychology, and anthropology. Specialists in higher education have tended to prize outcomes associated with teaching scientific, value-free investigation. Teachers, on the other hand, have reported that students are much more interested in value questions and in what implications content from the behavioral sciences has for them personally. Teachers drawing upon contents from the behavioral sciences have to strike a reasonable balance between the specialists' insistence on looking only at *what is* and the student's concern for *what ought to be.*

REFERENCES

AMERICAN PSYCHOLOGICAL ASSOCIATION. "Program on the Teaching of Psychology in the Secondary School." Monograph. Washington, D.C.: American Psychological Association, 1970.

BOHANNON, PAUL. "Anthropology." Publication 106 of the Social Science Education Consortium. Boulder, Colorado: University of Colorado, 1966.

DYNNESON, THOMAS L. "Anthropology and Openmindedness: A Restructuring of the Social Studies Curriculum." Paper presented at the Annual Meeting of the National Council for the Social Studies. Washington, D.C.: November 1976.

———. "Pre-Collegiate Anthropology: Trends and Materials." Monograph. Athens, Georgia: University of Georgia, Anthropology Curriculum Project, publication 75–1, November 1975.

FRASER, GRAEME S., and THOMAS J. SWITZER. "Inquiries in Sociology: Responses by Teachers and Students." *Social Education* (December 1970): 922–926.

KALSO, MILTON R. "Contributions from Anthropology to Elementary Social Studies Curricula." *The Social Studies* (November 1973): 254–257.

KLUCKHOHN, CLYDE. *Mirror for Man.* New York: McGraw-Hill Book Company, Inc., 1949.

LANGHORST, H. WALTER, and JOHN L. SULLIVAN. " 'Hey That's Me!'—A Relevant Course." *The Clearing House* (December 1968): 203–205.

PELTO, PERTTI J. *The Study of Anthropology.* Columbus, Ohio: Charles E. Merrill Books, Inc., 1965.

PERUCCI, ROBERT. "Sociology." Publication 101 of the Social Science Education Consortium. Boulder, Colorado: University of Colorado, 1966.

PHILLIPS, RICHARD. "A New Sociology Course for High Schools." *The Social Studies* (March 1969): 125–129.

ROSS, ROBERT J. "A Conceptual Program for High School Psychology." *Psychology in the Schools* (October 1972): 418–422.

SENESH, LAWRENCE. "Organizing a Curriculum around Social Science Concepts." In *Concepts and Structure in the New Social Science Curricula,* edited by Irving Morrissett, pp. 21–38. New York: Holt, Rinehart and Winston, Inc., 1967.

STERN, ADELE. "The Converging Paths of Humanity—Approaches and Materials for Studying Anthropology." *Media & Methods* (October 1974): 43–45.

ZUNINO, NATALIA. "The Teaching of Psychology in American High Schools: What's Happening?" *Social Education* (March 1974): 256–259.

The Profession

Chapter 22

THE SOCIAL STUDIES
TEACHER

Preparation of the professional social studies teacher does not end with the awarding of an academic degree. Professional development is a continuous process. Knowledge derived from history and the social and behavioral sciences changes. Interests of students vary over time. Social values refuse to stand still. Given a world in which there are few constants, the social studies teacher who wishes to maintain and improve on his or her ability to communicate with students must be adaptable.

Teachers who keep abreast of personal, social, and intellectual changes frequently find that this regenerating process rekindles their own enthusiasm for teaching. Teachers who rely on dated information passed on in college classrooms may find themselves less interested in their work with each passing year. When the fires of enthusiasm burn low in the teacher, student concern for the social studies will likely be minimal. The equation is a simple one: "My teacher isn't really interested; so why should I care?"

Patterns of professional behavior begin to develop during teachers' years of undergraduate preparation and, particularly, during the student teaching experience. Varying greatly from teacher to teacher, much subsequent development results from personal self-development programs. In the sections that follow, some characteristics of the student teaching experience and professional growth possibilities will be introduced.

Student Teaching

Student teaching, in most college and university programs, occurs toward the end of the undergraduate program. In some schools, student teaching is the last course a student takes before graduating. Programs vary in length from about eight weeks to about sixteen weeks. Regardless of their length and regardless of the special expectations of the program, all student teaching programs share one thing in common; that is, they enroll a group of undergraduates who, at the beginning of the experience, are extremely nervous if not downright terrified. This anxiety is a normal condition for beginning student teachers, and it is explained by the students' view of student teaching as an experience designed to separate those who "can cut it" in the classroom from those who cannot.

In reality, the system is not quite so harsh and threatening as many beginning teachers suppose it to be. For one thing, students in many programs throughout the country are now systematically exposed to students in the schools well before the quarter and semester in which they do their student teaching. Additionally, they are evaluated by their professors as they progress through their undergraduate program. In essence, a great deal of screening has gone on before student teaching begins. Consequently, in most colleges and universities, at least, there is an expectation that the student who is assigned to student-teach will have a successful experience. Because of this expectation, efforts of university supervisors and supervising teachers are directed toward supporting the efforts of the student teacher rather than at looking for reasons to prevent him or her from being certified. Consequently, there is no need for a student to feel that he or she will be operating in anything other than a supportive environment during student teaching. (Certainly, unfortunate incidents do occur involving conflicts of personality (in most cases), but given the large numbers of student teachers placed each year, these are blessedly few in number.)

Student teaching experiences typically involve close cooperation between three key people. First of all, there is the individual doing the student teaching. Second, there is the teacher with whom he or she is working. This individual may be called a master teacher, a supervising teacher, or a field supervisor or may be known by some other title. Third, there is the university supervisor, visiting professor, or some other representative from the college or university who may be known by any one of a number of titles. Each of these individuals has a specific role to play.

The student teacher. The student teacher has particularly delicate roles to play. This results because this individual must be able to switch back and forth from (1) status as a student charged with learning as much as possible from his or her supervising teacher and university supervisor and (2) status as a teacher charged with leading learning experiences for a group of youngsters under his or her direct supervision. Some guidelines regarding how each of these two roles is to be played usually are provided by the college or university. But, even given guidelines, these responsibilities are not easy ones.

Many beginning student teachers do not come to the experience prepared for the initial strain of their new responsibilities. From an undergraduate life characterized by note-taking in two or three classes a day, they are catapulted into a situation requiring them to (1) learn 160 or more names as quickly as possible, (2) prepare lesson plans daily for as many as three different kinds of classes, (3) manage paperwork relating to attendance and other matters, (4) maintain some sort of classroom decorum, and (5) interact more frequently and with more people than at any previous time in their lives. Not surprisingly, these new responsibilities do take their toll. Frequently, this results in feelings of extreme fatigue during the first week or two of student teaching. Many student teachers report feeling a desperate need to go to bed at 6:30 or 7:00 P.M. Fortunately, after a week or two of "settling in" time, most students overcome this initial fatigue phase and are heartened to discover that they can teach on something less than eleven hours of sleep a night.

A successful student teaching program requires that a good rapport be maintained with the supervising teacher. This is not a difficult working relationship to establish. First of all, supervising teachers ordinarily have been selected who have had enough classroom teaching experience to make them creditable models. Second, supervising teachers themselves were student teachers once. Most recall their own feelings at this time in their professional career and will go out of their way to make the experience a pleasant and productive one for student teachers with whom they are working. In the planning of lessons, consideration of the views of the supervising teacher help keep lines of communication open and, in many instances, will contribute to the success of classroom presentations.

For the beginning social studies teacher, relationships with the school and with the supervising teacher can get off on a solid footing when time is taken to determine the limits within which the teacher is able to operate. For example, it makes little sense to prepare lessons for which materials are unavailable or to spend time setting up field trips when no moneys are available to pay for transportation of students. Some time spent, at the beginning of the student teaching experience, determining the range of options available will make lesson planning more productive. Little is gained by preparing lessons that cannot be implemented.

The supervising teacher. As noted previously, most supervising teachers are selected because they have had an interest in working with student teachers and because they have demonstrated their competence in the classroom. The overwhelming majority are very supportive of their student teachers and fully appreciate that student teaching is a difficult and demanding experience. Most, too, take a professional pride in their ability to help their student teachers have a successful experience.

For a student teacher, one of the most intimidating experiences is to observe a supervising teacher, who has been in the classroom for years, walk over to a vertical file, pull open a drawer, and display perhaps fifty file folders of classroom activities focusing on a given topic. At such times, it is not unusual for the student teacher to experience a sinking feeling and a realization that "there's no way I will ever get together *that* much information on *any* topic." There is no need for any sense of inadequacy at this point. The supervising teacher had no exhaustive set of files available when he or she started either. Resource collections get built over years, not over months.

Doubtless, the supervising teacher gathered some of these materials from other teachers. The student teacher, too, should consider making a polite request for copies of as much of the good material as the supervisor might be willing to share. Few professional teachers are very possessive about materials they have gathered or special lessons they have developed. Most recognize the plight of the beginner and are willing to share some of the benefits of their years of experience in the classroom. In addition to the supervising teacher, sometimes social studies departments maintain excellent files of materials and lesson plans. A chat with the department head might well result in permission for a student teacher to make copies of some of these items.

Above all, the student teacher needs to work for a relationship with the supervising teacher that will make it possible for him or her to speak candidly with this individual. When there is a problem, it needs to be addressed immediately. When lines of communication between student teacher and supervising teacher remain open, a frank exchange of views frequently can result in a plan of action that can resolve a minor difficulty before it becomes a real problem.

The university supervisor. Typically, the student teacher sees much less of the university supervisor than of the supervising teacher. Most university supervisors have responsibilities for a number of student teachers who may be in several buildings. Many also teach some classes on the college or university campus. Consequently, university supervisors who visit student teachers more frequently than once a week are the exception rather than the rule.

A typical pattern for a university supervisor's visit involves a brief chat with the student teacher before a lesson is taught, an observation of the lesson being taught, and a debriefing session with the student teaching in which strengths and weaknesses of the lesson are discussed. Most university supervisors work very hard at building the confidence of their student teachers so that the latter have as successful an experience as possible. After a few visits from the university supervisor, most student teachers become much more comfortable in having this "outsider" sitting in on their classes.

A nightmare many students have involves a visit from the university supervisor on a day when a group of normally well-behaved youngsters decide to cut loose and literally climb the walls. Happily for student teachers, that nightmare almost never reflects the reality. If anything, secondary school students tend to be more responsive and better behaved when the university supervisor is present than at other times. The students recognize that the university supervisor is there to observe the student teacher. Most of the time they try to make the student teacher look as good as possible.

The author worked as a university supervisor for a number of years. On numerous occasions when he was visiting student teachers in social studies classes, classroom discussions were underway. In an effort to reflect credit on the student teacher, frequently every hand in the class would go up in response to a question asked by the student teacher. (To those who have not yet taught social studies, in "real life" considerably fewer than 100 per cent of the hands go up even in response to a question of the "Who's buried in Grant's tomb?" variety.) On many occasions, students stopped by after the lesson to say, "Mr. X or Ms. Y got an *A* today, right?"

The university supervisor works closely with the supervising teacher. Both seek to make the student teaching experience a good one. Both, too, ordinarily play a role in the final evaluation. There has been a trend in recent years for the student teacher as well to play a role in the evaluation process. Some programs feature a final three-way conference involving university supervisor, supervising teacher, and student teacher where all three parties explore dimensions of the student teaching experience and draft a summary statement reflecting collective and individual perceptions. Given a student teaching situation in which lines of communication have remained open, views of the three participants in such conferences tend to be highly similar. Certainly, if one considers the commitment of his or her supervisors to help the student teacher grow professionally, evaluation conferences at the conclusion of student teaching (or at various points throughout the experience) need not be viewed fearfully.

Professional growth, of course, does not stop after student teaching. Demands of teaching require educators to engage in a process of self-renewal throughout their entire careers. In the next section, some procedures for approaching professional improvement in a systematic fashion will be introduced.

Pursuing Professional Growth

Teachers who take the time to monitor and analyze their performance in the classroom typically find at least some aspects of their teaching less than they would hope them to be. Most recognize the need for continued professional development. After student teaching and graduation, most social studies teachers do not have available systematic counsel from university supervisors regarding how instructional skills might be refined. Occasionally, social studies department heads or other building administrators might sit in on a class and make a few observations. But such visits tend to be sporadic, and they are inadequate as guides to enhanced instructional effectiveness. For the career teacher, improvement in the instructional skills area involves self-development. This can take several forms, including self-directed study and active participation in social studies professional organizations.

Organizing Self-directed Study

In addition to formal programs, professional social studies teachers do a great deal of preparation on their own. Sources of information range from television, films, books, and articles to all sorts of life experiences that relate to the content of social studies classes. A productive self-directed study program requires the establishment of some priorities. One way to approach this task involves simply the identification of major topics being treated in social studies classes. This procedure may result in the identification of a large number of areas that might have to be refined further. Sometimes, it may be desirable to focus on a single broad topic and subdivide it into several subtopics. For example, a teacher interested in United States history might do something like the following:

Major topic: Development of the Great Plains in the Nineteenth Century
Subtopics: Railroad development.
Urban development.
Homesteading.
Folk music, folk tales, poetry, and other arts of the Great Plains region.
Inventions stimulated by the Plains environment.
Psychological adjustments to the Plains.

Of course, this major topic could be broken down in many other ways. The important thing is to establish some priorities that bear a relationship to both teacher and student interests and contents of courses. These topics can serve as basis for selecting reading material and involvement in other sorts of activities that can enhance understandings and build depth in these targeted areas.

Once a decision has been made regarding the focus of a self-directed study program, attention must be directed to the question of organizing information acquired. Organization is essential if the information is to be easily and quickly retrieved for use in planning for classroom lessons with students. A two-, three-, or four-drawer vertical file can be used to house and arrange systematically much information that is gathered. In addition to the more expensive metal files, less costly cardboard files are available from office supply stores and many major discount outlets.

When a decision has been made to use a vertical file, information must be gathered in a way convenient for storage in file folders. Certain important sections from books and magazines can be photocopied on 8½-by-11 inch paper and placed in individual folders. Similarly, notes can be taken and included in appropriate folders. Clippings from newspapers and magazines can be placed loose in folders or, alternatively, pasted on sheets of paper and then arranged in folders. Certain maps, brochures, and other loose items can be organized in individual folders with little difficulty.

Once materials have been placed in folders, flaps on each folder need to be labeled to indicate the contents. A number of systems are acceptable for doing this. Many teachers find it convenient simply to write the title of the item(s) included. Others prefer to label folders according to last names of authors of included items. Still others devise a scheme according to which individual folders are simply numbered and keyed to a master list of contents maintained elsewhere. (Maintenance of a master list for quick reference is a good idea regardless of which system is selected for labeling individual folders.)

If a teacher had decided to concentrate his or her efforts on information relating to the major topic "Development of the Great Plains in the Nineteenth Century" and had identified "Inventions Stimulated by the Plains Environment" as one of the important subtopics, file folders and a master list might include materials such as the following:

SUBTOPIC: INVENTIONS STIMULATED BY THE PLAINS ENVIRONMENT

Folder Number 1: Notes about windmills, revolvers, and barbed wire from W. P. Webb's *The Great Plains.*

Folder Number 2: "A Pioneer Remembers." Clipping from Houston *Light* (January 10, 1978. Sect. A, page 4, col. 4) about early days fights over fencing.

Folder Number 3: Burlingame, Roger. "Six Shooter." From *Machines That Built America,* pp. 100–115. (photocopy)

Folder Number 4: "Wind and Water." Pamphlet about windmills and the Plains distributed by Kansas State Historical Society.

Folder Number 5: Horn, Huxton. From *The Pioneers,* p. 214 and p. 218. (photocopy)

Folder Number 6: Monaghan, J. *The Book of the American West.* (extensive notes on inventions)

Folder Number 7: Wilson, Mitchell. *American Science and Invention.* (extensive notes on inventions related to the Great Plains)

These represent simply a sample of how files might be organized. Certainly, a variety of schemes might be devised. The important consideration is that individual items are easily accessible. There simply is not time when instructional planning is underway to get involved in a long search for a potentially useful time.

Materials gathered and organized as part of a self-directed study program have potential for adding some excitement and some depth to the social studies programs. Materials gathered in such an effort reflect the enthusiasms of the teacher. Further, they have not been stripped bare of potentially controversial content by a textbook author and a publisher concerned about the possibility of offending a broad and diverse audience. Given the potential emotive appeal of the materials and the interest in them on the part of the teacher who has gathered them together, such items can stimulate the development of some highly productive lessons.

Organizations of Interest to Social Studies Teachers

The premier national organization for social studies educators is the National Council for the Social Studies. This is an umbrella organization that includes classroom teachers, state and local social studies supervisors, and college and university professors with specialties in social studies education and in history and the social sciences. Each year the National Council (or NCSS, as it is popularly known to its members) holds an annual meeting that attracts thousands of social studies educators. Many meeting sessions focus on practical instructional procedures of interest to the classroom teachers. In addition to the national meetings, NCSS sponsors a number of regional conferences annually at various points throughout the country. Finally, there is a strong network of affiliated state and local councils throughout the nation that sponsor regular meetings focusing on improvement of social studies instruction. Certainly, affiliation with the National Council for the Social Studies and appropriate regional and local councils represents an appropriate step for the social studies teacher who seeks to professionalize his or her instructional practices.

In addition to its sponsorship of conferences, NCSS has an active publications program. For years the organization published an annual yearbook focusing on topics of interest. Some selected titles and years of publication suggest the range of concern reflected in these volumes:

Evaluation in Social Studies (1965).
Social Studies Curriculum Development (1969).
Teaching Ethnic Studies (1973).
Developing Decision-Making Skills (1977).

Many libraries have complete sets of these yearbooks. In addition, some of these titles are still stocked by the National Council for the Social Studies and can be ordered directly.

Recently, NCSS has made a decision to abandon publication of an annual yearbook. Instead, six publications called "bulletins" will be issued each year. Each bulletin will focus on a specific topic that will be treated in depth. This approach promises to add considerable flexibility by permitting many more topics to be treated annually than was possible when a single yearbook was organized around one central theme. Certainly, some of the bulletins that have been released since the adoption of the new policy have indicated the new approach has much to commend it. Bulletin 51, *Defining the Social Studies* (1977), prepared by Robert D. Barr, James L. Barth, and S. Samuel Shermis, exemplifies the potentials of the "bulletins" approach.

NCSS also publishes a journal for social studies educators, entitled *Social Educa-*

tion. The journal includes numerous articles relating to both curricular and instructional concerns in the social studies. Each issue includes practical ideas for presenting materials to students. Many professional social studies teachers maintain files of back issues that can be referred to as the need arises. In addition to *Social Education*, NCSS publishes *The Social Studies Professional,* a newsletter that seeks to apprise members of developments in the field.

In addition to the meetings and publications noted here, NCSS and its affiliates provide a number of other services for members. One area of interest, for example, is protection of social studies teachers' legal rights. For information about the total range of services offered and about membership requirements, write to:

The National Council for the Social Studies
Suite 400
2030 M Street N.W.
Washington, D.C. 20036

Social studies teachers with interests in geography profit from an association with the *National Council for Geographic Education* (NCGE). As the title implies, this group's primary mission is to serve the needs of teachers of geography in the schools. Additionally, NCGE attempts to stimulate interest in geography as a field of study.

Like NCSS, NCGE holds annual meetings that feature many presentations of instructional techniques that have proved their worth in the classroom. Additionally, NCGE publishes a number of materials targeted for use with secondary students. The organization's excellent publication, the *Journal of Geography,* is a featured item on the professional shelves of many social studies teachers. For information regarding the National Council for Geographic Education, write to:

National Council for Geographic Education
University of Houston
Houston, Texas 77004

The Social Science Education Consortium publishes many materials of interest to social studies educators. The consortium is a particularly rich source of information for individuals interested in developing social studies curricula. For social studies teachers, the three-volume *Social Studies Curriculum Materials Data Book* is an invaluable source of information. Rather expensive, the *Data Book* ordinarily is purchased by the school library or the social studies department rather than by individual teachers. Each volume is a three-ringed binder filled with removable pages. Periodic updates of material are mailed from SSEC at which time old pages can be removed and new ones inserted. Pages are organized into categories including such topics as "textbooks," "games and simulations," "supplementary materials," "teacher resource materials," and "social studies projects materials." Specific items are reviewed according to a standard format that includes (1) an overview of the material, (2) a description of the format of the material, (3) estimate of time needed to use material, (4) a description of assumed characteristics of the teacher and his or her students, (5) an explanation of the purpose of the materials, (6) a general description of the content of the materials, (7) an indication of intended teaching procedures, and (8) a summary of any available evaluation information regarding the material.

Information in the *Data Book* can prove invaluable when decisions are being made regarding future purchases. As all materials are reviewed according to the eight-part format just described, comparison of alternative materials is facilitated. The *Data Book* contains much useful information that has been gathered together in a single place. Certainly, it is a resource that the professional social studies teacher should know about. For information regarding the *Data Book* and other Social Science Education Consortium publications, write to:

> Social Science Education Consortium, Inc.
> 855 Broadway
> Boulder, Colorado 80302

Some periodicals of interest. There are many periodicals that social studies teachers find useful. A few of those that are intended specifically to meet the needs of social studies teachers are listed as follows:

> *The History Teacher*
> For information write: Department of History
> California State University, Long Beach
> 6101 East Seventh Street
> Long Beach, California 90840

> *Journal of Economic Education*
> For information write: Joint Council on Economic Education
> 1212 Avenue of the Americas
> New York, New York 10036

> *Journal of Geography*
> For information write: National Council for Geographic Education
> University of Houston
> Houston, Texas 77004

> *Simulation/Gaming*
> For information write: Simulation/Gaming
> Box 3039
> University of Idaho
> Moscow, Idaho 83843

> *Social Education*
> For information write: National Council for the Social Studies
> Suite 400
> 2030 M Street N.W.
> Washington, D.C. 20036

> *The Social Studies*
> For information write: Heldref Publications
> 4000 Albemarle Street N.W.
> Washington, D.C. 20016

Teaching Political Science
  For information write: Sage Publications, Inc.
                        275 South Beverly Drive
                        Beverly Hills, California 90212
Teaching Sociology
  For information write: Sage Publications, Inc.
                        275 South Beverly Drive
                        Beverly Hills, California 90212

Books for a professional social studies library.   Many outstanding books are available for the teacher interested in developing his or her instructional effectiveness in the social studies. Many teachers build splendid professional collections of their own throughout their teaching career. Sometimes, too, social studies departments make a commitment to purchase volumes for a departmental collection or for a professional collection to be housed in the school library. Though certainly any list of books that might be included in such a collection is open to question, still a case could be made for identifying some of the following titles for a basic secondary social studies collection:

BANKS, JAMES A. *Teaching Strategies for Ethnic Studies.* Boston: Allyn Bacon, Inc., 1975.
BANKS, JAMES A., and WILLIAM W. JOYCE, eds. *Teaching Social Studies to Culturally Different Children.* Reading, Mass.: Addison-Wesley Publishing Company, Inc., 1971.
BERELSON, BERNARD, and GARY A. STEINER. *Human Behavior: Shorter Edition.* New York: Harcourt, Brace, and World, Inc., 1964, 1967.
BEYER, BARRY K. *Inquiry in the Social Studies Classroom: A Strategy for Teaching.* Columbus, Ohio: Charles E. Merrill Publishing Co., 1971.
BRUBAKER, DALE L. *Secondary Social Studies for the '70's.* New York: Thomas Y. Crowell Company, 1973.
CLUBOK, ARTHUR. *Teaching World History Today: A Handbook for Teachers of Slow to Average Students.* Portland, Maine: J. Weston Walch, 1976.
ENGLE, SHIRLEY H., and WILMA S. LONGSTREET. *A Design for Social Education in the Open Curriculum.* New York: Harper & Row, Publishers, 1972.
FENTON, EDWIN. *The New Social Studies.* New York: Holt, Rinehart and Winston, Inc., 1967.
GILLIOM, M. EUGENE; JAMES DICK; JACK R. FRAENKEL; DONALD HETZNER; J. COLIN MARSH; ANNE R. PETERSON; and JOEL S. POETKER. *Practical Methods for the Social Studies.* Belmont, California: Wadsworth Publishing Company, Inc., 1977.
GROSS, RICHARD E.; WALTER E. MCPHIE; and JACK R. FRAENKEL, eds. *Teaching the Social Studies: What, Why, and How?* Scranton, Pennsylvania: Intext Educational Publishers, 1970.
HOMANS, GEORGE C. *The Nature of Social Science.* New York: Harcourt, Brace, and World, Inc., 1967.
HUNKINS, FRANCIS P. *Questioning Strategies and Techniques.* Boston: Allyn & Bacon, Inc., 1972.
HUNT, MORRIS P., and LAWRENCE E. METCALF. *Teaching High School Social Studies.* 2d ed. New York: Harper & Row, Publishers, 1968.
KELLER, CLAIR W. *Involving Students in the New Social Studies.* Boston: Little, Brown and Company, 1972, 1974.

Livingston, Samuel A., and Clarice Stasz Stoll. *Simulation Games: An Introduction for the Social Studies Teacher*. New York: The Free Press, 1973.

London, Herbert Ira. *Social Science Theory, Structure and Application*. New York: New York University Press, 1975.

Martorella, Peter H. *Concept Learning: Designs for Instruction*. Scranton, Pennsylvania: Intext Educational Publishers, 1972.

Morrissett, Irving, ed. *Concepts and Structure in the New Social Science Curricula*. New York: Holt, Rinehart and Winston, Inc., 1967.

Morrissett, Irving, and W. Williams Stevens, Jr., eds. *Social Science in the Schools: A Search for Rationale*. New York: Holt, Rinehart and Winston, Inc., 1971.

National Council for the Social Studies. *Social Studies Curriculum Guidelines*. Washington, D.C.: National Council for the Social Studies, 1971.

———— *Standards for Social Studies Teachers*. Washington, D.C.: National Council for the Social Studies, 1971.

Nesbitt, William A. *Interpreting the Newspaper in the Classroom: Foreign News and World Views*, 2d. ed. New York: T. J. Crowell, 1971.

Newmann, Fred M., and Donald W. Oliver. *Clarifying Public Controversy*. Boston: Little, Brown and Company, 1970.

Oliver, Donald, and James P. Shaver. *Teaching Public Issues in the High School*. Boston: Houghton Mifflin Company, 1966.

Raths, Louis E.; Merrill Harmin; and Sidney B. Simon. *Values and Teaching*. Columbus, Ohio: Charles E. Merrill Publishing Co., 1972.

Rokeach, Milton. *Beliefs, Attitudes, and Values*. San Francisco: Jossey-Bass, 1969.

Sanders, Norris M. *Classroom Questions: What Kinds?* New York: Harper & Row, Publishers, 1966.

Simon, Sidney B.; Leland W. Howe; and Howard Kirschenbaum. *Values Clarification*. New York: Hart Publishing, 1972.

Stanford, Gene, and Albert E. Roark. *Human Interaction in Education*. Boston: Allyn & Bacon, Inc., 1974.

Stephens, Lester D. *Probing the Past: A Guide to the Study and Teaching of History*. Boston: Allyn & Bacon, Inc., 1975.

Wesley, Edgar B., and Stanley P. Wronski. *Teaching Secondary Social Studies in a World Society*. 6th ed. Lexington, Massachusetts: D. C. Heath and Co., 1973.

White, Charles J. III, ed. *Teaching Teachers about Law*. Chicago: American Bar Association, 1976.

Wilson, John. *Thinking with Concepts*. Cambridge, England: Cambridge University Press, 1963.

Teaching the Social Studies: Some Final Thoughts

In some respects social studies teachers are like a ninety-year-old man planting an oak tree in his front yard. The ground must be prepared and fertilized in full knowledge that the tree (or the student) may never be seen in a state of full and mature glory. Social studies teachers believe in the future. Their commitment to act is premised on a conviction that students taught to respond rationally to divisive issues will develop into socially competent adults. Professional social studies teachers are sustained by a belief that their influences on students can compete successfully with others that go together to shape the nature of the adult human being. Given this conviction, social studies teachers "plant" even as they understand that it is their students who, in the final analysis, will determine the nature of the "harvest."

One of the most difficult lessons for the beginning social studies teacher is that all human beings—and students in particular—have the capacity to change. Without the perspective of seeing what happens to former students with the passage of time, it is tempting to "give up" on a student whose behavior, at the moment, shows scant promise. To get a little perspective on this change phenomenon, new teachers will find it a worthwhile undertaking to spend some time chatting with the "old hands" about some former students. Such conversations almost invariably include some discussion of individuals who appeared utterly beyond redemption as junior and senior high school students who today are running businesses, working for the government, or in some other ways making a significant personal contribution to the community.

The lesson to be learned from observations of student change is that those things that are emphasized in the social studies are learned later by some students than by others. In the short run, those students who demonstrate an eager and vital interest in the social studies program provide tremendous and necessary satisfaction to the social studies teacher. In the long run, satisfaction accrues out of a conviction that, in time, most of the students are "going to make it." The ability to work diligently in the present in the belief that socially responsible values and behaviors will, given time, "take hold" is a hallmark of the professional social studies teacher. It is for this perspective that the beginning social studies teacher should strive.

Summary

Professional development is an ongoing process for the social studies teacher. Many opportunities are available for the teacher to improve his or her understanding both of social studies content and of instructional methodology. In-service programs offered during the school year as well as summer school programs at colleges and universities are viable options.

Beyond student teaching, a good deal of professional development has to be of the "self-help" variety. A number of national organizations are dedicated to improving social studies instruction. These groups offer programs designed to enhance teachers' effectiveness in the classroom. Many offer excellent periodicals that include useful perspectives of social studies instruction.

Many individual social studies teachers and social studies departments are at work building rich libraries of books and other materials with a social studies education focus. Many outstanding books are available for the social studies teacher interested in professional development.

Social studies teachers have a long-term perspective. The fruits of their efforts will not be available at the end of the course or at the end of the school year. Rather, their influences may not be seen until years later when students they have taught take an active part in making rational decisions in the public arena. Much social studies instruction goes forward in the faith that, for some students at least, ideas that have been introduced will take root "later if not sooner."

REFERENCES

BARR, ROBERT D.; JAMES L. BARTH; and S. SAMUEL SHERMIS. *Defining the Social Studies.* Bulletin 51. Washington, D.C.: National Council for the Social Studies, 1977.
NATIONAL COUNCIL FOR THE SOCIAL STUDIES. *Standards for Social Studies Teachers.* Washington, D.C.: National Council for the Social Studies, 1971.

INDEX

Coleman, James S., 379, 390n
Community Futures Day, 335–36
Community use logs, 333–34
Concepts, 30–32, 212–20
  strategies for teaching, 212–20
    concept attainment, 216–18
    concept demonstration, 218–20
    concept diagnosis, 212–15
Conferences, see teacher-student conferences
Consumer education, see economics
Contour maps, 187–89
Cordasco, Francesco, 290
Cortez, Carlos E., 281, 293, 295n
Cost effectiveness, 11, 24
Council on Anthropology and Education, 405
Cramer, Robert E., 188n, 190n
Criterion-referenced grading, 128–30
Curr, George Lincoln, 302
Curriculum patterns, 20–23

Dante, Harris L., 349, 351, 374n
Davison, Susan E., 313
Decision making, 255–76
  informational component, 256–57
  intellectual education lesson, 262–68
  model for intellectual education, 263
  model for social education and personal education, 270
  personal education lesson, 273–75
  scope, 275–76
  social education lesson, 270–73
  values component, 257–61
Deductive learning, 193, 211
Deloria, Vine, Jr., 290
Denton, Jon J., 252n
Determining historical truth, 360–62
Dewey, John, 194, 210n
Diagnosing students, 71–87
  anecdotal records, 80–81
  attitudes, 73
  class profile sheet, 85–86
  interest inventories, 84–85
  knowledge, 72–73
  skills, 73
  table of prescriptions, 78–79
  teacher-kept checklists, 83
  teacher-made tests, 74–78
  teacher-student conferences, 81–83
Dick, James, 419
Dickleman, Mildred, 295n
Directed reading approach, 144–47
  establishing a purpose, 146–147

highlighting difficulties, 146
introducing new concepts, 145
surveying content, 144–45
Discipline-centered curricula, 21, 23–25
Discussion technique, 241–44
Dornbusch, Sanford M., 5, 13n, 209, 210n
Drimmer, Melvin, 289
Dunn, Kenneth, 244, 250–51, 252n
Dunn, Rita, 244, 250–51, 252n
Dynneson, Thomas L., 402, 404, 406n

Easton, David, 377, 379, 390n
Economics, 8, 375–76, 384–90
  course contents, 387–89
  teacher preparation, 386–87
  textbook difficulties, 384–86
Educational Policy Commission, 9
Engle, Shirley H., 255, 276n, 419
Environmental Law Reporter, 302
Essay tests, 111–13
Ethnic group information sources, 288–93
Ethnic studies, see multiethnic instruction
Evaluation, 106–30
  affective domain, 121–23
  essay tests, 111–13
  fill-in-the-blanks tests, 120–21
  grading, 125–30
  matching tests, 118–20
  multiple-choice tests, 113–16
  program review, 123–24
  relationship to desired behavior, 107–11
  relationship to teacher credibility, 106–107
  table of objectives, 108
  test types, 111–21
  true-false tests, 117–18
External validity, 360–61

Facts, 30, 32–34
Fenton, Edwin, 318, 326, 329n, 419
Fernández, Celestino, 5, 13n, 209, 210n
Ferre, Alan Victor, 54, 70n
Field trips, 343–44
Fill-in-the-blanks tests, 120–21
Fitzpatrick, Joseph P., 290
Flanders, Ned A., 234, 252n
Foerster, Leona M., 150n, 165n
Forbes, Jack D., 290
Fraenkel, Jack R., 326–27, 329n, 419
Franklin, John Hope, 289
Fraser, Dorothy M., 166, 190n
Fraser, Graeme S., 394–95, 398, 406n
Free enterprise, see economics

Price, Roy A., 9, 13n
Problematic areas of culture, 21
Program characteristics matrix, 15–20
Program organization considerations, 34–40
  availability of learning resources, 37–38
  student characteristics, 35–36
  teacher characteristics, 36–37
  thinking process factors, 40–46
Project Social Studies, 402
Proposition Thirteen, 11
Psychology, 391–92, 398–401, 405–406
  course patterns, 399–400
  problems of teaching, 400–401
  students' expectations, 398–99
  teacher preparation, 398–99

Raths, Louis E., 257, 277n, 316, 329n, 420
Reading difficulties, 133–48
  cloze procedure, 135–36, 140–43
  directed reading approach, 144–47
  Fry readability graph, 135–40
  major dimensions, 134–35
Real values, 173–75
Reinke, Robert W., 387, 390n
Relative and time chart, 363–64
Rest, James, 324, 329n
Rivera, Feliciano, 290
Roark, Albert E., 420
Robinson, Cecil, 290
Rokeach, Milton, 420
Role playing, 245–47
Rooze, Gene E., 150n, 165n
Ross, Robert J., 399, 406n
Rudwick, Elliot, 289

Sanders, Norris M., 420
Savage, Tom V., Jr., 15, 25n, 252n, 262n, 277n, 331, 333, 335, 337, 339, 345n
Senesh, Lawrence, 395, 406n
Shaver, Japes P., 420
Shermis, S. Samuel, 416, 422
Simison, Robert L., 138n, 148n
Simon, Sidney B., 257, 277n, 316, 329n, 420
Simulation, 247–49
Simulation/Gaming, 418
Sklare, Marshall, 292
Sleeper, Martin E., 6, 13n
Small-group instruction, 92–103
  combined with large-group instruction, 103–104
  group size, 93–95
  physical placement of individuals, 95

preparation of students, 99–102
  purposes of groups, 95–99
Smith, Frank, 134, 148n
Smith, John W., 378, 390n
Social Education, 15, 17–18
  attitudes and values, 18
  skills, 18
  understandings, 17–18
Social Education magazine, 292, 313, 416–18
Social Science Education Consortium, 35, 417–18
Social Studies, The, 292, 418
Social Studies Curriculum Materials Data Book, 417–18
Social studies history, 7–13
Social studies periodicals, 418–19
Social Studies Professional, The, 417
Social studies professionals, 409–22
  growth and development, 413–20
  organizations, 416–18
  periodicals, 418–19
  resource files, 414–16
  self-directed study, 414–16
  student teaching, 410–13
Sociological Resources for the Social Studies, 394–95
Sociology, 8, 391–98, 405–406
  classroom instruction, 396–98
  fundamental ideas, 395–96
  student motivation problems, 393–94
Sommer, Robert, 404
Sowell, Thomas, 292
Special retrieval systems, 160–61
Spicer, Edward H., 290
Stampp, Kenneth M., 289
Stanford, Gene, 420
Steiner, Gary A., 30, 34, 43, 46n, 419
Steiner, Stan, 290
Stephens, Lester D., 420
Stern, Adele, 406n
Stevens, W. Williams, 420
Stoll, Clarice, 248, 252n, 420
Structure of knowledge, 30–34
Student prescription card, 79
Student teaching, 410–13
Student views of social studies, 5–6
Sullivan, John L., 400
Switzer, Thomas J., 394–95, 398, 406n
Symbols, *see* map symbols

Taafe, Edward J., 366, 374n
Taba, Hilda, 30, 46n, 211–12, 228